NUTRITIONAL ANTHROPOLOGY

D1563281

CONTRIBUTORS

Claire M. Cassidy, Department of Anthropology and Department of Health Education, University of Maryland, College Park, Maryland; and Smithsonian Institution, Washington, D.C.

Kathleen M. DeWalt, Department of Anthropology and Department of Behavioral Science, University of Kentucky Medical School, Lexington, Kentucky

Wenche B. Eide, Institute for Nutrition Research, University of Oslo, Norway

Norge W. Jerome, Department of Community Health, School of Medicine, University of Kansas Medical Center, Kansas City, Kansas

Randy F. Kandel, Department of Sociology and Anthropology, Florida International University, Miami, Florida

Phyllis B. Kelly, Bucks Hill Farm, Southbury, Connecticut

Thomas J. Marchione, Department of Anthropology, Case Western Reserve University, Cleveland, Ohio

Gretel H. Pelto, Department of Nutritional Sciences, University of Connecticut, Storrs, Connecticut

Ellen M. Rosenberg, Western Connecticut State College, Danbury, Connecticut

Filomina C. Steady, Department of Anthropology, Wesleyan University, Middletown, Connecticut

Brian Weiss, Geography Department, University of California at Los Angeles, Los Angeles, California

David R. Yesner, Department of Anthropology, University of Southern Maine, Gorham, Maine

Cover Illustration, *The Bedford Oak,* rendered by Noel Malsberg
Cover Design by James Olsen and Tobias A. Wolf

NUTRITIONAL ANTHROPOLOGY

Contemporary Approaches to Diet & Culture

NORGE W. JEROME, Ed.
University of Kansas Medical Center

RANDY F. KANDEL, Ed.
Florida International University

GRETEL H. PELTO, Ed.
University of Connecticut

REDGRAVE PUBLISHING COMPANY , NY

ISBN 0-913178-55-1

Printed in the United States of America.

DEDICATION

Dedicated to Margaret Mead and Audrey I. Richards, two women who opened the doors in food and culture research, and to Dorothy Hussemann Strong, who saw the potential for Nutritional Anthropology.

CONTENTS

ACKNOWLEDGEMENTS

A book of this scope comes to fruition only through the patience and cooperative effort of many—contributors and reviewers, secretaries who patiently type and retype manuscripts, family members and close friends who nudge and push gently but steadfastly, institutional administrators, and a publisher who considers the effort of value. The editors acknowledge their support with gratitude.

We especially acknowledge the assistance and ideas of Michael Calavan, Carol Carter, Linda Darling, Leslie Sue Lieberman, Emma Jo Miller, G. Edward Montgomery, Robert Olson, Raymond Parmalee, Pertti J. Pelto, Stuart Plattner, Jane Savage and Joel Teitelbaum.

Introduction

R. F. Kandel
N. W. Jerome
G. H. Pelto

Most of the papers in this volume were originally presented in three symposia on Nutritional Anthropology organized by the editors at the Annual Meetings of the American Anthropological Association in 1973 and 1974. We organized these symposia because we realized that nutritional conditions are the result of both biological and cultural forces which are inseparably intertwined; moreover, we were committed to the idea that nutritional problems could only be understood and ameliorated when they are considered from a comprehensive biocultural perspective.

Food, by virtue of its pivotal place in human experience is, at once, a bundle of energy and nutrients within the biological sphere, a commodity within the economic sphere, and a symbol within the social and religious spheres. Food ideas and attitudes, socioeconomic structure, patterns of resource allocation, dietary intake, and nutritional status had to be studied holistically as part of a single system. Techniques of food production affect the natural environment, which, in turn, influences dietary requirements. Patterns of land tenure, food distribution within the society, family traditional cuisines, personal tastes, and financial pressures all influence what people will eat and how well nourished they will be. Differential nutritional status, by making some people more fit than others, has widesweeping social, political, and economic implications.

In organizing the symposia we hoped to draw together the scattered but growing group of researchers who were investigating nutrition-related problems from a contextual perspective, which combined the theory and method of both the nutritional and social sciences and to work together in developing the framework of a new theoretical approach.

At that time, we were acutely aware that a difficult task of cross-disciplinary education and communication lay before us because many nutritionists and social scientists lacked understanding of, and respect for, one another's fields. "Hard science" nutritionists tended to believe that requirements and standards could be established by experimental investigation, and good dietary habits could be taught by traditional didactic methods. They tended to discount the anthropologists' insights into the nonmaterial aspects of food beliefs and the importance of nonnutritional factors in dietary decision making. Anthropologists, for their part, often lacked even the rudimentary knowledge of nutritional requirements, the nutrient content of foodstuffs, or the techniques of collecting accurate dietary information that would enable them to collect field data useful for nutrition studies.

In developing a shared set of concepts and terms, it seemed possible to draw upon four parallel, but previously unintegrated, lines of food research. The first was a long tradition of dietary survey studies which had evolved within the nutritional sciences. The emphasis in these studies had been upon the precise description of sample populations, the accurate assessment of dietary intake, and the accurate measurements of the nutritional content of foodstuffs. Dietary adequacy was evaluated against the background knowledge of the processes of intermediary metabolism, the genetic makeup, diversity and health status of the studied population, and the environmental and activity factors which affected dietary needs. A history of investigation into the most accurate techniques of data collection and analysis lay behind these studies. It was essential to introduce the same degree of rigor, precision, and quantification into the field methods of nutritional anthropology if the "hard" and "soft" scientists were to communicate with each other.

The second line of research, which has been called "foodways" by anthropologists and "food habits" by nutritionists, was a wide-ranging investigation into the nonnutritional aspects of food as these related to ethnic identity, culinary tradition, social structure, social status, and culture change. It derived from the classic work of Audrey Richards (1932) in demonstrating that food production and distribution patterns were core elements of social structure, and the work of Bennett (1943), Cussler, and de Give (1952), and the Committee on Food Habits of the National Research Council, coordinated by Margaret Mead (NRC, 1945), in identifying the impact of ethnicity, household economics, status and prestige, work schedules, family composition, social pressure, and other similar factors on dietary choices. We felt it was necessary to recognize that dietary intake was not totally conditioned by outside forces. Rather, people make individual dietary decisions from among a limited range of possibilities in accordance with personal sets of values and goals—most of which do not concern nutrition. Personal preferences, tradition and appropriateness, status and prestige, finances and economics, and the availability and accesibility of foodstuffs all play a role in determining dietary selection and dietary need.

The third tradition, which derived from such seminal thinkers as F. Simoons (1961), stressed the cognitive aspects of food, analyzing the nonnutritional meanings of food as ideological systems unto themselves. The approach and results of these cognitive studies has recently been well summarized by Eliot A. Singer:

> Food has been studied not for itself, but as a medium for social and for cognitive expression. It has been shown to symbolize a wide variety of things, including clan and ethnic identities and social statuses. Food transactions have been found to express caste ranking, social distance, and community. Food taboos have been seen as maintainers of cosmic order and as reflectors of social order. Sacrifices, communions, feasts and fasts have been suggested to state the interdependence of humans, gods, and nature. Thus eating is to be seen not primarily as an instrumental behavior, but as an expressive act, which, in a conventionally organized way, is trying to say something about something. (1978:3)

It seemed as foolish to ignore the importance of these deeply entrenched cognitive systems for nutritional problems within the field context as it would be, within the clinical context, to attempt to get a hypertensive patient, who was also a deeply Orthodox Jew to abandon koshering his meat. Rather, we believed that nutritional anthropology should investigate the nutritionally-significant intersection of food beliefs and behaviors with a methodology that combined the grammatical rigor of cognitive studies with the mathematical rigor of dietary studies.

The fourth tradition upon which it seemed possible to draw was

that of ecological studies. The theory of human or cultural
ecology—originally formulated by anthropologists such as Leslie
White (1949), Julian Steward (1955), Elman Service (1962, 1971), and
more recently expounded by John Bennett in his profound book
The Ecological Transition (1976)—viewed human beings as in-
telligent, technologically equipped, and culturally conditioned
biological actors existing in open feedback systems with other
biological units of their environment. Thus, food becomes a means
for the transfer of energy among ecosystem components, and
nutritional requirements are conditioned by the multiplicity of
ecological factors.

The strength of the ecological approach is that it makes it
possible to relate biological and cultural factors on the same level
of analysis. Thus, an ecological explanation of early childhood
malnutrition in a Third World agricultural population might
include patterns of family size and composition, infant weaning
practices, cultural elaboration of high carbohydrate "superfoods"
methods of crop production, high levels of chronic parasitic
infection, and low levels of education and income as explanatory
factors of the same magnitude. Similarly, epidemic rates of midlife
overnutrition in the developed countries might be visualized as
embedded in a matrix which includes high cholesterol diets and
cocktail parties, high stress white collar jobs and sedentary lifestyles, and the advertising and distribution tactics of food-pro-
cessing corporations.

The essence of ecological theory is that human experience is not
only biocultural but evolutionary. Environmental transfers eventually result in environmental transformations when critical thresholds are crossed in both the biological and sociocultural realms.
Thus, diet has played a critical role in human biological evolution in
fostering our omnivorous habits, our eight essential amino acid
requirements, and population specific differences in lactose and
salt tolerances. It continues to play a role in patterning the genetic
nature of the human species as high carbohydrate-weaning diets
select out inviable children for early death, and as mysterious
malignancies—partially associated with chemical food additives—
alter the nature of urban populations.

Ecological transformations have played a critical role in sociocultural change as well. Changes in the predominant ways of
getting food have precipitated rapid increases in population,
which, in turn, have required increasingly complex systems of

social organization. Transactions between cultural and environmental systems, seen not as teleological determinants, but as mutable processes susceptible of modification by the human will, have led us irreversibly out of our hunting-and-gathering past to the brink of the global village.

From ecological theory it seemed possible to derive for nutritional anthropology a truly biocultural approach to nutritional problems in the field context, an evolutionary scheme for linking nutritional systems of the past, present, and future, and an overall orientation to the solution of the global food crisis.

Happily, the three Nutritional Anthropology symposia proved useful in coordinating a new biocultural thrust in nutrition research and in linking together an interdisciplinary network of concerned researchers. The eleven papers in this volume, therefore, are among the research efforts that launched a new direction in nutritional anthropology. The authors include anthropologists, nutritionists, and professionals with interdisciplinary training. Most of the studies combine the intensive long-term participant observation field methods characteristic of anthropology with the collection and quantification of hard data characteristic of the nutritional sciences. The analytical emphasis is upon the quantification and clear and rigorous delineation of all nutritionally relevant factors, whether these occur within the natural environment, the social, political and economic systems, the cultural ideology, or out-of-awareness behavior patterns. The papers attempt to integrate these areas into multifactorial explanations.

Although each study was conducted independently in a different area and employed a different set of methods, hypotheses, and midrange theories, they are unified in their theoretical foundations which have become the hallmark of contemporary research in nutritional anthropology. They unify the intellectual traditions discussed above into a new definition of the *nutritional system* as a series of biocultural transactions, mediated by human decisions at every stage from food production, through dietary intake, to nutritional status and its health and behavioral implications. Decisions within the nutritional system lead to a series of adjustments and readjustments which have biological and social consequences for individuals and population groups and evolutionary implications for the world community.

Over the past five years this new speciality of nutritional anthropology has grown by both reputation and result. Courses in

"culture and nutrition" have become fundamental parts of under-
graduate curricula for both anthropology and nutrition students.
Specialized training programs stressing the integrated use of
methodologies from both disciplines have produced a new breed
of well-prepared professionals. The field itself has yielded new
insights into areas which could barely be foreseen five years ago.
These include:

1. a new perspective on the cultural sensitivity of nutritional
standards and the question of biological adaptation

2. the role of maternal feeding practices in fostering differential
nutritional status among children within a single socioeconomic
community

3. the role of social networks in changing dietary models

4. the nutritional implications of the cognitive structure of meal
planning

5. the impact of dietary anomalies, such as chronic hypo-
glycemia, in influencing the culture focus of entire isolated
ethnic groups

6. the precise description of the behavioral consequences of
differential nutritional status.

Recently, it has become clear that the study of the nutritional
system has come full circle. While earlier studies have concentrated
upon the social and cultural factors which influence nutritional
status, the new thrust of research is toward the elucidation of the
social and cultural consequences of differential nutritional status.
We believe that nutritional anthropology can contribute significantly to these studies in at least three areas: *First,* it can analyze the
development of differences in economic statuses and occupations
caused by differential nutritional status, as mediated through
differences in physical activity, work output, and motivation.
Second, it can address the question of differences in cultural
practices, as these are influenced by differences in cognitive and
sensory capacity, and consequent learning skills, resulting from
differential nutritional status. *Third,* it can study the formation,
structure, and interactive processes within families, social networks, and communities, as these are influenced by differential
nutritional statuses mediated through the development of differential social competence. Work by Gross and Underwood (1971)
and others has already shown that close, quantified observation of

intrafamilial food distribution patterns can reveal the existence of different biocultural groupings within a single socioeconomic community. These can have profound effects upon the lifestyles and success potentials of family members.

In writing the introduction, the editors are acutely aware that we exist not merely in an academic context but within a broader human environment. The "food habits" field which lay dormant for twenty years after the Committee on Food Habits abandoned the formulation of a policy to "feed the world" has been spurred to life as *nutritional anthropology* not simply to address scientific questions, but also to address the pressing national and global issues of food production, distribution, and use.

The publication of *Hunger, USA* in 1968 and the White House Conference on Food, Nutrition and Health in 1969 publicized the existence of pockets of starvation and malnutrition in the United States. In those years food became ammunition in the government's "War on Poverty." A new popular consciousness in America saw dietary change as a route to health maintenance and "eating lower on the food chain" as a means to restore global ecological balance. Then, in the early 1970s, drought in the Sahara, massive secret purchases of American wheat by the Russians, and price-fixing by the OPEC nations created global economic shock waves. Between 1972 and 1973 the price of wheat in the international marketplace rose from $2.00 to $5.00 a bushel. A politics of global food scarcity was born! Food and petroleum purchasing nations responded in kind by raising prices of cash crops like coffee and sugar. The pinch in the pocketbook was felt round the world.

People are cognizant of the massive global inequities in food distribution between the rich and the poor; they realize that even the diets of the affluent are not conducive to optimum health and fear that the world is caught in a last ditch race for survival between population growth and increased food production. Books like the works by the Club of Rome and *Diet for a Small Planet* (Lappé, 1971) have argued back and forth over the primacy of population control and increased food production.

Against this dire backdrop, the inequities of distribution in a world—where overnutrition may be implicated in the death of two-thirds of the affluent, and undernutrition may be implicated in the deaths of two-thirds of the poor—appears a tragic injustice. Books like *Food First* (Lappé and Collins, 1977) and *How the Other*

Half Dies (George, 1977) have laid the blame on profit-seeking agribusiness and selfish governments. The need to develop a politically, economically, and environmentally secure world food reserve has been clearly manifested.

It is evident that the experimental establishments of nutritional requirements and standards and the development and dissemination of Green Revolution technology alone cannot improve the nutritional status of the large masses of needy human beings unless they are understood and employed in conjunction with social, cultural, economic, and political forces. It is in this dramatic context that the new *nutritional anthropology* has been born, and it is toward the solution of these critical problems that we hope its maturity will serve. We believe that the nutritional health of the international community will be facilitated by the search for solutions to improve our ability to operationalize the biocultural approach presented in these pages and to employ its insights in the formulation of a global nutritional policy.

The papers in this volume spotlight various points in the biocultural matrix of nutritional need. The papers are organized around an evolutionary scheme through past and current nutritional systems. Chapter 1 provides an ecological model for the biocultural discipline, nutritional anthropology. In addition to providing a framework for generating and organizing theory, the model contains guidelines for organizing research operations. A general methodological strategy based on this model is described and discussed in chapter 2. The biocultural approach of nutritional anthropology is addressed in chapter 3 as Eide, a nutritional scientist, and Steady, a sociocultural anthropologist, apply certain elements of the ecological model to a discussion of women's roles and functions in nutritional processes in rural African economies.

In chapter 4, Yesner, an archaeologist, places human dietary adaptations for different groups, localities, and conditions in evolutionary perspective. The archaeological evidence indicates that settlement patterns are "minimax" adaptive strategies that involve responses to external factors (e.g., environmental change), as well as to internal cultural factors (e.g., patterns of selection, exchange, or redistribution of resources) (cf. Alland, 1970). These settlement patterns maximize the use of dietary resources.

Cassidy, a biological anthropologist, expands on Yesner's discussion (in chapter 5) by providing data on nutrition and health for two prehistoric hunter-gatherer and agricultural skeletal populations obtained from two archaeological sites in Kentucky. The archaeological evidence indicates that agriculturalists had poorer health and shorter life spans than the hunter-gatherers, a difference apparently attributable to the inferior diet used by the agriculturalists. Cassidy indicates that agriculturists experienced population growth and increased cultural complexity *in spite of* unpredictable and low food supplies and the consumption of items of low nutritional quality, and *despite* increased rates of ill health.

The evolutionary perspective pursued in chapters 4 and 5 is advanced in chapter 6 by Weiss, a cultural anthropologist. Weiss provides a detailed description of food production, distribution, and consumption patterns of a contemporary group—the Miskito Indians of eastern Nicaragua. In this case, the theme is nutritional adaptation and cultural maladaption. By combining ethnographic and nutrition survey methods, Weiss shows that the aboriginal Miskito, who had achieved environmental adaptation through multiple resource exploitation. later became victims of external intervention.

Aboriginally, the Miskito had utilized a divergent set of local resources to supply their matter-energy requirements throughout the annual cycle. Later, with the onset of commercial turtling, the alteration of the evolutionary timeframe, and the virtual elimination of multiple subsistence pathways, maladaptation to the environment ensued. Weiss supplements Cassidy's conclusions on the nutritional consequences of tradeoffs in economic systems. However, he emphasizes the internal systems-breakdown factor in the evolutionary timeframe through external control.

The ethnographic evidence on adaptive mechanisms for controlling population size is fairly rich. However, there is a small body of data to indicate that sex-differential diets may yet be another form of population control. Rosenberg, a cultural anthropologist, explores the question of sex-differential diets by examining the ethnographic literature. Her findings are presented in chapter 7. The chapter presents descriptions of sex-differential nutrition for a variety of societies. Can these practices be considered mechanisms for population control? It is difficult to say. What are the nutritional consequences of these sex-specific diets? Again, given the data, it is difficult to say, but it is well worth exploring these diets beyond the currently available literature.

Although sex-differentiated diet patterns require further testing in the field, we have fairly reliable data on the nutritional consequences of microeconomic and minicultural differentiated diet patterns. Economic microdifferentiation and diet variation are probably key factors in preventing internal systems-breakdown in changing economies and living situations. Chapters 8 and 9 pursue these themes. DeWalt, Kelly, and Pelto (chapter 8) and Jerome (chapter 9) demonstrate that these twin situations are played out at the village level in a Mexican agricultural community and in an urban blue-collar black community in the American Midwest. Their findings are unique only in the sense that the researchers employed methodologies which penetrated "the culture" and constructs of "food beliefs," in order to unfold heterogeneity in situations which have been described as homogeneous. Combined ethnographic and nutritional methodologies as used by the authors permitted insights and perspectives which are usually indiscernible by uni-disciplinary procedures.

Nutrition correlates of intracultural variation and economic micro-differentiation probably reflect an individual or family's adaptation or maladaptation to the local environment. The correlates of nutritional intake with microeconomics and miniculture suggest that these factors could be used as sensitive indices of environmental adaption.

Marchione (chapter 10) takes us one step further by quantifying some intracultural and microeconomic factors influencing nutritional status. With the aid of factor analysis, he links young child malnutrition to ecological factors in one of Jamaica's western parishes. This method of analysis permits the reader to view food use and diet patterning within the context of the larger society. Highly specific household measures are integrated into macroscopic socioeconomic and environmental variability which are relatable to both young child malnutrition and socioeconomic conditions in Jamaica. The cultural anthropologist thus demonstrates that a biological condition (young child malnutrition) is an adaptational response to scarce food energy resources and material conditions which, in turn, is built into the socioenvironmental structure.

Chapter 11 should be considered the next logical step in expanding the use of nutritional-anthropological perspectives on food use by a contemporary group. Kandel and Pelto (chapter 11) compel us to view the health food movement of the early 1970s in the United States as a social revitalization force and a consumer-designed health maintenance system. The theme of this chapter is dietary change. The reader is presented with a wealth of data that show how ideology and dissatisfaction with the status quo lead to redefinitions of health and diet and the development of systems for social interaction and self-realization.

References

Alland, A.
    1970   *Adaptation in Cultural Evolution.* New York: Columbia University Press.
Bennett, J.
    1943   Food and Social Status in a Rural Society. *American Sociological Review* 8:561-569.
    1976   *The Ecological Transition: Cultural Anthropology and Human Adaptation.* New York: Pergamon Press.
Cussler, M. G. and de Give, M. L.
    1952   *Twixt the Cup and the Lip.* New York: Twayne.
George, S.
    1977   *How the Other Half Dies: The Real Reasons for World Hunger.* Montclair, New Jersey: Allanheld, Osmun and Company.
Gross, D. R. and Underwood, B. A.
    1971   Technological Change and Caloric Costs: Sisal Agriculture in Northeastern Brazil. *American Anthropologist* 73: 725-740.
Hunger, USA
    1968   A Report by the Citizens Board of Inquiry into Hunger and Malnutrition in the United States. Boston: Beacon Press.
Lappé, F. M.
    1971   *Diet for a Small Planet.* New York: Ballantine Books, Inc.
Lappé, F. M. and Collins, J.
    1977   *Food First: Beyond the Myth of Scarcity.* Boston: Houghton Mifflin Company.
National Research Council, Committee on Food Habits
    1945   Manual for the Study of Food Habits. Washington, D.C.: National Academy of Sciences, National Research Council.
Richards, A. I.
    1932   *Hunger and Work in a Savage Tribe.* London: G. Routledge and Sons, Ltd.
Service, E.
    1962   *Primitive Social Organization.* New York: Random House.
    1971   *Cultural Evolutionism.* New York: Holt, Rinehart & Winston.
Simoons, F.
    1961   *Eat Not This Flesh.* Madison: University of Wisconsin Press.
Singer, E. A.
    1978   Guest Editorial: Thoughts on the New Foodways. *The Digest: A Newsletter for the Interdisciplinary Study of Food* 1:3.
Steward, J.
    1955   *Theory of Culture Change.* Urbana: University of Illinois Press.
White, L.
    1949   *The Science of Culture.* New York: Farrar, Straus & Cudahy Company.
    1959   *The Evolution of Culture.* New York: McGraw-Hill Book Company.

1

An Ecological Approach to Nutritional Anthropology

N. W. Jerome
G. H. Pelto
R. F. Kandel

Introduction

Throughout the six million years of human existence, people have found means of producing adequate, palatable, ecologically adaptive, and ideologically acceptable diets within a vast range of environmental contexts and cultural patterns. When population growth made increased food production biologically imperative, ingenious strategies such as agriculture, animal domestication and industrial farming have been employed in order to expand food resources.

But today the threat of the Malthusian prophecy has raised serious questions about our continued ability to provide enough food for the ever-increasing world population. Malnutrition, caused both by global scarcity and pockets of overabundance, is widespread and well known. Efforts to deal with nutritional problems have met with mixed and often disappointing results. However, the failures as well as the successes of food programs have led to an increased understanding of these matters by the public and government and within the scientific community. The issues involved are complex and require a focus that incorporates biological, psychological, social, cultural and economic factors. More comprehensive models are needed to understand human food systems and to guide food production and food distribution policies and programs.

   Below, we present one potentially powerful model. It is based upon an ecological approach to human nutrition and integrates biological, psychological, social, cultural, and economic factors. We also review the major types of food production systems from this perspective.

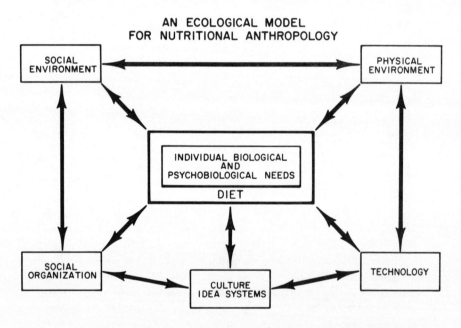

AN ECOLOGICAL MODEL
FOR NUTRITIONAL ANTHROPOLOGY

At the center of the diagram are individual biological require-ments for nutrients and psychological needs for nurturance which comprise the heart of the system. Individual requirements are conditioned not only by generalized species characteristics but also by developmental stage, activity level, reproductive demands, genetic characteristics, and various stress situations throughout the life cycle. Nutrient requirements are satisfied through the ingestion of food, which comprises the diet—the product of a particular food-producing system.

The surrounding boxes, which form part of an open system with the individual, represent the various aspects of a given society's food-producing system. The *physical environment* includes climate, water resources, soil characteristics, and related features which establish conditions for production. The broad *social environment* encompasses other societies whose food production and distribution behavior can have profound effects on the society in question. *Social organization* refers to a large set of features, including the economic and political structures related to food production and distribution, division of labor, and microlevel features of household structure. *Technology* embraces the tools and techniques of food production and distribution, including agricultural practices, food processing and transportation systems, domestic storage, and food preparation. *Cultural and ideological systems* include ideas about the role of food in health, religious beliefs involving food, food preferences and restrictions, and the use of food in social interactions, among others.

The ecological approach is valuable for delineating elements of a dynamic system, determining how the various elements work together, identifying hazards or potential stress areas, predicting types and direction of change, and assessing adaptive and deleterious responses to both planned and unplanned change.

The ecological perspective that Rappaport (1971a) describes for anthropology is especially pertinent to the study of nutritional ecology. His approach is to determine whether "behavior undertaken with respect to social, economic, political or religious conventions contributes to or threatens the survival and well-being of actors and whether this behavior maintains or degrades the ecological system in which it occurs" (Rappaport, 1971a:7). With this perspective it is possible to study biological, physical, and cultural environments in an integrated fashion (Baker, 1962). Nutritional ecology thus represents an endeavor that is aimed at contributing to a *holistic* understanding of human activity—one of the original goals of the science of anthropology.

Nutritional ecology should not be confused with a simplistic environmental determinism. As Sahlins has expressed it, we would exchange the notion of environmental determinism for one of "environmental possibilism, which holds that cultures act selectively, if not capriciously, upon their environments, exploiting some possibilities while ignoring others; that it is environment that is passive, an inert configuration of possibilities and limits to development the deciding forces of which lie in culture itself and in the history of culture" (Sahlins, 1977:215).

However, the potential for cultural selectivity varies in relation to environmental potential, the variety of edible foods, the level of technology, commerce, marketing strategies, and the extent of foreign intervention and intercultural contact. For example, until recently the Copper Eskimo subsisted primarily on an indigenous food supply and exercised only limited selectivity (Damas, 1972), whereas members of modern industrialized societies, who may also consume significant amounts of local foods, exercise a great deal of selectivity (Jerome, 1970, 1975, 1976).

Nutritional Adaptation and Maladaptation

Responses to the environment can be both adaptive and maladaptive. Adaptiveness is expressed in the ability of the human body to rally or respond positively to the insult of nutritional stress by altering physical or metabolic activity while maintaining function (Mitchell, 1964). When limited nutrient intake occurs for a delimited period of time, the body adapts by efficiently utilizing what is available. This form of adaptation is time-specific. When nutrients are limited for prolonged periods, these adjustive responses become maladaptive and can even lead to death. This conception of "nutritional adaptation" is an aspect of health. As defined by Audy, health is "a continuing property, potentially measurable by the individual's ability to rally from insults, whether chemical, physical, infectious, psychological or social" (Audy, 1971:142).

While examples of nutritional stress illustrate some of the dynamics of nutritional adaptation, they tend to present a limited picture of the intricacies of metabolic life. Nutritional adaptation also refers to the change in individual nutrient requirements in response to age, sex, activity, stress, disease, climate, altitude, and a wide range of socioenvironmental factors. The varied nutritional requirements of human groups living under a wide variety of environmental conditions are reflected in the variations of established recommended daily dietary allowances for different populations (Young, 1964:306-322).

In broad terms, nutritional adaptation applies to any situation in which an individual or population has adapted to the nutrients available in the diet, either metabolically or behaviorally and has expressed functional nutritional well being. Naturally, a wide range of nutritional health is manifest under varied conditions. A group could conceivably achieve functional nutritional health in a particular ecosystem and, at the same time, be considered malnourished in a different ecosystem. For example, the small stature of pre-war Japanese was an adaptation to the limited available supply of nutrients. MacPherson (1963) cites the unusual stamina and physical feats of apparently malnourished New Guineans as an indication of physiological adaptation to a particular way of life. At the opposite end of the continuum are those individuals and populations who have not been able to sufficiently adapt to the available quantity and quality of nutrients. Such people fail to manifest functional nutritional well-being in their ecosystems. Therefore, they suffer malnutrition.

Nutritional maladaptation can take many forms, including the classical deficiency diseases such as scurvy, beriberi, rickets, pellagra, marasmus, and kwashiorkor where dietary intakes are insufficient for metabolic needs. The more recent diseases of dietary excess such as obesity, dental caries, hypertension, coronary heart disease, and probably some types of cancer, also represent maladaptation.[1] Both classes of diseases—deficiency and dietary excess—reflect activities in the environment and responses to environmental elements that are nutritionally maladaptive.

The illustrations provided in this chapter depict some "processes of response to hazards and environmental perturbations," which Vayda and McCay (1975:293) perceive as the domain of ecology and ecological anthropology. Environmental hazards abound everywhere. They may be present in the form of nutrient deficits or excesses of specific food items, food combinations, or in the total food supply. They may also be present as naturally occurring or manufactured toxicants in food and drink. Intentional additives such as flavorings, sweeteners, preservatives, colorings, emulsifiers, stabilizers, and flavor enhancers could also contribute significant hazards. Accidental additives can be equally hazardous. These include pesticides, insecticides, rodenticides, fungicides, herbicides, antibiotics, hormones, toxic metals, and numerous components used in food processing and packaging. The sociocultural and psychological environments may be hazardous also if they lack the elements necessary for creative responses to changes in the system.

Sociocultural Factors in Nutritional Deficiency Diseases

A wide range of nondietary factors contribute to nutritional adaptation and malnutrition. These include sociocultural and aesthetic factors influencing what is used as food, by whom, in what amounts and under what circumstances. Economic and social relations regulating food production, supply, distribution and consumption, and dietary rules about food avoidances—especially among vulnerable groups such as pregnant and lactating women, infants, young children, and the ill, also lie in the sociocultural domain.

Throughout much of the world, spiritual or supernatural etiologies are applied to diseases that we recognize as due to nutritional deficiencies. In many parts of the developing world, protein-calorie malnutrition in young children is believed to be completely nondietary and brought on by breach of taboos or other insults to the supernatural. For example, among the northeast coastal Bantu, where kwashiorkor (*chirwa*) is endemic, malnutrition is thought to be caused by the breach of the taboo that forbids the parents from sexual intercourse during the period of gestation or before the child is weaned. It is believed that should a second pregnancy occur, the unborn fetus would "steal the strength" from the mother's milk, and the nursing child would suffer. Actually this taboo is adaptive in that it helps space pregnancies and is therefore beneficial to both the mother and the nursing child. However, if a second pregnancy does occur and the guilt associated with the breach of taboo (manifested in the child's kwashiorkor) inhibits the parents from taking appropriate action to restore their child's health, the adaptive potential is lost (Gerlach, 1964).

Another example comes from Buganda. The Buganda understanding of *obwosi* (kwashiorkor) is that it is caused by the jealousy that the unborn fetus feels toward the suckling sibling. The fetus takes revenge by making the child sick. To avoid illness when another pregnancy occurs, the nursing child is often separated from the mother and taken into custody by a grandmother or other relative who frequently does not provide a nutritious diet. Rather than serving as a preventive, this action may precipitate kwashiorkor. The inadequate diet, coupled with the psychological trauma of separation from the mother, often worsens the condition (Burgess and Dean, 1962; Cravioto, 1966; Amann et al. 1972). Kwashiorkor that results from separation is termed *omusana*, which is believed to be caused by the "cold" nights the child spends away from its mother (Burgess and Dean, 1962:25).

Nutritional diseases other than kwashiorkor are also attributed to nondietary causes. For example, Govil et al. (1958) report that in eastern Uttar Pradesh, night blindness is most prevalent during the dry summer season when green leafy vegetables cannot be grown. However, the villagers associate their night blindness with the heat of the sun.

A myriad of folk beliefs associated with intrinsic magical and semimagical properties of foods have characterized the rationale behind the dietary practices of all peoples. Some foods offer prestige (white bread and polished rice); others, security (milk in the U.S., rice in Asia), and still others a sense of group identification ("ethnic" foods) (Jerome, 1970). Food avoidance may be viewed as an expression of God's moral law (i.e., kashrut, Islamic abstention from pork and Ramadan, lenten abstention from meat, and totemic taboos of certain local religions). Frequently, beliefs concerning the intrinsic value of foods are associated with critical periods in the life cycle, i.e., pregnancy, lactation, disease, etc. Often, such beliefs are neutral in their nutritional impact, e.g., the Papago avoidance of salts and sweets by the mother until the umbilical cord falls off the infant (Gonzalez, 1972), or the avoidance of timid animals or repulsive-looking food to protect the infant from growing up timid or ugly (Hughes, 1963).

But some food taboos eliminate a much needed nutrient from the diet, especially at critical periods. These food taboos include the prohibition of eggs in the diets of women of childbearing age to avoid sterility and childbirth complications (HEW, 1973); the avoidance of milk by lactating mothers; the Burmese reduction of meat and fowl during pregnancy (Mead, 1955); the Papago diet of maize and wheat flour gruel for the first days following childbirth; the Tewa prohibition of milk for four weeks after childbirth (Gonzalez, 1972); the Navajo preferences for serving coffee and soft drinks to their children on the assumption that milk is a "weak" food (Reisinger et al. 1972); and the Zulu taboo against consuming milk from cows not owned by kin (Cassel, 1957). Because all cultures attach symbolic significance to their food, examples of food-linked taboos are virtually limitless.

The symbolic value of foods is also linked with healing. Many peoples associate the physical characteristics of a plant with specific healing properties (for example, heart-shaped leaves are believed to possess healing powers for the heart; red plants are believed to cure blood diseases). Often, however, foods are accorded qualities that are less easily identifiable. The *hot* and *cold theory of disease*, prevalent among some Latin American groups, is a classic example of this. Just as applicable is our own current obsession with the semimagical healing powers of vitamins C and E and ginseng products.

The examples cited clearly indicate that folk ideas and beliefs— and the behaviors emanating from these beliefs—work *in conjunction with* nonideational factors to influence food intake. Edibles are given, withheld, or provided in limited amounts based on ideas of their appropriateness for specific individuals at specific times. Sometimes symbolic and biological requirements coincide for sound ecological adaptation; at other times they conflict and maladaptation ensues.

Methods of preparation carry nutritional implications in terms of nutrient retention or loss; for example, parboiling rice retains important nutrients. The specific mix or combination of staple grains, seeds, and legumes is important to the protein content of the diet. Similarly, certain food combinations inhibit or enhance mineral absorption; for example, phosphates and phytates inhibit iron absorption and phytates inhibit calcium absorption. It has been reported that osteomalacia in the female Bedouin living in the Negev Desert of Israel is attributed to the high phytic acid content of the unleavened bread (similar to the Indian *chapati*) consumed by these women (Berlyne et al. 1973).

On the other hand, iron absorption is enhanced in the presence of ascorbic acid. The addition of certain ingredients during meal preparation can modify its nutritional composition; traditional alkali processing of maize in the preparation of tortilla increases the availability of lysine in its overall nutritional quality. In food preparation also, valuable nutrients, micronutrients, and fibrous material may be discarded as waste.

The temperature at which certain foods are stored may either provide safety and extend "shelf life" or furnish an appropriate environment for the growth of microorganisms. Inappropriate time-temperature relationships in the storage of foods also reduce or destroy important nutrients.

Within the family, patterns of food distribution have nutritional consequences. The order of eating, the identity or status of individuals allotted large quantities and first choice in food selection, and the method of serving food to individual household members affect who will be well or poorly nourished.

Patterns of food selection, distribution, and consumption vary in different types of societies. In peasant communities and in economies marked by subsistence agriculture, economically-productive household members are often given first choice of highly-prized meal items. Generally, this practice is reversed in high income or technologically-advanced societies. Infants, young children, and other "nonproductive" members of the group (e.g., the ill and the elderly) have some advantage when a family is faced with a limited supply of food. Both practices may lead to malnutrition in the form of overnutrition (among the favored) and undernutrition (among the neglected). For example, in Ethiopia (as in many East African nations) the father is granted priority in meal selection, followed, in order, by guests, the mother, the children, and finally the youngest children (Habte, 1969). During the critical growth years, the weaned child must consume the least desirable leftover adult foods without any special dietary supplementation.

In the developed world, obesity is now the most common pediatric disorder (Lloyd, 1969). Infant and childhood obesity in high-income countries stem from overconsumption of all foods, especially carbohydrate foods, sugary snacks, and milk. Purvis's (1973) analyses of diet records of 377 U.S. children thirteen months of age or younger showed that a majority of the infants and children consumed too much of a wide variety of foods. The group of babies studied was fed 563 different food items. Most babies greatly exceeded NAS Recommended Dietary Allowances for food energy, protein, vitamins, and minerals (except iron). A report of older children in Sweden also showed that the caloric density of foods consumed by young children was very high. Samuelson's report on health and nutrition of 1,401 children aged four to thirteen residing in three areas in a northern Swedish county revealed a trend toward consumption of diets rich in fat and refined sugar products. Carbohydrate-rich snacks and between-meal eating were common in all areas and age groups. The major part of the children's diet consisted of milk, cereal, and sugar (Samuelson,

1971). This pattern of food consumption is quite common in high-income countries.

Another feature of contemporary society that may contribute to obesity is a process that can be described as "individualizing" food selection and consumption. In a study of a U.S. midwestern, urban community, it was discovered that people respond to food abundance, diversity, and specialized food packaging by developing idiosyncratic and highly-individualized consumption patterns (Jerome, 1976). This feature may be characteristic of groups living in modern, urbanized societies.

The dynamics of food use in different ecological settings—combined with folk beliefs concerning the wisdom of excluding or including particular dietary items under specific conditions—expands or limits the actual diet consumed, thus promoting or inhibiting nutritional adaptation.

Nutritional Ecology in Different Types of Food Systems

Anthropologists find it useful to categorize societies in terms of their subsistence or food production systems (Harris, 1971; Pelto and Pelto, 1976). "Through the centuries several main types of societies developed as *relatively* stable adaptations based on complex interactions of food technology and environmental possibilities" (Pelto and Pelto, 1976: 225). Although the basic patterns are adapted to local conditions in myriad ways, certain features of social organization and nutritional ecology appear to be associated in nonrandom ways with each of the main types. In the following sections, the main characteristics of each of these systems will be sketched. However, it is important to recognize that understanding the dynamics of nutritional adaptation in any particular society requires careful and detailed analysis of a very large series of variables, as indicated in the ecological model described earlier.

Hunting and Gathering Food Systems

Hunting and gathering systems may be defined as the absence of deliberate and organized arrangements for long-term food production (e.g., agriculture or husbandry of animals). For more than 99 percent of human existence, Homo sapiens lived as a hunter-gatherer. Accounts of hunter-gatherers living today or in the historical past offer clues about the subsistence activities of prehistoric populations and suggest the dietary patterns and health standards of early humans. Naturally, direct correlations cannot be made because habitats, cultures, experience, and social organizations vary.

Hunting-gathering groups depend primarily on the indigenous foodstuffs of their local environment, affording them less control over diet than exists in other types of food systems. Their diets exhibit a great range in nutritional adequacy from abundance (sometimes coupled with high dietary selectivity) to chronic scarcity. Hunter-gatherers tend to be less destructive of their environments than food-producers and have developed numerous cultural mechanisms for maintaining a constant local food supply.

The Copper Eskimo illustrates successful adaptation to the sharply-limited food resources of their hazardous arctic tundra habitat—where white spruce and willow are the only vegetation. In the traditional diet (composed primarily of animal foods) caribou and ringed seal were most highly prized. The Copper Eskimo also hunted fox, wolf, and other small animals and fished for lake trout and char. Diet selectivity, limited by the harsh environment, was further restricted by seasonal variations in the food supply.

While the physical environment played a major part in determining diet, many other features of the ecological system were involved. The technology, developed in response to environmental imperatives, was designed for specific types of food acquisition. Bows, arrows, harpoons, lances, kayaks, knives, drills, and adzes (to name some of the tool kit) facilitated fishing and hunting in the arctic tundra (Damas, 1972).

The social organization, built on a system of reciprocal food distribution (termed *piqat*), helped to assure that everyone in the community received food. The successful seal hunter would bring his catch home to be divided among his family and his partners' families. If all his partners were present for the distribution, the hunter took only the least desirable sections—the fat, entrails, and skin. In return, he received choice sections of meat from his partners' catches. This system of food exchange offered more than security; undoubtedly it enhanced community relations and promoted the solidarity and cooperation that are so necessary in a marginal environment.

Perhaps related to the matter of food scarcity, the Copper Eskimo developed a series of religious sanctions and food taboos that further regulated diet. Food-linked prohibitions were associated with the meager products of a meager environment; e.g., fear of displeasing a deity, with resultant food loss, dictated that there be no contact between land and sea mammals. However, even with the cultural mechanisms for acquiring and distributing food, famine occurred fairly frequently. The practice of female infanticide helped to limit population size, but the cyclical nature of the food failed to provide year-around security.

Generally, the living conditions of the Copper Eskimo are typical of other arctic populations in the New World. Laughlin (1966) describes similar strategies of adapting to the habitat and acquiring food for other North American arctic populations.

The Guayaki Indians are also hunter-gatherers. Inhabiting the tropical forests of Paraguay, an environment that also offers surprisingly few edible fruits or vegetables, the Guayaki respond to concentrating their activity on hunting. Clastres (1972) reports that the economic life of the Guayaki is a continual food quest. Hunting is not only the focus of economic activity, but is also important in the socioreligious life and ritual activity of the group. Besides hunting and the generally unproductive fishing or gathering, Guayaki subsistence activities include a search for much-prized honey and larvae. Due to lack of surplus and storage facilities, food-getting activities start anew every day. For the Guayaki, as for the Copper Eskimo, the diet composition is directly related to the limited food sources. Guayaki cultural adaptations decrease the chance that any one member will go hungry. Clastres confirms their lack of options for diet selectivity by stating, "The life of the Guayaki depends directly upon a familiarity with their natural habitat—these Indians eat all animals of the forest, almost without exception." (The exception being the avoidance of birds with mythological significance.) (Clastres, 1972: 154).

The limitations of the environment, as indicated by a scarcity of plant sources, have been virtually overcome by the group's undiscriminating selection of animal foods. This assures the Guayaki an adequate and constant food supply.

Effective exploitation of the environment depends on a technological inventory—the bows and arrows of the hunters, plus spears, digging sticks, baskets, pottery, and other containers. The simple technological complex is consistent with the nomadic lifestyle that prohibits a large inventory of material possessions. Also, like the Copper Eskimo, the Guayaki system of game distribution includes rules prohibiting a hunter from consuming his own catch. The hunter's catch is divided among tribal members; each hunter relies on the catch of others for his own consumption. Again, this not only offers security in food but reinforces intragroup relations (Clastres, 1972).

To avoid the conclusion that a hunter-gatherer subsistence base implies minimal diet selectivity in marginal environments, we also must consider examples of hunter-gatherer groups who subsist in rich environments and exercise a great degree of selectivity from environmental possibilities. A classic example of such a group is the !Kung Bushmen of the Kalahari Desert. Lee (1972) has successfully destroyed the myth that all hunter-gatherer groups lived in constant peril of starvation and were forced to spend the majority of their waking hours in the food quest. Instead, he presents the picture, which he claims is common of hunter-gathers, of people who are well adapted to their environment and enjoy high health standards, while expending minimal time and energy in quest of food. In addition to the stable food supply, the dry climate and high elevation result in freedom from most infectious diseases endemic in tropical Africa.

While the !Kung Bushmen are both hunters and gatherers, the major portion of the diet by weight comes from reliable and nutritious plant sources. Though meat is highly relished, its supply is scarce and unpredictable, and it therefore plays a secondary role in the diet. The !Kung diet includes over 100 species of edible plants in the Dobe area. However, 90 percent of the diet by weight is obtained from twenty-three species; these include the very popular mongongo, baobob, and marula nuts. The abundance of food sources evidently allows a great deal of diet selectivity; less palatable foods are consumed only in times of scarcity. Factors contributing to this security are: (1) primary dependence on vegetable food over animal, (2) thorough knowledge and understanding of the local environment, and (3) reciprocal food distribution that pervades Bushmen social life. Further evidence of food security derives from the proportion of time spent in leisure. Women average two to three days per week in the food quest and enjoy their leisure time by visiting camps, sleeping, entertaining, or doing embroidery.

!Kung Bushmen subsistence activities demonstrate an appreciation of human-environment interrelationships. They make no
distinction between natural resources and social wealth. Un-
tampered or "unimproved" land is their means of production. The
land is communally owned and available to all; therefore, since the
habitat is nature's storehouse, there is no need to amass a surplus of
food. These concepts and practices tend to reduce food anxiety for
there is an implicit confidence in the ability of the environment to
provide for the group. Sahlins (1972) generalizes this confidence to
all hunters stating that "storage would be superfluous" when the
true surplus is everywhere. A stored surplus, like an abundance of
material goods, would only limit their mobility. The variety and
abundance of naturally available foods makes the tedious agricultural work of their Bantu neighbors quite unattractive.

Thus, the !Kung Bushmen stand out as an example of a hunter-
gatherer group that relies totally on naturally-occurring food
sources, yet exercises a great degree of cultural discrimination and
selectivity, while extracting a highly nutritious diet.

The Hadza represent another example of a hunter-gatherer
group able to practice great selectivity in gathering plant foods
from their rich environment. Ther diet by weight consists of 80
percent vegetable foods; meat and honey constitute the remaining
20 percent (Woodburn, 1968). Infant feeding is permissive and
nursing is prolonged until the mother becomes pregnant again.
Fat, marrow, gruel of baobob seed, and honey are introduced at an
early age, and infants consume the full adult diet by the age of
eighteen months (Jelliffe et al. 1962).

The search for food and its distribution among members of the
group is loosely organized. Men and women gather food individually and eat at the gathering site; only the women bring home
surpluses. Hunting is an individualized male activity; the hunter
eats his fill at the kill site and brings home only the leftovers. Men
and women are independent of each other in the food quest; food
exchange is not an important part of their way of life (Woodburn,
1968). The rich and stable environment, with its reliable food
resources, facilitate this type of individualized food acquisition and
loose distribution system.

Judging from two health and nutrition studies, the Hadza are a
well-nourished people. Jelliffe and associates (1962) conducted a
study of Hadza children, which was followed by a second study by
Cockburn (1971). In both studies the children receive high ratings

for nutritional status: there was no clinical evidence of protein-calorie malnutrition, rickets, scurvy, or vitamin B deficiencies. Jelliffe and colleagues report bitot spots (a symptom of vitamin A deficiency) in 13 percent of "preschool" age children and in 17.3 percent of the older children. Twenty-seven percent suffered from malaria and 30 percent from conjunctivitis—a percentage very similar to that reported by Cockburn. Cockburn also found some evidence of parasites, taenia, giardia, and ringworm, but no roundworm or hookworm. He concluded that the children were afflicted with infections that could thrive in a small mobile population. The lack of extensive nutritional deficiencies and the low rate of infectious disease compared to neighboring agriculture populations demonstrates a successful adaptation to the environment.

The Copper Eskimo and Guayaki represent groups inhabiting very different marginal environments who both usually manage to extract an adequate diet from the limited possibilities. Strict institutionalized distribution systems are adaptive to the insecurity of the food supply. The !Kung Bushmen and the Hadza both occupy relatively rich environments and are afforded a great degree of dietary selectivity. Both groups subsist primarily on vegetable foods with meat as a delicacy. Yet, their social organizations differ dramatically. The !Kung enjoy sharing their food, particularly meat, and food passes freely between camps. The food quest of the Hadza and much of their consumption is individualized.

The lifestyles of hunting-gathering groups are characterized by a slow rate of cultural change and by methods of food provisioning that tend to foster environmental stability. Reliance on non-domesticated food sources entails a minimum of direct environmental manipulation, which results in minimal alterations in the ecosystem.[2]

Dunn (1968) makes an essential point about hunting-gathering in the following statement: "The group utilizes environmental resources intensively but with minimal permanent disturbance of the environment; the individuals are well adapted to the conditions of the ecosystem in which they belong; the individual lives in intimate contact with his fellows and the environment" (Dunn, 1968: 223).

Malnutrition is rare among hunter-gatherers, although there are instances of starvation (more so in arctic regions than in the tropics). Malnutrition is considerably less frequent than among agricultural groups who depend on one or two staple food crops (Dunn, 1968). Strategies for survival result in diets that provide adequate nutrients to the population a majority of the time. "To date," state Lee and DeVore (1968: 3), "the hunting way of life has been the most successful and persistent adaptation man has ever achieved." Dubos (1959: 152) captures the underlying theme of nutritional adaptation to marginal conditions by stating that "primitive cultures manage to derive fairly adequate nourishment from even the most desolate areas if the ecological conditions under which they live are stable." Macpherson's review (1963) of the aborigines in Australia and New Guinea and Baker's review (1962) of indigenous South Americans emphasize the same point.

Pastoralist Food Systems
Pastoralism (or husbandry of migratory herd animals) is "a cultural adjustment to semiarid open country in which native vegetation will support large ruminants but in which hoe agriculture without advanced technologies cannot be satisfied or sustained" (Goldschmidt, 1968: 240). In other words, it is an adaptive response to the exigencies of an arid, marginal ecosystem.

Goldschmidt (1968) outlines the following pastoralist characteristics: (1) mobile, with the associated limited material possessions, (2) militaristic, particularly with regard to raiding and protecting their herds, (3) male dominated patrilineal societies, (4) little or no concept of land ownership, (5) dependence on an adequate water supply, and, Sahlins (1968) adds an additional characteristic: (6) political cohesion.

Pastoralists can be divided into two types: nomads and seminomads. The nomads do not occupy permanent dwellings and do not practice agriculture, while the seminomads set up semipermanent settlements near water with part of the group (usually women and children) cultivating crops (Griggs, 1974). Pastoralists often live in a symbiotic relationship with nearby sedentary villages. Pastoralist communities enter into regional arrangements of internal peace, collective defense, and periodic distribution of natural resources.

Today, pressure to disrupt pastoralist tribes and relocate them on sedentary ranches has greatly decreased their numbers. Yet for over 3,000 years, they inhabited the area from the Atlantic shore of the Sahara to the steppes of Mongolia and parts of North and South America (Sahlins, 1968; Griggs, 1974).

The typical pastoralist diet derives largely from the herd. Milk, milk products, and blood are staple foods. Although meat is eaten, slaughtering of livestock is expectedly uncommon since the herd is the primary source of wealth. The animal-based diet is supplemented with vegetable foods which have been grown, gathered, or acquired through trade. The arid land prohibits high yield agriculture and offers a limited indigenous food supply.

The Jie of Uganda are typical pastoralists. Their subsistence strategy is adapted to a dry barren environment. The group makes use of two climatic zones—the relatively moist west and semidesert east. They experience a rainy season between March and August and a dry season for the remainder of the year. Jie settlements are located in the center, bordered by the two climatic zones. Pasture land is communally held. Gulliver (1968: 264) has captured the subsistence strategy of the Jie in the following description: "The Jie attempt to make the best use of their meager natural resources by pastoral transhumance between east and west regions, which they use for their herds in the rainy and dry seasons, respectively."

The Jie combine the raising of livestock with the cultivation of crops. Economic activities are divided sexually, the men take full responsibility for the livestock, and the women take charge of all agriculture.

The diet consists primarily of sorghum, meat, milk (especially for children who can consume as much milk as they desire), milk products, blood (taken from the necks of living animals), finger millet from which beer is made, and peanuts. This traditional diet has had few changes in the twentieth century (Gulliver suggests this is due to the uselessness of the land for western exploitation). The diet is a remarkable example of the resourcefulness that converted arid, tropical land into a productive, inhabitable area.

Although limited by a harsh environment and dependent upon sparse rainfall (necessary for the survival of livestock and crops), the Jie have been able to create food sources for themselves. Unlike hunter-gatherers, they produce some of their foods. They have successfully integrated food production, nomadism, and the accumulation of wealth (livestock) in a harsh environment. The Jie subsistence exemplifies a form of human environment interrelations based on plant and animal domestication, which apparently does not produce serious environmental degradation while providing sustenance for the population.

Systems of Agricultural Food Production
The full-scale commitment to reliance on domesticated plants and
animals contrasts with the lifestyle of hunting-gathering peoples in
several respects: deliberate food cultivation; food production to
provide surpluses; independence from naturally occurring plants
and sedentarism. These features can have both positive and
negative consequences for dietary adequacy and nutritional status.

From a cultural standpoint, the development of agriculture led to
new patterns of social organization and new forms of technology
for cultivating food crops and for processing and storing food. The
distribution of foods also required different social arrangements.
The social relations of hunter-gatherers are heavily influenced by
seasonal cycles and fluctuations in available food and water;
however, agriculturalists had to adapt their social institutions to the
complexities of the agricultural economy (Cohen, 1968).

Physical environments undergo major changes as a result of
human agricultural practices. Indigenous species are replaced with
preferred types, which tends to upset the "natural balance" of the
ecosystem. Thus, agricultural processes developed in response, but
not also in harmony with the environment. Often, these processes
have resulted in overcultivation, overgrazing, and subsequent
erosion of the land—consequences that are often followed by
drought, hunger, and malnutrition.

The extent to which agricultural produces environmental degradation depends on a number of environmental and social factors,
and, as described by Griggs (1974), some agricultural systems have
been relatively nondestructive. For example, the style of shifting
cultivation practiced by many rain forest cultivators appears to
represent an effective use of land, adaptive to the conditions of the
tropics and to low population density.

Horticultural Systems
Horticultural or "gardening" systems of food production are
distinguished by a number of criteria. Technology is generally
simple. Production is intended for household consumption rather
than commercial sale. The production unit is self-sufficient in that
producers control the means of production (Wolf, 1966; Mellor,
1969). There is relatively little interdependency with outside groups
for food, so market networks are not developed and social relations
involving food production are primarily ceremonial and ritual. The
Tsembaga Maring of New Guinea, who practice horticulture or
"swiddening" (slash and burn agriculture) plus swine husbandry

exemplify the life of simple cultivators. Their form of agriculture makes relatively light demands on energy inputs, yet provides for almost all of the dietary needs of the people (Rappaport, 1971b).

The Tsembaga are well acquainted with the nondomesticated plants in their environment and can name at least 264 varieties of edible plants representing thirty-six species of domesticated and wild plants. The staples are taro and sweet potatoes, but they cultivate a wide variety of other tubers, legumes, and leafy vegetables. Maize and sugar cane (more recent introductions) are also grown. The wide variety of cultigens and the system of planting permit the best use of space, soil, and light and discourages plant-specific pests. Food production is therefore ecologically sound. It is also nutritionally sound. Gardens produce calorically-adequate diets for both sexes: 2,600 kilocalories per day for men who average 4'10½" in height and 103 lbs. in weight; 2,200 kilocalories per day for the women who average 4'6½" in height and 85 lbs. in weight. The combination of "swiddening" and swine husbandry, and the production and use of a wide variety of foods provide a subsistence base that is productive, self-sufficient, and nutritionally adequate.

The Sanio-Hiowe of Papua, New Guinea, present another example of subsistence agriculturists. Sago palm production is a highly productive subsistence technology in the simply organized economy of the Sanio-Hiowe. The high energy return of sago allows women working only one day in four or five to provide 85 percent of the calorie intake for their families. A woman can produce sufficient sago in one day to provide for 16.7 people (Townsend, 1974).

The use of simple technology in the production of food and the noncommercial nature of transactions involving food production are characteristics of many horticultural groups. They exemplify stability, self-sufficiency, efficiency, productivity, and richness—characteristics consistent with health and well being.

The Peasantry and the Transition to Cash Economics

Peasants are distinguished from subsistence agriculturists primarily because they form part of a larger, compound society and are mutually dependent on the larger society (Foster, 1966; Wolf, 1966). This dependence is the key factor distinguishing peasants from tribal people; the latter do not have economic arrangements with groups in the larger society. Wolf (1966) has described peasants as rural cultivators who raise crops and livestock in the countryside for household consumption—not as a business enterprise. However, their surpluses are transferred to a dominant group of rulers who use the surpluses to underwrite their own standard of living or for distribution to still other groups in the society.

In contrast, societies based on horticulture exchange surpluses directly among members of their own groups. The loss of control over surplus food sharply distinguishes peasants from tribal people and is key to the unbalanced transactions between peasants and economic elites. This characteristic also underlies the problem of inadequate and unbalanced diets, which are common among peasant groups.

Malnutrition and nutrition-related health problems of peasants are not new but appeared with the development of state societies. For the New World, for example, Haviland (1967) has argued that the decreasing average stature of Mayan males from the early Classic period (250-550 A.D.) to Late Classic times represents the effects of an increasingly inadequate peasant diet. More recently, the transition to a fully cash economy and the shift from subsistence food crops to cash crops appears to be bringing about even more serious nutritional problems.

Mead (1955: 244) notes some of the nutritional effects of transforming economies by stating: "In general, the effect of a cash-crop or wage economy on nutrition has been one of lowering the level by distributing the balance achieved under subsistence economy." Often, the most fertile land is used for the cash crop (coffee, peanuts, cotton, cocoa), thus lowering the production capacity of the land under food cultivation. The shift to a cash economy also means that a large part, if not the majority, of food is purchased instead of produced. The high cost of protein rich foods often makes them prohibitive, thereby forcing people into an affordable high carbohydrate diet, which is often much less nutritious than the original peasant diet. Thus, under the guise of economic progress, nutritional status becomes vulnerable. This ironic turn of events is what Hughes and Hunter call "the hidden cost of development" (Hughes and Hunter, 1970: 452). The following examples will illustrate this point.

Collis (1962) recounts the effects of cash cropping in a West Nigerian village. Initially the idea of growing cocoa for a cash profit carried promises of prosperity. Cocoa offers a high yield per acre per energy output. The crop was grown in the rich valleys, while food crops were cultivated in the less fertile highlands. Eventually, cocoa planting moved uphill and seriously diminished the already waning food supply. Since food crops did not grow well under the shaded branches of cocoa, food production was reduced even further, leading to heavy reliance on purchased foods, especially cheap carbohydrate foods such as cassava and yams. The nutritional status of the villagers was thus compromised by the economic transformation.

The West Nigerian villagers have a high rate of malaria and *loa-loa* and a high infestation rate of ascaris and hookworm. Fifty-four to 60 percent of the children between one and fourteen years of age suffer from spleen enlargement. Kwashiorkor, precipitated by inadequate weaning foods, diarrhea, and infectious or parasitic diseases are prevalent. Collis offers this comment: "The cash crop tends to kill the traditional life of the villagers; it merely puts money in their pockets for a short period in the year, during which time they enjoy themselves. When the money gets scarce, months before the next harvest, they find themselves short of everything" (Collis, 1962: 223).

A similar report on the consequences of the introduction of sisal agriculture comes from northeastern Brazil (Gross and Underwood, 1971). The principal economic activities prior to the introduction of sisal centered around cattle raising and subsistence farming. With the introduction of sisal as a profitable export crop, small landowners partially or completely abandoned subsistence agriculture in order to plant the profit-making crop. The most common form of sisal cultivation in Brazil is transplantion of vegetatively-reproduced suckers, which require about four years to reach maturity. Small sisal growers must enter the labor market to obtain supplementary work during the four years required for the plants to mature. Generally, the men entered the labor force to work at decorticating the sisal. Decortication involves a mobile, manually-fed rotating rasp driven by a diesel motor; this requires high human labor inputs. Harvesting takes place year-around. At harvest time, small landowners usually found that either the price of sisal had fallen sharply since planting, or that they could not harvest at a profit because decorticating unit owners discriminated against them. Continuous income was derived from work as laborers on decorticating units.

Obviously, the change from subsistence agriculture to a cash crop (sisal) was advantageous to the relatively small number of persons who owned equipment and could control production and prices. The laborers' wages were generally inadequate to meet the subsistence needs of their families. Energy costs of sisal laborers were so great in relation to wages that their "nonproductive" dependents were deprived of calories and an adequate diet; growing children were especially affected. The evidence indicates that without depriving their families, the laborers would not have had the stamina to function as wage earners. Clearly, the nutritional status of the peasant had suffered as a result of the introduction of the cash crop. Commenting on their findings, the authors state that "sisal production is part of a system whose effect is to expropriate energy in the form of manual labor in one part of the world and apply it to the general welfare of another people thousands of miles away" (Gross and Underwood 1971).

The transition to cash cropping has affected aspects of the ecosystem in addition to nutritional standards; it has also taken its toll on the environment. For example, the Sahelian drought of 1972-74 illustrates the impact that a cash-oriented economy can have on a delicately-balanced ecosystem. Though a drought is viewed as an uncontrollable natural calamity, certain imprudent actions precipitated the crisis. According to Wade (1974a), the Sahelian drought and desertification was caused by years of overgrazing and overplanting without adequate fallow periods. Cash crops (cotton and peanuts) had been grown on the most fertile land, leaving only the poorest land for food crops. The less fertile soil could not take the strain of intensive cultivation and resulted in poor crop yield, soil exposure, erosion, and eventually desert. In addition, the deforestation led to a loss of nitrogen from the soil, and the overgrazing of pastures created boreholes. The combination of these events left the Sahelian environment without any resistance to the mere suggestion of drought.

A cash-crop or wage economy frequently has a disastrous effect on the nutritional adequacy of the diet. Hughes (1963) has reviewed many of the earlier reports. The balance achieved under a subsistence economy can be disturbed by the reduced supply of traditional food crops that generally occurs with a shift to cash crops. Increased nutritional needs to meet the demands of increased work and activity further exacerbate the problem.

Lilimani's analysis of malnutrition in Kenya, where one-fourth to one-third of the families consume less than 60 percent of the "minimum daily requirements" (MDR) in preharvest periods and one-fifth consume less than 80 percent in postharvest times, sums up the transition problems in many developing countries:

> The rural population consists of subsistence farmers who, together with the urban wage earners, business contractors and tradesmen, do not have sufficient purchasing power to buy the surplus proteins and thus obtain a healthy, nutritious diet. The country must export protein foods as part of the Agricultural Export Plan and it also must request protein aid. A person who cannot understand this fact cannot comprehend the problems of the transition period to a monetary economy or the whole paradox of development. (1969: 45)

One solution offered by Dr. Muñoz of WHO is to convert food crops into cash crops through increased production (Muñoz, 1969). Small land-holders need to be advised about the appropriate types of food to grow in their areas in order to provide more foods and a balanced diet. Surpluses sold at the market would bring in hard currency which, through education, can be used to improve the nutritional standards and to invest in high-yield agriculture. This recommendation begins to get at the issue of balanced economic planning, if not ecological balance.

A study conducted by the United Nations' Food and Agricultural Organization (FAO) showed the dietary differences typically associated with different income levels (Willet, 1973):

Per Capita Income Level	Percentage of Calories from Given Sources			
	Fat	Carbohydrates	Protein Animal	Vegetable
$ 100	15	75	2	8
$ 600	30	60	–	–
$2,600	40	50	8	2

The rise in fat content was attributed to increased consumption of separated fats, milk, meat, fish, vegetable fats, and oils. Carbohydrate consumption was marked by a decrease in cereals, pulses, roots, and tubers, and an increase in sugar. It is important to note that total protein calories did not increase with income, but protein sources changed. The change in carbohydrate source—sucrose instead of roots, tubers, and grains is also worthy of note.

Industrialized Agriculturists

Industrialized agriculture may be conveniently divided into two types: (1) the large-scale farming of modern, industrialized nations, e.g., agri-business in the United States; and (2) large-scale farming developed as a result of international aid programs in developing countries, e.g., the Green Revolution.

Large-scale farming in modern industrialized nations is usually a capital and energy intensive business enterprise designed as a commercial venture that incorporates a wide range of knowledge and skills in agricultural science and business to achieve high productivity. Agricultural science and economics have provided tools for gaining more control over other biological species through selective plant cultivation and animal breeding, and through the use of a wide variety of chemicals to achieve specific economic objectives. Food engineering, a counterpart of industrialized agriculture, has further expanded food productivity and economic growth in modern industrialized societies in its application of food science and technology to the manufacture and synthesis of foods. These systems of production require large inputs of energy derived from fossil fuels.

In wealthy nations practicing industrial agriculture, food is generally abundant. In the U.S., for example, more than 32,000 food and beverage items are available to American consumers in the average supermarket (Ullesvang, 1970). Most of the items are produced under highly-mechanized, modern agricultural procedures, and they are manufactured, preserved, stored, distributed, packaged, prepared, marketed, and promoted with the aid of highly sophisticated technology. The key to food selection for a large segment of the U.S. population is convenience and fun, while the food industry's major goal is production, diversification, and profit.

Food supply and consumption are dictated by the market. For example, beef consumption reached an all-time high of 152 pounds per capita in 1974, following a substantial increase in beef production. In 1975, per capita consumption of beef was 145 pounds as a result of price increases. Consumption of refined sugar reached an all-time high of 102 pounds per capita in 1973 but declined to 88 pounds per capita in 1975, following the sharp increase in prices (USDA, 1976). The consumption of other commodities varies according to the dictates of the market.

The nutritional consequences of an industrialized food system are as much a product of interactions among the series of components that comprise the ecological framework as they are in simple hunting-gathering systems. Individuals achieve their potentials for growth; they mature early, but many ingest an excess and possibly imbalanced supply of nutrients and other chemicals.

Approximately 12 percent of the U.S. calorie intake is obtained from protein, 42 percent from fat, and 46 percent from carbohydrates. In most low-income countries, carbohydrates represent 60 to 75 percent of the diet of most peoples, and protein intake (especially animal protein) may be as low as 2 percent.

Diseases of affluence—obesity, coronary heart disease, and hypertension—are endemic in the United States. These diseases are all diet related and suggest that excess supplies of food energy, nutrients, and other dietary elements may be misused or maldistributed and become nutritionally maladaptive to the population.

Maldistribution of food energy and dietary elements is expressed in the distribution of weight within a population. Leanness and fatness present a real paradox in nutritional ecology. Garn and Clark (1974) have discussed this paradox as indices of malnutrition in poor and rich countries. In the United States (and some other affluent countries) poor women of different racial backgrounds are often fatter than rich women. The opposite situation holds in poor countries and among poor men in rich countries. The disparities (for the poor Afro-American male, at least) are due to variations in living and dietary styles, including relative frequency of food consumption away from home among poor black males and females (Jerome, 1967).

Malnutrition and nutritional well being under industrialized agriculture and its concomitant large-scale food manufacturing system present a complex picture to nutritional ecology and should be assessed through the analysis of the multiple components and interactions of these systems. This is a tremendous challenge.

The socioeconomic situation is different in developing countries. The introduction of advanced agricultural techniques in developing nations has led to a wide range of responses. It appears that although food production increased in many areas of the developing world where modern agricultural techniques have been applied, the local population failed to benefit from the increased food supply. The status of the poor and ill fed either did not change or changed for the worse. Only the relatively wealthy could afford to take advantage of the agricultural innovations. Basically, these failures stem from a lack of congruence between agricultural innovations and the local ecology, and from the wholesale transfer of technologies into areas unable to integrate them into existing systems.

There have been benefits, however. Improved agricultural techniques have succeeded in raising overall food production levels. Since 1947, India has experienced an increase in agricultural productivity of 3.5 percent per year, while the population has grown at a rate of 2.5 percent (Franda, 1974). It has been claimed that the high-yield crops are an overall improvement over traditional varieties, even without the use of fertilizers (Wade, 1974b).

However, the impact of the Green Revolution on the nutritional status of the majority of traditional farmers appears to be quite negative. The criticism that modern methods have widened the gap between the rich and poor seems to be based on empirical fact (Griffen, 1975). The initial costs of investing in high-yield seeds, fertilizers, pesticides, herbicides, and modern equipment are beyond the reach of most small farmers and peasants. Furthermore, the high-yield varieties are adaptive to specific ecological zones. This greatly limits the utilization potential over large areas. For example, the new "miracle" rice available in Asian countries (excluding China) are adaptive to only 20 percent of the available crop land. Similarly, high-yield wheat strains developed for use with irrigation or high rainfall constitute only 6 percent of the wheat sown in western Asia and North Africa (Freebairn, 1973).

The Green Revolution has also had an impact on traditional social institutions. In particular, the system of mutual obligations and responsibilities between landowners and laborers has been disrupted, thereby "undermining village social welfare systems established over centuries" (Freebairn, 1973: 103). Workers have been replaced with the expansion of mechanized techniques, thereby creating a system of capital intensive production at the expense of labor intensive production in economies that are poor in capital but rich in labor.

Other limitations include the unavailability of credit for the small land holder who desired to participate in improved agricultural techniques. The combination of high credit risk for lenders and the length of time and risk required to actually profit from the investment leaves the small holder in an immobile position with little leverage to enjoy what he feels is rightfully his (Mellor, 1969). In the Indian Punjab, it appears that the farmer with less than ten acres who adopted the new agricultural practices of the Green Revolution suffered an actual decline in economic position (Freebairn 1973). Overall, it appears that the efforts of the Green Revolution succeeded in raising production, but failed to meet many of the basic needs of the local populations. Understanding the dynamics of these complex problems also poses a serious challenge to nutritional ecology.

Programs are being developed to overcome some of the problems associated with the Green Revolution. For example, the International Crop Research Institute for the Semi-Arid Tropics (ICRISAT) is developing high-yield seeds that are resistant to insect and disease predation and that can grow with little fertilizer (Franda, 1974). Other international agricultural research programs designed to extend the Green Revolution have been described by Wade (1975). A recent report by Greenland (1975) describes a program of the International Institute of Tropical Agriculture (IITA) in Nigeria. It is aimed at developing farming systems that enhance the ability of the small farmer to benefit from improved crop varieties. Greenland correctly advocates that before attempting to replace the traditional "shifting" system of agriculture, a careful analysis must be made of all factors that led to a stabilization of the system, including the shifting cultivators' adherence to that system when offered alternatives. Obviously, the type of analysis advocated will include the interplay of technological, psycho-social, cultural, biological, and physical factors in a dynamic ecosystem.

Conclusions

In the preceding discussion we have attempted to develop a perspective for examining food and diet in a holistic fashion. In some circumstances the complex interactions in an ecosystem lead to nutritionally positive outcomes. However, in other conditions, malnutrition may be a consequence of such interactions. The linkages among the various components of a food system present challenges, hazards, and benefits at every stage of food production, processing, storage, utilization and consumption, as well as in refuse disposal.

In many instances economic change and modernization have had an adverse effect on the dynamic equilibrium of particular systems. "Economic development" has also had a negative effect on the nutritional status of subsistence farmers, fishermen, herdsmen, small landowners, and their families in many parts of the world. It is clear that as societies have developed more complex economic systems, nutritional well being has often been impaired. In many cases the rapid rate of change has prohibited adequate biological and cultural adaptation.

Nutritional ecology as described and discussed in this chapter provides a frame of reference for understanding how various human-food environment interactions influence dietary standards. Insults or assaults to any one constituent of the interacting system could ultimately disrupt the entire system and the established dietary standard. This perspective is valuable for systems analysis involving agriculture, food production and use, diet, and health. It is particularly useful for analyzing the direction of change and the nutritional consequences of changing systems.

Acknowledgments

This chapter has been adapted from an earlier paper by the senior author entitled "Nutritional Dilemmas of Transforming Economies," which appeared in *Food Policy: The Responsibility of the United States in Life and Death Choices*. P. Brown and H. Shue eds. New York: The Free Press, 1977.

Notes

1. If there is indeed a direct relationship between refined diet and colorectal cancer, this should be viewed as a deficiency disease. Breast cancer and cancer of the colon appear to be associated with high intakes of certain dietary components, e.g., animal fat, animal protein, and cholesterol.

2. There are exceptions, of course, including the possibility that big-game hunting by North American prehistoric populations was largely responsible for the disappearance of several species in the New World.

References

Amann, V. F., Belshaw, D.G.R., and Stanfield, J.P., eds.
       1972 *Nutrition and Food in an African Economy*. Vols. 1 and 2. Kampala, Uganda: Makere University.

Audy, J. R.
1971   Measurement and Diagnosis of Health. *Environ-Mental.* Shepard and McKinley, eds. Boston: Houghton-Mifflin.
Baker, P. T.
1962   The Application of Ecological Theory to Anthropology. *American Anthropologist* 64:15-22.
1966   Ecological and Physiological Adaptations in Indigenous South Americans. *The Biology of Human Adaptability.* Baker and Weiner, eds. Oxford: Clarendon Press.
Berlyne, G. M., Ben Ari, J., Nord, E., and Shainkin, R.
1973   Bedouin Osteomalacia Due to Calcium Deprivation Caused by High Phytic Acid Content of Unleavened Bread. *American Journal of Clinical Nutrition* 26:190-191.
Black, F. L.
1975   Infectious Diseases in Primitive Societies.*Science* 187:515-518.
Burgess, A. and Dean, R.F.A., eds.
1962   *Malnutrition and Food Habits.* New York: Macmillan, Inc.
Cassel, J.
1957   Social and Cultural Implications of Food and Food Habits. *American Journal of Public Health* 47:732-740.
Clastres, P.
1972   *The Guayaki. Hunters and Gatherers Today.* Bicchierri, ed. New York: Holt, Rinehart and Winston.
Cockburn, T. A.
1971 ·Infectious Disease in Ancient Populations. *Current Anthroplogy* 12:4562.
Cohen, Y.A., ed.
1968   Editor's Note to: Adams, R. McC. Early Civilizations, Subsistence and Environment. *Man in Adaptation: The Biosocial Background.* Chicago: Aldine.
Collis, W.R.F., Dema, J., and Omololu, A.
1962   On the Ecology of Child and Nutrition and Health in Nigerian Villages, Parts I and II. *Tropical and Geographical Medicine* 14:140-163, 201-229.
Cravioto, J.
1966   Malnutrition and Behavioral Development in the Pre-School Child. *Pre-School Child Malnutrition.* Washington, D.C.: National Academy of Sciences, National Research Council.
Damas, D.
1972   The Copper Eskimo. *Hunters and Gatherers Today.* Bicchierri, ed. New York: Holt, Rinehart and Winston.
Dubos, R.
1959   *Mirage of Health: Utopias, Progress and Biological Change.* New York: Harper.
Dunn, F.L.
1968   Epidemiological Factors: Health and Disease in Hunter-Gatherers. *Man the Hunter.* Lee and deVore, eds. Chicago: Aldine-Atherton.
Foster, G.
1966   Social Anthropology and Nutrition of the Pre-School Child. *PreSchool Child Malnutrition: Primary Deterrent to Human Progress.* Washington, D.C.: National Academy of Sciences, National Research Council.
Franda, M.F.
1974   Food Research in India. South Asian Series Field-Staff Reports, Vol. 18, No. 9. American Universities Field Staff, Inc.

Freebairn, D.K.
    1973   Income Disparities in the Agricultural Sector: Regional and Institu-
    tional Analysis. *Food, Population and Employment: The Impact of the Green
    Revolution.* Poleman and Freebairn, eds. New York: Praeger Publishing, Inc.
Garn, S.M.
    1968   Cultural Factors Affecting the Study of Human Biology.*Man in
    Adaptation: The Biosocial Background.* Cohen, ed. Chicago: Aldine.
Garn, S.M. and Clark, D.C.
    1974   Economics and Fatness. *Ecology of Food and Nutrition* 3:19-20.
Gerlach, L.P.
    1964   Socio-Cultural Factors Affecting the Diet of the Northeast Coastal
    Bantu. *Journal of the American Dietetic Association* 45:420-424.
Goldschmidt, W.
    1968   Theory and Strategy in the Study of Cultural Adaptability. *Man in
    Adaptation: The Cultural Present.* Cohen, ed. Chicago: Aldine.
Gonzalez, N.
    1972   Changing Dietary Patterns of North American Indians. *Nutrition,
    Growth and Development of North American Indian Children.* Moore,
    Silverberg and Read, eds. Washington, D.C.: United States Government
    Printing Office.
Govil, K.K., Prasad, B.G. and Pant, K.C.
    1958   Results of Diet Surveys in Uttar Pradesh. *Indian Journal of Public
    Health.*
Greenland, D.J.
    1975   Bringing the Green Revolution to the Shifting Cultivator. *Science*
    190:841-844.
Griffen, K.
    1974   *The Political Economy of Agrarian Change: An Essay on the Green
    Revolution.* Cambridge: Harvard University Press.
Griggs, D.B.
    1974   *The Agricultural Systems of the World: An Evolutionary Approach.*
    Cambridge: Cambridge University Press.
Gross, D.B. and Underwood, B.
    1971   Technological Change and Calorie Costs: Sisal Agriculture in North-
    eastern Brazil. *American Anthropologist* 73:725-740.
Gulliver, P.H.
    1968   The Jie of Uganda. *Man in Adaptation: The Cultural Present.* Cohen,
    ed. Chicago, Aldine.
Habte, D.
    1969   *Proceedings of the East African Conference on Nutrition and Child
    Feeding.* Washington, D.C.: United States Government Printing Office.
Harris, M.
    1971   *Culture, Man and Nature: An Introduction to General Anthropology.*
    New York: Thomas Y. Crowell.
Haviland. W.A.
    1967   Stature at Tikal, Guatemala: Implications for Ancient Maya Demo-
    graphy and Social Organization. *American Antiquity* 38:316-325.
HEW
    1973   Report on the Health, Population and Nutrition Activities of the
    Agency for International Development. Department of State for Fiscal Year
    1972.
Hughes, C.C.
    1963   Public Health in Non-Literate Societies. *Man's Image in Medicine and
    Anthropology.* Galdston, ed. New York: International Universities Press, Inc.

Hughes, C.C. and Hunter, J.M.
  1970   Disease and "Development" in Africa. Reprinted from *Social Science and Medicine* 3:443-488.
Jelliffe, D.B. et al.
  1962   The Children of the Hadza Hunters. *Journal of Pediatrics* 60:907-913.
Jerome, N.W.
  1967   Food Habits and Acculturation: Dietary Practices and Nutrition of Families Headed by Southern-Born Negroes Residing in a Northern Metropolis. (Ph.D. Dissertation 1967, University of Wisconsin, Madison.)
  1970   American Culture and Food Habits Communicating Through Food in the USA. *Dimensions of Nutrition.* Dupont, ed. Boulder Colorado Associated University Press.
  1975   On Determining Food Patterns of Urban Dwellers in Contemporary United States Society. *Gastronomy: The Anthropology of Food and Food Habits.* Arnott, ed. The Hague: Mouton Publishers.
  1976   Individuals, Not Families, Are the Key to Nutrition. *Community Nutrition Institute Newsletter* 6:4-5.
Laughlin, W.S.
  1966   Genetical and Anthropological Characteristics of Arctic Populations. *The Biology of Adaptability.* Baker and Weiner, eds. Oxford: Clarendon Press.
Lee, R. and deVore, I., eds.
  1968   Problems in the Study of Hunter-Gatherers. *Man the Hunter.* Chicago: Aldine-Atherton.
Lee, R.B.
  1972   The !Kung Bushmen of Botswana. *Hunters and Gatherers Today.* Bicchieri, ed. New York: Holt, Rinehart and Winston.
Lilimani
  1969   Proceedings of the East African Conference of Nutrition and Child Feeding. Washington, D.C.: United States Government Printing Office.
Lloyd, J.K.
  1969   Obesity in Children. *Obesity: Medical and Scientific Aspects.* McLean, Baird and Howard, eds. Edinburgh: E. and S. Livingstone.
MacPherson, R.K.
  1963   Physiological Adaptation, Fitness and Nutrition in the Peoples of the Australian and New Guinea Regions. *The Biology of Adaptability.* Baker and Weiner, eds. Oxford: Clarendon Press.
Mead, M., ed.
  1955   *Cultural Patterns and Technological Change.* New York: The New American Library.
Mellor, J.W.
  1969   The Subsistence Farmer in Traditional Economics. *Subsistence Agriculture and Economic Development.* Wharton, ed. Chicago: Aldine.
Mitchell, H.H.
  1964   Nutritional Adaptation. *Nutrition: A Comprehensive Treatise,* Vol. II. Beaton and McHenry, eds. New York: Academic Press.
Muñoz, C.
  1969   Proceedings of the East African Conference on Nutrition and Child Feeding. Washington, D.C.: United States Government Printing Office.
Nietschmann, B.
  1972   Hunting and Fishing Focus Among the Miskito Indians, Eastern Nicaragua. *Human Ecology* 1:41-67.
Pelto, G.H. and Pelto, P.J.
  1976   *The Human Adventure: An Introduction to Anthropology.* New York: Macmillan.

Plattner, S.
    1974   Wealth and Growth Among Mayan Indian Peasants. *Human Ecology*
    2:75-87.
Plog, F., Jolly, C. and Bates, D.
    1976   *Anthropology: Decisions, Adaptation and Evolution.* New York:
    Knopf.
Polgar, S.
    1964   Evolution and the Ills of Mankind. *Horizons of Anthropology.* Tax, ed.
    Chicago: Aldine.
Purvis, G.A.
    1973   What Nutrients Do Our Infants Really Get? *Nutrition Today* 8:28-34.
Rappaport, R.A.
    1971a   Nature, Culture and Ecological Anthropology. *Man, Culture and
    Society.* Shapiro, ed. London: Oxford University Press, Inc. (Warner Modular
    Publication).
    1971b   The Flow of Energy in an Agricultural Society. *Scientific American*
    225:116-132.
Reisinger, K., Rogers, K., and Johnson, O.
    1972   Nutrition Survey of Lower Greasewood, Arizona Navajos. *Nutrition,
    Growth and Development of North American Indian Chidren.* Moore,
    Silverberg, and Read, eds. Washington, D.C.: United States Government
    Printing Office.
Sahlins, M.D.
    1968   *Tribesmen.* Englewood Cliffs, New Jersey: Prentice-Hall.
    1972   *Stone Age Economics.* Chicago: Aldine.
    1977   Culture and Environment: The Study of Cultural Ecology. *Horizons of
    Anthropology.* 2d ed. Tax and Freeman, eds. Chicago: Aldine.
Samuelson, G.
    1971   An Epidemiological Study of Child Health and Nutrition in a Northern
    Swedish Country. *Acta Paed. Scand.,* Supplement No. 214.
Townsend, P.K.
    1974   Sago Production in a New Guinea Economy. *Human Ecology* 2:217236.
Ullesvang, L.P.
    1970   Food Consumption Practices in the Seventies. *Vital Speeches* 36:240-
    246.
United States Department of Agriculture
    1976   *National Food Situation* 156:9-16.
Vayda, A.P. and McCay, B.J.
    1975   New Directions in Ecology and Ecological Anthropology. *Annals of
    Review in Anthropology* 4:293-306.
Wade, N.
    1974a   Sahelian Drought: No Victory for Western Aid. *Science* 185:234-237.
    1974b   Green Revolution: Creators Still Quite Hopeful on World Food.
    Science 185:844-845.
    1975   International Agricultural Research. *Science* 188:585-589.
Weiss, B.
    1974   Selling a Subsistence System. Presented at the 73rd Annual Meeting of
    the American Anthropological Association, Mexico City, November 23, 1974.
Whyte, R.O.
    1974   *Rural Nutrition in Monsoon Asia.* London: Oxford University Press.
Willet, J.W.
    1973   Food Needs and the Effective Demand for Food. *Food, Population and
    Employment: The Impact of the Green Revolution.* Poleman and Freebairn,
    eds. New York: Praeger Publishing, Inc.

Wolf, E.R.
    1966   *Peasants.* Englewood Cliffs, New Jersey: Prentice-Hall, Inc.
Woodburn, J.
    1968   An Introduction to Hadza Ecology. *Man the Hunter.* Lee and de Vore,
    eds. Chicago: Aldine-Atherton.
Young, E.G.
    1964   Dietary Standards. *Nutrition: A Comprehensive Treatise,* Vol. II.
    Beaton and McHenry, eds. New York: Academic Press.

2

Methodological Issues in Nutritional Anthropology

G. H. Pelto
N. W. Jerome
R. F. Kandel

As a biocultural discipline, nutritional anthropology looks for theoretical guidance to both the social and biological sciences. Research methods and techniques are thus drawn from a variety of sources. For example, the analysis of people's diets requires research techniques from community nutrition, food sciences, agricultural economics, and related disciplines. The assessment of nutritional status involves research tools developed by nutritional biochemists, physical anthropologists, and biomedical scientists. The methods of sociocultural anthropology, as well as sociology, psychology, political science, and other social sciences are essential for study of the social, cultural, and psychological dimensions of food distribution and use.

   This chapter discusses a general methodological strategy for nutritional anthropology. It is not intended as a compendium of specific research tools and techniques. Moreover, it is but one of several different research approaches. There is no *one* method for the discipline, and different problems or questions call for different methodological perspectives. The chapters of this book illustrate a variety of different research designs, each compatible with the types of problems to which the authors address themselves.

Ecological Model as a Research Strategy

The ecological model presented in chapter one is useful as a framework for organizing research operations and for generating and organizing theory. The model contains guidelines for research design, including specifications of relevant units of analysis, types of variables, and data analysis techniques. Every society or community possesses a unique set of features in each of the five peripheral components of the model: culture/idea systems, social organization, social environment, physical environment, and technology. Furthermore, the individual components are in continuous interaction and are thus modified by each other, as well as by the biological and psychobiological needs of the individuals located at the heart of the model.

Individual human requirements for food energy and nutrients, and for psychological nurturance, do not vary significantly from one society to another when developmental stage, body size, gender, level of activity, reproductive demands, and genetic characteristics are taken into account. However, the resources available for meeting these needs may vary appreciably. Consequently, there is a continuous process of adjustment and modification of the biological and sociocultural aspects of a system. Therefore, the model should be viewed as a dynamic whole with complex feedback mechanisms among the six component sectors.

Our focus in this chapter will *not* be on specific techniques of data collection, as details about techniques are found in the specialized research literature. For each sector of data within the ecological model, there can be a wide variety of specific procedures, although they all fall within a more-or-less familiar range of field tools and instruments. The very difficult problems of dietary measurement, for example, have been the subject of much methodological-technical assessment. Fairly sophisticated comparative studies have examined the relative merits of the "twenty-four hour recall" method, the "food frequency" checklist, the "seven day diet record," and direct weighing and measuring of daily meals (cf. Garn, et al. 1978; Gersovitz and Madden, 1978; Marr, 1971). Of course, methods developed for use with literate populations have to be modified when they are used in "non-Western" research settings. Nutritional anthropologists are now working on the complex task of devising appropriate alternative techniques for observing and quantifying food intakes in a variety of research conditions ranging from urban industrialized to isolated, nonindustrial communities.

As a guide to the formulation of hypotheses and the design of research, the ecological model and each of its component parts can be and has been used to guide research design in several different ways. Some researchers concentrate on only one component. For example, some nutritionists study the individual requirements at the heart of the model, some anthropologists the symbolic aspects of food behavior, or the food-getting technology of an archaeological site.

If each component of the ecological model is regarded as the basic unit of analysis, the researcher may test hypotheses about relationships between any component and the dietary patterns and nutritional status of individuals in a given locale. For example, family structure, division of labor, and economic stratification can be related to the individuals within the system. The interrelationship of any two components may also be studied.

However, the holistic logic of the model calls for an integrated examination. It may be used to unravel the mechanisms, crosscutting many of the components, by which a specific system inhibits or facilitates an individual in fulfilling his/her biological needs for nutrients and psychological needs for nurturance. Through comparative analysis, the relative importance of the various components in different types of systems can be studied. Although specific features may vary significantly from one society to another, a common methodological strategy can be used to elucidate how and why individuals in different systems achieve or fail to achieve nutritional well being. The elements of the strategy include:

1. community-based or community-centered research
2. commitment to the use of both quantitative and qualitative data
3. careful operationalization of variables derived from the components of the ecological model

4. data-analysis techniques focusing on intra-group diversity
5. comparative analysis across communities and regions in order to identify commonalities as well as diversity of ecological processes
6. linking intracommunity analysis to broader macrolevel processes in order to identify the ways in which external forces impinge on local ecological systems.

Community-centered Research

It is in the context of the community that all of the above components interact. Although it can be said at a rather abstract level that a nation possesses "social organization" or "culture," the types of nutritional generalizations that can be made on this level have relatively limited application to *individual* nutritional status. For example, the relationship of vitamin A deficiency to socioeconomic status or income can be described for a nation. However, such statistical description tells us little about the specific processes whereby some individuals in a nation become vitamin A deficient while others do not. Furthermore, in large populations with various ecological and political-social environments, there may be different "pathways" to such a deficiency, which would be obscured by the macrolevel focus.

Organizing research on the basis of the community has been a main feature of cultural anthropological research for many years. Beginning in the 1920s with the work of Robert Redfield and the Chicago sociologists, led by Robert Park, anthropologists and sociologists have carried out intensive holistic community studies. This mode of research has a number of advantages, including the possibility of clearly defining the boundaries of the research population and of maintaining long-term, relatively intensive relationships with members of the population, a feature that increases the types of data that can be gathered, as well as their quality (cf. Pelto and Pelto, 1974).

In contrast to the social sciences, nutrition does not have a long history of community-based research. Surveys of nutritional status or of food use have usually focused on cross-sectional samples of large populations, while biochemical studies have concentrated on selected individual cases. There are some significant exceptions to this generalization, including the community-based studies that have been carried out for many years under the auspices of INCAP and the Institute of Nutrition in Mexico. Today, however, community nutrition is a recognized subfield of nutrition and dietetics, and an increasing number of nutritional scientists are doing community-based research.

Delimitation of the "community" will vary from one research problem to another. The selection and delimitation of the community will depend not only on the investigator's specific interests but also on the characteristics of the area itself. In large urban areas the "community" may be a neighborhood, since the ecological context may vary significantly from one neighborhood to another. Studies that purport to describe the situation of "minority" groups of a particular city often fail to consider the considerable diversity that occurs within the "minority" groups and neighborhoods of large metropolitan centers (Green, 1970). In thinly-settled, dispersed farming areas, the "community" may cover a large geographic area and include more than one political entity.

The community-centered approach does not mean that all significant factors are local. The ecological model should not be seen as a "reductionist" strategy. Rather, the concentration of data-gathering in defined community contexts permits assessment of the ways in which macrolevel factors, including international, political, and economic variables, impact on peoples' access to and use of food resources.

Quantitative and Qualitative Research Methods

Historically, both the strengths and the weaknesses of cultural anthropological research can be traced to the emphasis on qualitative, descriptive data, at the expense of attention to the more quantitative aspects of data-gathering. Conversely, nutritional science and nutritional epidemiology have been built on a firm quantitative base that has generated a verifiable body of knowledge. However, lack of attention to the descriptive, ethnographic aspects of community research has often resulted in studies that fail to reveal the underlying dynamics of the phenomena they seek to explain. "To develop meaningful and accurate measurements, we must take advantage of the qualitative methods of participant-observation, key informant interviewing, and archival and historical study that have been developed by ethnographers and wed these with the quantitative techniques that have proved to be indispensable to the development of verifiable, scientific knowledge" (Scrimshaw and Pelto, 1979).

A period of participant-observation and informal interviewing in the research community is an indispensable part of effective field research (cf. Jerome, 1967, 1975; Scrimshaw and Pelto, 1979; Pelto and Pelto, 1978). Such procedures have the following advantages:

1. They provide information about general patterns of food use, diet and lifestyle from which specific, testable hypotheses can be derived.
2. They provide information about the community from which to design specific questions for more structural interviewing. (For example, knowledge of a custom of labor exchanged for garden produce would lead to the inclusion of this feature in a formal interview schedule.)
3. They give the investigator information about local language use that is indispensible for designing questions that do not confuse or offend respondents.
4. They produce information about background factors that may influence individual responses to more formal questions (e.g., degree of literacy).
5. They increase rapport and improve the likelihood of obtaining true responses and of winning cooperation for time consuming or other disruptive procedures.
6. They identify locally specific "distorter variables" that may be controlled in hypothesis testing.
7. They provide a background of generalized information for interpreting the statistical results of the quantitative data.

While qualitative research techniques are particularly important in early phases of research, they also have a role to play in later aspects of data analysis and interpretation, as suggested in item 7 above. When the statistical picture emerges from the process of data manipulation, it should "make sense" in relation to life in the community. "It should be possible to identify cases (households and individuals) that exemplify the patterns revealed in the statistical analysis. Thus, the use of "case studies" or "case histories" (a type of qualitative data) not only provides a check on the statistical manipulations, it also gives a sense of reality . . . and helps . . . (to interpret the results)" (Scrimshaw and Pelto, 1979:204). Moreover, qualitative research techniques can provide information on changes in community life which could not have been anticipated at the beginning of the study.

Operationalizing the Variables Derived from the Model

Concepts like "social organization" or "culture" are abstract. For research purposes they must be broken down into specific elements that can be operationalized in the community. For example, within the general domain of social organization, it might be meaningful to study the ways in which specific features of family structure and composition affect the organization of food production, distribution, and consumption. Specific variables of "household composition" might include: (1) size, (2) complexity, (3) age structure, (4) number of adults, (5) number of children and child spacing. The data for classifying households by these variables would probably be best collected through a structured interview with an adult member of the household (cf. Scrimshaw and Pelto, 1979).

The relevant variables of the physical environment may include certain conditions regarded as stable for the entire community (e.g., "tropical rainforest habitat" or "located 150 miles from a primate city") and also those microenvironmental elements that vary within a community. For example, even small rural communities can have marked differences in "average date of killing frost" as well as significant variations in soil types (cf. Johnson, 1978). "Distance to nearest supermarket" may be a significant microenvironmental variable affecting peoples' food behaviors.

Generally speaking, nutritional status and dietary variables have received the most careful attention in nutrition studies, as compared to the frequent lack of attention to the effective operationalizing of social and cultural variables. On the other hand, some anthropological studies of food and diet have focused more attention on analysis of social stratification and cultural variables, while treating the problems of nutritional status only superficially.

The measurements of observations pertaining to specific variables are very frequently time-consuming since apparently simple items such as "household size" may require careful interviewing to sort out the list of persons actually resident on a continuing basis in each residential unit. Therefore, the total number of variables that can be included in a study may be sharply limited. Very careful research design, finely tuned through preliminary (qualitative) observations, can help researchers select key variables essential to their hypothesis testing.

Intracultural Diversity and Data Analysis Techniques
In our view, one of the most pervasive but misleading statistical habits is the automatic use of mean values or "averages" to characterize and compare populations. By its very nature the concept of "average" casts away much of the information about significant variations *within* research populations. Thus, the design— which compares mean values between, for example, "Indians" and "whites," between "high altitude" and "low altitude," or between "rural and urban" school children, will fail to show any significant variations that may exist within each group. With the household as the basic unit of analysis, Scrimshaw (1977) was able to demonstrate the diversities in family patterns and in children's health on a Guatemalan coastal plantation. Of course, most recent reports focus on the differences in average values of subgroups in terms of target variables.

The weaknesses in use of mean values for such groups include the following:

1. Variations within the identified groups or subgroups are simply ignored.
2. The major indepedent variable (e.g., ethnicity, "rural-urban," or "altitude" assumes the form of a nominal variable with no analytic flexibility.
3. Control variables are often introduced in a rigid fashion by breaking down the subgroups (e.g., rural or urban) into splinter groups (e.g., urban-young, urban-old) until such subgroups become too small for meaningful analysis.
4. Dichotomizing (or trichotomizing) such group variables encourages forms of relatively inflexible, two-variable statistical analysis.
5. Use of average values bars the researcher from penetrating to the individual and household level of analysis where the real interplay of biological, social, cultural, and other variables actually take place.
6. Use of mean values concerning social groups contributes inevitably to stereotypes about groups—allowing misleading generalizations about "diet patterns of Mexican-Americans" ("Indians") or other ethnic categories.

Statistical procedures for avoiding simple comparisons of mean values are not difficult to find. Many variables can be conceptualized as degree of "range of variation." For example, throughout

Latin America the concept of identity of "Indian" is sometimes measured in terms of "degree of 'Indianness.'" Detailed methods for operationalizing this concept are not relevant here, but interesting examples can be seen in the recent literature (e.g., B. DeWalt, 1979).

On the other hand, the significance of some variables disappears when more sensitive measures are sought. The work of Theodore and Nancy Graves and colleagues provided a striking instance in which the cultural identification of "Indian" was found to be irrelevant for understanding the dynamics of alcohol use of individuals. As Graves noted, "The vast majority of Navajo drunkenness, at least in Denver, can be accounted for *without recourse to the fact that the subjects are Indians*" (Graves, 1971, italics in original). Thus, analysis of intracultural variations can have the commendable side effect of refuting stereotypes about ethnic groups.

In many instances, the variable of ethnicity (or cultural group membership) may be significant, but can be regarded as *one of a series of independent variables* predicting variable in a dependent variable. In such cases the ethnicity variable may play a modest role, in conjunction with other factors, in the predictive model. DeWalt (1979) for example, found that the ethnic variable ("Indianness") played a role in affecting food production strategies but was not a major factor when compared with "political manipulation," "local leadership and wealth," and "extra-local orientation" of individual farmers.

The analysis of intracultural diversity does not necessarily require complex statistical analysis. For example, the research by Jerome (chapter 9) provides an example of the exploration of intragroup variables without complex statistical manipulation.

The strategy of intracommunity analysis does· not mean that researchers abandon the search for broader generalization or "uniformities" concerning food and nutrition. Rather, the search is precisely for general ecological processes, while seeking to place sociocultural factors into meaningful synchrony with other variables, as they impinge on (or are embodied in) particular individuals. As one example of a cross-cultural generalization with great significance, we should note that in practically all contexts where intracommunity, socioeconomic differentation has been effectively measured, this variable has been found to play a powerful role in diet and nutritional analysis.

Comparative Analysis across Communities and Regions
Research design of great potential power can be constructed wherever crucial ecological features show systematic variations within a region. For example, in a great many instances new technological innovations, commercialization, or other aspects of modernization are unequally distributed within a region, allowing for assessment of the impact through multicommunity research strategies (cf. Pelto and Poggie, 1974). Often features of the physical environment—such as available water, soil types, and wood supplies—are key variables that can be systematically examined within a region.

Occasionally the regional analysis model can be extended to the next level—interregional analysis. Such an extension usually requires extensive financial and human resources that are beyond the reach of many researchers. Since the definition of "region" is often arbitrary, and the term "interregional" comparison may take forms, great care must be taken in designing research that involves two or more *disconnected* or distinctly separate research locales. Research comparing "high altitude" and "low altitude" or "rural" and "urban," in which the locations are separated by many kilometers of intervening territory, runs the risk of having too many confounding and uncontrolled variables. Separate regions are generally different; many features of culture, such as genetic characteristics of populations, food supplies, economic structures, and so on, that comparisons are fraught with difficulties. On the other hand, when investigators are able to *demonstrate basic similarities of process* despite regional differences, the study design can be a powerful one. Thus, the focus of interregional comparative studies should be on delineating underlying similarities, rather than the documentation of differences.

Linking Intracommunity Analysis to Macrolevel Processes
Community-level research always runs the risk of being identified as "reductionist" or as failing to deal with the "real issues" at the level of national and international political and economic forces. Therefore, it is important for investigators to explore ways to link their research to broader, macrolevel analysis. The paper by Marchione (chapter 10) is an example of research in which two levels of analysis—household and individual—are linked to the effects of broad political-economic processes. The task of identifying the ways in which macrolevel processes affect individuals at

"the ground level" is frequently very difficult and requires knowledge and understanding about the general sociopolitical system within which the research is located and of the considerable qualitative data.

There are several reasons why linkage to the broader levels of analysis is important:

1. Processes at the microlevel are often *directly* affected by macrolevel events. For example, Marchione felt that the variables he examined at the local level in Jamaica were strongly affected by shifts in food prices and other political-economic factors.

2. Policy implications and suggestions arising from community-level research may be quite unrealistic if they do not take into consideration the ways in which system linkages facilitate or impede local-level changes.

Nutritional Anthropology and the Multidisciplinary Research Team

As we examine the complexities of research on food and nutrition, it is clear that the expertise of several disciplines is required for effective research. The expression "biocultural" suggests a breadth of theory and method beyond the capabilities of most individual investigators, however well they may be trained. Certainly there are important kinds of research that can be accomplished by individuals. On the other hand, it is important to be aware of the great need for effective multidisciplinary research efforts that bring together, in a single research site, methodological expertise from the biological and social sciences.

To make such collaboration effective, we believe that nutritional anthropologists should have considerable training and experience in both biological and sociocultural research. The primarily sociocultural anthropologist should have first-hand knowledge of the biochemical side of nutritional science in order to effectively interrelate his/her work with that of the nutritionists. Similarly, nutritionists and physical anthropologists must have an appreciation for the complexities of sociocultural research in order to collaborate effectively with community oriented anthropologists. In fact, the concept of "community oriented research" has been as difficult for many nutritional scientists as the definition and implementation of "community nutrition" as a subdiscipline.

The multidisciplinary research team needs other kinds of personnel in addition to nutritionists and anthropologists. Under varying conditions, depending on the ecological context and specific research questions, the team should include input from economists, physicians, epidemiologists, agronomists, and other specialists. The knowledge of the statistical-computer specialist is essential for data-analysis in ecological research. The nutritional anthropologist cannot afford to be ignorant of the fundamentals of statistics, even while relying on the specialist for data analysis. Many promising interactions between anthropologists and statisticians have foundered because the anthropologist could not conceptualize the data in a manner that made sense to the quantitative specialist.

These comments about the multidisciplinary team are a brief glance into a complex subject and are intended only to indicate the need for rethinking and refining training programs aimed at developing the new generation of nutritional anthropologists.

References

DeWalt, B.R.
    1979   *Modernization in a Mexican Ejido: A Study in Economic Adaptation.*
    New York: Cambridge University Press.
Garn, S. et al.
    1978   The Real Problem with One-Day Records. *Journal of the American Dietetic Association* 31:1114-1116.
Gersovitz, M. et al.
    1978 Validity of the 24-Hour Dietary Recall and 7-Day Record for Group Comparisons. *Journal of the American Dietetic Association* 73:48-55.
Graves, T.
    1971   The Personal Adjustment of Navajo Indian Migrants to Denver, Colorado. *American Anthropologist* 72:35-54.
Green, V.
    1970   The Confrontation of Diversity with the Black Community. *Human Organization* 29:267-272.
Jerome, N.W.
    1967   Food Habits and Acculturation: Dietary Practices of Families Headed by Southern-Born Negroes Residing in a Northern Metropolis. (Ph.D. Dissertation 1967, University of Wisconsin, Madison.)
    1975   On Determining Food Patterns of Urban Dwellers in Contemporary United States Society. *Gastronomy: The Anthropology of Food and Food Habits.* Arnott, ed. The Hague: Mouton Publishers.
Johnson, A.W.
    1978   *Quantification in Cultural Anthropology: An Introduction to Research Design.* Stanford, California: Stanford University Press.

Marr, J.W.
1971 Individual Dietary Surveys: Purposes and Methods. *World Review Nutr. Diet.* 13:105-164.
Pelto, P.J. and Pelto, G.H.
1975 Intracultural Diversity: Some Theoretical Issues. *American Ethnologist* 2:1-18.
1974 Ethnography: The Fieldwork Enterprise. *Handbook of Social and Cultural Anthropology.* Hoingmann, ed. Chicago: Rand McNally.
1978 *Anthropological Research: The Structure of Inquiry.* 2d ed. New York: Cambridge University Press.
Pelto, P.J. and Poggie, J.J.
1974 Models of Modernization: A Regional Focus. *Rethinking Modernization.* Poggie and Lynch, eds. Westport, Conn.: Greenwood Press.
Scrimshaw, M.W.
1977 Family Patterns of Nutrition and Health on a Guatemalan Coastal Plantation. Abstracts of the 76th Annual Meeting of the American Anthropology Association, Houston, Texas, 1977.
Scrimshaw, S. C. M. and Pelto, G. H.
1979 *Family Composition and Structure in Relation to Nutrition and Health Programs. Evaluating the Impact of Nutrition and Health Programs.* Klein et al., eds. New York: Plenum Publishing Corporation.

3

Individual and Social Energy Flows

Bridging Nutritional and Anthropological Thinking about Women's Work in Rural Africa, Theoretical Considerations

W. B. Eide
F.C. Steady

Introduction

This chapter explores the implications of an ecopolitical approach to nutritional anthropology as it applies to issues of development. We have developed a model that illustrates how an anthropological perspective on human activities can utilize, at least theoretically, certain nutritional-physiological information to show how individuals may be nutritionally deprived as a consequence of social factors and processes. The nature of the links is not often direct and clear, and it is insufficient to conclude, as nutritionists often do, that "malnutrition results from poverty." We need to know exactly how poverty leads to malnutrition in specific cultural settings and, in particular, who is most affected, in what way, and where and how action can be initiated—not as a palliative, but as a partial attack on the roots of the poverty complex.

Women in the African Context: Issues and Problems

We focus our discussion on the lives and work situation of rural women in Africa. Other contexts could fulfill the same objective. However, we have selected the problems related to "the women's issue" (particularly as they relate to rural Africa) because we have observed that some important aspects of women's roles in a variety of ecological settings in Africa have been masked by traditional research which had been mainly designed and constructed from a Western and often male perspective. Nutrition research in particular has contributed to the creation of an often false and biased image of women's roles as providers of food and of appropriate nutritional conditions for their children and other family members.

Some generalizations can be made about the role of women in the African setting, although we recognize diversities in social organization, in specific historical developments, and in ecological variations among African societies. We also recognize that generalizations on women's roles in the African context lose power when viewed within the framework of "development processes," since these processes have been influenced by both external and indigenous sociocultural phenomena.

The historical development of Africa can be broadly described by modern theories of underdevelopment. The colonial penetration of Africa extracted surplus that was expropriated to Western colonial powers (Frank, 1969; Amin, 1977; Rodney, 1974). This was largely achieved by diverting male labor from agricultural production and chanelling it into wage-earning activities. As a result, female labor became necessary to fulfill subsistence needs, and women's workload in agricultural production increased.

Wide ecological variations in Africa have further affected these colonial processes and their impact on women's roles. Three main geographical zones of cultivation can be identified: the African "green belt" corresponding to the Sudano-Sahelian zone; the African plantation belt in the tropical forest from west to east, and the African "reserve" belt corresponding to the southern part of the continent (UNRISD, 1978). The pattern of exploitation is similar in all of these areas—i.e., the introduction of cash crops, reservation of the best land for producing cash crops with the consequent reduction or loss of prize land traditionally owned by women; the introduction of private ownership of land; male migration from the rural areas to towns and cities; a demand for male labor in the extraction industries; and an increased workload for women in both subsistence agriculture and in the household (PAG Report, 1977). Technology transfer accompanying the introduction of cash crops was geared toward mechanizing agriculture and so favoring male rather than female labor in the new machine-controlled agricultural industries.[1]

Some might argue that the issue of women's roles is really part of the "class issue" and therefore of minor significance in the more pressing problems of general poverty and hardship. Without minimizing the class problem, it must be pointed out that women often experience poverty and hardship more severely than men. The consequence of poverty is more serious for women because they have—contrary to commonly held beliefs—a larger responsibility than men for ensuring the satisfaction of basic needs in many societies (PAG, 1977). This greater responsibility usually continues when economic processes alter the division of labor and traditional patterns of producing goods; these alterations often force men away from food production.

An examination of the more specific characteristics of women's roles in the household within this general context of role changes and double duty shows that the processes at work place some children "at risk" of malnutrition. However, this has not been properly understood by nutritionists and economic planners. Also, until relatively recently, the work of women in food systems has not been properly studied by social scientists or by investigators concerned with African rural economies. The neglect of women's productive roles reflects a long established male bias in most research. This bias has led to generalizations such as the following from de Garine (1971): "The traditional division of labor may seriously impair productivity, as when agricultural work is performed mainly by women." A male bias is reflected in numerous nutrition studies in which socioeconomic determinants are identified in variables such as "father's occupation," while ignoring women's extremely important economical (though often non-monetary) functions.[2]

Despite recent changes in the literature, relevant information about the role of women in food production and other tasks related to food throughout Africa are still relatively rare. Earlier anthropological studies failed to elucidate the women's role in production activities and their use of renewable and nonrenewable resources. Often the dynamic nature of the interaction between food and colonial exploitation was obscured in functionalist interpretations. More recent studies of women's roles in production in Africa have defrosted many of the early interpretations, and data documenting and analyzing the central role of women in food production and other food-related tasks throughout Africa are becoming increasingly available (Boserup, 1970; UNECA, 1974a; Bukh, 1977; Pala, 1975; Skjønsberg, 1977; see also PAG Report, 1977).

The Image of Women in Nutrition Research

The traditional focus of nutrition research in Africa, as well as in many other regions, has contributed to an image of women and their role in nutrition which is extremely limited and distorted. Women's biological reproductive functions have been the basic research "object," while the possible importance of their social role for nutrition has been limited to their role of feeders of infants, cooks for the family, and to some extent, nutrition educators for their children. In sum, it can be said that women have not been considered *social actors* in nutritional change, but merely as passive recipients of good food to ensure good fetal and child development, or as equally passive receivers of a type of nutrition education that has been expected to lead to automatic behavioral change. This limited perception of women's roles in food and nutrition may be partly responsible for the inadequate results of many nutrition intervention programs directed toward women.

In a very real sense women can be called "the true guardians of the family's nutritional needs." The household becomes very important as a unit of analysis since food is often consumed within this unit. Since the women's role is crucial in this unit, the nutritional status of a population is likely to be determined by the various elements and forces which act upon and influence the role and behavior of women. Hence, women and women's "spheres" should serve to integrate those sociocultural and biological factors that influence malnutrition.

Energy Considerations as a Bridge between Physiological and Social Reality

It is well recognized that women perform numerous time- and energy-consuming tasks during the day. In economically poor societies this is true for all women, but it is particularly manifest in rural areas in Africa where they are heavily involved in food production and other food-related tasks (Skjønsberg, 1977). This complex of tasks determines the degree to which women can involve themselves specifically in child care (Sharman, 1970; PAG Report, 1977) and also respond to educational programs and other innovations. We consider *time, motivation,* and *physical capacity* as primary determinants that must be taken into account in any nutritional program directed to women or in assessing women's productivity as agriculturalists.

The following questions are among those that can be raised concerning women's work and performance as they relate to food and nutrition:

- What determines women's *time expenditure* and *allocation of time?*
- What determines the *physical output* (working capacity) of a women involved in   food production/provisioning besides child-bearing and rearing?
- What determines their *motivation* to innovations, educational programs, visits to health stations, follow-up of rehabilitation center instructions, etc.?

The following hypotheses can be explored to elucidate the present reality of many rural women in Africa today:

- High time expenditure may be due to
  - numerous responsibilities in the home and in the field
  - unbalanced division of labor and responsibilities between the sexes
  - inappropriate technology
  - excessive distance to walk for farming and fetching fuel and water
- Low physical output in food production and provisioning may be determined by
  - excessive physical input in basic activities other than food production and provisioning

    —excessive demand for physical input due to inappropriate
      technologies
    —unbalanced distribution of food at the family level and the
      consequent malnutrition of women
    —closely repeated pregnancies and drain on mother's phy-
      sique
  • The behavior labeled as low motivation may be due to
    —general tiredness, ill health, and malnutrition (low energy
      intake, iron deficiency anemia)
    —lack of decision-making power over own produce or cash
      from produce
    —irrationality of a program as perceived by the woman

We have here a mixture of factors or aggregates of factors of
importance for the study of women's contributions to providing
food and ensuring good nutrition in various contexts. Some would
have to be studied by anthropological/sociological methods and
others by methods developed by nutritionists. Nutritionists and
anthropologists would, however, if working in isolation from each
other, initially give different emphasis to these determinants and
thus also to secondary factors conditioning the nature and relative
importance of these determinants.

Social scientists have been interested in the *time allocation* of
women's daily tasks (UNECA, 1974b). Such studies have demonstrated that women in Africa work longer hours than men, but they
do not increase our understanding about how the long hours spent
in productive activities affect the nutritional levels of family
members. Nutrition educators who are committed to achieving
behavioral change in nutritional practices often fail to understand
that their inability to alter women's nutritional behaviors after an
educational activity had taken place may be due to factors within
the recipient's social context rather than to motivation.[3]

The nutrition physiologist's interest has generally been confined
to the study of energy expenditure and *time/energy budgets* of
individuals. Such studies have been conducted in connection with
different work activities particularly of men.[4] We still lack a
substantial data base for energy expenditure of women in different
occupational and other activities. This is unfortunate, because it
would have given us an opportunity to consider, in a preliminary
fashion, the ways in which individual energy expenditure can be
linked to factors that influence time allocation. The analysis of daily

energy budgets, combined with consumption studies, can provide clues to how the various factors interplay in given economic and social situations.

Value Concepts of Women's Work

Since the three determinants selected here—time, motivation, and physical activity—are interlinked, they should be studied in an integrated manner. To arrive at such an integration, it is at first necessary to search for some unifying idea that makes it conceptually *logical* to integrate different methodological approaches and techniques. We believe that the concept of "the value of women's work" provides such a framework. Women's work has often been attributed a *use value* rather than an *exchange value* in the sense that women's labor is not valued within the context of the market. Thus, women are seen as reproducing the labor force rather than as active participants in producing goods (Steady, 1977).[5]

Use value and exchange value can be measured in terms of the energy expended during labor output. It is more customary, however, for some labor to be measured in terms of cash value (wages and salaries). Any labor that is not "traded" for cash (this usually includes a wide range of labor activities performed by women) has a value irrespective of the amount of energy expended during its output (see figure 2). A brief discussion of the transformation of the means of production will illustrate the main reasons for this discrepancy.

Since most societies have been influenced in varying degrees by the capitalist mode of production, it is necessary to understand its total effect on women's roles and work. In most cases the organization of the means of production along capitalist lines reinforced set patterns in the division of labor, but with differential value being given to women's work. In many African societies, in accordance with tradition, both male and female labor were necessary in food production. Communal ownership of the means of production assured the women a certain degree of control over her labor and of some decision-making power relative to her labor input. The sexual division of labor was based essentially on parallel rather than on hierarchical lines, thus granting equal value to male and female labor.

The growth and processes of capitalist modes of production

resulted in the reinforcement of patriarchal systems in which the command of women and children's labor became absolutely essential. Through this control, a hierarchy was established, and male and female labor were accorded different economic value. Under the conditions of wage labor, the family was no longer the production unit as was the case in subsistence agriculture. The individual was paramount, and male labor was in special demand. The latter was given an exchange value, while female labor was viewed in terms of its use value. The demand for male labor and new skills in agricultural production led to the migration of the young, and in many instances to the feminization of the labor force in subsistence agricultural production. The use value of female labor is a necessary concomitant of capital development since it subsidized male labor, increased profits for owners, and contributed to greater capital accumulation.

The "use value" concept of women's work has been unconsciously accepted by nutritionists whose research barely goes beyond women's biology and reproductive capabilities. For those nutritionists who have been deeply concerned with the need to provide arguments for persuading economic planners that nutrition is important and that nutritional considerations in economic planning will pay off in the long run, the concept of the *potential exchange value of women's work* could provide the basis for a powerful argument.[6]

A Model of Energy Flow in Relation to Women's Work

In order to give substance to the argument, we will now examine more closely how *energy*—in terms of working expenditure and in terms of food value—can provide one bridge to a better understanding of women's performance as an intervening variable between macro-processes and the nutritional micro-universe. By using energy considerations as components in a conceptual model, we illustrate the interplay between use value and the potential exchange value of women's work.

As has been said, the perspective on energy familiar to anthropologists is the total energy flow in a given economy. It is conceptually possible, though operationally laborious, to study the flow of energy in a relatively "closed" system, such as a small subsistence economy (Kemp, 1971). It is increasingly difficult to do so as the system "opens," and efforts to do so in complex systems (such as in US agriculture) have proven to be fruitless due to "hidden" inputs of energy in the technical and organizational machinery that form the basis of the system (Klausen, 1974).

Nevertheless, we employ an "open" system approach to conceptualize the energy flow in systems where women are part of the network of social actors. We first consider the situation in a hypothetically complete subsistence system, i.e., where all the food consumed by the family is obtained by home production and where nothing is sold. To simplify the case (but not diverting too far from the reality of rural Africa), we also stipulate that the total food supply is produced by the woman in the household (polygamic situations are ignored) and that the individual woman rather than the household is the "management unit," as far as food is concerned.[7]

Problem:

> With the limitations of the dietary energy available to a woman producer and mother (caloric intake), what are her options in transforming and allocating this energy for the different tasks for which she is responsible? More specifically, at what stages will environmental or systemic factors completely determine a woman's (potential) energy expenditure? By contrast, at what stages could she reduce her energy input voluntarily in order to "save" energy for higher priority tasks? What will be the consequences of such action?

Discussion of Example I (see figure 1)

While we recognize the danger of fragmenting the reality of women's working day and their methods of allocating resources, it may be useful nevertheless to consider the energy expenditure "items" singly. In each case, we can analyze the relative role and importance of the constraints imposed upon the women by the system and the environment on the one hand, and by her free choice, on the other hand.

Energy Cost of A. The biological energy cost must be assumed to be relatively fixed during pregnancy and lactation and has been estimated (Thomson and Hytten, 1973). However, the cost of physical activities during pregnancy and lactation is not known, whether these physiological states significantly alter the utilization and expenditure of energy during specific activities. On the basis of energy measurements of pregnant women in New Guinea, Durnin

Fig. 1.
Example I:
Food procured from subsistence farming only.

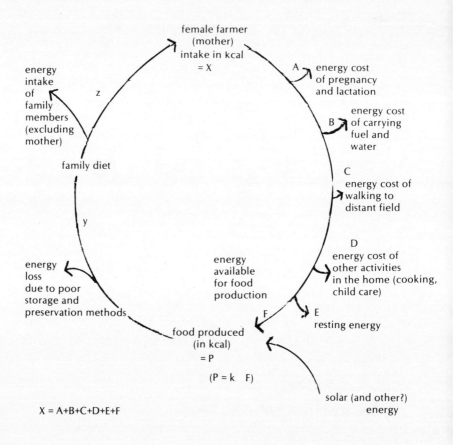

X = A+B+C+D+E+F

(1976) suggested that these women adapted to the situation by reducing their physical activity (sitting more, walking less). The degree to which women in general would do the same would probably be determined by cultural practices and expectations surrounding pregnancy (PAG Report, 1977).

Energy Cost of B. Fuel and water are both absolutely essential in the carrying out of basic daily tasks, and we would presume that the time and energy involved is fairly fixed. Any change in the use of energy would probably be in the upward direction as fuel becomes more scarce and is carried from longer distances to the home. In the latter case, and in cases where water is only available at some distance from the home, the prevailing environmental conditions set fairly narrow limits for the energy use involved. There is thus no real choice for the individual woman (only for the society) regarding ways to lower time and energy expenditure in fetching water and fuel.

Energy Cost of C. If the field is far away, the woman may go there less often than is optimal, which may mean suboptimal cultivation. Swantz (1975) gives an example of this from Tanzania, where fertile land on the slopes of Kilimanjaro is almost entirely used to produce cash crops (coffee and bananas) and is no longer available to women for maize production. The production of maize increasingly takes place on the lower plains. This does not so much affect the women who can afford transporation, as it does the poorer women who have more difficult access to the more distant fertile land.

Energy Cost of D. General home activities are of a somewhat different nature than fixed walks to the field or to the water source insofar as more or less "quality" comes into the picture, more or less time and energy can be put into food preparation, more or less attention and care can be given to children. Particularly in the latter case, the mother would see no immediate results of her activity (as compared to the fetching of a certain amount of water), and we may therefore assume that she might choose to "save" time and energy on home activities. We would also include here potential attendance at educational classes, meetings, etc., which would need strong motivation when time and energy become scarce.

Energy Cost of E. It is likely that this will be fairly constant. Available time budgets for women in rural areas show very limited resting time for women during the day. Concerning resting at night, it may be expected that the day/night rhythm is followed fairly rigidly where light may be a decisive factor.

Energy Cost of F. A woman may reduce her physical input in the field, but this would result in reduced food available to the family. Since such action would probably appear to be an obvious disadvantage to the mother, we postulate that she would try to maintain a relatively high input at this stage.

Discussion of Example II (figure 2)

We shall now look at a second type of situation, where some of the food produced by the woman is sold on the market. There is a relationship between cash value and energy value for food sold on the market. Within the total energy flow, part of women's work or energy input allocated to food production also attains a cash value. The cash obtained can be exchanged for new calories (i.e., other food items) for family consumption. Part of this will be consumed by the woman herself. This transformation of energy from the women's labor (energy expenditure) in the field (or post-harvest handling of food) through food energy sold, re-bought and partly re-fed into the woman for further transformation into energy for work in food production, will imply a net loss. Some of this loss may be due to low efficiency in energy utilization, to poor storage conditions, or to other waste at different stages in the "food path."

Our concern, however, is the point of market exchange. Here it should be possible to demonstrate whether the price received for the food energy sold is reasonable, so that the degree of "recovery" of energy in purchased food represents an exchange of goods of equal value, or whether it represents a net loss. In the latter case, it should be possible to identify what factors are responsible for the loss; i.e., why the price needed to buy food energy on the market is so much higher than that which the woman receives for her produce. The same factors could then be said to be directly responsible for the exploitation of women's labor expressed as its exchange value, and therefore, provide an opportunity to examine the nature and origin of these factors. An assessment might show that these factors are related to a variety of conditions—from local middle-men economic systems to the high profit margin on industrial products or to the high price of products

Fig. 2
Example II:
Food procured from subsistence production *and* from purchasing on the market.

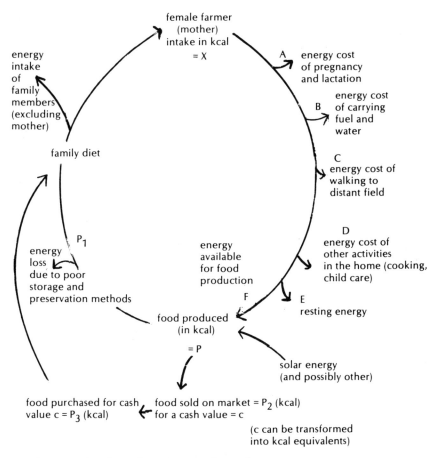

female farmer
(mother)
intake in kcal
= X

A energy cost
of pregnancy
and lactation

B energy cost
of carrying
fuel and
water

C
energy cost of
walking to
distant field

D
energy cost of
other activities
in the home (cooking,
child care)

energy
intake
of
family
members
(excluding
mother)

family diet

P₁

energy
loss
due to poor
storage and
preservation methods

energy
available
for food
production

F E
resting energy

food produced
(in kcal)

= P

solar energy
(and possibly other)

food purchased for cash
value c = P₃ (kcal)

food sold on market = P₂ (kcal)
for a cash value = c

(c can be transformed
into kcal equivalents)

If P₃ < P₂, then there is a net loss of energy.
(We ignore other nutritional assets.)

produced by costly modern agricultural inputs in the production system. These have already contributed to putting the woman producer at the marginally fertile land with limited returns.

Following this line of argument for purposes of changing the system, one would need to examine how women's labor could be better utilized or, to retain our terminology, how its potential exchange value could be maximized. In turn, this would also mean maximizing the local food supply and improving the women producers' place in the national economy. Options available to optimize the role of women in both the "productive" and "reproductive" spheres, without exploiting them as is being done today, are in theory legion, while the reality appears otherwise.

Limitations of the Model

Unfortunately, the model deals only with the energy part of food value. This represents a distinct limitation from a nutritional standpoint. Obviously, there may be energy losses through the purchase of low-energy food products which also contain other important elements; energy losses also result from the purchase of nonfood items. We have ignored these "other values" on purpose in this simplified model.

From an anthropological perspective, the model's limitation stems from a consideration of women's time and energy expenditure as freely convertible between different tasks. We have assumed that each woman will decide what, how, when, and where modifications can and should be made in her time and energy allocations (within the limits set by environmental and structural conditions). However, in practice this is not necessarily so, because different tasks may belong to different culturally well-defined sectors of "spheres" of society. Between these there may be "barriers" to conversion or transformation of different items or values. There might be social sanctions, e.g., moral reprobations in case an individual tries to cross such barriers (Bohannan and Dalton, 1965; Barth, 1967).

We may therefore hypothesize that there will be certain moral or other sanctions against a woman who tries to reallocate her attention, time, and energy to an activity that others in the household or community consider less important. For example, even if she *wants* to take more care of the children, the demands to put priority on cultivation in the field may greatly *limit* her ability to do so. Even if she *knows* that cultivation of leafy green vegetables would contribute to her children's health, her time may have to be used in petty trading in order to get enough cash for providing the staple, and so on.[8] In order to not complicate the development of our argument, we will eliminate further discussion about possible social barriers to exchangeability between, for example, the "domestic" and the "production" spheres (which by the way may be one and the same from the rural African woman's own perspective) or, if one likes, the reproductive-productive spheres.[9]

Placing Women's Role in Nutrition in a Wider Development Perspective

The model presented above could be developed further by looking at a variety of economic and social situations in which women find themselves—situations that have been determined by historical and political processes interacting with ecological and cultural conditions. For example, direct interventions like food aid or supplementary feeding programs add new dimensions to the models for energy flow. One major goal is to see how "food donations" substitutes or competes with local food production by the woman and determine what this means in terms of her energy expenditure and time allocation. Another goal is to determine to what degree the food aid relieves the woman of some of her burdens, or "relieves" her of additional income from the food she could have produced and sold on the market. When husbands are paid in food in certain "food for work" programs, does this interfere with the cash available to the family? Is women's work in food production increased when husbands—often migrant workers—go away?

Using the idea of energy budgets as one theoretical bridge between nutritional and anthropological methodologies and perspectives, we might ask the following questions:

1. What specific data are required for explanatory purposes?
2. What political considerations do the models generate?
3. What would be the consequence for nutrition research of the use of these models?

What data are required? In perusing the nutrition literature for energy expenditure data on women, one notes that there is a dearth of data on women engaged in agricultural work in the Third World. There is only one study on *hoeing* by women in Africa (Fox, 1953), while estimates of the cost of carrying water were calculated by Ritchie.[10] The hoeing value is recorded in Durnin and Passmore, *Energy, Work, and Leisure* (1967) and in FAO/WHO, "Energy and Protein Requirements" (1973). Norgan et al. (1974) measured energy expenditure of women during various agricultural tasks in New Guinea. Further work on energy expenditure by women during various activities at different agricultural cycles are in progress in Guatemala, partly in connection with pregnancy (McGuire, 1977),[11] and in Ghana (Orraca-Tetteh, 1977).[12] However, at present there is not an adequate set of energy data available to put substance to the models.

Are more data then needed? Some people concerned with the exploitation of women may feel that current information on time budgets suffice to demonstrate their arguments. However, we believe that new energy expenditure studies might add significantly to these arguments, as well as demonstrate the uneconomical nature and sometimes aggravating nutritional effects of many present day agricultural development policies. There is certainly a limit to *how many* of the same type of energy studies would be needed, and we would caution against using this approach to an extreme which could lead to a proliferation of respirometers or other devices all over the African continent or other parts of the Third World! Nevertheless, it seems warranted to suggest that a minimum amount of data be provided to clarify actual work input of women in various farm and domestic activities.

What political considerations do the models generate? We would like to see systematic studies carried out to amplify our conceptual models and to further demonstrate the often uneconomical nature of many current development policies as they apply to women's situation, the local food supply, and nutrition in general.

With this objective, however, one would enter into arguments of a more political nature. Several of the reasons suggested above for existing patterns of allocation of time, low productivity (not necessarily low physical output), and apparent low motivation among women can be traced back to two main types of determinants:

—those related to the prevailing production system and its

historical roots
—those related to existing patriarchal ideologies.

This is, of course, a very simplified categorization but will suffice for the points we want to make here. In practice, the conditions of women are likely to be influenced by the combined and mutually reinforcing effects of both types of factors. We have to recognize the existence of fundamental *conflicts of interest* where women normally will play the weaker part—whether it is vis-a-vis "the system" or vis-a-vis their men at the domestic level.

As we pointed out earlier, studies of women's situations have demonstrated that modern agricultural developments seldom reach women, even where they are the main food producers. They lack training, access to agricultural extension services, appropriate tools, and opportunities for credits and loans. These conditions might be remedied by improving the technology, bringing agricultural extension services to women farmers, and developing credit opportunities in cases where there is little economic security to start with.

These suggestions, however, require a fundamental reorientation of priorities within the existing agricultural extension service, totally new criteria for obtaining credits and loans, and a much stronger emphasis on the development of a technology appropriate for local production and consumption, and suited to women. But such a reorientation would necessarily be in conflict with the objectives of a national economy based on income from export agriculture. An emphasis on food production for local use does not necessarily ensure a large enough surplus to be exported or to be fed into secondary food production to satisfy the demand from the rich within the country.

At the domestic level, a "rational" way out of the women's dilemma, as seen from a Western perspective, would be to change the patterns of division of labor, so that women get more help from their husbands in basic food production. This is probably unrealistic in many societies where the original division of labor, developed as a way of optimizing the use of human resources, led to inequality in the new economic situations but were justified on the basis of maintaining traditional values.

There is another relative conflict of interest: women might want to change their work situation (e.g., in order to take better care of their children), but they have no freedom to do so because of their husbands' dominance in family decision-making. He expects his wife (or wives) to engage in agricultural activities thus making it possible for him to engage in other activities, such as wage earning, village affairs, or leisure.

In both types of conflict—within "the system" or at the domestic level—the strongest will win, and they will usually not be the women. Strength may be shown in various forms at various levels: through economic exploitative power, nationally, in the family, or as a physical strength. The latter can again take various forms according to the "level" of the conflict. The military apparatus being developed for external as well as internal oppression in many countries is a dramatic demonstration of this point.

What would be the consequences of the use of the models for nutrition research?   Nutritionists must recognize that research is nearly always motivated by multiple interests. In addition to the desire to increase understandings of physiological processes, nutrition research may also be motivated by economic, political, social, emotional, and other concerns. This feature of research undertaking is not necessarily bad, but the nature of such additional motives should be recognized and analyzed. Economically-oriented interests have often stood behind many of the energy expenditure studies, such as those aimed at the examination of how certain improvements in industrial workers' conditions, including food intake, could improve productivity. Detailed data on energy expenditure during various types of work operations have been needed, and therefore now abound.

We believe that available methodologies in nutrition research should be used for socially-beneficial purposes, including the exposure of inadequate development policies. A few efforts along this line have already been made in areas of energy expenditure. Gross and Underwood (1971) studied male workers on sisal plantations in Brazil and estimated that their energy expenditures effectively reduced the energy intake of young children, given prevailing economic conditions. Thus, they demonstrated a direct relationship between child malnutrition and the exploitation of sisal workers.

Taussig (1978) has examined the energy inputs of males as wage laborers on sugar plantations and as peasant farmers in Colombia. He points out that the sugar workers' self-provisioning on their own or on shared small plots, not only covers part of the cost of maintaining and reproducing the wage labor which otherwise would have had to be met by the capitalist plantation farming, but that it also increases malnutrition in the workers' families. In general, peasants with less land than is required for subsistence will redouble their efforts to make the land pay. When plantation work is combined with home production, it appears (from still imperfect data) that the nutritional balance that must be maintained by working adults to manage the combined effort is achieved at the expense of pregnant women and children.[13]

The models we have presented here are intended to be helpful for concerned nutritionists and anthropologists who would like to understand, in a more systematic way, how human beings as social actors within food and nutrition systems are tied to the wider network of economic, social, and political processes that bear upon the nutritional micro-universe. We feel that it is imperative to look at *totalities* rather than *fragments of realities*. Applied to our example, energy budgets of women's productive activities within the social system make possible a total perspective, while conventional energy studies precisely confined themselves to an examination of fragments of the total picture. This can lead to serious misinterpretation of the effectiveness of some nutrition interventions. For example, feeding workers at the workplace may lead to greater worker productivity, but when the program is viewed in a broader perspective, adverse effects may be discovered: payment in food may reduce cash income, which otherwise might be used for buying food for the family.

The Value of Models in Evaluation

Diagnosing a problem correctly is an important step toward its solution. Of equal importance is the effective evaluation of an action program, including an assessment of its unexpected, unforeseen, or "latent" impact.[14]

It is important not to lose sight of the purpose of the evaluation. A better evaluation methodology must not be thought of as an end in itself. The kind of perspectives we have presented in this paper may seem academic and purposeless for action. Even with a broadened perspective, studies of consumption and energy expenditure as implied in our models would be too costly to be used in regular evaluation activities.

That does not reduce the value of such models as guidelines for designing nutrition evaluation programs by researchers and planners. Nutrition intervention must be tailored realistically to suit the needs and resources of each country in a way that is most expedient and cost effective. By the same reasoning, basic research and evaluation must be appropriate to specific situations. When research planning is developed with an absence of information about local situations, it may be difficult to implement or prove to be disappointing in terms of outcomes.

For example, a recent document based on a study undertaken by an FAO consultant (ACC/SCN, 1978) represents a beginning effort toward developing a methodology for assessing the nutritional impact of agricultural and other programs on groups within different production systems. Although it poses certain questions concerning overall caloric availability as a result of changes, it completely omits a discussion of the role of sexual differentiation of labor within the various systems. Thus, it misses crucial aspects of the analysis that must precede the establishment of operational guidelines for assessment. A model such as the one presented here could help in making the initial analysis more complete and the subsequent approach to evaluation design more appropriate.

Therefore, while we do see the risk that more research on evaluation methodology may serve mainly to advance professional careers, we maintain that a certain amount of relatively sophisticated thinking and research is still needed in order to unveil hitherto unrecognized mechanisms that play a role in the development of malnutrition. This can, in turn, lead to the development of operationally useful indicators that can be used in evaluation work. Our point is that such indicators are not necessarily obvious but will often emerge following an analysis that might at first seem academic and useless in the field.

It is against this background that our considerations in this paper should be viewed and not as another justification for exotic research projects that could end up in "scientism"—or "a parody of positivism, quantification and socio-biology" (Taussig, 1978)—that will serve nobody.

Notes

1. Jette Bukh has described from Ghana the change from yam to cassava cultivation followed by the introduction of commercial cocoa production and massive male out-migration to cocoa plantations. Women became responsible for food crop production, but their available time resources prevented them from taking over yam production. They could only put in labor in small portions and in a way which would give the highest possible output per labor hour since time was their scarcest resource. They, therefore, replaced yam with cassava (traditionally

regarded as a low value hunger crop) since cassava gives a much higher output of starch per labor hour than yam. However, in spite of this resulting in higher food energy gain per labor hour, it is well known that cassava has a very low nutrient content and this in practice may imply a lowered nutritional value of the diet as compared to one based on yam (Bukh, 1977).

2. See PAG, 1977, for selected examples from village studies in Africa.

3. Several papers at a recent workshop held in Tanzania on "Food and nutrition education under changing socio-economic conditions" brought up the issue of structural constraints to changing behavior as contrasted to the belief in the message and the media as sole determinants for change (Jonsson, Maletnlema, Eide, among others, IUNS Workshop, Dar es Salaam, June 1978; Bantje, 1978).

4. See for example Durnin and Passmore: *Energy, work and leisure*, 1967.

5. The normative expectations surrounding women's roles as wives and mothers may have been generated by the colonialists, whose wives did perform mainly in the domain of the kitchen and the nursery room. In spite of a different situation in Africa, this may have reinforced the continuing existence of patriarchal ideologies that exist in a number of African societies (Steady, 1978).

6. We recognize that "economic arguments for increased emphasis on nutrition must not be the only ones used to persuade planners. Good nutrition is first and foremost a basic human right for everybody and should be approached as such. Yet in real politics and with scarce budgets, such arguments may be needed in addition.

7. This is an oversimplification in most situations, although justification for it exists (e.g., Barth, 1967, in his analysis of economic spheres in Darfur).

8. In addition, women may have their own strategies for optimizing their situation in very rational ways depending on the circumstances (Lamphere, 1974) although the basis of the rationality may not be understood by male food planners or Western (or Western-trained) nutrition educators—male or female! People in the latter category are usually quick to tell an "ignorant" mother what is best for her to do in order to ensure good child nutrition, and they become very surprised if the same mother does not respond and behave in the expected way. They are thus ignoring that within the mother's social and economic context, other strategies may in fact be more useful from her perspective.

9. Meillasoux (1972) has suggested that subsistence cultivation and women's labor force belong to the reproductive sphere, insofar as both are necessary to reproduce the labor force. For our purposes, we will restrict the word reproduction to its use by nutritionists, i.e., biological reproduction and tasks immediately related to child nurturing.

10. Cited in White et al. (1972)

11. J. McGuire, 1977, personal communication

12. R. Orraca-Tetteh, 1977, personal communication

13. It is interesting to note that in this Latin American situation the men contribute heavily to the maintenance and reproduction of the wage labour force. In rural Africa, the main burden in this sense would typically fall on women due to the traditional and prevailing patterns of division of labor.

14. For a discussion of the use of manifest versus latent consequences in nutrition evaluation, see Pelto and Jerome, 1978.

References

ACC-SCN
    1978 Towards Criteria and Practical Procedures for the Systematic Introduction of Minimal Consideration in the Preparation and Appraisal of Agricultural Projects. Paper presented by the Food Policy and Nutrition Division,

Food and Nutrition Assessment Service, FAO, for the Third Seminar of the ACC-Subcommittee for Nutrition, Rome, March 1978.

Amin, S.
1976   *Neocolonialism in West Africa.* New York: Pathfinder Press.
1977   *Imperialism and Unequal Development.* New York: Monthly Review Press.
1977   *Unequal Development: An Essay on the Social Formation of Peripheral Capitalism.* New York: Monthly Review Press.

Bantje, H.
1978   Constraint Mechanisms and Social Theory in Nutrition Education. Service Paper No. 78/4. Bureau of Resource Assessment and Land Use Planning. University of Dar es Salaam. Paper prepared for the Eleventh International Congress on Nutrition, Rio de Janeiro, Brazil.

Barth, F.
1967   Economic Spheres in Darfur. Six Themes in Social Anthropology, A.S.A. Monographs. London: Tavistock Publications.

Bohannan, P. and Dalton, G. eds.
1965   *Markets in Africa.* New York: Anchor Books.

Boserup, E.
1970   *Women's Role in Economic Development.* New York: St. Martin's Press.

Bukh, J.
1977   Report to the PAG Project on Women in Food Production, Food Handling and Nutrition. United Nations, New York.

de Garine, I.
1972   The Sociocultural Aspects of Nutrition. *Ecology of Food and Nutrition* 1:143-164.

Durnin, J.V.G.A.
1976   Sex Differences in Energy Intake and Expenditure. Symposium on Sex Differences in Response to Nutritional Variables, *Proc. Nutr. Soc.* 35:145-154.

Durnin, J.V.G.A. and Passmore, R.
1967   *Energy, Work and Leisure.* London: Heinemann Educational Books.

Eide, W. B.
1978   Wanted: A Framework for Food and Nutrition Education. Education as a Neutral Activity—Does It Exist? Paper presented at the IUNS Workshop, Rethinking Food and Nutrition Education under Changing Socioeconomic Conditions, Dar es Salaam, Tanzania.

FAO/WHO
1973   Joint Ad Hoc Expert Committee on Energy and Protein Requirements, FAO Nutrition Meetings Rep. Ser. No. 52, WHO Techn. Rep. Ser. No. 477.

Fox, R.J.
1953   Study of the Energy Expenditure of Africans Engaged in Various Rural Activities. (Ph.D. 1953, London University.)

Frank, A.G.
1969   *Latin America: Underdevelopment or Revolution.* New York: Monthly Review Press.

Gross, D.R. and Underwood, B. A.
1971   Technological Change and Calorie Costs: Sisal Agriculture in Northeastern Brazil. *American Anthropologist* 73:723-740.

Jonsson, U.
1978   The Planning Approach to Nutrition Education: National Potentials and Constraints. Paper presented at the IUNS Workshop, Rethinking Food and Nutrition Education under Changing Socioeconomic Conditions, Dar es Salaam, Tanzania.

Kaberry, P.
1952 *Women of the Grassfields.* Her Majesty's Stationery Office, London.
Kemp, W.B.
1971 The Flow of Energy in a Hunting Society. *Scientific American* 225:104-115.
Knutsson, K.E.
1974 Det Anthropologiska Perspektivet—Reflektioner Omkring et Emnas Identitet. Vetenskapliga Perspektiv.
Lamphere, L.
1974 Strategies, Cooperation and Conflict among Women in Domestic Groups. *Women, Culture and Society.* Rosaldo and Lamphere, eds. Stanford: Stanford University Press.
Malentnlema, T.N.
1978 Who Is Ignorant? Paper presented to the IUNS Workshop, Rethinking Food and Nutrition Education under Changing Socioeconomic Conditions, Dar es Salaam, Tanzania.
Meillasoux, C.
1972 From Reproduction to Production: A Marxist Approach to Economic Anthropology. *Economy and Society.* London: Routledge and Kegan.
Norgan, N., Ferro-Luzzi, A. and Durnin, J.V.G.A.
1974 The Energy and Nutrient Intake and the Energy Expenditure of 204 New Guinean Adults. *Phil. Trans. R. Soc. London* 268:309-348.
Pala, A.O.
1975 A Preliminary Survey of Avenues and Constraints on Women's Involvement in the Development Process of Kenya. M 75-2449 IDA, University of Nairobi.
Pelto, G. H. and Jerome, N.W.
1978 "Nutrition Education and Evaluation Research: Some Theoretical Concerns." Paper presented at the XIth Meeting of the International Union of Nutritional Sciences, Rio de Janeiro.
Rodney, W.
1974 *How Europe Underdeveloped Africa.* Washington, D.C.: Howard University Press.
Sharman, A.
1970 Nutrition and Social Planning. *Journal of Development Studies* 5:77-79.
Skjønsberg, E.
1977 Women and Food and the Social Sciences. Oslo, mimeographed paper.
Steady, F.C.
1968 The Social Position of Women: Selected West African Societies. Unpublished B. Litt. Thesis, Oxford University, England.
1977 Research Methodology from an African Perspective. Paper presented at the 1977 Conference on the Decolonization of Research of the Association of African Women for Research and Development (AAWORD), Dakar, Senegal.
1978 Decolonizing Education: Implications for Nutrition Education. Paper presented at the IUNS Workshop, Rethinking Food and Nutrition Education under Changing Socioeconomic Conditions, Dar es Salaam, Tanzania.
Swantz, M., Henricsson, U., and Zalle, M.
1975 Socioeconomic Causes of Malnutrition in Moshi District. Research Paper No. 38, Bureau of Resource Assessment and Land Use Planning (BRALUP), Dar es Salaam, Tanzania.

Taussig, M.
  1978   Nutrition, Development and Foreign Aid: A Case Study of U.S.-Directed Health Care in a Colombian Plantation Zone. *International Journal of Health Services* 8:101-121.
Thomson, A.M. and Hytten, F.E.
  1973   Nutrition During Pregnancy. *World Review of Nutrition and Dietetics* 16:22-45.
UN Economic Commission for Africa (UN/ECA)
  1974   Africa's Food Producers: The Impact of Change on Rural Women. Paper prepared by the Women's Programme Unit, Human Resource Division, for the American Geographical Society.
  1974   The Data Base for Discussion on the Interrelations Between the Integration of Women in Development, Their Situation and Population Factors in Africa.
UN Protein-Calorie Advisory Group (PAG)
  1977   Women in Food Production, Food Handling and Nutrition. United Nations, New York, mimeographed paper.
UNRISD
  1977   The Impact on Women of Socioeconomic Changes. Background Document Board 1978/WP6.
White, G.F., Bradley, D.J., and White, A.U.
  1972   *Drawers of Water: Domestic Water Use in East Africa.* Chicago: University of Chicago Press.

4

Nutrition and Cultural Evolution

Patterns in Prehistory[1]

D. R. Yesner

This chapter serves two purposes. It seeks to illustrate the importance of adding time depth to the study of nutrition in contemporary human communities, and it describes an archaeologist's views on human dietary adaptations. In doing so, three major approaches are undertaken. First, the archaeological record is examined for evidence relating to prehistoric diets and their nutritional value. Second, methods are considered for establishing relationships between various diets and patterns of population size, density, distribution, growth, and mobility. Finally, some dietary trends in cultural evolution and in patterns of nutritionally-related disease among hunter-gatherers and agriculturists are discussed. Wherever appropriate, the discussion will focus on various possible strategies for obtaining nutritional data directly from the archaeological record.

Reconstruction of Prehistoric Diets and Their Relation to Population Configurations

Reconstruction of prehistoric human diets from archaeological remains is based upon a record that is of necessity incomplete. The magnitude of the data deficiency or insufficiency is related both to local conditions of preservation and to the nature of the occupation(s) being considered (Schiffer's "n-transforms" and "c-transforms," respectively, 1976). In spite of the problems associated with prehistoric dietary reconstruction, however, generalizations on dietary trends over time and space can be made. The accuracy of such generalizations is inversely proportional to the size of area or length of time being considered. As far as size of area is concerned, the "regional" dietary analyses frequently employed by archaeologists serve as an effective compromise between the minimum size necessary for accurate reconstruction and a maximum size necessary for a sufficient sample. If it is well defined ecologically, a region may also serve as a useful operational unit. Population distributions for various time periods may be determined through regional surveys. Within each period of human occupation of the region, individual settlement loci serve different functions, and some of these loci change in function over time as well. Typically, archaeologists determine these functions by first examining indications of the season of site occupation, such as age distributions of fauna, presence or absence of migratory fauna, incremental growth ring patterns of fish or mollusks, pollen profiles, presence of absence of seeds, and so on (Evans, 1978). Archaeologists also make use of data about activities at each settlement locus, as reflected in assemblages of technological and dietary refuse. Human population sizes and densities may be indirectly estimated through densities of various kinds of archaeological remains such as bones, potsherds, or habitations (Cook, 1972; Heizer, 1960), or through the application of ethnographic analogy (e.g., Yellen, 1977). Skeletal populations may occasionally enable archaeologists to make more direct population estimates (Howells, 1960).

In arriving at estimates of population size, density, distribution, or mobility, the nutritional constituents of the diet itself are rarely taken into consideration. This is surprising when one considers that the structure of preindustrial human settlement patterns is in large part a reflection of nutrient availability in terms of both quantity and quality. Factors of quantity include the density, aggregation, accessibility, reliability, and storability of resources (Hassan, 1975). Factors of quality involve maintenance levels for physiological requirements for various vitamins and minerals. Calories produced by the synthesis of proteins and fats may be to some extent a floating requirement, depending on biological demand for energy related to factors such as body size, which in turn, respond to caloric availability. However, the balance of essential amino acids, the building blocks of proteins, is a critical biological requirement which must be maintained by human populations. That is, for optimal utilization by adults, eight essential amino acids must be present in the diet in the proper ratio. According to a joint report of the World Health Organization (WHO) and Food and Agriculture Organization (FAO) of the United Nations (1973), the following relative proportions in mg. of amino acids per g. of protein seem adequate: isoleucine, 18; leucine, 25; lysine, 22; methionine and cystine, 24; phenylalanine and tyrosine, 25; threonine, 13; tryptophan, 6.5; and valine, 18.

Optimal Foraging Theory

Human settlement patterns are best viewed as "minimax" adaptive solutions to problems of optimal location for best exploiting the environment. As such, studies of prehistoric subsistence and settlement tend to reflect what has been termed "optimal foraging theory." The concept of optimal foraging patterns has been applied by biologists to various species of animals (Pyke et al., 1977; Pulliam, 1974; Cody, 1974; Rapport, 1971; Emlen, 1967); in particular, it has been applied to various nonhuman primates (Gaulin and Kurland, 1976; Coelho et al., 1976; Altmann, 1974). Some suggestions have been put forth on the application of the concept of hunter-gatherer societies both ethnographically (Smith, 1978; Winterhalder, 1978) and archaeologically (Keene, 1977, Jochim, 1976). Most authors' conception of an "optimal diet" is one in which energy return is maximized while energy outlay is minimized; in other words, a "least effort" or energy-efficiency behavioral model (Emlen, 1966; Norberg, 1977). In exploring possible "minimax" settlement patterns, therefore, anthropologists have generally suggested calculating the caloric expenditures required in exploiting each resource by clocking the time required for search, retrieval, and processing operations; this information would then be balanced against the energy provided by each resource (Hill, 1971; Perlman, 1978). However, since more than caloric input and output are at stake in human dietary adaptations, it is necessary to calculate the specific *nutritional* value of given food items (Pulliam, 1975). Unfortunately, few archaeologists have yet recognized this fact. Ideally, studies of prehistoric subsistence and settlement should elicit whether site locations at various time periods ensure availability and balance of nutrients such as vitamins, minerals, and essential amino acids (Reidhead, 1977; Reidhead and Limp, 1974).

In sum, settlement patterns are "minimax" adaptive strategies that involve responses to nutritional changes, whether those changes are the result of external factors (e.g., environmental change) or internal cultural factors (e.g., patterns of exchange or redistribution of resources). Throughout hominid history, population sizes, densities, and distributions have evolved in tandem with nutritional changes. These responses may be viewed as selective in nature (Hayden, 1972). Nutrition can be linked to population dynamics through infant mortality, either directly (through reduced availability of important resources to dependent members of the population) or indirectly (through increased maternal mobility due to conscription of resources or through a deficient prenatal environment). In some cases, nutrition can be linked to fertility patterns as well (Nag, 1962).

Subsistence Shifts in the Post-Pleistocene:
A First Approximation

One result of this inattention to nutritional factors by archaeologists is that diets are described in very general terms in the literature. In point of fact, hunting-gathering diets referred to as "littoral," "riverine," or "lacustrine" differ significantly in the distribution of critical nutrients such as vitamins, minerals, and essential amino acids. Furthermore, most authors have made the mistake of dealing with habitat zones such as forests or sea-coasts in very broad ecological terms; the fact is, forests differ greatly from other forests, and sea-coasts from other sea-coasts in terms of specific complexes of nutrients that are available to the human diet (Yesner, 1977a).

To illustrate this point, let us consider the cast of post-Pleistocene subsistence shifts. What is the meaning, in nutritional terms, of the presumed shift from specialized hunting of large-sized, high-biomass herbivores to so-called "broad spectrum" subsistence during the terminal Pleistocene and early post-Pleistocene in Europe and the Near East?

It is necessary to delineate at the outset the differences in post-Pleistocene adaptations to different forest environments. To begin with, the only vegetal resources available to any significant extent and utilized by human populations in the dense western European forests during the period in which the area was undergoing initial postglacial successional change were hazelnuts (*Corylus* sp.), acorns (*Quercus* sp.), a few greens such as dock (*Rumex* sp.) and various plantains, as well as some essentially unstorable berry species (Newell, 1973; Iversen, 1949). In fact, the mixed European forest of this period (the Atlantic—Boreal transition) had a lower total biomass in kg./km.² than the tundra of the preceding terminal Pleistocene (Butzer, 1971; Bourliere, 1963). The relative dearth of vegetal resources must have taken on increased importance as the biomass of game species declined. In contrast, the upland oak-pistachio open park woodlands of the post-Pleistocene Near East contained a high density and wide variety of resources utilizable by human populations, including a large number of storable resources (Flannery, 1969). Hence, human post-Pleistocene adaptations probably proceeded quite differently in the two areas.

In western Europe, for example, forest Mesolithic sites are present, but coastal midden sites predominate. Human groups exploited shellfish almost exclusively at most of these coastal sites. At some sites, ocean fish were added to the diet, but this occurred only where the level of technology and local socioeconomic organization permitted their exploitation. The same is true of seals, which were added to the diet only in specific localities such as northwestern Europe. What did this mean in nutritional terms? Shellfish are low in both protein and fat content—and hence caloric content—per unit weight; one would have to eat enormous quantities in order to maintain sufficient energy levels (Parmalee and Klippel, 1974). Furthermore, they do not contain a full complement of essential amino acids; while high in lysine and tryptophan, they are low in isoleucine and the sulphur-containing amino acids. Deep-sea fish are generally higher in protein content per unit weight than most shellfish, but if low in fat (as most species are), they may also be low in caloric content per unit weight. Deep-sea fish often contain more of the sulphur-containing amino acids than do shellfish, but they tend to be deficient in iron and vitamin C, which must be obtained elsewhere (WHO-FAO, 1973; Watt and Merrill, 1963).

Forest cultures of the western European Mesolithic would have been able to exploit some vegetal resources high in vitamins A and

C, as well as a variety of game such as deer, chamois, mountain goat, and wild boar (Butzer, 1971). Littoral populations, cognizant of these resources, must have exploited forest products, despite their limited biomass, in order to ameliorate their nutritional situation. Many of the early post-Pleistocene coastal sites in Spain and Portugal contain evidence of these species (Straus, 1977; Freeman, 1973). A similar pattern emerges from Gorman's (1971) studies of post-Pleistocene "broad spectrum" coastal adaptations in southeast Asia (Thailand), with interior cultures exploiting only interior resources, and coastal groups exploiting both coastal and interior resources.

The settlement picture, then, for post-Pleistocene western Europe does not necessarily demonstrate the degree of sedentism that some archaeologists have suggested. It even renders unlikely the alternate interpretation that coastal sites represent seasonal settlement loci (Gabel, 1958; Clark, 1972). Rather, the coastal sites of the period probably represent home bases from which hunting parties simultaneously exploited both coastal and interior resources and may have thus coexisted with scattered interior-adapted populations. This may be what Newell (1973) is getting at when he refers to a "continuity of combined inland and coastal adaptation and exploitation" and notes that "coastal exploitation was an integral and functional element in the total Mesolithic economy (adaptive strategy)."

The nutritional evidence for a combined nuclear-dispersed settlement pattern is corroborated by technological evidence which suggests that different early western European Mesolithic settlement loci represent specialized activity areas. For example, the central base settlements, which contain macrolithic as well as microlithic tools, may reflect food processing as well as food producing activities, whereas the smaller, purely microlithic sites, frequently found in forested areas but in close proximity to central base sites, may have been used for food-procuring activities such as bow-and-arrow hunting (cf. S.R. Binford, 1968, for a similar analysis of the Mousterian of Levallois Facies). A similar nuclear-dispersed settlement pattern has also been postulated for certain areas of aboriginal North America, particularly the Pacific Northwest (Yesner, 1977a) and certain coastal areas of eastern North America (L. R. Binford, 1968a) where shell-heaps and forest hunting campsites indicate isolated task-specific loci of a single culture.

If a pattern of nuclear-dispersed settlement can be verified for western Europe, it follows that the adoption of even a rudimentary horticulture may have enabled some late Mesolithic populations to become fully sedentary where previously they were not. They could supplement their littoral diets with agricultural products (Troels-Smith, 1967). Two assumptions are being made here; first, following the principle of least effort, that human populations will become sedentary whenever and wherever resource configurations allow; and second, all other things being equal (i.e., if the level of technology and perception of available resources so permits), human populations will strive to maintain nutritional sufficiency.

An entirely different picture of resource availability from that of western Europe is shown in southwest Asia—specifically southwest Iran. In response to slight environmental amelioration, the oak-pistachio park uplands seem to have expanded beginning ca. 11,000 B.P. (Wright, 1978). According to archaeological data from the site of Tepe Alikosh in southwestern Iran, the available vegetal resources included not only cereal grains, such as wild wheat and barley, but also wild legumes, such as lentils, peas, alfalfa, fenu-greek, vetches, plantains, burnets, and clover; fruits, such as jujube, tamarisk, wild caper, and wild licorice; and wild grasses, such as canary grass, bermuda grass, brome grass, goose grass, oat grass, and rye grass (Flannery, 1969). The upland forest of south-western Iran certainly provided caloric sufficiency, and a fairly wide variety of vegetal products provided vitamins and minerals as well as a full complement of essential amino acids. Furthermore, many of these vegetable foods were storable for long periods. In addition, until the vegetative cover became adversely affected by expanding human settlements, game of various sorts was available in the upland forest; this included gazelle, onager, aurocks, wild boar, wild sheep, wild goat, fallow deer, porcupine; some turtles, crabs, fish, and mussels; and various species of birds (Flannery, 1969). Solely on the basis of nutritional information gleaned from archaeological data, one can readily see that a high potential for sedentarism in the exploitation of local resources existed at an early time in the southwest Iranian uplands and other parts of southwest Asia. Early sedentary villages, in fact, led to rapid population expansion in southwest Asia, culminating in events that contri-buted to the origins of agriculture.

The situation with regard to postglacial nutrition and population dynamics in the intermediate area of eastern Europe is just beginning to emerge as more paleoenvironmental reconstruction is undertaken and new data on postglacial cultural adaptations come to light. It is no accident that the data reveal a heretofore unsuspected closeness in the timing of the emergence of food production in eastern Europe and in southwest Asia. The forest of eastern Europe, with its open parklands and scattered woodlands, allowed the buildup of significant population densities, particularly in coastal, riverine, or lacustrine locations (Tringham, 1971; Binford, 1968b). Such locations were ecotones high in species diversity, where complementary nutrients were available to sedentary populations. When food production emerged in these areas, particularly in response to increased population densities, woodlands were essentially clearable by swidden techniques (Tringham, 1971).

Aleut Adaptations: A Second Approximation
The preceding discussion has provided some approaches used in examining archaeological data to assess prehistoric diets. By using the inductive approach, regional settlement systems and prehistoric exploitation patterns may be reconstructed from data obtained from individual archaeological sites. Or, one may opt for a deductive approach that infers the mix of dietary resources from settlement location alone. In order to undertake the latter type of analysis, the paleoenvironment must first be accurately reconstructed; this is followed by an examination of the "goodness of fit" between the observed settlement location and the hypothesized optimal location for resource exploitation. Again, subsistence refuse are examined, but this time to test a hypothesis of optimal settlement location.[2] Ideally, both inductive and deductive approaches should be combined to permit continuous testing and readjustment of nutritionally-related hypotheses.

Such a combination of approaches has been undertaken in studies conducted in the Aleutian Islands (Yesner, 1977b). There, maritime-adapted populations exploited a wide variety of sea-mammals, sea-birds, fish, and invertebrates and developed efficient systems whereby caloric levels and nutrient balances were maintained in the population. Adequate nutritional levels were maintained through the deployment of populations to various settlement loci at various times of the year to exploit localized resources (Aigner, 1974). In areas where species diversity and biomass were higher, the local population established centrally based villages that were continuously occupied. In areas where resources were less diverse and less abundant, seasonal and/or activity-specific campsites were established. When population levels at the central base strained the "carrying capacity" of the local microenvironment, populations exploited the marginal (species-poor) sites more intensively in order to extract maximum nutrition from available resources. The temporary camps then became year-round sedentary villages until population levels were reduced again by natural factors. Sudden population increases of this nature were enabled by the fact that, unlike Eskimo populations, mechanisms of social mortality such as infanticide or senilicide were never adopted by the Aleuts.

The sex and age composition of the Aleut population was important in determining actual population levels at given points in time. The sex/age population profile was in turn the result both of nutritional factors (i.e., the nutritional adequacy of various sex/age classes of the population), various stochastic demographic processes (i.e., sex ratio at birth), and random mortality factors such as navigational accidents, which were of great importance in these relatively small breeding isolates. For example, a probable large increase in population of the Aleutian chain occurred ca. 4,000 B.P., soon after geological stabilization of the coastline allowed a slowing of relative sea-level rise, the cutting of wave-based strandflats, and the development of extensive invertebrate populations on those strandflats. The population increase was a product both of the opening of a new resource niche and of the resultant increased viability of young, old, pregnant, and infirm members of the population who could collect this resource with little difficulty and thus support themselves (Laughlin, 1972).

In order to determine to what extent Aleut exploitation patterns were based on simple resource abundance as opposed to specific nutritional factors, an analysis was undertaken of the relative biomass attributable to each Aleutian resource both in the natural ecosystem and in the record from Aleutian archaeological sites (Yesner and Aigner, 1976). Faunal remains were analyzed from various sites in the southwest region of Umnak Island in the Aleutians and compared with biological data from Aleutian National Wildlife Refuge surveys. When the two types of biomass ranks are compared, one notes that, in general, most species are exploited according to their relative abundance in the ecosystem. The exceptions appear to be those species that are particularly large in size (and thus yield an increased energy return per unit invested) as well as those that have particular nutritional value to the population. A detailed dietary analysis (Yesner, 1977b) showed that the latter group included sea-mammals and birds with greater fat content; migratory species were present during the critical times of the year, especially the late winter and early spring when caloric levels were low.

Overall, there seems to be some response of Aleut populations to nutritional factors in their resource selectivity. Much of this archaeological inference receives support from the Aleut ethnographic record (e.g., Veniaminov, 1840; Jochelson, 1933). Unfortunately, certain data that are crucial to a full comprehension of population responses to nutrient availability are *not* present in the ethnographic record. The exact resource preference schedules of the Aleut population are largely unknown and must be inferred from archaeological data. For example, it would be extremely useful to know at what point of invertebrate resource depression would the population turn to other resource(s) as a substitute, to what specific resources, and how much would be consumed? At present, the archaeological approach to questions of nutrient optimization seems to yield the most tangible results.

Nutrition and Cultural Evolution: The Nutrition of Hunter-Gatherers and Agriculturalists

Subsistence Resources of Hunter-Gatherer Populations
The problem of determining resource preference schedules of hunter-gatherers is by no means peculiar to the Aleutian Islands. In fact, our knowledge on this subject is derived largely from a few quantitative studies such as those reported by Lee (1969) and Tanaka (1976) on the Kalahari San. As a result, we know little about the generalizability of these models to other hunter-gathering populations. For example, the diet of nomadic !Kung San consisted primarily (ca. 65 percent by weight) of vegetal matter (Lee, 1969). While most investigators are willing to concede that arctic populations vary considerably from this pattern, fewer researchers seem cognizant of the fact that hunters in certain temperate and tropical zones subsisted largely on animal flesh. Examples include large areas of temperate North America where populations subsisted on diets containing large quantities of fish (Casteel, 1972) or large

game animals such as bison. On the South American pampas, populations apparently subsisted on game with little or no use of vegetal materials. Among some of these populations, special adaptive physiological responses to high levels of fat ingestion may have occurred; this seems to be true of certain arctic and pastoral populations subsisting almost entirely on a meat diet (Taylor and Ho, 1971; Ho et al., 1972; Draper, 1974). At any rate, depending upon region and resource, hunting groups must have utilized widely different diet patterns, and adaptive responses must have varied widely.

The example of Mesolithic populations cited earlier, demonstrated primarily how hunter-gatherer populations with different ecologies adapted to different nutrient quality combinations through different population distributions and settlement patterns. Other sets of adaptations, however, were made by hunter-gatherer populations to different *total* levels of dietary resources. These included biological adapations in body size and form, growth patterns, and various mechanisms for regulating population size. Except for populations relying primarily on animal protein, hunter-gatherers seem to have optimized local group sizes in relation to resources within certain adaptive limits. Hunting and gathering is an omnivorous compromise between the more nutritionally-efficient hunting of animals with proper amino acid ratios and the more ecologically-efficient gathering of vegetal materials at low trophic levels. On the one hand, large group size is necessary in cooperative hunting for maintenance of "territorial integrity" (Williams, 1968:126) and, in some environments, for protection against the loss of individuals in hunting accidents. On the one hand, a slightly smaller group size is adaptive for gathering, since less mobility is required and the local environment is degraded less readily. Actually, as Martin (1973) has pointed out, these limits are in fact sufficiently close that most hunter-gatherer populations maintain a relatively small overall range of total group size. Many populations maintain an optimal group size based around the minimum number of hunters necessary to be efficient in cooperative search-and-kill procedures while not over-exploiting local resources (Martin, 1973). The result of this "optimization" of local group size is a minimizing of energy expenditures of movement while distributing population aggregates to match the clustering of resources and adjusting the total population level to minimally available resource densities, following Liebig's "Law of the Minimum" (Odum, 1971).

Demographic Features

Because hunter-gatherer populations were generally maintained above minimal levels, people probably rarely starved outright. Occasional gross deficiencies of essential amino acids, vitamins A, B, and E, and a few minerals, such as magnesium, sodium, and potassium, may have had effects on population fertility levels through the reduction of spermatozoa production (Farris, 1950) or through increased miscarriages and stillbirths (Kyhos et al., 1945). Hunter-gatherers in simple ecosystems with low diversity such as deserts or the high arctic probably did encounter more frequent episodes of starvation, however (Laughlin, 1968), and in the high arctic this was compounded by depressed calcium levels (Foulks, 1972) which may have had significant effects on fertility (Rumney, 1935).

What biological regulatory mechanisms may have come into play, then, so that hunter-gatherers did not overexploit their resources? Frisch's work (1975) has demonstrated close linkages between the fat content of the female body and the onset of menstruation, as mediated by the production of estrogens. It has been suggested that the reduced fat content of the female hunter-gatherer body, as a result of diet and exercise patterns, coupled with the prolonged lactation characteristic of hunter-gatherers (which itself has a depressing effect on fertility), would have been sufficient to control fertility levels and widen birth spacing (Coale, 1974). In contrast, the high carbohydrate diets and more limited exercise patterns of sedentary agriculturalists would have resulted in increased fat storage to trigger population increases. With soft gruels and porridges of cereal grains available for early weaning of infants, length of lactation time would have been reduced and further population increase stimulated. Spontaneous abortion due to mobility, another possible regulator of hunter-gatherer populations, may also have been reduced among early sedentary agricultural populations, giving rise to further population increase.

Not all of the constraints on hunter-gatherer population size were ecological or biological, however. Some females may have limited family sizes in order to minimize stresses of carrying infants between settlements (Lee, 1972). Upper limits of population size also warded off increased psychological stress, increased aggression, and the need for settling disputes (Savishinsky, 1971; Chagnon, 1972). This can be viewed as a proximate response mechanism, ultimately adjusting populations to the food supply. Lower limits on the size of local Mendelian populations, "required on the basis of a strictly mechanical model of man" (Williams, 1968:131), were needed to overcome various kinds of stochastic processes, such as reduction in genetic variability due to random genetic drift (Roberts, 1968) or imbalances in sex ratios and age distributions within populations.

Two problems are involved in assessing the meaning of age/sex composition and other demographic features of hunter-gatherer populations. One problem is that differences in population profiles are related to different ecologies. For example, where juvenile and aged persons were more important as producers, they were more highly represented in the population age structure (Laughlin, 1968; Thomas , 1974). Another problem is the likelihood that the population profiles of surviving hunter-gatherers may be quite different from those of extinct populations. For example, certain kinds of social mortality (such as infanticide) may have occurred more frequently in marginal resource habitats. Furthermore, it is likely that surviving hunter-gatherer populations in marginal areas use quite different resources than did extinct populations in more beautiful regions. Related to this is the probability that nutritional deficiencies, particularly the gross temporary deficiencies, of a "feast-or-famine" nature that have been cited for modern hunter-gatherer populations (Dunn, 1968) may not have been characteristic of "the first 99% or more of man's life on earth" in which "periods of gorging alternated with periods of greatly reduced food intake" (Neel, 1962: 355).

It is necessary, however, to make a distinction between acute "feast-or-famine" situations and regularized fluctuations, primarily of a seasonal nature, in the density and distribution of resources. In the first case, *excess* nutrients may result in acute physiological stress, with

> serious consequences for the organism in the long run. The necessity to respond repeatedly to intake of one or another substance in amounts larger than the tissues are adapted to tolerate is likely to result in physiological disturbances. (Dubos, 1965: 84).

The famine part of the "feast-or-famine" situation would also have contributed such physiological disturbances as hepatic and pancreatic lesions, lack of appropriate immunological response, and excessive fat storage in the liver.

Adaptation to Seasonal Resource Fluctuations

Seasonal resource fluctuations also may have occasionally in-curred some of the same physiological responses as did longer term fluctuations. In addition, both acute and seasonal resource vari-ability may have resulted in increased prenatal mortality rates, due to physiological stresses on mothers and increased requirements for female work output and mobility (resulting in higher levels of spontaneous abortion). It appears that in some cases of regular seasonal resource fluctuations, populations responded by altering births to take place during certain times of the year (Cowgill and Hutchinson, 1966). This minimized the likelihood that the addi-tional caloric requirements of pregnancy (an average additional requirement of 80,000 kcal.) would coincide with periods of resource deprivation and make females available for additional energy expenditure (i.e., work effort) during such periods (Tho-mas, 1970). Regularized response to seasonal resource fluctuations include the production of alternating periods of positive and negative caloric balance through cultural means (differential energy expenditures) and/or biological means (storage of calories in fats and storage of protein reserves in lymphatic and extracellular fluid systems).

A different type of cultural response to seasonal resource changes is the "scheduling" of resources (Flannery, 1968) or shifting of populations as the biota and diet change during the course of the year following animal migration and plant maturation sequences. This may involve shifting the population within a given ecological zone (as in the Aleutians), movement of part of the population into adjacent ecological zones (as in the vertical systems of the Andes), or movement of the entire population into a different ecological zone during part of the year (the "seasonal rounds" typical of many hunter-gatherers). The last of these frequently entails the alternate aggregation and fragmentation of populations during the year into what have been termed micro-bands and macro-bands (MacNeish, 1972).

A final category of cultural adjustments to seasonal resource fluctuations (or to annual fluctuations among agriculturalists) is storage of resources. However, as evidenced from the !Kung data (Lee, 1968), in many cases it is easier to respond to resource fluctuations by shifting populations rather than by storing food.

Hunter-gatherer populations have to deal with long-term as well as seasonal resource fluctuations. One cultural solution to this problem is interpopulational resource exchange, which may be manifest in ceremonial activity (Suttles, 1960; Rappaport, 1969). However, hunter-gatherer societies have also developed *internal* structional solutions for dealing with the problem of long-term nutrient imbalances. The Aleutian archaeological data are particularly instructive in this regard. The fluctuating settlement system which the data demonstrate is apparently the result of changing population/resource ratios. The point is this: unlike agriculturalists, hunter-gatherers have developed a structural solution for dealing with temporary increases in population or reductions in general nutritional levels through more intense utilization of marginal zones. Among agriculturalists, who often have all locally arable land under cultivation, further support of an increasing population, even on such a temporary basis, may be difficult without concomitant technological change and/or political centralization.

The methodological lesson of the material on hunter-gatherer ecology is that the diet of prehistoric populations must be studied by careful analysis and viewed in highly regionalized terms. The same can be said about the diets of horticulturalists. Rather than speaking of the general systemic effects of grain diets on human populations, it is necessary to speak of the effects of specific grain diets, such as corn, rice, or sorghum diets, or of grain combination diets, or of diets combining grains with other specific dietary substances. Many diseases of early horticulturalists, such as pellagra or beriberi, are highly localized phenomena strongly related to local resource patterns.

Certain generalized statements, however, can be made about the nutritional effects of the transition from hunting-and-gathering to agriculture. In all areas, except those where shellfish or low-fat fish were the primary preagricultural resources, there was a substantial reduction in dietary proteins and fats, but an increased consumption of carbohydrates, thus providing an adequate caloric intake.

Diet Patterns, Nutrition, and Infection
Among Subsistence Agriculturists

One major result of a high-starch, low protein diet is an imbalanced immunochemical system leading to impaired disease resistance through depletion of antibodies (more commonly in children than adults) and interference with macrophage metabolism. Also involved is an interference with mucopolysaccharide and collagen synthesis, and therefore an interference with the body's inflammatory response, since this response involves the deposition of these substances. Hormonal response patterns are also affected; acute starvation is known to activate the pituitary-adrenal system, while chronic undernutrition is known to decrease adrenal activity. Both pituitary and adrenal glands play important roles in the resistance to infection. In sum, protein deprivation appears to be involved in impaired disease resistance, although vitamin A and to some extent vitamin C are involved as well. When protein deprivation is in fact, responsible, it is generally the case that "the proper balance of amino acids is probably at least as important as the total amount of these nutrients in determining resistance to infection" (Dubos, 1965: 156).

Major effects of nutritional deprivation include aggravation and prolongation of infection as well as increased likelihood of contracting infection in the first place. Nutritional deficiencies have a synergistic effect with bacterial, rickettsial, and helminthis infections, and this synergistic effect is particularly strong in children, for whom requirements for protein (and particularly certain essential amino acids such as leucine) are elevated (Scrimshaw et al., 1968; Latham, 1975). This situation was exacerbated by the fact that, with the advent of food production came an increase in certain kinds of infections such as zoonoses spread from domesticated animals; disease (such as malaria) borne by mosquitos whose breeding grounds were increased as a result of forest clearance (Angel, 1972); and infections from increasing human waste among sedentary village populations (Polgar, 1964).

In sum, the transition to agricultural production probably increased the spread of infectious disease as a result not only of sedentism but also nutritional changes (Pfeiffer, 1975). In addition, disturbed prenatal development may have occurred as a result of amino acid imbalances. For the pregnant woman, the National Research Council considers that 50 percent of all amino acids in the diet must be essential amino acids. When the excess of a single amino acid depresses the availability or utililization of other amino acids, particularly its analog, retarded intrauterine growth and disturbed development may occur (Giroud, 1973; Goldsmith, 1968).

Among hunter-gatherers, for whom the full complement of

amino acids were generally available, relative dietary deficiency leading to malnutrition was probably rare (Dunn, 1968). In addition, weak individuals among hunter-gatherers tend to be selected out of population during the prenatal period either by cultural means, such as infancticide, or by natural means, such as mobility-induced spontaneous abortion (Sussman, 1972; Nurge, 1973). The extent to which this occurred in any hunting-and-gathering population depended on the local ecology and the group's particular cultural pattern of population regulation. However, with the development of highly productive and efficient mono-crop agricultural systems (e.g., maize in Mesoamerica), the risk of famine became much greater than among hunter-gatherers, since the stability of ecosystems (including artificial ones) is related to their diversity, albeit in a complex manner. The risk of famine, however, only affected certain members of agricultural populations (i.e., individuals of lower socioeconomic status) to any extent. Furthermore, in many early agricultural populations, food storage largely minimized the risk of famine.

As the risk of famine increased for many agricultural groups, their ability to fall back on natural resources in an emergency decreased. This was because human population growth, increased settlement size, forest clearance, and the production of salt pans from irrigation systems all acted to modify or even destroy the vegetative cover in many areas (Adams, 1966). In some areas this modification of the vegetative cover also exaggerated the effects of dry seasons (Dunn, 1968). In addition, since wild animal populations were dependent on vegetative cover, such modification or destruction generally precluded the maintenance of a great deal of animal protein in the diet. This problem was alleviated in areas where domesticable animals were available. The symbiotic relationship between early agriculturalists and pastoralists (Adams, 1966) can be explained as a means of simultaneously insuring proper dietary balance and maintaining high productivity levels. Of course, the grazing animals themselves took a toll of the ecosystem. Furthermore, as animals became increasingly used as beasts of burden, an ever greater proportion of the group's caloric output became channeled through the animals themselves. Where domesticable animals were not readily available, however, the problems were much worse, and chief among those problems was a much higher risk of nutrient imbalances.

Socioeconomic Stratification

As indicated above, not all members of early agricultural populations were equally affected by nutritional and other changes that
accompanied the advent of food production. The severity of
unequal resource distribution that resulted from increased socioeconomic stratification can be estimated from status differentials
revealed by archaeological items such as habitations, grave goods,
or subsistence data from floral and faunal remains (Brown, 1971;
Saxe, 1977). In some places, such as Tikal (Haviland, 1967), at several
Woodland sites in midwestern North America (Cook 1971), or in
cemeteries from medieval Germany (Huber, 1968), the nutritional
effects of unequal resource distribution have been more precisely
determined by correlating the status differentials revealed in grave
goods with stature differentials in the skeletons that accompanied
them.

Paleopathology

The nutritional and demographic effects of the transition from
hunting-gathering to agricultural production can thus best be
assayed through detailed examination of human skeletal series,
where a record is available within a given region, and where the
economic base of populations at various points in the archaeological record can be reconstructed with some accuracy. This has
been attempted by archaeologists in different regions with varying
degrees of success. In the long series from the Tehuacan Valley in
highland Mesoamerica, for example, dating from ca. 6,500 B.P. to
the time of the Spanish conquest, there is little evidence of change
in nutritional status, except for a slight increase in dental caries with
the transition to agriculture (Anderson, 1967). However, the incidence of periodontal disease, alveolar abscesses, and premortem
tooth loss declines simultaneously.

Part of the problem in assessing these data is that often only
severe nutritional deficiencies, and then only specific substances,
show up in the skeletal record as osteoporotic changes, osseous
lesions, or gross morphological changes (Brothwell, 1961). Dental
anomalies, whether subclinical hypomineralization of the denti-
tion or clinically-evident enamel hypoplasia, may also be more
closely related to the absence of specific substances, such as
vitamin A, although metabolic changes brought about by certain
infectious diseases may also be involved. The same is true of
transverse lines of growth arrest of the epiphyseal plate, which may

be related equally to childhood disease episodes as to nutritional deficiencies per se (Palkovich, 1975; Cassidy, 1974 and this volume). However, the presence of transverse lines may, in some cases, be a key to pinpointing generalized protein-calorie deficiencies, since general deficiencies seem to be involved in their etiology.

Transverse lines are primarily due to periodic nutritional deficiencies and debilitating disease followed by periods of recovery. Chronically suboptimal nutrition is more likely to result in slowed rate of skeletal growth and hence reduced stature. Anderson found no such reduced stature in the Tehuacan materials, but two workers in the Maya region, Haviland (1967) at Tikal, and Saul (1972) at Altar de Sacrificios, found reductions in stature in the populations during periods of greater population density, with the greatest changes occurring among males.[3] They postulated a period of dietary stress. Similarly, Angel (1946) attributed an 8 percent stature increase over a 4,500-year period in ancient Greece, from the early Neolithic to Classical times, to an increase in agricultural productivity. In all cases, researchers have claimed that the essential genetic continuity of the populations was maintained, i.e., they were unaffected by heterosis. However, there are other problems in stature analysis; it is well known, for example, that rates of growth as well as intrapopulational variances in skeletal proportions may change over time and within a given region. Changes in socioeconomic differentiations may lead to changes in intrapopulational nutrient distributions, which may in turn affect intrapopulational variances in skeletal proportions Huber, 1968). Finally, the reconstruction of infant mortality patterns for prehistoric populations on the basis of skeletal remains is exceedingly hazardous, because of poor preservability and because infants were frequently disposed of in a manner different from other members of the population.

Recently, great success has been achieved in relating the quality of prehistoric diets to the strontium content of human bone. High strontium values tend to be characteristic of a herbivorous diet, while low values tend to be characteristic of a carnivorous diet. Because quantities of bone strontium are so minute, techniques for measuring strontium (or other trace mineral) content involve X-ray fluorescence, atomic absorption spectrometry, or neutron activation analysis. Results have been only somewhat encouraging when applied to fossil hominids (Boaz and Hampel, 1978), but in both midwestern United States "Woodland" populations (Lambert et al., 1979) and Mesoamerican populations from Chalcatzingo (Schoeninger, 1979) there is a very strong inverse correlation between bone strontium content and social status, as determined from burial goods associated with the human skeletons. The results suggest that higher status individuals in both areas had diets with higher meat protein content. Correlations with social status and bone magnesium content may also be indicated (Lambert et al., 1979).

The importance of specific plants in the human diet may also be reflected in the elemental constituents of bone. The ratio of Carbon 13 to Carbon 14 isotopes in bone appears to reflect the dietary importance of plants which themselves utilize different metabolic pathways in photosynthesis. A higher ratio of C^{13} to C^{14}, for example, may reflect increased consumption of maize as a dietary item; such a trend has been found in prehistoric skeletons dated to 5-2,000 B.P. from the Viru Valley in Peru (DeNiro and Epstein, 1978). The calcium content of human bone may also reflect increased maize consumption (Lambert et al., 1979), since traditional maize processing utilized large amounts of lime (Katz et al., 1974). The benefit of this processing technique is an increase in both dietary calcium and the ratio of lysine to other amino acids, which is generally very low in maize but improves with the addition of alkali. However, alkali treatment simultaneously reduces the content of several vitamins (thiamine, riboflavin, and niacin). More important, maize itself contains large quantities of phytic acid, an iron chelating agent, which adversely affects the absorption of iron by making it unavailable for metabolism. The result of a long-term maize diet, then, was the development of porotic hyperostosis, a symptom of severe iron deficiency anemia, as evidenced in cranial lesions in skeletal series from the United States southwest, Mesoamerica, and Peru (El Najjar et al., 1976 a, b). There is also evidence that iron is a critical determinant in susceptibility to infectious disease (Weinberg 1974).

In regions where soils (and hence the flora) are nutrient deficient, agriculturalists and pastoralists would be expected to display skeletal abnormalities. Specifically, defiencies of three trace elements—copper, manganese, and zinc—may show up directly in skeletal material. Although the research is more extensive for animals than for human populations, it seems quite clear that at least manganese and zinc deficiencies can result in osteoporosis, osseous lesions, and epiphyseal dysplasia. Deficiencies of these substances are related to infertility, in some cases through defective ovulation, in other cases through reduced production of spermatozoa; zinc deficiency, for example, has been linked to the malproduction and dysfunction of several hormones, notably gonadotropin, progesterone, and testosterone (Underwood 1977). Even at a subclinical level, is it not possible that deficiencies in certain trace elements could lead to suppressed human fertility, and hence reduction of potential for human population growth? It has also been suggested by Dubos (1965) that certain leguminous plants grown by horticultural peoples may have had some effects on human fertility because they contain estrogen-like substances that have stimulated estrus in animal populations.

The "Demographic Transition"

Life expectancies of early subsistence agriculturalists were not substantially different from those of hunter-gatherers in general (Weiss, 1973), but in specific cases they were probably lower because of the nature of the particular crops that were grown or because of changes in food distribution enforced by elite groups. Life expectancies, however, may be relatively poor indicators of the nutritional adequacy of human populations. For example, malnourished peasant populations of today tend to have higher average life expectancies than early horticulturalists (Weiss, 1973). One compounding factor is that these figures usually average out the rural and urban segments of the population; since the time of the earliest cities, mortality rates have been higher and life expectancies generally lower in urban areas. Overall, the situation is quite complex, and frequently depends upon the position of a particular area vis-a-vis the so-called "demographic transition." Infant mortality rates seem to be highest, and problems of malnutrition greatest, in areas that are only beginning in transition. These nations, involved in the international market in production of cash crops but not yet industrialized, often demonstrate the population expansion and strain on resources concomitant with high infant mortality (Polgar, 1964).

The existence of an international trade market is a crucial factor that must be taken into account in assessing the dietary adequacy of prehistoric agricultural populations and making comparisons with data from modern peasant populations. Today all agricultural populations are involved in the world economy to some extent;

often nutritional quality of the diet seems to be associated with economic modernization. Changes in traditional subsistence crop complexes (e.g., deletion of squashes from Mesoamerican diets), total deletion of animal protein from the diet in many places, increased reliance on high-carbohydrate processed foods, and changed patterns of sex-differential nutrition all have significant effects on nutritional adequacy. Changes in infant feeding practices can be directly traced to the effects of acculturation; which, in turn, influences infant growth, development, disease, and mortality patterns. The extent of these influences is largely unknown (Behar, 1968).

It can be established through archaeological data, that more land per capita was available for cultivation during prehistoric times; however, the market systems which existed then functioned much differently than the markets today. Markets, of course, arose as symbiotic systems enabling the trading of goods, including subsistence items, between ecologically differentiated regions; this helped to maintain overall nutrient balances (Sanders, 1955). Subsequently, the structure of those markets became changed through the activity of local elites and the markets were used to redirect the flow of "surplus" goods (i.e., forced excess production) to elites, rather than to benefit the subsistence of the producers. Finally, with the incursion of capital, the production of peasants became directed toward national and world markets with the substitution of cash crops for subsistence goods, and modern peasant markets have become competitive systems in many ways more detrimental than beneficial to peasant groups.

Archaeological data has established the fact that there was a substantial shift in the nature of nutritionally-related epidemiological patterns between hunter-gatherers and agriculturalists. Archaeological data also allow us to trace the antiquity of the nutritional deficiency diseases of tropical populations such as kwashiorkor and marasmus.

Present evidence indicates that kwashiorkor probabiy has some antiquity in various tropical zones. The best current guess that could be made about the antiquity of kwashiorkor in the tropical Amazonian region, for example, is that it may have accompanied the initial domestication of manioc and sweet potato sometime before 1300 B.C. when these crops diffused from the Colombia coast (Meggers, 1971). However, because of continuously low population densities due to low soil productivity, populations in the Amazonian region have generally been able to maintain a diet which included a component of animal protein such as riverine fish and small forest animals. It is believed that this type of diet precluded any widespread dietary imbalances in the region down to the present day (Gross and Underwood, 1971).

Similarly, in west Africa, kwashiorkor may have accompanied the origins of yam cultivation in rain forest areas ca. 3000 B.C. (Clark, 1971). Again, however, until west African populations increased substantially, thus straining the available resources and reducing the remaining animal component of the diet, it is likely that substantial dietary imbalances occurred. Whether this were true to any significant degree before the recent beginnings of demographic transition (and recent immigration of Europeans) into west Africa is a moot issue.

In contrast to the above cases, marasmus—involving generalized protein-energy deficiencies—is simply an extension of the famine conditions affecting individuals of low socioeconomic status since the advent of food production. It may well be the case, however, that modern peasant and urban populations suffer more from generalized malnutrition and undernutrition than did the early subsistence agriculturalists.

Conclusion

The archaeologist interested in reconstructing the total picture of human adaptation must be able to do several things. He/she must be able to assess accurately the effect of different nutrient substances and dietary combinations on human physiology. He/she must be able to relate nutritional deprivations of various kinds to different patterns of nutritionally-related epidemiology. He/she must be able to determine the relationship between the density and distribution of resources across the landscape to dietary differentials, and then to population size, density, distribution, and mobility. He/she must be able to assay the effects of dietary differentials over time on potentials for population growth and changes in settlement pattern. Finally, he/she must have a good handle on feedback between social organization and dietary adequacy.

Several years ago, Osborne (1968) suggested that archaeologists and physical anthropologists have a unique opportunity for co-operating in the "determination of diet and natural resources." The same statement could well be repeated with respect to archaeologists and nutritionists. Archaeologists need to work more closely with nutritionists to establish the nutritional significance of prehistoric dietary adapations. Nutritionists, too, need to work more closely with archaeologists to define more precisely the adaptive response of human populations to different nutritional configurations.

Notes

1. The present paper owes much to several individuals who reviewed the original form of the paper, as delivered to the 72nd annual meeting of the American Anthropological Association in New Orleans, especially G. Pelto and P. Kelly of the Section of Archaeology and Human Ecology, Department of Anthropology, University of Connecticut, and N.W. Jerome, convener of the symposium on nutritional anthropology. Thanks are also due J.S. Aigner of the Department of Anthropology, University of Alaska, for making available archaeological materials on which the Aleutian research was based. That research was carried out under Grant GB28426, National Science Foundation, and Dissertation Grant 077, Connecticut Research Foundation. The Maine research was carried out under grants from the Maine Historic Preservation Commission and the University of Southern Maine.

2. These kinds of analyses could also be applied to incipient agricultural populations. In that case, data would be gathered on local soils and geomorphology as well as the location of various wild sources of nutrients. This type of information could then assist in determining whether the population was fully exploiting either wild resources, areas suitable for agricultural production, or some mix of the two. This kind of analysis is particularly useful in regions where continuous sequences exist from hunting-and-gathering to fully horticultural societies.

3. It is generally accepted that males are more subject to reduction in stature as a result of nutritional stress than are females. The underlying physiological mechanisms are the result of natural selection. Statural reductions are the result of reduced growth rates during adolescent years, in turn the result of reduced protein availability. Males, who grow more slowly to a slightly greater height (the ratio ranges from 1.09:1 to 1.04:1 for various societies) can afford such a protein reduction because most male tasks are well performed below the maximum capacity of even small males (Stini, 1974). For females, as actual reduction in skeletal muscle also serves as the amino acid reserve for infant nutrition, including both prenatal placental feeding and postnatal milk production. As a result, it appears that "females are better buffered against the effects of nutritional stress" (Stini, 1974:18).

References

Adams, R.
    1966   The Evolution of Urban Society. Chicago: Aldine.

Aigner, J.S.
   1974   Studies in the Early Prehistory of Nikolski Bay: 1937-1971. *Anthropological Papers of the University of Alaska* 16:9-25.
Altmann, S.A.
   1974   Baboons, Space, Time and Energy. *American Zoologist* 14:221-248.
Anderson, J.E.
   1967   The Human Skeletons. *The Prehistory of the Tehuacan Valley, Vol. I: Environment and Subsistence.* Austin: University of Texas Press.
Angel, J.L.
   1946   Skeletal Changes in Ancient Greece. *American Journal of Physical Anthropology* 41:69-97.
   1972   Ecology and Population in the Eastern Mediterranean. *World Archaeology* 4:88-105.
Béhar, M.
   1968   Food and Nutrition of the Maya Before the Conquest and at the Present Time. *Biomedical Challenges Presented by the American Indian.* Washington, D.C.: Pan American Health Organization.
Binford, L.R.
   1968   Archaeological Visibility of Food-Gatherers: Comments. *Man the Hunter.* Lee and DeVore, eds., Chicago: Aldine.
   1968   Post-Pleistocene Adaptations. *New Perspectives in Archaeology.* Binford and Binford, eds. Chicago: Aldine.
Binford, S.R.
   1968   Variability and Change in the Near Eastern Mousterian of Levallois Facies. *New Perspectives in Archaeology.* Binford and Binford, eds. Chicago: Aldine.
Boaz, N. T. and J. Hampel.
   1978   Strontium content of fossil tooth enamel and diet of early hominids. *Journal of Paleontology* 52: 928-933.
Bourlière, F.
   1963   Observations on the Ecology of Some Large African Mammals. *African Ecology and Human Evolution.* Howell and Bourlière, eds. Chicago: Aldine.
Brothwell, D.R.
   1961   Diseases in Earlier Man. *New Scientist* 233:238-240.
Brown, J.
   1971   Approaches to the Social Dimensions of Mortuary Practices. Memoirs of the Society for American Archaeology 25, *American Antiquity* 36(3): Part 2. Washington, D.C.: Society for American Archaeology.
Butzer, K.W.
   1971   *Environment and Archaeology.* Chicago: Aldine.
Cassidy, C.M.
   1974   Determination of Nutritional and Health Status in Skeletal Populations: The Use of Multiple Techniques for Data Analysis. Paper presented to the American Association of Physical Anthropologists, Amherst, Mass.
Casteel, R.W.
   1972   Two Static Maximum Population Density Models for Hunter-Gatherers: A First Approximation. *World Archaeology* 4:19-40.
Chagnon, N.A.
   1972   Tribal Social Organization and Genetic Microdifferentiation. *The Structure of Human Populations.* Harrison and Boyce, eds. Oxford: Clarendon Press.

Clark, J.D.
  1971   *The Prehistory of Africa.* New York: Praeger.
Clark, J.G.D.
  1972   *Star Carr: A Case Study in Bio-Archaeology.* Reading, Mass.: Addison-Wesley.
Coale, J.A.
  1974   The History of the Human Population. *Scientific American* 231:40-51.
Cody, M.L.
  1974   Optimization in Ecology. *Science* 187:1156-1164.
Coelho, A.M., Jr., Bramblett, C.A., Quick, L.B., and Bramblett, S.S.
  1976   Resource Availability and Population Density in Primates: A Socio-Bioenergetic Analysis of the Energy Budgets of Guatemalan Howler and Spider Monkeys. *Primates* 17:63-80.
Cook, D.C.
  1971   Patterns of Nutritional Stress in Some Illinois Woodland Populations. (M.A. Thesis 1971, University of Chicago.)
Cook. S.F.
  1972   *Prehistoric Demography.* Reading, Mass.: Addison-Wesley.
Cowgill, U.M. and Hutchinson, G.E.
  1966   The Season of Birth in Man. *Memoirs of the Connecticut Academy of Arts and Sciences* 17:232-240.
Denham, W.D.
  1975   Population Structure, Infant Transport and Infanticide Among Pleistocene and Modern Hunter-Gatherers. *Journal of Anthropological Research* 30:191-198.
DeNiro, M. J. and S. Epstein.
  1978   Carbon isotopic evidence for different feeding patterns in two *Hyrax* species occupying the same habitat. *Science* 201: 906-908.
Draper. H.H.
  1974   Aspects of Adaptation to the Native Eskimo Diet: Energy Metabolism. *American Journal of Physical Anthropology* 43:475.
Dubos, R.
  1965   *Man Adapting.* New Haven: Yale University Press.
Dunn. F.L.
  1968   Epidemiological Factors: Health and Disease in Hunter-Gatherers. *Man the Hunter.* Lee and DeVore, eds. Chicago: Aldine.
El Najjar, M. Y. and A. L. Robertson, Jr.
  1976   Spongy bones in prehistoric America. *Science* 193: 141-143.
El Najjar, M. Y., D. J. Ryan, C. G. Turner II, and B. Lozoff
  1976   The etiology of porotic hyperostosis among the prehistoric and historic Anasazi Indians of the southwestern United States. *American Journal of Physical Anthropology* 44: 477-488.
Emlen, J.M.
  1966   The Role of Time and Energy in Food Preference. *American Naturalist* 100:611-617.
  1967   Optimal Choice in Animals. *American Naturalist* 102:385-389.
Evans, J.
  1978   *Environmental Archaeology.* Ithaca, New York: Cornell University Press.
Farris, E.J.
  1950   *Human Fertility and Problems of the Male.* White Plains, N.Y.: The Author's Press.
Flannery, K.V.
  1968   Archaeological Systems Theory and Early Mesoamerica. *Anthropo-*

logical Archaeology in the Americas. Meggers, ed. Washington, D.C.: Anthropological Society of Washington.

1969   Origins and Ecological Effects of Early Domestication in Iran and the Near East. *The Domestication and Exploitation of Plants and Animals.* Ucko and Dimbleby, eds. Chicago: Aldine.

FAO/WHO
1973   *Amino Acid Content of Foods and Biological Data on Proteins.* Rome: United Nations.

Foulks, E.F.
1972   *The Arctic Hysterias of the North Alaskan Eskimo.* Washington, D.C.: American Anthropological Association.

Freeman, L.G.
1973   The Significance of Mammalian Faunas from Palaeolithic Occupations in Cantabrian Spain. *American Antiquity* 38:3-44.

Frisch, R.
1975   Demographic Implications of the Biological Determinants of Female Fecundity. *Social Biology* 22:17-22.

Gabel, W.C.
1958   The Mesolithic Continuum in Western Europe. *American Anthropologist* 60:658-667.

Gaulin, S.J.C. and Kurland, J.A.
1976   Primate Predation and Bioenergetics. *Science* 191:314-317.

Giroud, A.
1973   Nutritional Requirements of the Embryo. *World Review of Nutrition and Dietetics* 18:195-262.

Goldsmith, G.A.
1968 . The New Dietary Allowances. *Nutrition Today* 3:16-19.

Gorman, C.F.
1971   The Hoabinhian and After: Subsistence Patterns in Southeast Asia During the Late Pleistocene and Early Periods. *World Archaeology* 2:300-320.

Gross, D.R. and Underwood, B.A.
1971   Technological Change and Caloric Costs: Sisal Agriculture in Northeastern Brazil. *American Anthropologist* 73:725-740.

Hassan, F.A.
1975   Determination of the Size, Density and Growth Rate of Hunting-Gathering Populations. *Population, Ecology and Social Evolution.* Polgar, ed. The Hague: Mouton.

Haviland, W.F.
1967   Stature at Tikal, Guatemala: Implications for Ancient Maya Demography and Social Organization. *American Antiquity* 32:316-325.

Hayden, B.
1972   Population Control Among Hunter-Gatherers. *World Archaeology* 4:205-221.

Heizer, R.F.
1960   The Quantitative Analysis of Habitation Residues. *The Application of Quantitative Methods in Archaeology.* Heizer and Cook, eds. Chicago: Viking Fund Publications in Anthropology.

Hill, J.N.
1971   Research Propositions for Consideration by the Southwest Anthropological Research Group. *The Distribution of Prehistoric Population Aggregates.* Gumerman, ed. Prescott College Anthropological Reports No 1. Prescott, Arizona: Prescott College Press.

Ho, K.J., et al.
1972   Alaskan Arctic Eskimo: Responses to a. Customary High Fat Diet. *American Journal of Clinical Nutrition* 25:737-745.

Howells, W.W.
1960 Estimating Population Numbers Through Archaeological and Skeletal Remains. *The Application of Quantitative Methods in Archaeology.* Heizer and Cook, eds. Chicago: Viking Fund Publications in Anthropology.

Huber, N.M.
1968 The Problem of Stature Increase: Looking from the Past to the Present. *The Skeletal Biology of Earlier Human Populations.* Brothwell, ed. Oxford: Pergamon Press.

Iverson, J.
1949 *The Influence of Prehistoric Man on Vegetation.* Danmarks Geologiske Undersogelso Ser. 4(3).

Jochelson, W.
1933 *History, Ethnology and Anthropology of the Aleut.* Washington, D.C.: Carnegie Institute of Washington.

Jochim, M.A.
1976 *Hunter-Gatherer Subsistence and Settlement: A Predictive Model.* New York: Academic Press.

Katz, S. H., M. L. Hediger, and L. A. Valleroy
1974 Traditional maize processing techniques in the New World. *Science* 184: 765-773.

Keene, A.S.
1977 Economic Optimization Models and the Study of Hunter-Gatherer Subsistence-Settlement Systems. Paper presented to the Society for American Archaeology, New Orleans, Louisiana.

Kyhos, E.D., et al.
1945 Effects of Malnutrition Upon Mothers and Infants in Naples. *American Journal of Digestive Diseases* 16:436-441.

Lambert, J. B., C. B. Spuznar, and J. E. Buikstra
1979 Chemical analysis of excavated human bone from Middle and Late Woodland sites. *Archaeometry* 21: 115-129.

Latham, M.C.
1975 Nutrition and Infection in National Development. *Science* 188:561-565.

Laughlin, W.S.
1968 The Demography of Hunters: An Eskimo Example. *Man the Hunter.* Lee and DeVore, eds. Chicago: Aldine.
1972 Ecology and Population Structure in the Arctic. *The Structure of Human Populations.* Oxford: Clarendon Press.

Lee, R.B.
1968 What Hunters Do for a Living, or, How to Make Out on Scarce Resources. *Man the Hunter.* Lee and DeVore, eds. Chicago: Aldine.
1969 !Kung Bushman Subsistence: An Input-Output Analysis. *Environment and Cultural Behavior.* Vayda, ed. Garden City, New York: Natural History Press.
1972 *Work Effort, Group Structure and Land Use in Contemporary Hunter-Gatherers.* Andover, Mass.: Warner Modular Publications.

MacNeish, R.S.
1972 *The Evolution of Community Patterns in the Tehuacan Valley of Mexico and Speculations About the Cultural Processes.* Andover, Mass.: Warner Modular Publications.

Martin, J.F.
1973 On the Estimation of the Sizes of Local Groups in a Hunting-Gathering Environment. *American Anthropologist* 75:1448-1468.

Meggers, B.J.
1971 *Amazonia: Man and Culture in a Counterfeit Paradise.* Chicago: Aldine.

Nag, M.
   1962   *Factors Affecting Human Fertility in Non-Industrial Societies: a Cross-Cultural Study.* Yale University Publications in Anthropology No. 66. New Haven: Yale University Press.

Neel, J.V.
   1962   Diabetes Mellitus: A "Thrifty" Genotype Rendered Detrimental by Progress? *American Journal of Human Genetics* 16:52-140.

Newell, R.R.
   1973   The Post-Glacial Adaptations of the Indigenous Population of the Northwest European Plain. *The Mesolithic in Europe.* Kozlowski, ed. Warsaw: Warsaw University Press.

Norberg, R.A.
   1977   An Ecological Theory on Foraging Time and Energetics and Choice of Optimal Food-Searching Method. *Journal of Animal Ecology* 46:511-529.

Nurge, E.
   1973   Abortion in the Pleistocene. Paper presented to the Ninth International Congress of Anthropological and Ethnological Sciences, Chicago, Illinois.

Odum, E.P.
   1971   *Fundamentals of Ecology.* Philadelphia: W.B. Saunders.

Osborne, D.
   1968   The Archaeological Determination of Diet and Natural Resources and the Case for Cooperation. *American Journal of Physical Anthropology* 30:439-442.

Palerm, A.
   1967   Agricultural Systems and Food Patterns. *Handbook of Middle American Indians.* Austin: University of Texas Press.

Palkivich, A.M.
   1975   Evaluating the Nutritional Status of a Prehistoric Population: Skeletal Biology and Demography. Paper presented to the American Anthropological Association, San Francisco, California.

Parmalee, P. and Klippel, W.
   1974   Freshwater Mussels as a Prehistoric Food Resource. *American Antiquity* 39:421-434.

Perlman, S.M.
   1978   Mobility Costs and Hunter-Gatherer Group Sizes. Paper presented to the Society for American Archaeology, Tucson, Arizona.

Pfeiffer, J.
   1975   The First Food Crisis. *Horizon* 17:32-47.

Polgar, S.
   1964   Evolution and the Ills of Mankind. *Evolution After Darwin.* Vol. II. Tax, ed. Chicago: Viking Fund Publications in Anthropology.

Pulliam, H.R.
   1974   On the Theory of Optimal Diets. *American Naturalist* 108:59-74.
   1975   Diet Optimization with Nutrient Constraints. *American Naturalist* 109:765-768.

Pyke, G.H., Pulliam, H.R., and Charnov, E.L.
   1977   Optimal Foraging: A Selective Review of Theory and Tests. *Quarterly Review of Biology* 52:137-154.

Rappaport, R.A.
   1969   Population Dispersal and Land Distribution Among the Maring of New Guinea. *National Museums of Canada Bulletin* 230:113-126.

Rapport, D.J.
   1971   An Optimization Model of Food Selection. *American Naturalist* 105:575-587.

Reidhead, V.A.
  1977   Labor and Nutrition in Food Procurement: Did Prehistoric People
  Optimize? Paper presented to the Society for American Archaeology, New
  Orleans, Louisiana.
Reidhead, V.A., and Limp, W.F.
  1974   Nutritional Maximization: A Multifaceted Nutritional Approach to
  Archaeological Research. Paper presented to the American Anthropological
  Association, Mexico City, Mexico.
Roberts, D.F.
  1968   Genetic Effects of Population Size Reduction. *Nature* 220:1084-1088.
Rumney, J.
  1935   The Problem of Differential Fertility. *Population* 2:3-23.
Sanders, W.
  1955   The Central Mexican Symbiotic Region: A Study in Prehistoric
  Settlement Patterns. *Prehistoric Settlement Patterns in the New World.*
  Willey, ed. New York: Wenner-Gren Foundation.
Saul, F.P.
  1972   *The Human Skeletal Remains of Altar de Sacrificios: An Osteo-
  biographic Analysis.* Cambridge, Mass.: Peabody Museum Press.
Savishinsky, J.S.
  1971   Mobility as an Aspect of Stress in an Arctic Community. *American
  Anthropologist* 73:604-618.
Saxe, A.A.
  1977   On the Origin of Evolutionary Processes. *Explanation of Prehistoric
  Change.* Hill, ed. Albuquerque: University of New Mexico Press.
Schiffer, M.B.
  1976   *Behavioral Archaeology.* New York: Academic Press.
Schoeninger, M. J.
  1979   Diet and status at Chalcatzingo: some empirical and technical aspects
  of strontium analysis. *American Journal of Physical Anthropology* 51: 295-310.
Scrimshaw, N.S., Taylor, C.E., and Gordon, J.E.
  1968   Interactions of Nutrition and Infection. World Health Organization
  (WHO) Monography No. 57. Geneva: United Nations.
Smith, E.
  1978   Optimal Foraging Theory and the Study of Human Hunter-Gatherers.
  Paper presented to the American Anthropological Association, Los Angeles,
  California.
Stini, W.A.
  1974   Adaptive Strategies of Human Populations Under Nutritional Stress.
  Biosocial Interrelations in Population Adaptation. Johnson, ed. The Hague:
  Mouton.
Straus, L.G.
  1977   Of Deerslayers and Mountain Men: Palaeolithic Faunal Exploitation in
  Cantabrian Spain. *For Theory Building in Archaeology: Essays on Faunal
  Remains, Aquatic Resources, Spatial Analysis and Systemic Modeling.* Bin-
  ford, ed. New York: Academic Press.
Sussman, R. W.
  1972   Child Transport, Family Size and Increase in Human Population During
  the Neolithic. *Current Anthropology* 13:258-259.
Suttles. W.
  1960   Affinal Ties, Subsistence and Prestige Among the Coast Salish. *American Anthropologist* 62:296-305.
Tanaka, J.
  1976   Subsistence Ecology of the Central Kalahari San. *Kalahari Hunter-*

Gatherers: Studies of the !Kung San and Their Neighbors. Lee and DeVore, eds. Cambridge, Mass.: Harvard University Press.

Taylor, C.V. and Ho, K.J.
1971 Studies on the Masai. *American Journal of Clinical Nutrition.* 24:1291-1293.

Thomas, D.H.
1973 An Empirical Test for Steward's Model of Great Basin Settlement Patterns. *American Antiquity* 38:155-176.

Thomas, R.B.
1970 El Tamano Pequeno del Cuerpo como Forma de Adaptacion de Una Problacion Quechua a la Altura. Acta y Memorias del 39 Congreso Internacional de Americanistas, Lima, Peru.
1974 Human Adaptation to Energy Flow in the Andes: Some Conceptual and Methodological Considerations. *Energy Flow in Human Communities.* Jamison and Friedman, eds. University Park, Pa.: International Biological Program.

Tringham, R.
1971 *Hunters, Fishers and Farmers of Eastern Europe: 6000-3000 B.C.* London: Hutchinson.

Troels-Smith, J.
1967 The Ertebolle Culture and Its Background. *Palaeohistoria* 12:505-528.

Underwood, E.J.
1977 *Trace Elements in Human and Animal Nutrition.* New York: Academic Press.

Veniaminov, I.
1840 *Notes on the Islands of the Unalaska District.* St. Petersburg: Russian-American Company.

Watt, B.K. and Merrill, A.L.
1963 *Composition of Foods: Handbook No. 8.* Washington, D.C.: United States Government Printing Office.

Weinberg, E. D.
1974 Iron and susceptibility to infectious disease. *Science* 184: 952-956.

Weiss, K.M.
1973 *Demographic Models for Anthropology.* Washington, D.C.: Society for American Archaeology.

Winterhalder, B.
1978 Optimal Foraging in a Patchy Environment: An Analysis of Cree Hunting and Gathering. Paper presented to the American Anthropological Association, Los Angeles, California.

Williams, B.J.
1968 The Birhor of India and Some Comments on Band Organization. *Man the Hunter.* Lee and DeVore, eds. Chicago: Aldine.

Wright, H.
1978 Environmental Change and the Origin of Agriculture in the Old and New Worlds. *The Origins of Agriculture.* Reed, ed. The Hague: Mouton.

Yellen, J.
1977 *Archaeological Approaches to the Present.* New York: Academic Press.

Yesner, D.R.
1977 Resource Diversity and Population Stability Among Hunter-Gatherers. *Western Canadian Journal of Anthropology* 7:18-59.
1977 *Prehistoric Subsistence and Settlement in the Aleutian Islands.* Ann Arbor, Michigan: University Microfilms.

Yesner, D.R. and Aigner, J.S.
1976 Comparative Biomass Estimates and Prehistoric Cultural Ecology of the Southwest Umnak Region, Aleutian Islands. *Arctic Anthropology* 13:91-112.

5

Nutrition and Health
In Agriculturalists and
Hunter-Gatherers

A Case Study of Two
Prehistoric Populations

C. M. Cassidy

Agriculture as a subsistence activity has long been viewed very positively because of the increases in population size and cultural complexity it is believed to have fostered (see, e.g., Childe, 1941; Cole, 1959; Braidwood, 1959; Harris, 1971). In contrast, hunting-gathering has been described as an inefficient and precarious means to wrest sustenance from the land.

However, recent ethnographic work has largely called into question past images of both hunter-gatherer and agricultural economies.[1] These studies have considered production, types of foods used, and some aspects of social structure, but have tended to omit detailed discussion of variables of health and food nutritional value. In this paper I consider the latter topics. My points will be illustrated with a case study of two prehistoric populations, one of which practiced hunting-gathering, and the other agriculture. This study indicates that the agriculturalists had poorer health and shorter life-spans than the hunter-gatherers, a difference apparently attributable to the inferior diet used by the agriculturalists. The argument is expanded to include other hunter-gatherer and simple agricultural populations, and, in the last section, I consider circumstances under which an inferior diet could become acceptable to a group.

According to the conventional view, agriculture is and was practiced by sedentary (settled) or at least seasonally-sedentary peoples. They are sedentary because care of their crops requires it. This is not a disadvantage, since crops can be depended upon to produce food that can be stored for gradual use. Agriculturalists thus have a stable food supply and often even have produced a surplus. The surplus is used to support population increases or to raise the caloric intake. It can be used to feed full-time artisans and other nonfarming specialists. The assurance of the daily availability of food reduces anxiety about food, and this, combined with the fact that the crops require tending for only a part of the year, produces leisure. Extra energy can be directed toward other goals—specifically, toward the building of complex societies. The existence of a stable food supply, accompanied by the production of surplus food, is considered the greatest strength of the agricultural method because it allows and supports the other changes.

The same model, in contrast, has hunter-gatherers living at the mercy of the environment, having none of the assurance that a stable food supply can give. They must be nomadic in order to take advantage of sparse wild food resources. They have little spare time, often go hungry, and live harried, short, simplified and rough lives (Cassidy, 1972 and Sahlins, 1972 review and discuss negative attitudes to the hunter-gatherer in more detail). The tendency to undervalue the way of life of the hunter-gatherer is so marked that Sahlins suggests:

> The traditional dismal view of the hunters' fix . . . was (probably) one of the first distinctly neolithic prejudices. (1972:3)

Much information now contradicts the above model. Ethnographic data on modern hunter-gatherers indicates that except in rare cases (e.g., Birhor of India, Netsilik Eskimos), these peoples have (more than) adequate food supplies of large variety and suffer malnutrition very much less often than do agriculturalists (see, e.g., discussions in Lee and DeVore, 1968; Sahlins, 1972). Some store food, but others, such as the Bushmen of the Kalahari desert in Africa, merely gather enough at one time to last for the next few days, and then go out again when necessary (Lee, 1968, 1969). There is actually more free time available than among agriculturalists. The food supply is not stable in the sense of being stored and instantly available, but it is relatively predictable to the hunter-gatherer (by season and location), and may be more stable in the face of drought, floods, or other natural disasters than are cultigens.

Little material is available that directly compares the health of hunter-gatherers and agriculturalists. The health of agriculturalists has usually been considered "good" in relation to what was perceived to be typical of hunter-gatherers. Hunter-gatherers were said to live short, tough lives, to be "forced" to eat foods the reporters considered unfit for normal human consumption, to starve frequently, to exhibit high infant mortality rates because of infection and malnourishment, and to need to practice population control by infanticide or gerontocide because food supplies were so limited. Again, ethnographic field data on hunter-gatherers contradicts this image. Some 10 percent of Bushmen live over sixty years (Lee, 1968); the health of the Hadza of Tanzania is considerably better than that of surrounding agricultural tribes (Woodburn, 1968; Scudder, 1971). Archaeological evidence shows that the introduction of corn agriculture to Illinois Woodland Indians led to a decrease in growth rate and size in childhood (Cook, 1972), while in Greece, people living in early Neolithic times had shorter life spans than those living either later (during industrialized periods) or earlier (pre-Neolithic; Angel, 1972).

From another point of view, (e.g., in Africa or Central America) studies of health in modern peasant villages indicate the people often have short life-spans, high rates of infectious and other diseases, high infant mortality rates, and much malnutrition. (Case studies can be found in, e.g., Burgess and Dean, 1962; Scrimshaw and Gordon, 1967; McCance and Widdowson, 1968; Patwardhan and Darby, 1972. Kryzwicki, 1934, provides much statistical comparative data on hunter-gatherers and agriculturalists.) Epidemiological reconstructions of the disease possibilities for peoples of the past (see, e.g., Polgar, 1964; Cockburn, 1971) indicate that hunter-gatherers suffered from a number of diseases derived from other animals (zoonoses), through contamination of foods, or wounds, or by vector routes. However, agriculturalists had all of these and had, in addition, a large number of so-called "crowd" diseases— diseases which require populations over a certain threshold size for propagation. Since hunter-gatherer groups tend to be small, the threshold is seldom if ever reached, and they are usually free of these diseases. Scourges such as plague, tuberculosis, typhoid fever, influenza, measles, and others probably were rare or nonexistent in human populations in pre-Neolithic (pre-agricultural) times. Further, there is growing evidence that specific nutritional disorders—beriberi, sprue, even kwashiorkor—did not appear until humans began living on diets consisting largely of grains. Several authors have speculated that some of the problems of malnutrition seen in modern agriculturalists result from an incomplete selective adjustment of the human organism to grain diets since the beginning of the Neolithic (Newman, 1962; Shatin, 1967).

Finally, the actual stability of food supply among agriculturalists can also be questioned. Famine is an ever-present threat if crops fail and the food supply cannot be replaced by trade or altruism. "Returning to the land" is an avenue closed to most agricultural groups—both because population sizes are too large to be supported by available wild foods, and because the people have forgotten how to hunt and gather successfully. Further, if when caloric supplies are adequate, a proper balance of nutrients cannot be maintained, malnutrition will occur in the population. This can happen because of poor soil, food preparation techniques that damage foods, or deleterious food habits. Scrimshaw and Gordon comment on these points:

> During the recent droughts in East Africa the semi-civilized tribes suffered greatly and some individuals survived by learning from the African Bushmen how to exploit long-forgotten food sources in the environment. The Bushmen themselves apparently do not suffer more malnutrition during droughts because they eat more low-preference foods and cover more ground to obtain food and water. (1967:109)

Thus, there is information to suggest that hunter-gatherers are not only better off than previously imagined, but also that living in a society dependent on agriculture is not an unmixed blessing. The conventional contrasting view of the hunter-gatherer and agriculturalist, which in so many ways gives the agriculturalist the advantages, needs to be reexamined. The following study examined health and nutrition in two pre-Columbian Amerindian groups, one pre-agricultural and the other agricultural, to determine the extent to which differences (if any) could be attributed to differences in diet.

The Research Populations

In order to study differences between hunter-gatherers and horticulturalists, it is necessary to limit the differences between the study populations as much as possible to those of subsistence method alone. Differences between the groups on other variables—as of race, natural environment, other cultural factors, and, in the case of Amerindians, amount of exposure to Europeans—must be minimal. Only under these circumstances can we be reasonably sure that the nutrition and health differences observed are primarily effected by the difference in subsistence methodology, and not by other factors. In addition, large skeletal populations in good condition are needed. These conditions were adequately met by the skeletal populations of two archaeological sites in Kentucky: *Hardin Village*, whose inhabitants practiced agriculture, and *Indian Knoll*, inhabited by hunter-gatherers.

Hardin Village is an archaeological site of the Fort Ancient Tradition,[2] located on the banks of the Ohio River in eastern Kentucky, across from the modern city of Portsmouth, Ohio. Fort Ancient villages are found abundantly in Ohio, Kentucky, and West Virginia, and have been dated from about AD 950 into the historic period (Prufer and Shane, 1970). Marquette and Joliet, the famous explorers, listed thirty-eight Shawnee villages in Ohio in the seventeenth century (Hanson, 1966). Work by Griffin (1943) indicates that in all probability Shawnee villages and Fort Ancient sites are the products of the same people.

There is general agreement that Fort Ancient peoples regularly practiced agriculture. According to Prufer and Shane, while early sites provide equivocal evidence on the degree of agricultural dependency, "for later Fort Ancient communities the evidence for intensive food production involving a developed corn-beans-squash complex is over-whelming" (1970:249).

Hanson's analysis of Hardin Village indicates that it was inhabited from approximately AD 1500 ± 50 years to AD 1675 ± 5 years (1966). The later date overlaps the historic period, but, although a few

122   Nutritional Anthropology

implements of brass were found in the highest levels of the village site, Hanson has concluded: "The European brass fragments and artifacts found at the Hardin Village site were probably the result of trade with other Indians, who acted as intermediaries, rather than directly with Europeans" (1966:175). Apparently, there was no significant contact with Europeans before site abandonment—a fact of importance in interpreting health data since it is well known that the arrival of Europeans usually usually signaled an abrupt increase in the frequency and types of diseases experienced by the Indians.

The village covered over eleven acres near the river bank, of which about one-tenth was excavated in 1939. It was surrounded by a stockade and contained an estimated ten to twenty dwellings that probably housed several nuclear families of the same kin group (Hanson, 1966). Population size can be reconstructed using house floor areas and assuming a minimum of 10m² of floor space per individual (Naroll, 1962; Puleston, 1973). From this it appears that the size of the village nearly tripled in 150 years, from about 118 at settlement to as many as 359 just before abandonment (Table 1).

The Indian Knoll site consists of a large shell midden (refuse heap) of Archaic age, located on the Green river in western Kentucky. Culturally, it is classed with the Shell Mound Tradition of the Archaic[3] (other sites are found in Georgia, Tennessee, Kentucky, Indiana). There are numerous other Shell Mound sites in this valley and in neighboring river valleys. Archaic peoples were hunter-gatherers and are believed to have usually been nomadic. In the Shell Mound Tradition, in contradistinction to some other Archaic Traditions, river mussels and snails apparently provided stable food sources, allowing either sedentary or semisedentary occupation of sites and supporting relatively large populations. As the name implies, all these sites characteristically include large mounds of shells left over from the river harvest.

Nearly the whole of the Indian Knoll site—a midden heap with accumulations of up to eight feet in depth—was excavated between 1939 and 1941 (Webb, 1946). Carbon-14 dates give a maximum average age of 5,302 ± 300 radiocarbon years: B.C. 3352, and a minimum age of 3,963 ± 350 radiocarbon years: B.C. 2013 (Libby, 1955:94, 99). There is some argument as to whether the site was occupied on a permanent (Webb, 1946) or seasonal (Winters, 1969) basis. There is no evidence for substantial houses as at Hardin Village. Because of lack of agreement as to permanency of occupa-

TABLE 1. Estimation of population size at Hardin Village from house floor area.

House (listed in order of occupation)	Size in Feet	Size in Meters	Area in Meters	Number of Inhabitants	Estimated Village Population
1. House 6	24.5 x 51.0	7.5 x 15.7	117.8	11.8	118
2. House 4	27.0 x 66.0	8.3 x 20.3	168.5	16.9	169
3. House 1	27.5 x 57.0	8.4 x 17.5	147.0	14.7	147
4. House 5	30.0 x 70.5	9.2 x 21.7	199.6	20.0	359
House 7	29.5 x 57.0	9.1 x 17.5	159.2	15.9	

Method from Naroll, 1962; Puleston, 1973. House order of occupation and floor areas from Hanson, 1966. One more house was occupied during this time but Hanson was unable to decide to which occupation level it belonged since it contained no artifacts. Hanson considers the one-tenth of the site excavated to have been representative of the whole site (1966: 176); therefore the population estimate consists of house inhabitants times ten in each case.

tion of Indian Knoll, it is not possible to make a useful population estimate for the site.

Racially, the groups have been treated as similar since both are Amerindian and both lived for long periods in the same area of the continent. Current knowledge about population movements in Kentucky in prehistoric times does not permit any statement about the degree of genetic relationship between Hardin Villagers and Indian Knollers. However, the skeletal characteristics chosen for study were expressly picked because they are *known to vary primarily in response to nutritional stress.*

Available fauna and flora, water, and climate were so similar in the two areas (Table 2) that it may be assumed that whatever natural stresses existed at one site were probably existent at the other also, and therefore, in themselves, these should not affect health and nutrition differentially.

As mentioned earlier, population size and degree of sedentarism affect disease spread. In the cases of Hardin Village and Indian Knoll, since *both* are sedentary or semisedentary, this variable should be negligible in explaining differences in disease experience between the sites.

Archaeologically-reconstructable variability in material culture is also fairly small (though Indian Knollers used the spear-thrower and spear, while Hardin Villagers had pottery, permanent houses, and the bow and arrow). Thus in all probability the most significant difference between these two populations is in subsistence technique, with agriculture at the later site, and hunting-gathering at the earlier.

Diet in Hardin Village and Indian Knoll

The difference in subsistence technique also suggests a difference in diet. Though it is difficult in archaeological studies to determine the relative contributions of different foods to the diet, some data from these sites, taken in conjunction with faunal and floral data from nearby culturally-related site provide a general picture (Table 3). At Hardin Village, primary dependence was on corn, beans, and squash. Wild plants and animals (especially deer, elk, small mammals, wild turkey, box turtle) provided supplements to a largely agricultural diet. It is probable that deer was not a quantitatively important food source to Fort Ancient peoples. At Hardin Village,

TABLE 2. The natural environments of Indian Knoll and Hardin Village.

	Ohio County	Greenup County
Location:	Western Coalfields	Eastern Coalfields
Site of Interest:	Indian Knoll, on Green River	Hardin Village, on Ohio River
Geography:	Low hills intersected by broad alluvial valleys	Maturely dissected low mountains with steep slopes and narrow alluvial valleys
Mean Altitude:	370' above sea level on Green River at site	570' above sea level on Ohio River at site
Parent Rocks:	Sandstones and shales	Sandstones and shales
Soil Division:	Grey-brown podzolic	Grey-brown podzolic
Soil Types:	River: Waverly	River: Huntington
	Elsewhere: Tilsit, Muskingum	Elsewhere: Muskingum
Minerals:	Bituminous coal, oil, asphaltic pitch, iron oxides as red ochre	Bituminous coal, cannel coal, oil, natural gas, iron oxides as red ochre
Former Climate at Occupation:	Atlantic IV--Sub-Boreal	Pacific II--Neo-Boreal
Modern Climate:		
Mean summer temperature	70-80°F	70-80°F
Mean winter temperature	30-40°F	30-40°F
Mean annual freeze period	180 days	180 days
Mean days w/snow cover	10-30 days	10-30 days
Normal annual total precipitation	40-48"	40-48"
Mean annual relative humidity	70-75%	70-75%
Potential natural vegetation:	Southern Hardwood Forest	Southern Hardwood Forest
Potential natural wildlife:	Black bear, bobcat, mountain lion, bison, wapiti, white-tailed deer, wolf, beaver, raccoon, opossum, cottontail rabbit, wild turkey, prairie chicken, Bob-white, passenger pigeon, dove, rattlesnake, box turtle, . . .	

Reference: Cassidy, 1972; with minor changes.

TABLE 3. Floral and faunal remains from selected Fort Ancient and Archaic sites.

	Fort Ancient					Shell Mound Archaic	
(Date of Study)	1967 Blain	1902 Gartner	1901 Baum	1917 Feurt	1918 Fullerton	1946 Indian Knoll	1961-63 Riverton
FLORA--cultivated							
corn (Zea mays)	x	x	x	x	ND		
beans (Phaseolus vulgaris)	x	x	x	x			
pumpkin (Cucurbita pepe)	x						
FLORA--wild							
hickory nut	x	x	x	x		x	x
black walnut	x	x	x	x		x	x
acorn	x	x		x		x	x
butternut		x	x	x			
chestnut			x				x
hazelnut		x	x				x
pignut							
wild grape	x		x				
wild red plum		x	x				
wild cherry	x			x			x
elderberry							x
persimmon				x			
pawpaw	x	x	x	x			
blackberry				x			
wild morning glory	x						x
wild sunflower	x						
smooth sumac	x						
Chenopod							x
Polygonum							x
bulb (lily or onion)							x

Key: ND--no data for category.
      x--presence; blank space--absence.
Reference: Cassidy, 1972, Table 3.

TABLE 3. Floral and faunal remains from selected Fort Ancient and Archaic sites. (Continued)

(Date of Study)	1967 Blain	1902 Gartner	Fort Ancient 1901 Baum	Fort Ancient 1917 Feurt	1918 Fullerton	Shell Mound Archaic 1946 Indian Knoll	Shell Mound Archaic 1961-63 Riverton
MAMMALS							
white-tailed deer	x	x	x	x	x	x	x
wapiti (elk)	x	x	x	x	x		x
raccoon	x	x	x	x	x	x	x
beaver	x	x	x	x	x	x	x
squirrel	x	x	x	x	x	x	x
opossum	x	x	x	x		x	x
porcupine			x	x			x
bobcat (wildcat, lynx)	x	x	x	x		x	x
mountain lion (puma)	x	x	x	x	x		x
cottontail rabbit	x	x	x	x		x	x
woodchuck (ground hog)	x	x	x	x		x	x
muskrat	x	x	x	x			x
fox	x	x	x	x		x	x
dog	x	x	x	x		x	x
wolf	x	x	x	x	x		x
coyote							x
skunk	x	x	x	x		x	x
mink		x	x	x		x	x
weasel			x				x
fisher			x	x			
otter		x	x	x			
black bear	x	x	x	x	x	x	x
mole							x
pocket gopher							x
chipmunk						x	x

TABLE 3. Floral and faunal remains from selected Fort Ancient and Archaic sites. (Continued)

(Date of Study)	Fort Ancient					Shell Mound Archaic	
	1967 Blain	1902 Gartner	1901 Baum	1917 Feurt	1918 Fullerton	1946 Indian Knoll	1961-63 Riverton
BIRDS							
wild turkey	X	X	X	X	X	X	X
goose		X	X	X	X	X	X
duck			X				X
trumpeter swan		X	X	X			X
owl		X	X	X			
turkey vulture	X					X	
crane						X	X
bald eagle		X	X	X			
great blue heron		X	X	X			
bittern		X					
prairie chicken	X						
passenger pigeon	X						X
bobwhite							X
8 more species							X
TURTLES AND FISHES							
box turtle	X	ND	ND	ND	ND	X	X
snapping turtle						X	X
6 other turtles							X
drumfish	X	ND	ND	ND	ND	X	X
buffalofish	X					X	X
15 other fishes							X
6 other fishes	X						
MOLLUSCS							
Snails (Gastropods)	12 species	ND	ND	ND	ND	X	29 species
Mussels (Pelecypods)	26 species					X	37 species

Some of these plants and animals may not have been used for food (e.g., smallest mammals, some birds), see the reference for further discussion.

remains of deer were sparse. At the somewhat earlier Fort Ancient Blain site in Ohio, only remains of very young or aged deer were recovered (Prufer and Shane, 1970). These authors have interpreted this to indicate hunting by stalking—a relatively inefficient technique when contrasted to, for example, trapping or driving game animals. There was also little evidence for storage of wild plant foods at Hardin Village.

At Indian Knoll it is clear that very large quantities of river mussels and snails were consumed. Other meat was provided by deer, small mammals, wild turkey, box turtle, and fish; dog was sometimes eaten ceremonially. Deer remains were relatively very sparse— possibly the paucity of large mammal remains in the site reflects negatively on Indian Knoll technology, or it may be that the easy source of meat in mussels limited the appeal of hunting. The wild plant list is incomplete—more likely because of archaeological problems of preservation and collection than because of lack of utilization by the Indians themselves (Yarnell, 1964).

There are several other dietary differences. The Hardin Village diet was high in carbohydrates, while that at Indian Knoll was high in protein. In terms of quality, though Clark believes primitive agriculturalists got plenty of protein from grain diets (1963), most recent writers, such as Altschul (1962, 1965), emphasize that the proportion of essential amino-acids is the significant factor in determining protein-quality of the diet, rather than simply the numbers of grams of protein eaten. It is much more difficult to achieve a good balance of amino-acids on a corn-beans diet than when protein is derived from meat or eggs. The lack of protein at Hardin Village signaled by the archaeological data should prepare us for the possibility of finding evidence of protein deficiency in the skeletal material.

Health and Disease in Hardin Village and Indian Knoll

At Hardin Village 296 skeletons and at Indian Knoll 285 skeletons were studied. They were analyzed morphologically and by x-ray. (The techniques used are described below and in greater detail in Cassidy, 1972; only the most significant findings of the 1972 research are discussed here.)

Let us define malnutrition as a general term for physical states that result from lack or scarcity of food or deficiencies of specific nutrients. It may range from starvation with gross clinical states to mild subclinical states that affect individual functioning but are difficult to identify. Malnutrition and infections or other disease are closely interrelated:

a. Individuals who are ill are also typically malnourished because of loss of appetite or inability to take in or utilize nutrients. In such cases malnutrition may be acute—lasting just a few days—or prolonged if the disease is more chronic.

b. Persons who are malnourished, for whatever reason, are less resistant to infections and to some other diseases than are the well nourished. (See Scrimshaw, Taylor and Gordon, 1968, for a detailed discussion of nutrition-disease interrelationships.)

Modern peasant populations characterized by diets of limited variety and high carbohydrate content are also those in which infections of many kinds are commonest.

Malnutrition can be studied in skeletons in several ways. Mortality profiles, life expectancies, evidence for growth arrest, and frequency of nutritional and infectious disease will be discussed here (the following figures and statistical data are from Cassidy, 1972):

1. Figure 1 shows life expectancies for the sexes at different ages in the two groups.

These life expectancies have been derived using a composite life table, which does not require knowledge of the exact year of birth or death, as do conventional life tables (Swedlund and Armelagos, n.d.). This is important, since there are a number of good methods for aging skeletons, but they cannot give more than a close estimate of age. Therefore, skeletal material is grouped into age intervals. As can be seen in Figure 1, aging of children (based mainly on tooth eruption sequence and bone maturation) is more precise than aging of adults (based on pubic symphysis wear and tooth wear), and the age identification intervals grow from months to years as age advances. Similarly, the sex of a skeleton can be identified fairly reliably, but in this case, only in the adult. To derive sex ratios for death in childhood, I have assumed a ratio of 92 males: 100 females. This ratio is derived from karyotype (chromosome count) studies of aborted fetuses (McKusick, 1970).

Life expectancies for both male and female Indian Knollers exceeded those for Hardin Villagers at all ages. It is also interesting that the women at Hardin Village appear to have had a slight advantage over the men. A large loss of life between ages two to four (12 months-47months)[4] at Hardin Village shows here in the failure of the life expectancy curve to rise sharply after infancy as it does for Indian Knoll.

Fig. 1.   Life Expectancies at Succeeding Ages ($\overset{o}{e}_x$) for Indian Knoll and Hardin Village, by Sex.

o--o Indian Knoll Males
o—o Indian Knoll Females
•--• Hardin Village Females
•—• Hardin Villages Males

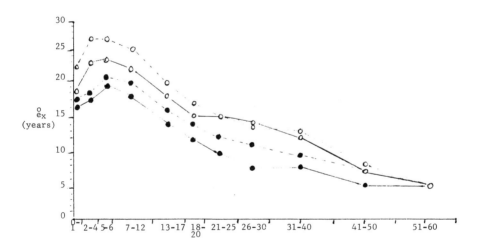

2. Figure 2 shows the mortality profiles for the samples at each site. These are derived simply by adding males and females at each age interval, within population samples.

At Indian Knoll 44.6 percent of the children died before age 17, while at Hardin Village the corresponding figure is 53.7 percent. The difference is statistically significant (p < 0.05). The major difference in age at death occurs in the first four years. At Indian Knoll 70 percent of mortality under age four occurs in the first year (under 12 months), while 60 percent of Hardin Village infant and toddler mortality occurred in the next three years. The difference is highly significant (p < 0.001).

Fig. 2. Mortality Profiles for Hardin Village and Indian Knoll

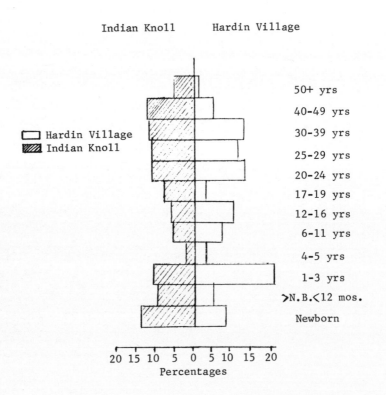

Fig. 3. X-ray photograph showing Harris Lines in a tibia.

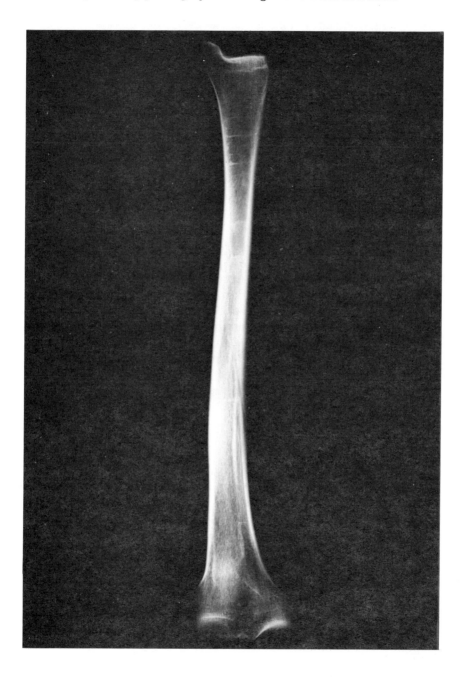

3. Iron-deficiency anemia is a true deficiency disease, often an accompaniment of low-meat diets, long-term infection, or chronic disease (Brown, 1971). It is also frequently found in cases of protein-energy malnutrition (especially in kwashiorkor). Chronic cases can be identified in skeletons from changes in the skull (Eng, 1958; Moseley, 1966). Iron-deficiency anemia chronic enough to alter the skull bones was identified in 8.2 percent of Hardin Villagers, but was absent from the Indian Knoll sample. Of the twenty-four cases at Hardin Village, twelve occurred in children under five years of age.

4. Growth arrest was analyzed by consideration of Harris' Lines (bone scars) in the tibias and of enamel hypoplasia in the teeth.

Harris' Lines (also called growth arrest lines or transverse lines) are lines of heavier deposition of calcified material which occur in long bones and are visible on x-rays as opacities spanning the marrow cavities (Figure 3). They appear in childhood following a bout of malnutrition (whether from infection or lack of food). Each line in the shaft and end of the bone indicates the person underwent one event of growth arrest lasting approximately ten days or more. Because the lines appear only *after* malnutrition is ended, they cannot provide information on the duration of the provoking event. Also, during bone remodeling, which continues throughout life, lines may disappear. Nevertheless, a summation of the lines in an individual gives at least a minimum figure on number of malnutrition events serious enough to have stopped growth temporarily during childhood. An average for a population, called the Index of Morbidity (Wells, 1967), allows interpopulation comparisons.

The deposition of the enamel of the teeth can also be interrupted during development by episodes of ill health or hunger. Such damage shows itself as horizontal lines, pits or grooves on the cheek or lip surfaces of the teeth (Figure 4. Mellanby, 1929; Wells, 1967). These defects, called enamel hypoplasia, are analogous to Harris' Lines in that they represent episodes of growth arrest in childhood. They have the advantage, though, of giving some impression, by the degree of their development, of the duration, and thus severity, of the growth arrest episode. Mellanby distinguishes three degrees of development—mild, moderate, and severe—which can be quantified to make possible intra- and inter-population comparisons.

Fig. 4. Lines of Enamel Hypoplasia, comparing a normal tooth (bottom) with two affected teeth.

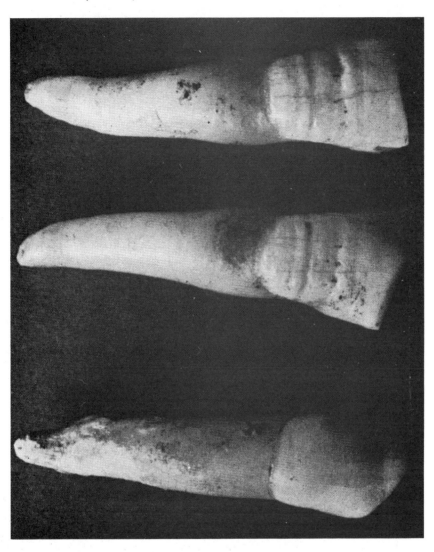

An average of 11.3 bone scars were found in Indian Knoll shinbones, while the mean at Hardin Village was only 4.1. This means that in both groups growth ceased frequently but briefly during childhood. However, in contrast to the other data presented here, the higher rate at Indian Knoll might indicate more malnutrition there than at Hardin Village.

But two other pieces of information—one from the bones, and one from the teeth—alter this interpretation and bring it into line with other data indicating less good health among the Hardin Villagers: 1) The distribution pattern of scars in Indian Knoll tibias is extremely regular, indicating that malnutrition occurred at periodic intervals, perhaps as a "normal" part of life. At Hardin Village the lines occur randomly—a sign that intermittent malnutrition caused the growth arrest. 2) Equivalent numbers of jaws at Hardin Village and Indian Knoll had hypoplastic teeth, but the frequency of severe episodes of arrest was significantly higher at Hardin Village (p 0.05). Thus, when growth arrest occurred at Indian Knoll, it was temporary and soon made up; at Hardin Village severe and long-lasting states of malnutrition, such as might be caused by long illness, were not uncommon.

The most parsimonious interpretation of this information is that mild food shortages occurred at regular intervals at Indian Knoll; perhaps late winter was a time of danger. McHenry (1968), using growth arrest lines, and Winters (1969) using archaeological data, have similarly concluded that in the hunter-gatherer populations they studied, food shortages occurred regularly, probably on a yearly basis. At Hardin Village growth arrest was caused by illnesses or crop failures which resulted in long-lasting, but randomly-occurring, episodes of growth arrest.

5. Infections are identified in bones by the typical inflammatory changes that they provoke. Evidence for infections (other than those characteristic of the Syndrome of Periosteal Inflammation [below]) occurred with comparable frequency at the two sites (p> 0.95), but affected signficantly more children at Hardin Village than at Indian Knoll (p< 0.02). Though differences between the sexes in frequency of infection within sites was not statistically significant, there was a tendency for Hardin Village males to have more infections than Hardin Village females (p< 0.10); this is of interest since life expectancy for Hardin Village males was lower at all ages than for Hardin Village females.

6. A distinctive infectious disease, here identified as the Syndrome of Periosteal Inflammation, occurred at both sites but affected approximately thirteen times as many Hardin Villagers as Indian Knollers.

This syndrome is characterized by changes in the long bones, particularly those of the legs, consisting of thickening, and the development of either stripes of smooth billowed material or patches of rough porous material on the surfaces of the bones. Some diminution of the marrow spaces occurs in advanced cases by endosteal apposition. In very young children the bones, on x-ray, show layering, the so-called "onion-skin effect." This morphological picture, taken together with historical and medical data (Cassidy, 1972) suggests the identification of the disease as a treponematosis, similar to but not identical with contempoary treponematoses, which include pinta, yaws, endemic syphilis and venereal syphilis.

Part of the difference in incidence between the two sites may be explained on the basis of increase in possibilities for infection with population increase and sedentism among the Hardin Villagers. One might also propose that the infectious organism had become more common or contagious over time. But taken in conjunction with the other evidence presented above, it becomes probable that many of the cases owed their origin to lack of resistance in the host because of poor diet and general health.

7. Finally, teeth can provide information on type of diet by the kind of wear they exhibit and by their health. Unhealthy teeth are associated with poor-quality diets and are themselves often the cause of general ill health.

Tooth decay was rampant at Hardin Village, but uncommon at Indian Knoll. Adult males at Hardin Village had an average of 6.74 carious teeth/mouth, while at Indian Knoll the corresponding frequency was 0.73 per mouth. For women the rates were 8.51 and 0.91 per mouth, respectively. No Indian Knoll children under twelve years of age had caries, whereas some Hardin Village children already had developed caries in milk teeth in their second year of life. Tooth decay is closely associated with sugar content and consistency of food, occurring with higher frequency in sweet or high carbohydrate diets which are soft and sticky. Ethnographic data about methods of corn preparation among the Seneca (geographic, and in many ways, cultural neighbors of the Fort Ancient people) indicates that the typical food was indeed high in starch, sweet, and sticky (Harrington, 1908).

Tooth abscessing (infection of the pulp cavity which often drains into the tooth socket, producing characteristic damage) was frequent at both sites, and commoner at Indian Knoll than at Hardin Village in the older age group. Abscessing at Hardin Village occurred as a result of the development of massive caries which exposed the pulp cavities; this caused much tooth loss in early adulthood. At Indian Knoll, the gritty diet associated with eating river molluscs promoted rapid wear of the teeth. When enamel and dentine were worn away, and pulp cavities exposed, abscessing began. But this did not usually occur until the fourth decade of life or later; and until then tooth health was good.

To summarize the data on health derived from the skeletons:

1. Life expectancies for both sexes at all ages were lower at Hardin Village than at Indian Knoll.
2. Infant mortality was higher at Hardin Village.
3. Iron-deficiency anemia of sufficient duration to cause bone changes was absent at Indian Knoll, but present at Hardin Village, where 50 percent of cases occurred in children under age five.
4. Growth arrest episodes at Indian Knoll were periodic and more often of short duration and were possibly due to food shortage in late winter; those at Hardin Village occurred randomly and were more often of long duration, probably indicative of disease as a causative agent.
5. More children suffered infections at Hardin Village than at Indian Knoll.
6. The syndrome of periosteal inflammation was more common at Hardin Village than at Indian Knoll.
7. Tooth decay was rampant at Hardin Village and led to early abscessing and tooth loss; decay was unusual at Indian Knoll and abscessing occurred later in life because of severe wear to the teeth. The differences in tooth wear rate and caries rate are very likely attributable to dietary differences between the two groups.

Overall, the agricultural Hardin Villagers were clearly less healthy than the Indian Knollers, who lived by hunting and gathering.

Comparison of Archaeological and Contemporary Data

While the data are revealing in themselves, they become more useful if the characteristics of health and diet at these sites are compared with data on contemporary groups.

Modern hunter-gatherers usually live in marginal areas, yet, as mentioned above, they typically have adequate food supplies and enjoy balanced diets. Lee's study on the Bushmen (1968) showed many lived to old age, another parameter of good health; while

Jelliffe's medical survey of the Hadza showed high levels of health and good nutritional states in this group compared to surrounding agricultural peoples (Scudder, 1971). The picture at Indian Knoll is likewise characterized by good overall health and a good chance of living into middle or old age once past the first twelve months. This leads me to conclude that nutrition must also have been good; and the archaeological evidence on diet supports such a conclusion. Furthermore, it is quite likely that at least some of the infant mortality is attributable to infanticide; Birdsell (1968) and Washburn (1968) believe that some 15 to 50 percent of hunter-gatherer infant mortality was voluntary.

The health and nutrition situation at Hardin Village may profitably be compared with that in modern peasant villages. In many of these, children are typically fairly healthy until weaned. At this time they are introduced to a soft diet consisting largely of carbohydrates (in much of Africa and Central America, a pap is made of sugar, water, and maize flour; in Jamaica green bananas replace maize). In many cases, within a few weeks or months these children develop diarrhea, lose weight, suffer multiple infections, and may eventually develop the form of protein-energy malnutrition called kwashiorkor. In this disorder caloric intake is usually adequate, but protein and other nutrient intakes are extremely limited; without modern hospital care many victims die. The first description of this disease, in 1933, correlated its occurrence with children weaned onto maize diets (Williams, 1935). Kwashiorkor is frequently accompanied by iron-deficiency anemia.

At Hardin Village the highest rate of death occurs between the second and fourth years of life. This is typical for a population experiencing weaning problems. Considering the softness of the adult diet and the high caries rate of both children and adults, it is not unlikely that the children were weaned onto a corn pap of some type. Perhaps it was much the same as that given to children in some Central American villages today. The high prevalence of childhood infection, severity of growth arrest in the first few years of life, and the existence of iron-deficiency anemia all point to a situation at Hardin Village analogous to those in modern peasant villages. In other words the evidence supports a hypothesis that malnutrition began with weaning at Hardin Village, sometimes resulted in kwashiorkor, and continued at a low level—just enough to reduce the resistance of the population to infectious disease—throughout the life of the individual.

Since the groups were chosen in such a way as to minimize input from other sources, most of these health differences can be attributed to subsistence technique as it is expressed in dietary quality. The health data provides convincing evidence that the diet of the agriculturalists was the inferior of the two. The archaeological dietary data support this conclusion. As far as the skeletal and archaeological data will take us at this time, the inferiority of the agricultural diet lies in the lack of adequate supplies of high-quality protein.

Cultural Complexity and Health

The data from Indian Knoll and Hardin Village provide us with an interesting question to ponder and point up the need for more research on the comparative advantages of being a hunter-gatherer or being an agriculturalist: How could such an inferior diet become acceptable to a group?

The population at Hardin Village increased over the 150 years of its occupation from just over 100 people to over 300. Further, it was just one of many such villages dotting the major river valleys of Ohio and northern and eastern Kentucky. The increases in population size called for increases in hunted foods as well as in cultivated foods. At the time Hardin Village was being settled, Fort Ancient peoples had already been exploiting surrounding lands for some 600 to 700 years. Under these circumstances there must have been pressures on both wild and cultivated food sources from several directions.

As human population densities rise, many species of animals, including large game animals, leave the area (Naumov, 1972). Overhunting must have occurred in the neighborhood of the village. As time passed Hardin Villagers must have had to travel farther and farther to bag a single deer or elk; at some point the reward must rarely have been worth the effort. Warfare could have removed so many young men from the work force that hunting was to all intents and purposes out of the question. Hanson's occupational reconstruction of the Hardin Village site indicates an increase in evidence for violence just before abandonment (1966). Historical data show that the Iroquois and Shawnee were at war in the seventeenth century, the time when Hardin Village was still inhabited. Eventually the Shawnee moved south to the Cumberland River Valley, and the Iroquois extended their warfare west to the lands of the Illinois. Finally, we must also wonder if people didn't begin to prefer corn and beans to meats? There is some evidence that carbohydrates can become so palatable to humans that they eat them in preference to other foods (Shatin, 1967); such a situation may have further limited the appeal of hunting.

Thus population expansion, inefficient hunting techniques, loss of game from the area by migration and overkill, and warfare, all may have contributed to force the Hardin Villagers to become more and more dependent on a small number of high-carbohydrate agricultural foods of limited quality, and *this may have been so even were they aware of an increase in physical ill-health in the group.*

Further, at the same time that wild foods, especially meats, were becoming harder to procure, there may have been pressures on farm land that also reduced the quantity and quality of cultivated foods. Possibilities include natural or man-made disasters (the result of warfare or poor land management, for example) which could have destroyed a year's crops; loss of soil fertility on intensively cultivated lands such as those nearest the village, which would lead to a decline in nutritional quality of foods produced on that land; and the use of food processing techniques which damaged food quality.

To expand this argument: Population increase and overkill/ migration of game are typical experiences and may in large part explain the overdependence of many simple agricultural groups (not practicing animal husbandry) on certain food crops even when they are well aware of the dangers of undependable climate and poor soil in producing poor quality foods. Food production, it appears, forces its practitioners into a vicious circle. Once population expansion occurs, the group cannot return to the land. Techniques of hunting-gathering are forgotten, and population size may exceed the ability of wild lands to supply adequate amounts of food. Large animals often desert the area. Gradually the agriculturalists come to depend more and more on their crops. Then, vicissitudes in weather and soil quality become more and more significant in determining the quality of life. In this situation, should an inadequate diet develop, they can do very little about it.

In the past, anthropologists gave major credit for the social changes accompanying the development of agriculture to the existence of a stable food supply. I have presented some evidence that indicates not only that the food supplies of simple agriculturalists may not be so stable as was formerly assumed, but also that even if stable, these food supplies may be of such low quality as to lead to malnutrition and other forms of ill-health. In view of current data, we should seriously consider the possibility that agriculturalists experienced population growth and increased cultural complexity *in spite of* unpredictable food supplies and supplies of low nutritional value and *despite* increased rates of ill-health. It is a curious and bitter paradox that humans, in the transitional periods to food production, exchanged many components of good physical health for opportunities to increase cultural complexity. The development must have been so slow as to blind experiencers to its occurrence. Indeed, we are only now, as we come out on the other side of what might be called "agricultural-superiority ethnocentrism," in a position to realize the fatal bargain we, as agriculturalists, seem to have made.

Notes

1. Throughout this paper, agriculturalist or agricultural economy should be taken to mean simple, early, or primitive agriculturalist or agricultural economy including contemporary peasant farmers who practice slash-and-burn techniques. Since the discussion centers on two New World groups, pastoralists are also excluded.

With slash-and-burn technique, future farm land is first cut over, fallen plant-life is allowed to dry somewhat, and then the land is fired. The resultant ashes provide fertilizer for subsequent crops. Such fields are used for two to three years and then allowed to revert to brush for a longer period, after which they may be reclaimed once again. Slash-and-burn farming has been practiced in both temperate and tropical climates, and remains common in many parts of the world.

2. Archaeologists use a taxonomy to organize sites into groups sharing spatial, temporal and/or cultural configurations. See Willey and Phillips (1958) for detailed exposition of this subject. A *tradition* is a "temporal continuity represented by persistent configurations in single technologies or other systems of related forms" (Willey and Phillips, 1958:37). A *stage* is a large division designating a major level of cultural development.

The Fort Ancient Tradition belongs to the Formative Stage, a stage in which agriculture was certainly practiced and people lived in settled villages. Peoples of the Fort Ancient Tradition lived over much of the Ohio River Valley, built their villages on the banks of large streams or rivers, and used shell-tempered pottery and small triangular projectile points (more details in Griffin, 1943).

3. The Shell Mound Tradition belongs to the Archaic Stage, which is a developmental stage characterized by nomadic but increasingly seasonally sedentary populations, practicing hunting and gathering with an emphasis on gathering, and lacking pottery and the bow and arrow. In the Shell Mound Tradition (broadly spread over Indiana, Illinois, Kentucky, Tennessee, Alabama, and Georgia) settlement occurred along streams capable of supplying large quantities of molluscs.

4. The demographer counts the first year of life as "age 1," while in the vernacular this would be counted in months. Thus the demographer's "age 2-4" corresponds to the vernacular "age 1-3." In either case the interval refers to months 12-47, roughly the age of weaning.

References

Angel, J.L.
   1972   Teeth, Health and Ecology: Pitfalls of Natural Experiments. Paper presented at the 1972 meeting of the American Association of Physical Anthropologists, Lawrence, Kansas.
Birdsell, J.B.
   1968   Discussion. *Man the Hunter*. R.B. Lee and I. DeVore, eds. Chicago: Aldine-Atherton, p. 243.
Braidwood, R.J.
   1959   *Prehistoric Man*. Chicago Natural History Museum, Chicago, Anthropology Series 37.
Cassidy, C.M.
   1972   *A Comparison of Nutrition and Health in Agricultural and Pre-Agricultural Amerindian Skeletal Populations*. Ph.D. dissertation, University of Wisconsin. University Microfilms, Ann Arbor.
Childe. V.G.
   1941   *Man Makes Himself*. 2d ed. London: Watts and Co.
Clark, C.
   1963   Agricultural Productivity in Relation to Population. *Man and His Future*. G. Wolstenholme, ed.
Cockburn, T.A.
   1971   Infectious Diseases in Ancient Populations. *Current Anthropology* 12:45-62.
Cole, S.
   1959   *The Neolithic Revolution*. London: British Museum of National History.
Cook, D.
   1972   Subsistence Base and Growth Rate in Four Illinois Woodland populations. Paper presented at the 1972 meeting of the American Association of Physical Anthropologists, Lawrence, Kansas.
Eng, L.L.
   1958   Chronic Iron-Deficiency Anemia with Bone Changes Resembling Cooley's Anemia. *Acta Hematologica* 19:263-268.
Griffin, J.B.
   1943   The Fort Ancient Aspect. *University of Michigan Museum of Anthropology, Anthropological Papers 28*, Ann Arbor.
Hanson, L.
   1966   The Hardin Village Site. *University of Kentucky Studies in Anthropology 4*.
Harrington, M.R.
   1908   Some Seneca Corn Foods and their Preparation. *American Anthropologist* 10:575-590.
Harris, M.
   1971   *Culture, Man and Nature*. New York: Thomas Y. Crowell Co.
Kryzwicki, L.
   1934   *Primitive Society and its Vital Statistics*. London: Macmillan and Co., Ltd.
Lee, R.B.
   1968   What Hunters do for a Living, or How to Make Out on Scarce Resources. *Man the Hunter*. Lee and DeVore, eds. Chicago: Aldine, pp. 30-48.
   1969   !Kung Bushman Subsistence: An Input-Output Analysis. *Environment and Cultural Behavior*. Vayda, ed. Garden City: Natural History Press, pp. 47-49.
Lee, R.B. and I. DeVore
   1968   *Man the Hunter*. Lee and DeVore, eds. Chicago: Aldine.

Libby, W.F.
   1955   *Radiocarbon Dating.* Chicago: University of Chicago Press.
McCance, R.A. and E.M. Widdowson
   1968   *Calorie Deficiencies and Protein Deficiencies.* McCance and Widdowson, eds. London: J. and A. Churchill.
McHenry, H.
   1968   Transvers Lines in Long Bones of Prehistoric California Indians. *American Journal of Physical Anthropology* 29:1-18.
Mellanby, M.
   1929   Diet and the Teeth: an Experimental Study. *Medical Research Council Special Report Series* 140.
Moore, C.V.
   1973   Iron and the Essential Trace Elements. *Modern Nutrition in Health and Disease.* 5th ed. Goodhart and Shils, eds. Philadelphia: Lea and Febiger. pp. 297-323.
Moseley, J. E.
   1966   Radiographic Studies in Hematologic Bone Disease: Implications for Paleopathology. *Human Paleopathology.* Jarcho, ed. New Haven: Yale University Press.
Naroll, R.
   1962   Floor Area and Settlement Pattern. *American Antiquity* 27:587-589.
Naumov, N.P.
   1963   *The Ecology of Animals.* Springfield: University of Illinois Press.
Newman, M.T.
   1962   Ecology and Nutritional Stress in Man. *American Anthropologist* 64:22-34.
Park, E.A.
   1964   The Imprinting of Nutritional Disturbance on the Growing Bone. *Pediatrics* 33:815-860.
Patwardhan, V.N. and Darby, W.J.
   1972   *The State of Nutrition in the Arab Middle East.* Nashville: Vanderbilt University Press.
Polgar, S.
   1964   Evolution and the Ills of Mankind. *New Horizons in Anthropology.* Tax, ed. Chicago: Aldine-Atherton Publishers, pp. 200-211.
Prufer, O.H., and Shane, O.C., III
   1970   *Blain Village and the Fort Ancient Tradition in Ohio.* Cleveland: Kent State University Press.
Puleston, D.
   1973   Ancient Maya Settlement Patterns and Environment at Tikal, Guatemala: Implication for Subsistence Models. Unpublished Ph.D. dissertation, Department of Anthropology, University of Pennsylvania.
Sahlins, M.
   1972   *Stone Age Economics.* Chicago: Aldine-Atherton Publishers.
Scrimshaw, N.S. and Gordon, J.E.
   1967   *Symposium in Malnutrition, Learning and Behavior.* Scrimshaw and Gordon, eds. Cambridge: MIT Press.
Scrimshaw, N.S., Taylor, C.E., and Gordon, J.E.
   1968   *Interactions of Nutrition and Infection.* Scrimshaw, Taylor, and Gordon eds. Geneva: WHO.
Scudder, T.
   1971   Gathering Among African Woodland Savannah Cultivators, a Case Study: The Gwembe Tonga. *Zambian Papers* 5.

Shatin, R.
1967   The Transition from Food-Gatherers to Food-Production in Evolution and Disease. *Vitalstoffe-Zivilisationkrankheiten* 12:104-107.

Swedlund, A.C. and Armelagos, G.I.
n.d.   Use of the Life Table in paleodemography, with an example from Sudanese Nubia. Unpublished paper.

Washburn, S.L.
1968   Discussion. *Man the Hunter*. Lee and DeVore, eds. Chicago: Aldine-Atherton, p. 84.

Webb, W.S.
1946   Indian Knoll, site Oh2, Ohio County, Kentucky. *University of Kentucky Reports in Anthropology* 4(3): Part I, Lexington.

Wells, C.
1967   A New Approach to Paleodemography: Harris' Lines. *Diseases in Antiquity*. Brothwell and Sandison, eds. Springfield: C. C. Thomas, pp. 390-404.

Willey, G.R. and Phillips, P.
1958   *Method and Theory in American Archaeology*. Chicago: University of Chicago Press.

Williams, C.D.
1935   Kwashiorkor: Nutritional Disease of Children Associated with Maize Diet. *Lancet* ii:1151.

Winters, H.D.
1969   The Riverton Culture. *Illinois State Museum Reports of Investigations* 13. Springfield.

Woodburn, J.
1968   An Introduction to Hadza Ecology. *Man the Hunter*. Lee and Devore, eds. Chicago: Aldine-Atherton, pp. 49-55.

Yarnell, R.A.
1964   Aboriginal Relations Between Culture and Plant Life in the Upper Great Lakes Region. *University of Michigan Museum of Anthropology Anthropological Papers 23*. Ann Arbor.

6

Nutrition Adaptation and Cultural Maladaptation

An Evolutionary View[1, 2]

B. Weiss

Both the evolution and the extinction of cultures have been
frequent topics of inquiry for anthropologists. While evolutionary
explanations have long taken the form of attempts to identify
general processes and laws, extinction has more frequently pro-
voked particularistic, case-by-case formulations. Yet extinction is
simply one alternate outcome of evolution, and it should be
possible to identify those processes that culminate in selection
operating against a culture.

Parsimony and Occam's Razor notwithstanding, there is certainly
no single explanation of why cultures perish. In seeking processual
rather than particulate explanations, we must attempt to identify
phenomena that are common to many systems, in many places, at
many times. I will outline in this paper one of the processes by
which a human culture undergoes maladaptation and becomes less
likely to survive.

To do that, it is necessary to first provide some working definitions for the terms "adaptation" and "maladaptation." Although common currency in discussions of biological evolution, what do we mean in applying these terms to cultural systems?

Ecologist Ramon Margalef has written that "in cybernetic systems that occur naturally . . . the only test to pass is the ability to remain" (Margalef 1968:3). Adaptation may be defined as the sum total of biological and behavioral mechanisms by which a population secures its ability to persist. For many organisms, adaptation is almost entirely by biological means. Other animals may include in their adaptational repertoire cooperation and communication. For humans, culture is an additional factor in facing the test of persistence.

What is needed for persistence? Every living system, plant and animal alike, must provision itself with the matter and energy required to sustain it. The first problem to be solved in assuring persistence is subsistence, and the subsistence function might well be called the primary adaptation of every living system.

Adaptation, then, is first and foremost a matter of locating food. If persistence is to be the measure of adaptation, however, we must add a proviso: for a population to be adapted, it must maintain its subsistence resources in an undegraded condition. If matter-energy is removed at a rate in excess of production, the relationship is obviously untenable over time. When a system enters into a set of matter-energy relationships that degrade the resources being utilized, and which therefore could not be sustained over time, we may say that maladaptation has taken place.

Persistence is a matter of probabilities; evolution offers no guarantees, only chances. A matter-energy relationship that degrades resources is maladaptive because it must inevitably terminate, whereupon a system either locates new resources or perishes. The acquisition of new resources involves a risk, and thus the probability of persistence is lessened.

When a resource is being rapidly depleted, the effect is to confront the system with evolutionary decisions that might otherwise have been met over much longer periods of time, and perhaps through other mechanisms. With the time frame compressed, a system may lack information that would otherwise have been acquired and stored. Dalton notes that for cultural systems:

> Where degenerative change occurs, it is, obviously because the situation is such that traditional institutions designed to deal with traditional sorts of stress and

conflict are unable to deal with the novel change because it embodies forces
which are at the same time without precedent, irreversible, and overwhelming to
traditional organization. (1971:214)

This failure of the information processing system due to an
altered time frame decreases the probability of re-establishing a
stable system. On the other hand, it should be noted that those
systems which *do* re-establish themselves probably do so by
making the sorts of major evolutionary "great leaps" that later
confuse investigators by the gaps they create. Domestication of
plants in many places may well be evidence not of man's inevitable
rise to civilization, but rather of his original energy crisis.

More complex systems may be buffered against many of these
effects by their internal complexity, which allows a degree of
resource interchangeability. For less complex systems, however,
diminution of a single resource creates a marked fluctuation in
energy flow and "the process of self-organization stops when
fluctuations are unpredictable or insurmountable" (Margalef,
1968:33.).

One such system is that of the Miskito Indians of eastern
Nicaragua. The coastal population of Miskito numbers between
10,000 and 15,000 living in a series of villages from the Rio Coco
border with Honduras in the north to near the town of Bluefields in
the south (see Figure 1).

Throughout most of their history, the coastal Miskito have
derived a large part of their subsistence from the green sea turtle
(*Chelonia mydas*), a reptilian herbivore that often weighs in excess
of 200 pounds. One indication of the important role of the sea
turtle is found in the spatial distribution of villages, which corresponds closely to the availability of the offshore cays (islands)
around which turtle congregate.

French buccaneers and English traders who first traveled the
Coast frequently took note of the consummate skill of the Miskito
as turtlemen and found the Indians to be well provisioned in spite
of their infrequent attention to agriculture. The adequacy of the
Miskito's stores is a function of the capability of the turtle to
convert the vast undersea carpets of turtle grass, which blanket the
offshore littoral zones, into high quality protein that is available
throughout the year. These sea grasses are rarely utilized by marine
animals (Margalef, 1968:95), and the turtle thus provides a unique
means for tapping an otherwise-unavailable resource.

Today, pirates and traders no longer ply the Caribbean. Only

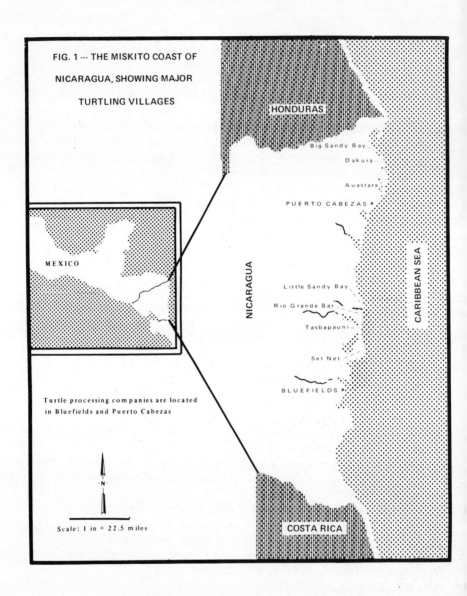

FIG. 1 --- THE MISKITO COAST OF
NICARAGUA, SHOWING MAJOR
TURTLING VILLAGES

turtles and Indians remain, and both are in jeopardy. In late 1968, commercial firms arrived on the Miskito Coast and began buying turtles; meat was exported to North America as a high-priced delicacy, and the calipee[3] from beneath the shell was sent to Europe to be processed into soup for the burgeoning gourmet market.

The Miskito, with no other source of cash, have been eager salesmen, and the companies have been insatiable consumers. The result has been a precipitous rise in the number of turtles harvested each year—an increase that now endangers both the turtles and the human population which has subsisted on them throughout its history.

With the arrival of "The Company," the diet and nutrition of the Miskito has been profoundly altered. The result might well be called "The Development Paradox," in which the availability of more money results in lowered nutritional status.

Historical developments have put the Miskito into the market-place to sell turtles, and the ecological and nutritional consequences threaten to put them out. A complex latticework of cultural, economic, and political factors are combining to create, and perpetuate, the development paradox.

Aboriginal Adaptations

The history of the Miskito Coast is nearly as intricate as the lacework pattern of rivers and lagoons that criss-crosses the area. For hundreds of years, the Miskito have been buffeted by the winds of exploration, exploitation, and domination that have periodically descended on the Coast from near and far. Each of these visitations has left a distinctive mark on the Coast and on its people, and many of the problems the Miskito face today result from the accumulated debt of 450 years of culture contact.

The history of the Coast is an adventure story, replete with the mystery and mystique of pirates, privateers, and men of fortune. Even today, as you walk the isolated beaches, there is a feeling that a distant boat on the horizon could easiy turn out to be the sailing ship of Henry Morgan. The Miskito still speak of buried treasure; nobody has every found any, but everyone knows a story of some old person who has.

The original, precontact inhabitants of the Coast were organized in a series of small, scattered, seminomadic groups that spoke a variety of dialects (Helms, 1971:15). There is linguistic evidence (Greenberg, 1960; Swadesh, 1962) for a relation with the Chibchan languages of South America, and ethnographic (von Hagen, 1940; Adams, 1956; Kroeber, 1963) and serological (Matson and Swanson, 1962) evidence that supports the conclusion of a South American origin.

The Miskito name and language reflects the variegated history of the area. There is no agreement as to the origin of the name *Miskito*, nor even whether or not it was in use before European contact. Various authors trace the name to the French (a corruption of the term for "musket bearing"), the British (referring to the malarial mosquito found in abundance inland), and the Spanish (from the term "indios mixtos"). There are numerous variations on the spelling in the literature—*Mosqueto, Mosquito, Musketo, Mustique, Moskito*—but current usage (Helms, 1971; Nietschmann, 1973) favors *Miskito*.

The earliest available accounts from the buccaneers tell of small, mobile groups that moved about with the seasons, exploiting the riverine and marine environments with only casual attention to any land crops. The Miskito, de Lussan complained, were "extremely lazy and only plant and cultivate sparingly" (1930:287 orig. 1688).

The Indians, Dampier wrote:

> delight to settle near the Sea, or by some River, for the sake of striking Fish, their Beloved Employment.
>
> Sometimes the Miskito man seeks only for Fish, at other time for Turtle, or Manatee. (1968:16 orig. 1703)

Those who spoke the same dialect seem to have considered themselves a unit (Dampier, 1968 orig. 1702; M.W., 1732; Esquemeling, 1893), and other groups were distrusted. These populations were egalitarian in their political organization, with leadership being exercised primarily by respected elders or warriors.

There were at least ten of these linguistically-distinct groups aboriginally, including the Twahka, Panamaka, Ulwa Kukra, Bawihka, Yusku, Prinsu, Boa, Silam, and Ku (Conzemius, 1929:64, 1932:15). These people were later known collectively as Sumu, and they are today culturally distinct from the Miskito. Whether this distinction is aboriginal in origin is a point of considerable contention.

Nietschmann (1973:26; personal communication) feels that the aboriginal Miskito had a unique subsistence adaptation, based on exploitation of the littoral environment in general, and turtling in particular, that distinguished them from the Sumu. Helms, on the other hand, argues in favor of a postcontact origin of the Miskito (1971:18) who she feels were a subtribe of the Sumu before Europeans arrived.

My own view is that there existed a series of populations each of which utilized the available microenvironments in different ways. The Coast is an area of very high ecological diversity measured both from north to south and from sea to interior. By being mobile, these populations were each able to garner their own subsistence by exploiting the seasonal variations in resource availability that characterize each resource zone. Population density was low and contact minimal, which contributed to linguistic isolation and differentiation while minimizing conflict and overexploitation.

Some of these populations clearly made use of marine resources during at least part of the year, but I doubt that any population had the type of marine adaptation that was the hallmark of later Miskito subsistence efforts. I believe this marine adaptation is a function of sedentism, with its concomitant increase in population density and demand for greater energy extraction from a given territory. Use of marine resources in general, and the turtle in particular, taps a resource that is extremely high in productivity and that is available throughout most of the year. These were the necessary, if not sufficient, conditions for the conversion of one of those nomadic groups into the people known as Miskito.

The Europeans contributed to the rise of the Miskito both directly, by the arms they provided, and indirectly, by the black slaves they brought to the West Indies, many of whom escaped to or were shipwrecked on the Coast. The intermarriage of blacks and Indians produced a physically-distinctive population that rapidly became identified as Miskito by the other populations.

By the early seventeenth century, the English were engaged in a search for natural resources in the New World. In 1633, the Providence Island Trading Company sent an expedition to the region of Cape Gracias á Dios on the northern coast. Anthropologist Mary Helms feels that the Miskito, as an identifiable group, arose from this contact with the British. Having acquired firearms in trade, a population of perhaps 1,000 around Cape Gracias rapidly became the scourge of the Coast. Neighboring populations were raided and either assimilated or driven far inland.

Eager to consolidate their claim to this New World territory, the
English created and crowned a Miskito "King" in 1687. Traditional
social-political organization had been entirely at the village level. A
king was a new concept for the Miskito, but they admired the
wealth and power of the British and thought a king might work as
well for them. It continued to work better for the British, who
crowned the first Miskito king in Jamaica, and promptly had him
invite them to come and stay, which they did for almost 100 years.

During this early phase of contact, the Miskito gathered small
amounts of local resources, or extracted them from surrounding
populations as "tribute" for the new king. This was the first of
several significant shifts in Miskito lifeways. They now became
traders, bartering the dyewood, sarsaparilla and "tortoise shell"[4]
obtained as tribute for "fish-hooks, small glass beads, Dutch
looking-glasses, salt, and other articles which, except to them, were
of very trifling value" (Roberts, 1965:34 orig. 1827).

These European goods quickly became cultural necessities for
the Miskito, as did other things they felt necessary to live "English
gentleman fashion." Whether through trade or tribute, the Miskito
obtained what the traders wanted from the Sumu who had been
forced inland. "In a word, the Miskito became middlemen, living
off the 'profits' of directed exchange between coastal traders and
interior groups" (Helms, n.d.: 9).

This intensification of an already-established pattern of exploitation is a process that was to be repeated at a later time, but
with a very different ecological result.

During this time, the Miskito subsistence system remained intact.
Although the men were absent from the villages for long periods of
time, bartering, raiding, or seeking turtle shell, agricultural pursuits
were seen to by the women and children.

Helms suggests that the matrilocal residence pattern found
among the Miskito is an adaptation to a situation in which the men
were periodically gone from the village:

Matrilocality has proved to be of positive value for the Miskito during centuries
of contact. On the one hand it assured the continuation of traditional culture in
the face of an increasingly heterogeneous world; on the other it provided
Miskito men in particular with the necessary individual freedom not only to hunt
and fish as they had always done, but also to take advantage of diverse new
activities which would yield European goods. (1971:26)

Population and Subsistence

Miskito population, growing by both reproduction and acquisition, swelled rapidly from the 1600-1700 estimated by Esquemeling in 1856 (p. 167) to as many as 10,000 in the 1800s (Salvatierra, 1937:106). Bound to the Coast by trade relations and their desire for European goods, the mobile Miskito gradually settled down into sedentary villages, a process that brought with it new subsistence patterns.

The coastal populations, I argue, became increasingly specialized in their subsistence selection, shifting from emphasis on a wide variety of riverine, agricultural, and marine resources to concentration on the sea turtle. This subsistence shift is a matter of emphasis and should not be interpreted as an argument that the Miskito abandoned agriculture entirely, or that they no longer used riverine resources.

The soils of the Coast proper are poorly suited to agriculture, a fact noted long ago by Roberts:

> The soil in the neighborhood (of Cape Gracias) is extremely bad; and with the exception of a few spots on which there are small patches of cassava, is incapable of producing anything better than coarse rank grass. (1965: 150 orig. 1827)

> I may here observe, that all the pine savannahs in the neighborhood of the sea, on the Mosquito Shore, are sandy, and, comparatively speaking barren . . . in consequence the inhabitants on the coast are obliged to have their provision grounds, and plantain walks, on the banks of rivers, or streams, many miles up from the sea; with the exception, however, of cassava, which thriving on sandy soil, can be planted close to the coast settlements. (1965:115)

The riverine Miskito and other inland groups grew "Plantains, bananas, cassava, sweet potatoes, ginger, oranges and other fruits" (Young, 1847:18) which they traded to the Coast where "very little bread kind (starchy staples) is grown . . . by reason of the sandy nature of the soil" (Young, 1947:19).

This need for subsistence resources from beyond their immediate environment reinforced the patterns that were established by trade and tribute between the coastal and inland populations. The integration of seasonal cycles and the combination of varying microenvironments that was once achieved through population movement now came about through the movement of foodstuffs. The people became sedentary and the resources became mobile.

Combining land and sea resources, these people had little

trouble subsisting. The ease with which they made a living was a
point of constant irritation to Europeans in general, and mis-
sionaries in particular, who came to the area:

> The men . . . are abominally lazy, subsisting by hunting and fishing and the
> produce of their plantations, which the women attend to. (Young, 1847: 28)

> They are excellent swimmers, archers and persevering rowers. It is a pleasure to
> watch them at these activities; then one sees what these otherwise lazy and
> apparently dull men are capable of. (Schneider, 1900:7)

> The men, after they had secured food sufficient for a few days by fishing or
> hunting were content to spend their time lying idle in their hammocks until a
> fresh supply was needed. (Joyce, 1971:42 orig. 1916)

As the Miskito expanded geographically, each village that
emphasized the exploitation of marine resources had access to a
particular set of offshore cays, where turtling activity was centered.
This distribution remains unchanged today. There is virtually no
overlap in the use of the cays, and villages located on the Coast that
do not have access to this resource zone obtain their subsistence
from the rivers or lagoons, despite their proximity to the sea. The
differential capacity of these ecosystems to provide protein may be
the major factor that accounts for turtling villages having an
average population over twice that of those using lagoon and
riverine resources (739 vs. 296).

"The Company"

In 1894, the Miskito Coast was incorporated into Nicaragua as the
Department of Zelaya. It was previously a reservation, as a result of
1859 and 1860 treaties with England. This passing of political control
was perhaps more in symbol than in substance, since the Nicaraguans have even today not assumed effective administration of
the area. Economically, however, there was a revolution as large,
foreign-owned companies came to the Coast.

Wage labor replaced barter as a series of economic boom and
bust cycles swept the region. Rubber, mining, bananas, and lumber
each had their day:

> The most immediate effect of boom-and-bust economic cycles on Miskito life
> was to provide a range of job opportunities for Miskito men who, for example,

could contract as laborers in the mines, or with mahogany gangs, work in the bush tapping rubber, or hire out as boatmen for foreigners traveling the rivers. (Helms, 1971:28)

These new economic relationships were voluntary, in the sense that there was no political coercion, and yet there was a very definite need for material goods—a "need" that had been created by the years of contact with traders and pirates. Helms (1969, 1971) identifies as "purchase societies" those populations that voluntarily enter the marketplace through the sale of local resources or labor, while retaining political autonomy and cultural identity:

> The definitive characteristic of any purchase society is the articulation of local society with the wider complex world through economic channels of trade and wage labor, while political autonomy and a stable social organization are maintained. (1971:7)

In a purchase society, acquisition is a cultural necessity:

> The term "purchase society" is suggested because it emphasizes both the economic referent in general, and the specific aspect of that referent which appears most important from the point of view of the local society, and toward which local adaptations will be directed, i.e., the need to obtain, to 'purchase', through one means or another, foreign manufactured goods which have acquired the status of cultural necessities. To be sure, something must be exchanged or sold in order to acquire these goods, but to the local population, that which is sold is merely a means to the all important end of purchasing. (Helms, 1971:7)

Purchasers, then, *must* purchase. But they must also sell. What is sold is a major determinant of the degree of autonomy yielded to the outside system. Because purchasing is obligatory, such populations readily relinquish their ecological autonomy—the making of decisions about the rate at which local resources are utilized—in exchange for money.

The Booms Begin

In the first two booms after 1894—mahogany and gold— the Miskito provided wage labor. Parsons (1955:55) reports that the George D. Emery Company of Boston exported close to 1,000 mahogany logs monthly from the Rio Grande area in the years 1894 to 1902. This was probably the first activity on the Coast that caused substantial ecological degradation, as major stands of marketable mahogany were stripped from the land, floated down the river and loaded onto waiting ships.

The largest impact, ecologically and culturally, came from the operations of foreign banana companies, beginning in the 1890s and ending in 1940. Aided by the advice and technology of the banana companies, the Miskito cleared huge tracts of forest and put them into bananas. By abandoning the relatively small and temporary plots that characterized their aboriginal subsistence efforts, the Miskito became ecologically vulnerable, and between 1938 and 1940 Panama and Sigatoka (soil) diseases swept through the banana plantations, bringing a virtual halt to commercial operations.

The cultural changes, initiated by contact with Europeans, accelerated as Americans appeared on the Coast with canned goods and leather shoes. Banana company commissaries were well stocked, and for a few years the boom flourished. Many of the older Miskito still speak fondly of a time when villages like Rio Grande and Karawala were "well fix up" with bulging commissaries and loud dance halls. As one woman told me, "I think that time can never end, but, well it end now. That's the world."

Today, Karawala is almost eerie in its silence. The rusting hulks of old banana barges still sit at the foot of the dock. Rio Grande, too, is a virtual ghost town, with decrepit buildings and barren foundations as the reminders of stores that once held thousands of dollars in goods for a population of Americans and Miskito which had the money to buy.

The last major boom on the Coast was the cutting of pine lumber, beginning in the 1920s and ceasing as the stands gave out around 1959. Again the Miskito provided the labor—to cut the logs and run the mills—and their ecosystem provided a resource that was simply exploited until exploitation was no longer economically feasible. The companies left, and the Miskito stayed, mulling over memories of dollars and canned ham, and with no ready source of cash.

As each of these booms faltered, the Miskito returned to their local ecosystem for subsistence, while awaiting another chance to purchase. Each time, the ecosystem continued to provide the necessary food, and

The very recurrence of economic cycles which has at times led to insecurity, restricted sociability, and economic depression is perhaps also responsible for the maintenance of the Miskito subsistence economy and, by extension, a certain amount of self-sufficiency which permits cultural identity to continue. (Helms, 1971:233)

Although the Miskito subsistence system was intact, their eco- system underwent severe degradation during this time, as resources were removed without thought for the consequences. The pine savannas were stripped for lumber, the forests cleared for bananas. Caymen Islanders, having depleted their own fishing grounds, came to the Coast in 1837, and began the first significant intensification of turtle exploitation (Parsons, 1962:30).

degraded ecosystem

> As each boom ended, it left the Miskito . . . their subsistence system together with an overburden of desires for luxury and foreign goods as a result of contact. (Nietschmann, 1970: 56)

> Now, foreign objects and luxury foods obtainable through participation in the market economy are no longer available. Hence life is not completely satisfying. A feeling of want and of isolation has become dominant. (Helms, 1967: 235).

There is ample evidence of this "ethic of poverty" in the village of Little Sandy Bay. Most of the residents recall the last two booms, and they always recall them happily. Work was plentiful, and goods were cheap. The currency was U.S.: "gold money, not this Nicaragua monkey money." Things were "well fix up" then, with plenty of goods to purchase and plenty of money to purchase them with.

Little Sandy Bay—Subsistence-by-the-Sea

There are three ways to get to little Sandy Bay, all of them by boat. You have your choice of outboard motor, diesel motor, or sail. Little Sandy Bay is a part of the main, yet it is also an island surrounded by water.

It is quite appropriate to arrive in Little Sandy Bay by water, since the coastal Miskito have a lifestyle oriented almost entirely toward the sea, lagoons, and rivers that dominate the landscape. To the coastal Miskito, water is a source of both subsistence and transportation. The Miskito are equally adept whether traveling a riverine railway, or sailing the Caribbean in their 20-foot dories,[5] flour sack sails set to capture the skyborne current. For the Miskito, land is what you travel over to get to water.

Little Sandy Bay is isolated on the Miskito Coast, and the entire coast in turn is isolated from the country of which it is ostensibly a

part. Although recent ethnographic work (Helms, 1971; Nietschmann, 1973; Weiss, 1975) makes the area better known anthro-
pologically, it remains *tierra desconocido* to most Nicaraguans,
who prefer the more temperate western climate to the humid
tropical lowlands of the east. An estimated 35,000 Miskito live in
Nicaragua (Nietschmann, 1973:47), divided between riverine populations (25,000) who combine swidden agriculture, fishing and
hunting, and coastal villages (10,000), who seek their subsistence
primarily from either sea or lagoon. My research focused on the
subsistence pattern of Little Sandy Bay, whose inhabitants depend
on the green sea turtle (*Chelonia mydas*) for a major part of their
food.

There are 377 people in the village, divided almost equally by sex
(184 males, 193 females). The population pyramid is extremely
bottom-heavy; 36 percent of the population are below the age of
eleven, and 62 percent are under twenty-one. This distribution is
highly significant, since under the current subsistence strategy,
more and more of the younger people are contributing less to the
subsistence effort.

Comparison with the data of Nietschmann (1973:51) from
Tasbapauni shows that this age distribution is common to coastal
villages. Tasbapauni has 59 percent of its population under the age
of twenty-one. It is difficult to estimate the rate of population
increase for the Miskito on the basis of current data, but it
approximates 3 percent annually. During the period of my research, there were twelve births and three deaths in Little Sandy
Bay, a net gain of nine people.

Aboriginally, the subsistence system returned food for the labor
of anyone old enough to walk. Even young children made a
contribution in maintenance of agricultural plots, and the proportion of producers in the population was thus quite high. The
availability of additional labor could be converted, quite directly,
into additional food.

Now, the situation has shifted quite suddenly and quite pre-
cipitously. The Miskito are planting less and less agricultural
ground as they devote more and more time to pursuit of the turtle.
At the time of year when the clearing and planting of ground must
be accomplished, the weather and sea conditions are also the most
favorable for turtling. Faced with a choice about the expenditure of
a finite amount of time, the men most frequently choose turtling.
As the amount of agricultural ground being planted is reduced,

the labor of women and children can less often be invested in subsistence efforts. It is men who initiate and determine the agricultural cycle, since only men are considered capable of the initial clearing of trees and underbrush from a plot. Women whose labor might once have helped produce pounds of manioc and dasheen now sit home while the men pursue turtles. The same is true of children.

In effect, the consumer/worker ratio has undergone a sudden upward revision under the new subsistence regime, and the very high percentage of young people in the village is a measure of the tremendous impact that change is having. In one fell swoop, producers have become consumers just as surely as if an accident had rendered them immobile.

The Social System

Kinship and age were once the major factors in defining day-to-day, face-to-face relationships among and between the Miskito. To a certain extent this remains true, but recently economics has entered into the calculation. Economic acts and social acts were once inseparable for the Miskito, and the recent separation has left a residue of confusion and unhappiness.

The Miskito have a strong sense of what constitutes proper traditional values, and most of the definitions have to do with behavior toward kin. Although observable behavior conforms less and less often to the spoken ideal, it is clear that until quite recently there were specific rights and obligations between a wide-ranging set of relatives.

The largest kin group currently recognized is the *taya*, which includes all descendants of ego's maternal and paternal grand-parents and their siblings and half-siblings, and of ego's great-grandparents. The *taya* is of importance because it is reckoning at this level that usually allows a traveling Miskito to find a kindred in another village and to obtain the hospitality and support that stems from that relationship.

The *kiamp* is the most frequently referenced kin group within the village. *Kiamp* members share the same surname and represent a subset of the *taya*. *Kiamp* membership includes all offspring of a male, and a married woman remains a member of her father's *kiamp*. This relationship is extremely important in the distribution of food, and there is often tension because men feel that their wives are sending food to another *kiamp,* and there are frequent accusations that the man's *kiamp* is being shorted, since it is the women who do the food distribution.

Traditionally, there were strongly-felt sets of obligations among all *kiamp* members, and this was exemplified and emphasized through the giving of turtle meat. The Miskito subsistence system was once intimately tied to this kin-based distribution network, in which turtle meat and other provisions were freely provided to *kiamp* members one day, and received another. This served to smooth irregularities of supply for the individual family units and made the most efficient use of the available resources. The prevailing rule was "If anybody has, everybody has."

There is a geographic reality that corresponds to the *kiamp,* since members of one *kiamp* often reside in a cluster within the village. Spatial proximity serves as a reminder and a reinforcer of the social bonds that link *kiamp* members.

The major functional unit of Miskito society today is the nuclear family. Like all Miskito villages, Little Sandy Bay encompasses most of the possible living arrangements, from individuals to extended families, but the prevailing form is man, woman, and children living under one roof. Of the sixty-seven households in Little Sandy Bay, fifty-one (76 percent) are of this type.

On a day-to-day basis, these household units are the focal point of Miskito social and economic behavior. Despite the men's complaints that their wives "too much give," the distribution of turtle meat remains an important means of reaffirming relationships, particularly at a time when economic and social demands often call for conflicting behavior. At the same time, this kin network plays an important role in providing for village subsistence.

Records kept on the distribution of butchered meat showed that 78 percent of the meat was either used in the household or given away as gifts (gifts 35 percent, household use 43 percent). The competition between meat for sale and meat for food is strong, however, and as a result subsistence is a little less certain for the individual Miskito. There is simply less meat available to distribute, and as a result the amounts given are declining and distant relatives are often not provided for as they once would have been.

The economics of turtling thus enter into social calculations. *Kiamp* ties are weakening, and the nuclear family is increasingly an independent economic unit in a system where "every man for himself" substitutes for an ethic that emphasized sharing with everyone.

The other major mode of reckoning, besides kinship, is age. The categories include child (*tukta,* which indicates either sex but can be modified to make it sex-specific), adolescent (*tiara,* female, *wahma,* male), and adult (*almuk,* either sex). The latter two are actually kinship terms, but by convention they are used as terms of respect to any elder, particularly by children.

These are both social and economic categories, and the behaviors associated with each are shifting rapidly. Children, for example, are not differentiated terminologically by sex, and to adults they are an amorphous group. This group, however, once had a much larger role in productivity than it does today. All but the youngest of children accompany their parents to help in the working of agricultural plots. Although unable to heft a hoe, children are particularly adept at weed pulling, a constant chore whose prompt execution can make a considerable difference in harvest yields. Now, however, with decreasing amounts of agricultural ground under cultivation, this labor is unused. Although no longer producers, these children remain consumers, and the subsistence load is thus being carried on fewer shoulders and often with less success.

Kinship and age crosscut and reinforce one another, providing the social and economic fabric of Miskito society. These factors of kinship and age were an indigenous property of Miskito organization, although their meaning has shifted considerably with changing circumstances.

Selling Subsistence Resources

> The company no help nothin'.
> Only want your turtle.
>
> **A Miskito man**

The most recent phase of Miskito history began in late 1968, when a commercial company set up the first factory to procure and process green turtles. Again, the Miskito were invited into the economic marketplace, and again they entered. Once a subsistence resource, gathered for food, the turtle quickly became an economic commodity, sought for sale. Once, the food needs of a local population determined when turtlemen went out and how many turtle they brought back. The demand was finite and within limits that the turtle population could sustain. Now, the virtually unlimited demand of a world market defines production, and turtle populations are being decimated.

The Miskito pursue the turtle because it can be converted to money with which to purchase. The presence of a commercial outlet for turtle has acted to amplify the demand, and the impact has been both sudden and sharp; from less than 1,000 in 1968, exports of turtle rose to an estimated 10,000 in 1972. In Little Sandy Bay, 913 turtle were taken in a one-year period, of which 170 were consumed and 743 (81 percent) were sold to the commercial companies (see Figure 2).

Figure 2.   Number of Green Turtles Caught, Sold and Consumed in Little Sandy Bay, April, 1972 through March, 1973.

MONTH	TURTLES SOLD	TURTLES CONSUMED	TOTAL	% SOLD
January	52	10	62	84
February	18	6	24	75
March	41	13	54	76
April	71	12	83	86
May	102	35	137	74
June	20	20	40	50
July	8	7	15	53
August	106	15	121	88
September	102	16	118	86
October	32	12	44	73
November	157	18	175	90
December	34	6	40	85
TOTAL	743	170	913	81

Turtle herds cannot withstand such drastically increased predation. Zoologist Carr predicted twenty years ago that the "once-teeming hordes" of green turtles "will be pursued with harpoon and stop net, and the centers of activity will invade ever more remote waters until the animal is backed against the wall" (Carr, 1952:353). Today, on the Miskito Coast, his vision is becoming a fact.

The turtle is a reptile, a ponderous reminder of life as it was on earth 200 million years ago. Evolution has left the sea turtle a hard shell but a fragile life cycle. Green turtles are wholly aquatic, except for the few hours necessary for the female to come on shore to lay her clutch of eggs, which will number in excess of 100. The performance will be repeated several times in one nesting season, and the female will then retire to the sea, reappearing on the same beach to repeat the cycle two to four years later.

From the clutch of eggs, hatchlings emerge in about two months. The coordinated thrashing of dozens of flippers carries the tiny turtles from their underground nest to the surface, where they begin a dangerous dash to the sea, dodging a wide range of predators. It is estimated that less than 1 percent of the emergent turtles ever reach adulthood.

These survivors are the end result of a careful evolutionary calculation that has balanced predator and prey. Man, however, has sharply altered the balance. The green turtle has been pushed, by human activity, from feeding and breeding grounds throughout its range. Today, there remains only one major nesting beach in the entire western Caribbean, at Tortuguero in Costa Rica. There, for almost twenty years, Archie Carr has tagged, measured, and protected turtles in an attempt to understand their life history and restore their diminished numbers.

Guided by a still-unknown navigation system, turtles from the Miskito Coast and northward to Cuba and the Yucatan of Mexico migrate hundreds of miles from their feeding grounds to Tortuguero's desolate twenty-two miles of sand, responding to an evolutionary demand that they attempt to perpetuate themselves. Ecological and economic factors have combined to make existence precarious for the green turtle, and commercial exploitation now threatens to make it completely untenable.

In a very real sense, the outcome for the turtles may be the outcome for the Miskito. Human populations, too, are the end point of a complex evolutionary calculation that ultimately balances people and resources. The large population of coastal Miskito is sustained because of the abundant supply of turtle. Turtle plays a critical role in Miskito subsistence ecology because of its unique ability to convert the vast carpets of undersea vegetation which lie off the Nicaraguan coast to protein which is available to the human population. The turtle at sea, like the cow on land, is the ecological link through which a human population is joined to a highly productive resource that occurs over a large area. This resource provides not only energy, but high-quality protein.

Protein is a critical resource. It is probably more often the limiting resource for subsistence populations than energy (see Carneiro, 1957, 1960; Denevan, 1966). Protein is available from fewer sources than calories, which are obtained from any consumable material.

Another factor often overlooked is that human populations are at the hunting-and-gathering stage in terms of protein resources long after they are able to deliberately cultivate calories. The much-touted "agricultural revolution" would have (and on several occasions probably did) failed had protein been unavailable in quantities sufficient to complement the increased caloric resources. Even the most modern industrial populations remain partially "hunter-and-gatherer" in terms of their protein resources. Protein is the least available, most costly, and least dependable resource needed by human populations.

Selling Food To Get Money To Buy Food

Now the Miskitos are taking home a little cash instead of meat, and with it buying an inadequate diet to replace the good one provided for ages by the turtle colony with which their society had evolved. (Carr, 1972: 29)

Rivers of sunlight ran from nearby coconut palms, filling the face of an old Miskito Indian. He was telling me about his village, Little Sandy Bay. His head swung slowly from side to side. "Nothin'—Mister, we got plenty of that here."

I was in Little Sandy Bay to find out exactly how much "nothin'" was and how the Miskito came to have so much of it.

Finding out exactly how much of what foods was being consumed every day by the 377 people in Little Sandy Bay proved to be a complex task, but one which was essential in order to understand the way Miskito subsistence patterns had been affected by the shift from a subsistence to a market economy. The proof of subsistence success is in the eating, but few studies have provided satisfactory data on food consumption.

The reasons for this are mostly methodological. Keeping track of all the food consumed in a human community, even a small one, is a huge task. In field studies whose primary focus was on other factors, the gathering of nutritional information did not command the amount of research time that would have been necessary for complete data gathering. As a result, previous research (Rappaport, 1968; Nietschmann, 1973; Gross and Underwood, 1971; Williams, 1973) had reported what a few people ate for a little while, but samples were either too small, nonrandom, or taken over too brief a time period to permit statistically valid generalizations about a community's yearly intake of food.

The major considerations in preparing the research design were that the study (1) take place continuously over most or all of a one-year period, (2) sample in such a way that the results were valid for the entire population, and (3) have an independent means of verifying the results obtained from the sampling program.

The data on nutritional consumption were gathered during an eleven month period from April 1972 through March 1973. I numbered all the houses in the village and drew a 10 percent sample weekly, using a random number table. Each house was visited daily, late in the afternoon, and whoever was responsible for food preparation was asked to recall the food that had been used that day.

The accuracy of such a recall technique is often questioned in many studies, but I believe that it was accurate for the Miskito. A large proprotion of their food is purchased in measured units from village stores and from each other, and women recall quite clearly how much (or little) they have spent and on what it was spent. (This ability to recall dietary intake accurately is common among people with limited dietary options, a fairly standard food purchasing and consumption pattern, limited numbers of serving utensils, and/or measuring units and standard eating times.)

In the cases of foods gathered or harvested, I estimated the amounts by recording the number of tubers, bananas, or other appropriate unit consumed and later converted these using an average weight found from fifty or more measurements of each food. For a very limited number of foods, it was necessary to express the amount used in some local unit of measurement (such as the number of calabash [gourd] bowlsful) and to later convert this, as with bananas.

Each person eating in a household on a sample day was recorded as belonging to one of six age categories: adult (male/female), teenage (male/female), child, and infant. These categories corresponded closely to those of the Miskito. The data were recorded on a preprinted form, converted into a numerical code, and later keypunched for computer analysis. A more detailed presentation on the methods of this study and the verification of the data will be presented in a paper now in preparation.

With these data in hand, it was possible (with the aid of a computer) to determine from a table of food values tailored to the region, the quantity of protein, calories, fats and carbohydrates consumed in each household each day, and the average amount consumed per adult male or equivalent in other consumers. Because the data are from a random sample of acceptable size, the results are valid as a generalization about consumption in the entire village.

Nutrition Survey—Results

There is no one measure of nutritional intake that suffices by itself, but the one most nutritionists turn to first is caloric intake.

Calories—the energy contained in food—are essential for the functioning of all bodily systems. Minor and temporary deficiencies can be made up by drawing calories stored in the body as fat. Chronic, severe shortages can lead to illness and death.

Caloric intake in Little Sandy Bay was 1,500 calories per adult male (or equivalent in other age-sex category) per day. This level is approximately 45 percent below that recommended by the Food and Agriculture Organization of the United Nations (1973).

Most of the village's calories previously came from their fields. Today, 65 percent of the calories are purchased from one of the small stores in the village. Flour provides 24 percent of the calories, 23 percent comes from rice, and 17 percent comes from sugar.

There are some significant monthly variations from these figures (which are the averages over the period of a year). In two months—May and June—turtle contributed close to 17 percent of the caloric total. It is during these months that commercial turtling is banned,[6] and any turtle the Miskito catch they must consume. When it is not an economic resource, turtle once again becomes a subsistence resource, making a signficant contribution of not only protein, but calories.

Other local resources are utilized when available. In August and September, breadfruit accounted for almost 25 percent of the village's calories. Breadfruit are harvested from trees planted upriver many years ago. They require no investment of time that might otherwise be spent turtling, since these months are a period of inclimate weather when dories rarely venture out.

The Miskito now depend on the store for calories and on the turtle for money to go to the store. As a result, average monthly caloric intake varies tremendously as weather and other conditions oscillate (see Figure 3). On a monthly basis, weather is the major determinant, though weekly variations often reflected whether or not a company boat made it to the village to purchase turtles. From the first of the year through April, the weather was good, and 20 percent of the year's catch was made in this period.

Turtles could not be sold to the company from May 15 to July 15. Average daily intake dropped as low as 895 calories per adult male equivalent in May. Consumption rose slowly until August, when improving weather and the renewed turtle season opened the cash spigot again. September usually brings a "little dry season" and although it was not as pronounced as usual in 1972, the weather was good enough for almost 16 percent of the entire year's turtle catch to have occurred in that one month. There was a corresponding increase in caloric consumption.

This improvement continued for the remainder of the year. The only exception was in November when a large number of turtles were caught, but no supply ships came to Little Sandy Bay. One by one the major staples were exhausted, and the people began walking the ten mile round trip to Rio Grande to obtain an ounce of coffee and a few spoons of sugar.

There were similar supply gaps—of varying durations—throughout the year, since boats serviced Little Sandy Bay at their own convenience. The trip to and from Bluefields is an arduous one that tests both the crew and the leaking hulks with which they face the unpredictable Caribbean sea.

Calories are now bought, not made, in this village, and the ability to buy them is directly related to the availability of the turtle.

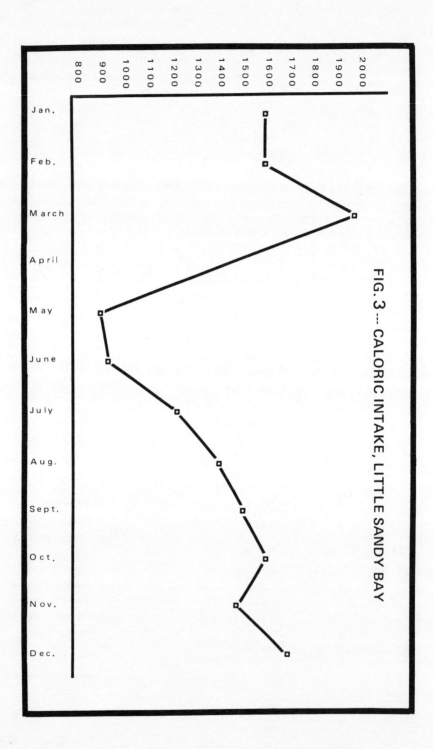

FIG. 3 — CALORIC INTAKE, LITTLE SANDY BAY

Protein

If calories are the most obvious measure of dietary intake, protein may well be the most important. Protein, composed of chains of amino acids, is the material from which body tissue is made. It is also critical to the operation of many vital chemical systems within the body; as hormones, proteins regulate a host of bodily processes, and as neurotransmitters proteins carry messages that move muscles and think thoughts.

Protein is a critical resource, particularly for children, whose mental and physical systems are in the process of building. Most authorities agree that there is a definite connection between childhood protein insufficiency and impaired mental functioning in adulthood (Food and Agricultural Organization, 1973; Montagu, 1972).

The Miskito of Little Sandy Bay obtained a daily average of 45 grams of protein per adult male equivalent, about 30 percent below the amount recommended in international standards.

The shortage was not only one of quantity, but also of quality. There are eight amino acids that cannot be synthesized by the human body and must be supplied in the food. Each protein contains different amounts of these essential amino acids, and the more closely the proportions conform to those we require, the greater the percentage of the protein that can actually be used.

The Miskito are obtaining over one-third of their protein from rice and flour, both of which are very low in the amino acid methionine. Since there are no other foods correspondingly high in methionine, this protein is not completely available. The Miskito are selling a food with a high content of high-quality protein (turtle) and using the money to purchase a food with a low quantity of low-quality protein (rice and flour).

Only 36 percent of the protein is purchased, and this is reflected in the much more consistent monthly pattern of intake (see Figure 4). The Miskito obtain 30 percent of their protein from turtle meat, and another 13 percent from fish. Although hunting contributed very little (slightly over 1 percent) of Little Sandy Bay's protein, Nietschmann (1973:165) found that it made a significant contribution in the village of Tasbapauni. The difference is largely one of ecology. The men of Little Sandy Bay do not have the same access by water to the game-rich tropical forest as do Tasbapauni's hunters.

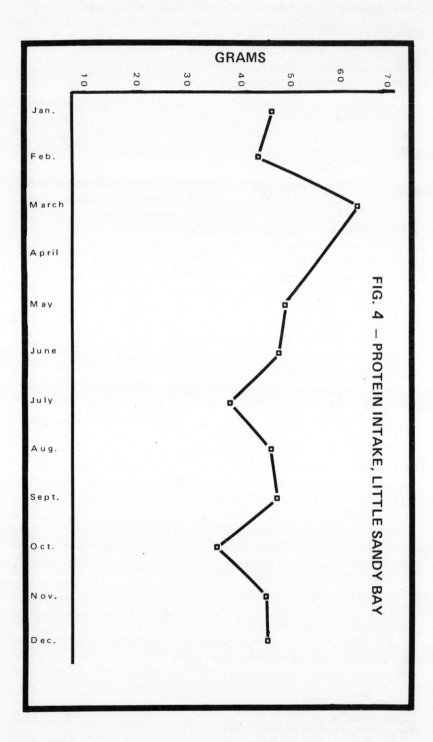

GRAMS

FIG. 4 — PROTEIN INTAKE, LITTLE SANDY BAY

Unlike caloric intake, protein is available in spite of prevailing weather conditions, reflecting the more localized and diversified resources from which it is obtained. In only one month (July) did protein consumption fall below 40 grams.

Almost 60 percent of the protein was derived from eight resources *within* the Miskito ecosystem, with an additional 4 percent from a scattering of seasonal items. By contrast, 64 percent of the calories were purchased from *outside* the ecosystem in the form of just three resources—flour, sugar, and rice. Other purchased foods contributed another 1 percent of the calories.

The major store foods purchased are flour, rice, and sugar (see Figure 5). The flour is mostly used for buns, either plain or sweetened. Sugar is used virtually every meal, most frequently as a sweetener for coffee. Many people will use their last few cents to purchase a small quantity of coffee and sugar, explaining that by drinking the mixture they won't feel as hungry.

Figure 5.   Major Store Foods Purchased in Little Sandy Bay During One Year, 1972-73.

ITEM	PRICE (Córdobas)*	AMOUNT SOLD	TOTAL SPENT (Córdobas)
Beans	.75/lb.	2,125 lbs.	1,594
Coffee	3.50/lb.	2,404 lbs.	8,414
Flour	1.00/lb.	18,500 lbs.	18,500
Rice	1.00/lb.	11,700 lbs.	11,700
Sugar	1.00/lb.	16,300 lbs.	16,300
Cigarettes	2.00/pack	5,009 packs	10,018
			C$66,526

*One córdoba = U.S. $0.14

The 16,000 pounds of sugar consumed by villagers amounts to just over 42 pounds per year for each man, woman, and child in Little Sandy Bay. Sugar and coffee have replaced manioc and turtle meat as the staples of Miskito subsistence.

The Miskito remain autonomous in protein productivity, but are dependent on the turtle and the marketplace for calories. There is an interaction between the two, however; lacking calories, the body will utilize incoming protein to provide for its energy needs first (protein, when broken down in the body, provides an average of four calories per gram of protein). Caloric insufficiency thus aggravates a marginal protein deficiency, producing a nutritional status that can hardly be described as good.

Fats and Carbohydrates

The remaining two categories of foodstuffs are mainly providers of calories, and their availability is reflected in the section on calorie intake. The major source of fat (60 percent of the total) is coconuts, which are ubiquitous, appearing in one form or another at almost every meal. Only 13 percent of the fats utilized are purchased, whereas 73 percent of the carbohydrates come from the store.

Nutrition and Maladaptation: An Analysis

Its natural resources largely depleted, the Miskito Coast suffered "benign neglect" from the late 1950s until late 1968, when a factory opened in Bluefields for the processing of green turtles. The meat was sent to North America, and the calipee to Europe for the preparation of turtle soup, to supply a burgeoning gourmet market.

Almost immediately, a profound alteration of energy flow patterns took place. Aboriginally, the Miskito had utilized a divergent set of local resources to supply their matter-energy requirements. This multiple resource exploitation served to smooth irregularities in the seasonal availability of plants and animals while reducing the demand on any one resource to a level that could be sustained by the ecosystem. The aboriginal Miskito, then, were adapted—they had established a pattern of energetic relationships that could have been sustained through time.

With the onset of commercial turtling, however, the Miskito increased the energy flow through one pathway while reducing or eliminating others. Demand has now accelerated to a rate that cannot be sustained. This population has, in other words, mal-adapted.

Zoological data leave little doubt that the turtle population is being depleted, and will not withstand commercial exploitation at current levels. A geographer who studied the situation reports, "There simply are not enough green turtles to support such excessive exploitation" (Nietschmann, 1972:1). Zoologist Archie Carr, who has studied green turtles for more than twenty years, feels "it is now very clear that the present day dilute stocks of *Chelonia* do not constitute a marine resource that will withstand efficient harvesting for an export market . . . they cannot keep pace with the power of the people to consume" (Carr, 1969:16). In villages up and down the coast, turtlemen now report spending a week at sea to capture the turtles they once took in a day.

Commercial exploitation has altered the evolutionary time frame; the instantaneous increase in exploitation in effect mimics population growth of a magnitude that might be expected over a period of 500 years. In so doing, it bypasses a series of homeostatic regulators that might otherwise maintain exploitation at a lower level, and it foreshortens to an almost negligible length the amount of time the system has to acquire and store new information that would enable it to make an adaptive response.

Lacking the buffering devices of a larger, more differentiated system, drastic fluctuations are already taking place in the Miskito subsistence system. Expanded exploitation has, in fact, brought a reduced energy intake.

Why has this occurred? What is the *process* by which the Miskito have maladapted?

Human cultures are systems, and they share certain organiza-tional similarities with all natural systems (Parsegian, 1973; Laszlo, 1972). Cultures share with other organized complexity certain ways of articulating, and certain processes for gaining and regulating those articulations. It has recently been suggested that such systems may suffer "pathologies" (Rappaport, 1969; Flannery, 1972). When variables within a subsystem pass beyond a goal range, higher level controls may be activated in an attempt to restore the previous values. However, the "cure" may be at the expense of disrupting yet other subsystems, and a spiraling pattern of positive feedback loops may generate. If control is not re-established through evolution, the system proceeds to extinction.

One of the pathologies posited by Rappaport (1969:24) is "meddling." In meddling, variables normally regulated by lower order controls come to be governed by higher order controls. This process is quite evident in the Miskito case. For several hundred years, the flow of energy and matter through the Miskito cultural system was regulated entirely within that system. Through various cultural mechanisms, the Miskito acquired and stored information about the ecosystem, and that information regulated the utilization of matter and energy from the local ecosystem.

Abruptly, control was acquired by a higher level. When commercial companies appeared, the number of turtles taken ceased to be regulated in any way by information stored within the Miskito system—the Miskito had, in fact, become a subsystem of a yet larger system. The number of turtles extracted was now determined not by population size and local nutritional needs, but by the demands of a distant and unseen market about which the Miskito system has imperfect information and over which it has no control.

There was thus initiated a flow of matter and energy out of the system. The "meddling" system, however, received no feedback on the status of the local ecosystem. Declining resources of turtle are not information to the acquiring system, nor would maintenance of the turtle population be a necessary goal even if the information were available.

Because of the tremendous disparity in size between the two systems, it is not surprising that this new demand for energy was far in excess of that which could be supplied without degrading the local ecosystem. By altering the pattern of energy flow, a meddling system acquires energy for its own needs while causing a fluctuation in flow that may destroy the acquired system. For a brief period, one system's adaptation becomes another's maladaptation.

Meddling, then, is one of the processes by which maladaptation can occur. In the case of the Miskito Indians, meddling resulted in intensification of energy flow along one pathway with simultaneous simplification of the subsistence resources being used. Compression of the time frame resulted in failure of the information system, reducing the probability of a suitable adaptive response.

Cultural and biological arrangements for acquiring matter and energy are subject to constant evolutionary review, with selection inevitably operating against those systems that fail to make the primary adaptation. Any system supplying its food needs while degrading subsistence resources has maladapted, and such a population has a lessened probability of passing the evolutionary test of persistence.

Notes

1. A 16mm sound and color film ("The Turtle People") showing the village and situation described in this paper is available for sale and rental from B&C Films, 3971 Murietta Ave., Sherman Oaks, CA. 91423.
2. The field research described in this paper was supported by a grant from the National Institutes of Mental Health.
3. Calipee is a cartilagenous material from beneath the shell. It provides the taste, color and thickening that characterize turtle soup.
4. "Tortoise" shell is in fact the shell of the sea-dwelling Hawksbill turtle, *Eretmochelys imbricata.*
5. Dori is the term by which the Miskito refer to their dugout canoes, with which they sail to the offshore cays in pursuit of turtle.
6. As a conservation measure, turtling is banned by Nicaraguan law from May 15 to July 15, to protect the gravid females that migrate to Costa Rica at that time to lay their eggs. Enforcement of the ban is lackadaisical at best, and the Miskito often stockpile turtles to be sold when the season reopens.

References

Adams, R. N.
    1956   Cultural Components of Central America. *American Anthropologist* 58: 881-907.
Carneiro, R. L.
    1957   Subsistence and Social Structure: An Ecological Study of the Kuikuru Indians. Unpublished Ph.D. dissertation (anthropology), University of Michigan.
    1960   Slash-and-Burn Agriculture: A Closer Look at its Implications for Settlement Patterns, F. C. Wallace, Ed. Men and Cultures: Selected Papers of the Fifth International Congress of Anthropological and Ethnological Sciences. Philadelphia: University of Pennsylvania Press.
Carr, A.
    1952   *Handbook of Turtles.* Ithaca: Cornell University Press.
    1969   Survival Outlook of the West Caribbean Green Turtle Colony. Proceedings of the Working Meeting of Marine Turtle Specialists, Morges, Switzerland. International Union for the Conservation of Nature.
    1972   Great Reptiles, Great Enigmas. *Audubon* 74: 24-35.
Conzemius, E.
    1929   Notes on the Miskito and Sumu Languages of Eastern Nicaragua and Honduras. International Journal of Linguistics 5: 57-117.
    1932   Ethnographical Survey of the Miskito and Sumu Indians of Honduras and Nicaragua. Smithsonian Institution, U. S. American Ethnology Bulletin 106. Washington, D. C.: Smithsonian Institution.

Dalton, G.
    1971 Theoretical Issues in Economic Anthropology. *Economic Develop-
    ment and Social Change,* G. Dalton, ed. New York: The Natural History Press.
Dampier, W.
    1968 *A New Voyage Round the World.* New York: Dover Publications (orig.
    1703).
De Lussan, R.
    1930 *Raveneau De Lussan, Buccaneer of the Spanish Main and Early French
    Filibuster of the Pacific.*Translated and edited by M. E. Wilbur. Cleveland:
    Arthur H. Clark Co.
Denevan, W. M.
    1966 A Cultural-Ecological View of Former Aboriginal Settlement in the
    Amazon Basin. *The Professional Geographer* 18: 346-351.
Esquemeling, J.
    1856 *The History of the Buccaneers of America.* Boston: Sanborn, Carter,
    and Bazin.
    1893 *The Buccaneers of America.* H. Powell, ed. London.
Flannery, K. V.
    1972 The Cultural Evolution of Civilizations. *Annual Review of Ecology and
    Systematics* 3: 399-425.
Food and Agriculture Organization of World Health Organization
    1973 Energy and Protein Requirements. W. H. O. Tech. Rep. Series No. 522,
    Geneva.
Greenberg, J.
    1960 The General Classification of Central and South American Language.
    A. F. C. Wallace, ed. *Men and Cultures.* Philadelphia: University of Penn-
    sylvania Press.
Gross, D. R. and B. A. Underwood
    1971 Technological Change and Caloric Costs: Sisal Agriculture in North-
    eastern Brazil. *American Anthropologist* 73: 725-740.
Helms, M. W.
    n.d. Origins of the Miskito and Sumu Indians of Eastern Nicaragua and
    Honduras. m.s.
    1967 Frontier Society: Life in a Miskito Village in Eastern Nicaragua.
    Unpublished Ph.D. dissertation (anthropology): University of Michigan.
    1969 The Cultural Ecology of a Colonial Tribe. *Ethnology* 8: 76-84.
    1971 *Asang.* Gainesville: University of Florida Press.
Joyce, T. A.
    1971 *Central American and West Indian Archaeology.* Freeport, New York:
    Books for Libraries Press. (originally 1916)
Kroeber, A. L.
    1963 *Cultural and Natural Areas of Native North America.* Berkeley and Los
    Angeles: University of California Press.
Laszlo, E.
    1972 *The Systems View of the World.* New York: Braziller.
Margalef, R.
    1968 *Perspectives in Ecological Theory.* Chicago: University of Chicago
    Press.
Matson, G. and J. Swanson
    1963 Distribution of Hereditary Blood Antigens among Indians in Middle
    America: V in Nicaragua. *American Journal of Physical Anthropology* 21: 545-
    559.
Montagu, A.
    1972 Sociogenic Brain Damage. *American Anthropologist* 74: 1045-1061.

Nietschmann, B. Q.
    1970 Between Land and Water: Subsistence Ecology of the Miskito Indians, Eastern Nicaragua. Unpublished Ph.D. dissertation (geography): University of Wisconsin.
    1972 Hunting and Fishing Focus Among the Miskito Indians, Eastern Nicaragua. *Journal of Human Ecology* 1: 41-67.
    1973 *Between Land and Water. The Subsistence Ecology of the Miskito Indians, Eastern Nicaragua.* New York and London: Seminar Press.
Parsegian, V. L.
    1973 *This Cybernetic World.* Garden City: Anchor Books.
Parsons, J. J.
    1955 The Miskito Pine Savanna of Nicaragua and Honduras. *Annals of the Association of American Geographers* 45: 36-63.
    1962 *The Green Turtle and Man.* Gainesville: University of Florida Press.
Rappaport, R. A.
    1968 *Pigs for the Ancestors.* New Haven: Yale University Press.
    1969 Sanctity and Adaptation. Prepared for Wenner Gren Symposium, The Moral and Esthetic Structure of Human Adaptation. New York: Wenner Gren Foundation.
Roberts. O. W.
    1965 Narrative of Voyages and Excursions on the East Coast and in the Interior of Central America. Gainesville: University of Florida Press. (originally 1827)
Salvatierra, S.
    1937 La Costa de Mosquitos. *Revista de la Academia de Geografia e Historia de Nicaragua*, Volume II: 208-259.
Swadesh, M.
    1962 Afinidades de las Lenguas Amerindias. Proceedings, Thirty-fourth International Congress of Americanists, 1960. pp. 729-738.
Von Hagan, V. W.
    1940 The Mosquito Coast of Honduras and Its Inhabitants. *Geographical Review* 30: 208-259.
W., M.
    1732 The Mosquito Indian and His Golden River. A. Churchill, ed. *A Collection of Voyages and Travels* 6: 285-298.
Weiss, B.
    1975 *Selling a Subsistence System.* Los Angeles: B&C Films.
Williams, A. W.
    1969 Dietary Patterns in Three Mexican Villages. Man and His Foods: Studies in the Ethnobotany of Nutrition-Contemporary, Primitive and Prehistoric Non-European Diets. C. Earle Smith, Jr., ed. Papers presented at the Eleventh International Botanical Congress, Seattle, Washington. University of Alabama: University of Alabama Press.
Young, T.
    1847 *Narrative of a Residence on the Mosquito Shore with an Account of Truxillo, and the Adjacent Islands of Bonacca and Roaton.* London.

7

Demographic Effects of Sex-Differential Nutrition

E. M. Rosenberg

Although population may increase geometrically while food supply increases only arithmetically at best, it is well known that the Malthusian triumvirate of war, pestilence, and famine needs to be invoked, but rarely as population control mechanisms. In balanced ecosystems, where bioforms are interdependent, their interaction usually maintains interspecific population ratios in dynamic equilibrium. When these fail, it appears that widespread physiological stress caused by overcrowding may curb population through deaths from shock, decreased fertility, increased spontaneous abortions, and disturbances in mating and maternal behavior (Hoagland 1966). These stress factors may also operate in human populations, but in human societies, more subtle population control mechanisms also operate on the cultural level.

I will discuss one such mechanism—differential nutrition for males and females in a variety of cultures. The basic question I will try to answer is simple: Is female (and especially maternal) nutritional deprivation a cross-culturally important means of population control? My preliminary assumption is well stated in the words of Frederick Stare and Margaret McWilliams:

> From a nutritional viewpoint, one of the significant concerns is the distinction made between men and women in some cultures. . . . If food is plentiful this does not create problems, but if food is short, nutritional needs of the women and children, particularly the young children, will not be met. (1973:37)

In examining the ethnographic literature dealing with differences in foodways between men and women, I have tried to answer the following questions: (1) is there evidence of differential nutrition between the sexes? (2) if so, what are the cultural values by which differential nutrition is justified? and (3) what are the consequences of differential nutrition? Because the data dealing with the subject are scanty and have often been collected for purposes relating only tangentially to this topic, sampling is necessarily serendipitous, and the conclusions drawn are only suggestive and speculative at best. Nonetheless, discussion of the data provides a feeling for the style and reliability of existing data, a sense of the urgency of the problem, and a stimulus to further research.

Cultural Values Associated with Sex-Differential Nutrition

Two major explanations have been offered for sex-differential nutrition. The first links the male's high status in most societies with priority over the best foods, while the second links women's special status as child bearers, coupled with their customary proximity to the best foods, with the jural rules or supernatural sanctions which limit access to certain foods or to those close at hand.

In recognition of their high status, men are allowed to eat first, of the best foods. As Hutton Webster notes:

> The custom of men and women eating apart (is common), the former almost always before the latter. This sexual separation in eating may sometimes be simply an outcome of the inferior status of the female sex: the men satisfy their hunger first and with the best of food. (1942: 110-111)

Simoons, speaking particularly of the Old World, similarly remarks:

> There is impressive documentation for the statement that women, especially of childbearing age, are singled out for avoidance customs. (1967: 171)

There are other ways by which males acquire the best food. For example, although the female may have direct access to the best food sources of forest, stream, field and garden plot, access rights are often curtailed through jural rules or supernatural sanctions based upon the contaminating or polluting nature of the female essence. Specific food taboos are often imposed on women. While these tend to be of limited duration, they occur primarily at the most nutritionally sensitive periods—during pregnancy and lactation when both mother and child are vulnerable. As Jensen notes:

> Some of the most harmful taboos for primal folk deprive especially pregnant women of the nutrition so necessary in prenatal development. (1953: 153)

Foods are most commonly proscribed during the pregnancy-lactation period for symbolic reasons, often related to their magical properties. Their extent and intensity may also be related to psychological factors. Thus, Barbara Ayres believes:

> The causal sequence involved in the production of food cravings and food taboos would thus seem to be the following: pregnancy—frustration and anxiety—increased need for nurturance and affection—demands on relatives and husband in the form of food cravings—increase in food consumption—excessive weight gain with discomfort and threat of toxemia—social sanctions in the form of taboos which further the interest of society of safeguarding both mother and infant. . . . The reason why women in some societies are more prone to this type of increased dependency during pregnancy may be sought in childhood experience. (1967: 114-115)

Since the specific foods proscribed are chosen for symbolic or psychological reasons, their nutritional impact may be good, bad or indifferent and can only be evaluated for well-defined groups living under specific conditions.

In many ways, the two explanations are intertwined although the first deals directly with social structure and the second with taboos.

The two major reasons attributed to sex-differential nutrition will now be discussed, using sampling of facts and descriptions from the literature as background. Literature citations are grouped into two categories: (a) social stratification and (b) pregnancy and lactation proscriptions.

Examples of Sex-Differential Nutrition Based upon Social Stratification

Hunters and Gatherers

Ethnographic evidence indicates that sex-differential nutrition obtains in hunter-gatherer economies.[1]

Dunn (1968: 224) believes that among hunters and gatherers in general, life expectancy is lower for females because of "male-female dietary disparities." A number of ethnographic accounts appear to support his stance. Simoons, again discussing the Old World, says:

> Restrictions are more commonly applied to women as a group. . . . Even where women are not prohibited a flesh food, they may be discriminated against in the division of the meat. The Chukchee of Siberia carry this to great lengths. The chukchee woman skins the slaughtered reindeer, cuts up the flesh and prepares it, and in return receives the leftovers and the bones after her husband has selected and eaten the choice parts himself. The Chukchee have a saying: "being women, eat crumbs," which portrays the position not only of their women but of women among many other Old World peoples. (1967: 110)

Webster's comments are similar:

> Food restrictions observed by men are occasionally more numerous or more burdensome than those imposed upon women. As a rule, however, it is the women who must abstain from certain articles of food, especially delicacies. No doubt masculine selfishness largely accounts for their dietary disabilities, but these are sometimes to be explained by fear of feminine uncleanness. . . . The ill effects of certain foods on the female sex, considered as the weaker vessel, are also sometimes alleged to be the reasons for forbidding them to women. . . .
>
> In the Encounter Bay tribe of South Australia old men appropriated to themselves the roe of fishes: if women, young men, or children ate of this dainty they were believed to grow prematurely old. Some Queensland aborigines in the neighborhood of Cape York did not allow women to eat many kinds of fish, including some of the best, "on the pretence of their causing disease in women, although not injurious to the men." (Macgillivray, 1852: II, 10) In North Queensland, though a food taboo is generally declared by men, it can sometimes be declared by women, but then only in the interest of the male sex. Among the natives of Arnhem Land the more savory kinds of food are often reserved for men, particularly for the older men. (Webster, 1942: 117)

And Nieboer's statement also supports this interpretation:

> Among some tribes of Queensland and South Australia, women and children are forbidden to eat some kinds of food, especially such things as the men are very

fond of. . . . In Moore River District of Western Australia the husband gives his
wife only the offal of the chase. Central Australian men eat alone, and throw what
they can't eat to the women. (1900: 11)

Among the Hudson Bay Eskimos, Freuchen reported that "wom-
en are not allowed to take part in . . . feasts. It is thought that boiled
meat is man's food, too good for women to have" (1961: 97).
Josephy noted similar attitudes on the part of sub-Arctic Indians:

Among some groups, women and old people were treated harshly. The women
dragged the toboggans, built the shelters, split the firewood, and sometimes ate
only after the men were finished. (1968: 69)

The quality of the materials makes it difficult to assess the health or
nutritional impact of such dietary inequities on females.

Herders and Agriculturalists
Women seem to fare no better in herding and agricultural
societies. For East Africa, in general, Trant writes:

Most food taboos fall on the women. , . . The chief foods forbidden to all women
are eggs, fowls, mutton, pork, and to a lesser extent, goat's meat . . . a fairly
common taboo is that of milk and certain kinds of fish (generally the fish worth
eating!). (1954: 704)

The following remarks illustrate the prevailing picture in particular African societies.

"Nuba women receive but small portions of meat or none at all" (Simoons, 1967:
12). Among the Karamojong, "most cattle are slaughtered at public ceremonies.
The men eat most of the meat" (Dyson-Hudson 1970:103). In the Dodos herding
group, "young men who work with the herds use more blood than the rest of the
population. Women and children receive very little" (Deshler 1965: 162). And
with the mainly agricultural Azande, "men are still recognized as having the first
right to food, and it is bad manners for women to eat with the men, or until they
have finished" (Baxter and Butt 1953: 47).

The situation is possibly at its most extreme among the Kikuyu.
Here "meat cannot . . . be regarded as forming a regular part of the
dietary. The amount eaten by women and children must be
insignificant" (Orr and Gilks, 1931: 27).

Kenyatta cites one sacrifice, praying for rain, in which women are
sometimes allowed, but they "must be only those who have passed
childbearing age" (c1935: 235).[2] As a rule, "men and women never
eat together. A woman is not allowed to see a man eat meat, still less

does she cook it for him" (Routledge and Routledge 1910: 61). Although, according to Kenyatta, cows' milk is reserved for the warriors, Middleton notes that goats' milk is drunk by women and children, and sums up: "the diets of men and women differ considerably, the women eating no meat, but eating several kinds of vegetables not used by men" (Middleton 1953: 19). It is this fact that led Orr and Gilks to conclude that "the dietary of young children, the girls and the women, is better balanced than that of the older boys and men" (1931:35). This is accomplished principally by a special "women's stew," which adds certain green leaves rich in sodium and calcium to the customary starchy mixture.

Among the Nyakusa, "well-to-do men are expected to entertain generously, inviting fellow villagers to drink beer or to a 'dinner party'—an ample meal with delicious dishes" (Wilson 1951: 68) in which women do not participate.

In Bemba land, noted for its hungry period, although "sex distinctions are not marked," and "there are no foods specially tabooed to women . . . the man gets a larger share of meat or any favorite relish" (Richards 1939:35). Richards goes on to say: "Men and women eat separately. Even husband and wife never share a meal, except at night in the privacy of their own hut" (1939: 122).

There are age-linked rules about how much of the relish (which will contain any meat there is) it is proper to scoop up with each bite of millet dough. On the rare occasions when husband and wife do eat together, "she is supposed to merely dip her porridge in the stew like a child" (Richards 1939: 76).

> It is part of the legal duty of a wife to cook porridge for her husband and to allow him a predominant share of it. . . . Each wife in a polygamous household will cook for her husband even if she has insufficient for herself, so that a husband may get two or three dishes of porridge while a wife and children may go short (ibid., p. 129)

This all takes place in a society in which average caloric consumption averages approximately 1700 calories per day, and the average daily protein intake for three villages at different times of the year was 50 g. per person, only a fifth of which was of animal origin.

Male-female differences in food distribution are also widespread in Oceania. On Yap, according to Lorimer (1954: 139) "men and women eat apart, and individuals of widely different ages also eat separate food. This separation occurs even within the family." Webster gives many examples:

It was formerly the rule among the Torres Strait Islanders for the father and his sons to take their meals before the mother and her daughters. This rule did not prevail in the Murray Islands, but even there the husband reserved to himself the right of choosing certain tidbits. On the island of Meli, one of the New Hebrides, the men prepare all their food in their own clubhouses, access to which is forbidden to women. . . .

Some Samoan chiefs of inferior rank permitted their wives to eat with them, but, generally speaking, women and children did not eat with men. In the Marquesas Islands the rule prevailed that a wife must not eat in the same place as her husband or prepare her food at his fire. . . . (Webster 1942: 111)

According to an early visitor to the Hawaiian Islands, the women were forbidden "when in their houses, to eat in company with men, and even to enter the eatingroom during meals. The men, on the contrary, may enter the rooms in which women dine, but must not partake of anything." (Lisiansky 1814: 127)

In the Society Islands women never ate with the men. The fires at which the men's food was cooked, the baskets in which it was kept, and the house where the men ate,—all were "sacred" and prohibited to women under pain of death. "Hence the inferior food, both for wives, daughters, etc., was cooked at separate fires, deposited in distinct baskets, and eaten in lonely solitude by the females, in little huts erected for the purpose." (Ellis 1831: 129)

Simoons describes the great desirability of pork for most of these people, and states that the "restrictions on women eating pork further confirm the association of pork with a position of prestige in society" (1967: 34). He further notes that in the Society Islands, among the Biara of New Britain, women are allowed no pork, and that its consumption by women is rare among the Buin of Bougainville, in the Marquesas, and the Hawaiian Islands.

Webster's details support this general conclusion:

Concerning some of the tribes of what was formerly German New Guinea we are told that the "menu" is so arranged that the good things, the dainties, are reserved for men. In New Britain women are not allowed to eat pork, which is greatly esteemed: "the men are very angry when women eat it" (Brown 1910: 126). Some articles of food, "mostly dainties," including turtle, dugong, and human flesh, are tabooed to New Caledonian women. (1942: 117)

One of the most startling cases is described by DuBois for the Alor. Here, sexual division of labor starts very early, and because of the different, segregated eating patterns, food serves as an incentive to work and as a reward even for the young. Boys may receive meals as guests of adult men for whom they have performed some service; girls are more likely to get a vegetable lunch as a reward for helping with the weeding.

During feasts the boys who help with the butchering are given some of the less desirable portions of the animal to roast on the spot. . . .

Although a girl has more regular access to food she does not have the guest privileges of the small boy. She gets no presents during butchering unless an unusually indulgent and thoughtful male kin happens to remember her and give her a bit of meat. The meat at feasts is always distributed to the women but only in terms of the males in their households. That is, women get meat for their husbands and sons but not for themselves or their daughters. This is consistent with the theory that flesh food is the property of men. Since feasts are primarily occasions for food distribution and actual consumption is at home, women do get a share, but only as dependents of the men. Also, since meat is eaten primarily in connection with feasts or sacrifices and is definitely a treat, the way is open for it to become set in children's minds as a symbol of masculine prerogative. The system of meat distribution helps to reinforce early in life, and on a very basic level, the role of masculine prestige in the culture. Men are not the providers; in fact, they are quite the contrary. They are the ones provided for, but they are also the purveyors of a delicacy. (DuBois 1944: 57-58)

The pervasiveness of this pattern is most clear among the great agrarian societies of the Old World. For example, "everywhere in Arabia it is the universal custom for the father and older sons to eat first and for the women and children to eat only what the men leave" (May 1961: 460). The differential treatment begins in infancy: throughout Arabic Islam, "although a girl baby is likely to continue nursing for as long as one or one and a half years, the boy is nursed until he is two or two-and-a-half, and gets far more tender treatment" (Goode 1963: 143). Similarly, in West Pakistan "the adult male certainly has a priority in helping himself to the available fare . . . especially damaging for pregnant women and infants" (May 1961: 312).

In India, things seem to be similar. Noting the extraordinary sex imbalance in India (260 million males to 213 million females in the 1961 Census): "it has been suggested that in some areas and under some circumstances female children do not receive the same degree of attention and care extended to male children and therefore succumb more easily" (American University 1964: 76). This is an old pattern, as the following passage from the 1911 Census indicates: "The boys . . . are allowed to eat their fill before anything is given to the girl. In poor families, when there is not enough for all, it is invariably the girls who suffer" (cited by Goode, 1963: 237-238). In Bangladesh, although men have three meals a day,

The women take two meals a day, one at noon and the other in the evening.

without any refreshment in between. In poorer households, they have to go shorter still, when due to the shortage of foodstuff at about September-October they are the first to starve by going without one meal or taking very little in one and still supplying the men and the children with food. (Mukherjee 1958: 22)

A like situation existed in traditional China:

What happens is that the small amount of food available to the family is unequally distributed; the son gets the larger share and the daughters are practically starved. Hence the frequent epidemics take a heavier toll of girls than of boys. (Lang 1946: 150)

Yang corroborated this picture. "Women die earlier than men. This may be because they bear children, work hard, and usually have a diet that is inferior to that of men" (1945: 12). During the harvest, "a family may deny certain food to the children and women in order to satisfy the laborers . . . . Women, especially young women, usually have less choice food than their men have" (1945: 34, 77).

Contemporary societies exhibit an unfortunately similar picture. For example, May and McLellan (1973) revealed the same underlying trend for the Caribbean. Investigators reported that in one locality in the Caribbean, with the exception of vitamin A, the diets of adult men were considered to be adequate but the diets of women and children were found to be low in calcium, vitamin A and riboflavin. In another area, it was also shown that women were not reaching the minimum required in any nutrient except ascorbic acid and thiamine. As everywhere else, young children and adult women were the heaviest sufferers (1973:277).

A work on the history of diet in Britain shows that the same forces may operate in industrial societies in situations of scarcity. Burnett reports that during the worst part of the Depression, in many cases parents, and particularly mothers, were literally starving themselves in order to feed and clothe their children reasonably (Burnett 1966: 305). The pattern was intensified during World War II.

One is willing to hypothesize that almost anywhere there is a fixed order of precedence, those who eat last get the short rations. There were only two cases where women and children eat first. The first was in rural Haiti, a society in which women's economic status and religious power are known to be unusually high. The second was the Mae Enga, a New Guinea group who had suffered a disastrous epidemic and thus desired to increase its population.

Sometimes the proscriptions leveled against women extend not only to the foodstuffs being prepared but to the foods being produced. For example, among the Tiv, where "women don't get all that much meat under any circumstances" (Bohannon and Bohannon 1969:488), the women control only the supply of less desired vegetable foods. Millet, which is characterized as the hungry season staple, is under male control. Most meat is eaten in the context of sacrifices, and men cook it: they "complain that women cannot cook meat" (Bohannon and Bohannon, 1969: 254). It certainly appears as if this situation reflects not merely a division of labor, but a mechanism by which a social subgroup controls the access to scarce or desirable food resources.

Another illustrative example comes from the Venda of the Transvaal. Here "a man's plot . . . worked by his youngest wife . . . is always larger than that of any of his wives. He may enter their gardens at will and take food, but no wife may enter her husband's garden without permission" (Saucier, 1972: 240). Among the Chimbu of New Guinea, "women sit . . . preparing vegetable food for cooking; men arrange and distribute the food and valuables butcher and cook pork" (Brown, 1972:30).

Powdermaker discusses the situation in Lesu (New Ireland), where women cook the vegetable food, mostly taro, while men are responsible for the baking of fish and animals. Most meat is eaten in the context of "feasts," which are sex-segregated. A leader speaks to the group in the men's house during such a feast:

> All of you look at these two pigs . . . . We will eat them here in the enclosure and finish eating them here. These other two pigs on the ground, we will eat half here and the remaining half will be taken out to the women . . . . (Powdarmaker, 1933:122)

At other feasts,

> Now comes the distribution of the food by the people . . . the parents of the newly initiated boys being particularly active. It is uncooked food, yams, taro, and coconuts. . . and is given to the other women . . . . The men go into the enclosure and eat pig and taro. (Powdermaker, 1933: 114) Part of the taro, but none of the pig, is taken to the women outside. (ibid., 117).

Again,

> The pigs are now cut up and distributed . . . . Uncooked taro tied together in bundles and bundles of baked taro, bananas, and small pieces of pig are given to

the women. When the distribution is over, everyone goes home; the women with their heavily loaded baskets, and the men carrying the large portions of pig. (Powdermaker, 1933: 129-130)

Turtle is not a part of the everyday diet, but is caught occasionally and usually eaten at a feast. It is always cooked by the men. . . . It is eaten by the men, although not taboo to the women. The men like it too much to give it to the women. (Powdermaker, 1933: 184)

At the final rites of marriage it is the women who have the stellar roles. . . the food is given to the women. At most of the rites in this society the feasts are exclusively masculine, with the women getting the leftovers. When the exception occurs, it therefore makes the occasion a significant one. (Powdermaker, 1933: 154)

Even a trivial geographical taboo is illuminated by this perspective:

For men the cemetery serves as a banqueting hall and most of the men's feasts are held there. Women are never permitted in the cemetery for a feast, or at any other time, except at a burial, and then they leave immediately after the interment. (Powdermaker, 1932: 241)

Hutton Webster treats all these matters within the framework of "Separation of the Sexes," emphasizing "the supposed uncleanness of women at certain periods of their reproductive life" (1942: 110).

He describes the practices of six groups in different parts of the world:

In the Hawaiian Islands women might not engage in agricultural work or in fishing. . . .

As for women (Toda), they take no part in the dairy ritual nor in the operations of milking and churning, and they are regularly excluded from the dairies themselves. They may approach a dairy only at appointed times when they receive buttermilk given out by the dairyman, and they must keep to a particular path.

Among the Bantu-speaking tribes of South Africa the care of the cattle and dairy is the highest post of honour amongst them, and this is always allotted to the men. . . . The women are never (under the pain of heavy chastisement) permitted to touch a beast.

Among the Banyoro of Central Africa the milking of cows falls entirely to men. . . . The Baganda forbid girls and women to herd the cows or milk them. The Dinka of the White Nile think it very desirable for their cows to be milked by boys and girls who have not reached puberty. Women must never do the milking. . . .

In Morocco the general uncleanness of women subjects them to many taboos. They may not enter on the threshing floor to go into the granary. . . . Some tribes do not allow women to work in a vegetable garden or gather vegetables from it. Women are also supposed to be injurious to bees; consequently the honey is always gathered by the men.

In Mala, one of the Solomon Islands, ordinary fishing nets are avoided by women lest their touch should cause the nets to become ceremonially defiled. . . . In Tikopia bonito fishing is exclusively a masculine pursuit, for the presence of a woman in a canoe at this time is taboo. . . . Marquesan women might not enter canoes and consequently could neither engage in fishing nor travel. . . . In the Hawaiian Islands canoes were taboo to women except under exceptional circumstances. . . . The canoe was associated in the native mind with fishing (men's work). . . . (1942: 112, 113, 114, 115-116)

Among the Jie, the ethnographer suggests:

We may contrast the rights of a wife in respect of her stock with her rights over agricultural land and its produce. A wife owns her garden land absolutely and in no way at the discretion of her husband. . . . Where the domestic stock are concerned, a wife has none of these powers as of right and even her de facto control is strictly limited. . . . Jie often say "women do not own cattle. They own gardens," or, "grain is the stock of women." (Gulliver, 1955: 60-61)

Women do get some milk, and occasional meat, but much of the meat is consumed at "purely male feasts" for ritual reasons.

These facts cannot be explained simply by reference to what is presumed to be a logical or plausible division of labor. If women were physically incapable of performing these tasks it would not be necessary to proscribe them. The taboos increase the dependency of women on men, and strengthen the social stratification system. They also give men greater control over critical parts of the food supply.

If, as has been postulated, limiting the dietary intake of women is a means of population control, then negative cases should prove the rule by occurring in situations where increased population is desired. India is one society from which ethnographic tidbits seem to indicate that women were fed first at a time when children were desired, and last when they were unwanted.

According to Manu (sometime between 200 B. C. and 200 A. D.), precedence at the dinner table should be given to "newly married daughters and daughters-in-law, diseased and pregnant women" (Kapadia, 1966: 235). In Buddha's time, the sixth century B. C., a householder:

before he dined should feed his guests, young lads of the family, diseased persons, old people and persons of low caste. (idem)

The situation in modern India is contrastive. When widow burning was outlawed, many groups returned to a pattern of shaving the widow's head, dressing her in white, and limiting her to one meal a day. According to Sen Gupta (1970), the 1921 census showed some 329,000 widows under the age of fifteen.

No authoritative statement can be made about the comparative prevalence of sex-differential nutrition among societies at different levels of sociocultural integration or at different prehistoric and historic periods, given the data base. Textor's (1967) cross-cultural survey of the existence of "totemism with food taboos," however, reveals that the "totemism with food taboos" complex is absent in 81 percent (sixteen societies) of his sample which have a daily protein intake of 90 g. or more, and "tend toward food gathering." On the other hand, the "totemism with food taboos" complex is present in 81 percent of the thirty-nine societies which have a per capita daily protein intake of 80 g. or less, and "tend toward food production." This leads us to hypothesize that patterns of sex-differential nutrition are more intense in agrarian than in hunting-and-gathering societies. Social stratification distinctions on the basis of sex are also more extreme in agrarian than in hunting-and-gathering societies. But the data presented above support the view that sex-differential diets could occur in any situation of scarcity at any level of social complexity.

Examples of Sex-Differential Nutrition Based upon Pregnancy and Lactation Proscriptions

Several writers have commented in general terms upon the food restrictions placed on pregnant women. Webster states:

> Pregnant, puerperant, and menstruating women may be required to avoid certain food of general consumption, such as fish and game, because eating them would spoil the luck of the fisher or hunter; the impurity of the women would be transmitted in some way . . . to the animals forming the chief source of his food supply. (1942: 117)

About East Africa, Trant makes the following remarks:

> The lot of the pregnant women is especially hard. Not only is she denied all the foodstuffs denied to other women, but during her pregnancy she is subjected to extra taboos either for fear of the effect of certain foodstuffs on the unborn child or to guard against trouble during her pregnancy and confinement. (1954: 704)

Commenting on Trant's discussion, Ellis states:

> Deprivation falls particularly heavily on the pregnant women. . . . The extreme degrees of anemia of pregnancy which are common in most tropical areas are often largely attributal to local custom which may insist that the foods of higher nutritional value are reserved for men or sold as a cash crop and that pregnancy (far from necessitating a better diet) is a period of prohibitions. (1962: 423)

There are many statements in the ethnographic literature about such taboos. For example, Mace and Mace say "a mother-in-law in India . . . might starve her son's young wife, in the belief that this would result in a smaller fetus and so make birth easier" (1959: 283). Robson notes that in parts of Ethiopia "pregnant and lactating women . . . are not . . . permitted to eat beans, a good source of protein in the predominantly vegetable diet (1972: 87-88).

The most complete documentation for any one region comes from the medical geographer May, in delineating a Southeast Asian pattern:

> In Burma, expectant and nursing mothers often starve themselves because they fear a rich diet may cause abnormal growth of the fetus. . . . They favor polished rice, dried fish (in small amounts) or mutton if available. Some pulses may be eaten, but green vegetables, fruit, eggs and milk, even if they could be bought, are frowned upon. (May, 1961: 193)

Mead (1955: 39) corroborates this, in describing the small amounts of meat and fowl permitted the pregnant Burmese woman and noting that father and sons eat first. In rural Vietnam, May reports the pregnant woman's fear of eating too much:

> During pregnancy the diet is limited to a small amount of rice, soya sauce, some vegetables and *nuoc mam* (fish sauce) of inferior quality. Fish and meat are said to generate poisons in the child. (May, 1961: 95)

Similarly, in Cambodia, the "diet of pregnant women is limited by the desire to keep the child small" (ibid., 125). In Thailand, the pregnant woman is limited to rice, spices, and a few pulses. Eggs might be a welcome supplement, but they are sold for cash; "pregnant women and children are prevented from eating them by an age-old taboo" (idem.). An interesting example of an interdiction extending into the next generation is given by Simoons:

> The Chaldean Christians of modern Turkey, Iraq and Iran still require that a candidate for the patriarchate of their church shall never have eaten meat, and that his mother shall not have done so during her pregnancy and nursing. (1967: 11)

Although examples of the dietary cravings and food proscriptions placed on pregnant women appear in numerous articles and monographs, they have almost always been discussed from a symbolic, psychological, or ethnoscientific perspective. As a result, it is impossible to judge the nutritional consequences of the taboos which have been described in the proceeding sections. These difficulties are further compounded by the reporting of incomplete data. For example, Whiting (1958) has referred to a decrease in calories and protein during pregnancy and lactation for some populations with no apparent nutritional reason. Thirty-three percent of her sample "with good data" (which includes those with both nutritional surveys and ethnographic accounts) showed a decrease in protein intake during pregnancy. Unfortunately, the base from which the decrease is effected is not specified. Textor (1967) gives a protein base for 21 of the 32 societies in Whiting's sample that decreased protein intake during pregnancy; for 12 of that 21, intake was more than 90 g. daily, for 9, less than 80 g. Both could represent adequate protein intakes; however, reference to a decreased consumption is meaningless without additional data.

There are other sources of error. Unless both the regular and special status diets are recorded in both qualitative and quantitative terms, it would be difficult to make meaningful comparisons. Often, that which appears inferior by the standards of the community may be nutritionally adequate. The opposite also holds true. To illustrate, Ford (1945: 47) cites the following case of the Andaman Islanders (one of the groups in Whiting's study which had decreased protein intake) from Man:

"During pregnancy, the women eat in moderation, but delight in as great a variety of food as possible, telling their husbands day by day what to procure for them."

He goes on to note that "the same society, however, forbids the consumption of pork, turtle, and honey during pregnancy." Radcliffe-Brown (1922), who of course had Man's report to work from, gives a more complex picture.

During the latter part of the period of pregnancy, and for about a month after the birth of the child, the mother and father must observe certain restrictions. . . . According to an . . . informant the men and women may not eat dugong, honey and yams; they may eat the flesh of small but not of full-grown pigs and turtles. An informant of one of the Northern tribes said that the woman may not eat fullgrown pig, *Paradoxorus* (civet cat), turtle, dugong, the fish *komar*, monitor lizard, honey and yams, her husband may eat these things but must carefully avoid eating certain fishes. (1922: 89)

However, if his more detailed account of the seasonal food acquisition pattern is studied, it would be shown that women were still able to eat molluscs and fish (and they have their own nets), snakes and rats, birds when they can be caught, insect larvae at certain times of year, and *small* pigs, in addition to a great variety of vegetable foods. There is a decrease, to be sure, but the diet appears adequate in quantity and variety.

Another report poses similar problems. Douglas (1966) provides an "ethnoanalysis" of the Lele's natural world (Kasai Province, Zaire). to the Lele, dogs, rats and lizards as food are "unthinkable," chickens are all right for males to eat but "unseemly" for females. Goats are kept for exchange only and are not expected to be part of the diet. On the whole, meat should be wild game, "spirit animals," "burrowing or nocturnal or water-loving." Men make cults of them and eat them; females avoid them and do not eat them. For pregnant women, it is dangerous to eat creatures of the earth, but the creatures of the sky are considered "nourishing" (ibid., 200). The situation is nutritionally unclear, but it sounds as if women are extremely limited by taboos in their sources of animal protein at any time, and especially during pregnancy. They are extraordinarily dependent on men to capture approved forms of meat.

A third perplexing case is that of the Wai Wai of Guyana. Here the taboos are visited on both parents, but their impact is necessarily quite different; indeed, the ethnographer describes the complex as the couvade. In the last trimester of pregnancy, both father and mother must give up eating large animals and fish. According to Fock (1967: 135) "the dieting tabu rules are stricter in the case of the mother than of the father. The ideal demand on the mother is that she must not eat meat for a space of three years with the exception of two species of small bird." It is conceded that the rules are not strictly followed.

Like the example from India which suggested an exception to the pattern of life-long nutritional deprivation for females, there are other instances where the nutritional supplementation of the diets of pregnant and lactating women is associated, culturally, with the desire for population increase. For example, in traditional China:

A public health nurse in a Chinese district was rejected because she tried to persuade parturient mothers to eat vegetables instead of a diet of fried chicken; these women had been eating mainly vegetables all their lives, and had looked to this period when their special status would be acknowledged by this special diet. (Mead 1955: 203)

Osgood (1963) supports that observation. After birth, he says, Chinese women were given an improved diet with pork, eggs, brown sugar, and chicken if the family could afford it. Vegetables were banned.

If sex-differential diets indeed have something to do with controlling numbers, then it might be predicted that societies passionately wanting to maintain or increase the size of their population would take special precautions to supplement rather than reduce diets. The literature surveyed provided only a few examples of traditional societies where the diets of pregnant and lactating women were purposely enriched. The Enga of New Guinea is an example. Among the Enga, a "society in biological decline," in which the lethal neurological disease, *kuru*, "decimates adult women" (Lindenbaum, 1972: 244). She notes:

Annual ceremonies are observed for the safety of children and pregnant women. Infants and future mothers eat special foods, and receive a share of the feast before other women and all men. The ceremonies are held if there is news of infant illness in surrounding areas, or at the beginning of the dry season, presumably a time of increased sickness. (idem)

The extreme rarity of this order of precedence is telling evidence of the main thesis of this discussion.

Statistical data on the prevalence of food taboos during pregnancy and lactation are as scarce and inconclusive as that dealing with social structure. For example, in Ford's (1945) sample of sixty-four societies, thirty-three societies had food proscriptions only during pregnancy, five had food taboos only during lactation, and five had proscriptions during both pregnancy and lactation. In general, among the great agrarian societies, pregnancy proscriptions seem to be imposed on top of a lifelong pattern of female deprivation.

Although quantitative data are scant, the ethnographic evidence suggests that special prescriptions designed to enrich the diets of pregnant and lactating women are associated with a desire to increase the population. Conclusions cannot be drawn about diet proscriptions for women of similar status. The restrictions imposed by the society could also be viewed by the group as being protective of women who had achieved a special status. Certainly, it can also be argued that the practice permitted men greater access to the food supply.

Discussion and Conclusions

The ecological and demographic effects of sex-differential nutrition are difficult to assess, especially for populations whose nutritional level is of borderline adequacy. Since men are generally larger, and engage in heavier physical labor, their caloric needs are greater than those of women. If the men do not have sufficient energy to do the work required to produce food or earn a living, everyone in the group may starve. Limiting the women's access to food, especially during the circum-childbirth period when their appetites may be large for nonnutritional reasons, may thus have positive survival value for the group. At the same time, if the men require more than their fair share of food simply to get through the work day, everyone else may suffer from nutritional impairment. As Gross and Underwood (1971) have shown for sisal growers in Brazil, the nutritional status of poor families may directly reflect the energy expended by husbands at work.

Providing a nutritional reserve for the male worker, to the jeopardy of his family, has clear detrimental consequences. Habitually malnourished females may be weaker, smaller, more lethargic, more disease prone, and shorter-lived than their husbands. All this clearly contributes to and justifies their inferior social status and mitigates against possible sexual equality. At the same time, the biological work of the female is the production and bearing of children—and it is the children who suffer most visibly from maternal food deprivation, both during the fetal period and during the nursing period, through the mother's reduced ability to produce milk.

To summarize the argument: Is there evidence of differential nutrition between the sexes? The answer is unequivocally yes. However, it is difficult to identify the specific values supporting the practice or to delineate the consequences of differential nutrition between the sexes. For some societies, the goal of population increase is implemented by supplementing women's diet. In most traditional societies, however, women's diets are inferior to the men's. These diet patterns are often sanctioned by religious beliefs and built into the prestige structure of the society. However, their real demographic and nutritional impact has not been ascertained.

Notes

1. However, even hunting groups which practice extreme segregation of labor, and in their eating patterns, may make allowances for special needs. Although "it seems to be certain that the differentiation of the activity field according to sex is a universal phenomenon among modern food gatherers" (Watanabe 1968: 75), among the East African Hadza, where 80 percent of the food is of vegetable origin, "only when more animals are caught than are needed to satisfy the appetites of the hunters are they brought back to camp" (Woodburn 1966: film narration), yet "meat should be shared with those who ask for it. In particular pregnant women have the right to eat meat belonging to everybody." (Woodburn 1968: 53)

2. In general, Kenyatta's text tends to mask the discrepancy in male and female dietary patterns. For example, when he writes "sheep and goats . . . are used for various religious sacrifices and purifications. They are the chief means of supplying the people with meat" (1935: 235), the reader remembers only with difficulty that this is a male-dominated gerontocracy and that by "the people" Kenyatta means the male elders.

References

American University
    1964   Area Handbook for India. Washington D. C.: U. S. Department of the Army. Pamphlet. 550-552.
Ayres, B. C.
    1967   Pregnancy Magic: A Study of Food Taboos and Sex Avoidances, A Comparative Study of Human Production. C. S. Ford, Ed. New Haven, Conn.: Human Relations Area Files Press.
Baxter, P. T. W. and A. Butt
    1953   The Azande, and Related Peoples. Ethnographic Survey of Africa, IX. London: International African Institute.
Beardsley, R. K., J. W. Hall and R. E. Ward
    1959   Village Japan. University of Chicago. Phoenix edition 1969.
Bohannon, P. and L. Bohannon
    1969   A Sourcebook on Tiv Religion. New Haven, Human Relations Area Files Press.
Brown, G.
    1910   Melamesians and Polynesians. London.
Brown, P.
    1972   The Chimbu, Cambridge, Mass.: Schenkman Publishing Co., Inc.
Burnett, J.
    1966   Plenty and Want. Harmondsworth, Middlesex, England: Penguin Pelican edition.
Deshler, W. W.
    1965   Native Cattle-Keeping in Eastern Africa, and Animals: Man, Culture, and Animals: The Role of Animals in Human Ecological Adjustments.

Publication No. 78 of the American Association for the Advancement of Science. A. Leeds and A. P. Vayda, eds.

Douglas, M.
  1966   Purity and Danger. Baltimore, Md.: Pelican Press.

DuBois, C.
  1944   The People of Alor. New York: Harper Torchbook edition 1961.

Dunn, F. J.
  1968   Epidemiological Factors: Health and Disease in Hunters and Gatherers. *In* Man the Hunter, R. B. Lee and I. DeVore, eds. Chicago: Aldine-Atherton Publishing Co., pp. 221-228.

Dyson-Hudson, K.
  1970   Food Production System of a Semi-normal Society: the Karamojong, Uganda. *In* African Food Production Systems. P. McLoughlin, ed. Baltimore, Md.: Johns Hopkins Press.

Ellis, R. W. R.
  1966   Child Health and Development. New York: Gruen and Stratton.

Ellis, W.
  1831   Polynesian Researches. London, 2nd ed. vol. I.

Fock, N.
  1967   South American Birth Customs in Theory and Practice. Cross-Cultured Approaches, C. S. Ford, ed. New Haven: Human Relations Area Files Press.

Ford, C. S.
  1945   A Comparative Study of Human Reproduction. Yale University Publications in Anthropology 32. New Haven: Human Relations Area Files Press reprint, 1964.
  1967   Cross-Cultural Approaches. New Haven: Human Relations Area Files Press.

Freuchen, P.
  1961   Book of the Eskimos. Fawcett edition 1965.

Geertz, C.
  1960   The Religion of Java. Free Press edition 1964.

Geertz, H.
  1961   The Javanese Family. Glencoe, Ill.: Free Press.

Goode, W.
  1963   World Revolution and Family Patterns. Free Press edition 1970.

Gourou, P.
  1961   The Tropical World. New York: John Wiley.

Greep, R. O.
  1963   Human Fertility and Population Problems. Cambridge, Mass.: Schenkman.

Griffis, W. E.
  1882   Corea: The Hermit Nation. New York: Charles Scribner's Sons.

Gross, D. R. and B. A. Underwood
  1971   Technological Change and Caloric Costs: Sisal Agriculture in Northeast Brazil. American Anthropologist 73: 725-740.

Gulliver, P. H.
  1955   The Family Herds. Westport, Conn.: Negro University Press edition 1970.

Hoagland, H.
  1966   Cybernetics of Population Control. Human Ecology. J. Bresler, ed. Reading, Mass.: Addison-Wesley.

Jensen, L. B.
  1953   Man's Foods. Champaign, Ill.: The Garrard Press.

Josephy, A.
1968   The Indian Heritage of America. New York: Alfred A. Knopf.
Kapadia, K. M.
1966   Marriage and Family in India, 3rd ed. London: Oxford University Press.
Keir, R. M.
1914   Modern Korea. Bulletin of the American Geographical Society (New York), vol. XLVI.
Kenyatta, J.
1935   Facing Mt. Kenya. Vintage edition 1962.
Lang, O.
1946   Chinese Family and Society. New Haven: Yale University Press.
Leary, J. R.
1961   A Cross-Cultural Study of Protein Consumption: the Role of Cultural Taboos in the Differential Use of Animal Protein in a Sample of 100 Societies, unpublished manuscript, New Haven: Human Relations Area Files, H. 100.
Lee, R.
1968   What Hunters Do for a Living . . . . R. B. Lee and I. DeVore, eds.
Levine, D. N.
1965   Wax and Gold. University of Chicago edition 1972.
Lindenbaum, S.
1972   Sorcerers, Ghosts and Polluting Women: an Analysis of Religious Belief and Population Control. Ethnology, XI.
Lisiansky, U.
1814   A Voyage Round the World. London.
Lorimer, F.
1954   Culture and Human Fertility. F. Lorimer, ed. Paris, UNESCO.
Mace, D. and V. Mace
1959   Marriage East and West. Garden City, New York: Doubleday Dolphin Press.
MacGillivray, J.
1852   Narrative of the Voyage of the H. M. S. Rattlesnake. London.
Man, E. H.
1883   Aboriginal Inhabitants of the Andaman Islands.
May, J.
1961   The Ecology of Malnutrition in the Far and Near East. New York: Hafner Press with the American Geographical Society.
May, J. and D. McLellan
1973   The Ecology of Malnutrition in the Caribbean. New York: Hafner Press with the American Geographical Society.
McLoughlin, P.
1970   African Food Production Systems. Baltimore: Ed., Johns Hopkins Press.
Mead, M.
1955   Cultural Patterns and Technical Change. New York: Mentor Books.
Middleton, J.
1953   The Central Tribes of North East Bantu. Ethnographic Survey of Africa, part V. London: International African Institute.
Montagu, M. F. A.
1972   Sociogenic Brain Damage. American Anthropologist, October.
Moore, F. W.
1970   Food Habits in Non-Industrial Societies. Dimensions of Nutrition. Boulder: University of Colorado Press. pp. 181-221.
Mukherjee, R.
1958   Six Villages of Bengal. J. Asiatic Society (Calcutta), XXIV, 1 and 2.

Mussey, R. D.
    1949   Nutrition and Human Reproduction: An Historical Review. American
    Journal of Obstetrics and Gynecology, 57: 6, June.
Nag, M.
    1962   Factors Affecting Human Fertility in Non-Industrial Societies: A
    Cross-Cultural Study. New Haven: Yale University Publications in Anthro-
    pology No. 66. Human Relations Area Files Reprint 1968.
National Academy of Sciences
    1970   Maternal Nutrition and the Course of Pregnancy. Washington, D. C.
Nieboer, H.
    1900   Slavery as an Industrial System. The Hague, Martinus Nijhoff.
Orr, J. B. and J. L. Gilks
    1931   Studies of Nutrition: The Physique and Health of Two African Tribes.
    Great Britain Medical Research Council, Special Report Series no. 155.
    London, H. M. S. O.
Osgood, C.
    1963   Village Life in Old China. New York: Ronald Press.
Powdermaker, H.
    1932   Feasts in New Ireland: The Social Functions of Eating. American
    Anthropologist 34.
    1933   Life in Lesu. Norton Library edition 1971.
Radcliffe-Brown, A. B.
    1922   The Andaman Islanders. New York: Free Press edition 1964.
Richards, A.
    1939   Land, Labour and Diet in Northern Rhodesia. London: Oxford
    University Press.
Robson, J. R. K.
    1972   Malnutrition: Its Causation and Control. New York: Gordon and
    Breach Publishers.
Routledge, W. S. and K. Routledge
    1910   With a Prehistoric People: the Akikuyu of British East Africa. London:
    Edward Arnold.
Saucier, J.-F.
    1972   Correlates of the Long Postpartum Taboo: a Cross-Cultural Study.
    Current Anthropology 13.
Sen Gunto, S.
    1970   A Study of the Women of Bengal. Calcutta: Indian Publications.
Simoons, F. J.
    1967   Eat Not This Flesh. Madison: University of Wisconsin Press.
Stare, F. J. and M. McWilliams
    1973   Living Nutrition. New York: John Wiley.
Textor, R. B.
    1967   A Cross-Cultural Summary. New Haven: Human Relations Area Files
    Press.
Trant, H.
    1954   Food Taboos in East Africa. Lancet (London), 2 October.
Watanabe, H.
    1968   Subsistence and Ecology of Northern Food Gatherers. R. B. Lee and I.
    DeVore, eds. Chicago: Aldine-Atherton Publishing Co., pp. 69-77.
Webster, H.
    1942   Taboo: a Sociological Study. Stanford University Press.
Whiting, M. G.
    1958   A Cross-Cultural Nutrition Survey of 118 Societies Representing the
    Major Cultural Areas of the World. D. Sc. Thesis, Harvard University School of
    Public Health, Boston.

Wilson, M.
    1951   Good Company. Boston: Beacon Press.
Woodburn, J.
    1966   The Hadza (film).
    1968   An Introduction to Hadza Ecology. *In* Man the Hunter. R. B. Lee and I.
    DeVore, eds. Chicago: Aldine Publishing Co. pp. 49-55.
Yang, M.
    1945   A Chinese Village. New York: Columbia edition 1965.

8

Nutritional Correlates of Economic Microdifferentiation in a Highland Mexican Community

K. M. DeWalt
P. B. Kelly
G. H. Pelto

The purpose of this paper is to examine dietary patterns in a mixed Indian-Mestizo agricultural village in central Mexico. Variations in food use among households in the *ejido* community of Puerto de las Piedras are demonstrably related to social, economic and cultural variables, especially differences in economic means. Micro-economic differentiation, often not particularly apparent to outsiders, may have long-term effects on people's health, nutrition and fertility. These small-scale differentials in access to resources also affect programs of planned change. The examination of these issues requires detailed data from samples of households in order to analyze the covariations in economic resources, food use and other characteristics. The data for this study were collected during fieldwork in 1973.[1]

Food Use Research in Anthropology

In the past, anthropological investigation of nutritional issues focused primarily on cultural beliefs about food (e. g., Adams 1952, 1959; Currier 1966; Wilson 1971, 1973; Walter 1973. See also Bonfil 1966). The assumption underlying a number of anthropological studies (of the 1940s and 1950s) was that non-Western cultural beliefs about food were major obstacles to the establishment of sound nutritional habits (e. g., Adams 1952, 1959; Cassel 1955; Jelliffe 1957). Thus, nutrition programs sought to change food habits by introducing new foods and educating people to "Western" principles of nutrition.

Anthropological studies in health and nutrition in Latin America have put heavy emphasis on cultural beliefs, such as the humoral system which classifies foods, herbs, illnesses and situations as "hot" or "cold." In most cases, researchers have assumed that beliefs like the hot/cold classification scheme have important causal effects with respect to nutritional problems and are therefore the most important factors to investigate. Although the 2.5 percent of rural Mexican children who develop severe cases of malnutrition generally come from the *poorest* segments of the rural poor, many attempts to ameliorate the nutritional state of the Mexican child have called attention to the "lack of cultural resources" of their mothers, mothers' erroneous beliefs about proper feeding and "magical" ideas about the origins of illness (Perez, Hidalgo, Chavez and Madrigal 1970; Cravioto 1958). Many health programs in the Third World have centered on efforts to educate mothers, apparently because of the assumption that food use patterns are heavily determined by cultural beliefs.

In addition to assuming that beliefs are the primary forces, most anthropological studies concerning food use have assumed homogeneity of food use in particular cultural groups. Variation in food use and nutritional status *within* groups has been largely ignored. Ethnographers tend to report a "typical diet," including a list of common foods. Usually little attention is given to the place of these foods in the diet or to individual and familial variations in consumption. An exception to this tendency is Oscar Lewis (1951), who outlined the diets of two Tepoztecan families, documenting differences in the complexity of their diets as well as quantities of food consumed. At the same time, however, he emphasized the underlying homogeneity of food consumption. On the other hand, several authors (e. g., Hernandez et al. 1975; Jerome, this volume; Beaudry-Darisme et al. 1972; Chassey et al. 1967) have documented wide variation in dietary patterns. These studies involve situations of rapid modernization and industrialization, and variations in diet are therefore attributed to acculturative processes.

It is our contention that dietary homogeneity and the assumption that food practices are the result of food beliefs should be regarded as hypotheses. Pilot investigations in a Mexican town (DeWalt 1971; DeWalt and Pelto 1977) indicate that reported consumption of particular foods has little relationship to beliefs about the flavorfulness or the healthfulness of the foods. Particularly striking, for example, is the extent to which meat and fish may be considered delicious and healthful, yet are rarely consumed in most households. In this paper we will explore some of the constraints and forces that appear to have significant effects on intra-group differences in eating habits in a small Mexican village.

The Research Community

El Puerto de las Piedras,[2] with a population of about 1,300, is located in the northwest part of the state of Mexico, about 100 miles from Mexico City. The community is located on a hillside a kilometer from the municipal center of the valley, a town of some 33,000 people. The people of El Puerto are primarily agriculturalists. Half of the families have access to cooperative (ejido) land on the fertile valley floor. Some families in the village own their own land or rent privately-owned land. Persons with no access to farm land work as wage laborers on the large farms of wealthy townspeople. A few make their living, or add to agricultural incomes, by working as stone cutters, masons, weavers, and vendors.

A generation ago the inhabitants of the community were mostly identifiable as Mazahua Indians. Since the construction of a road nearly forty years ago, the community has lost much of its Indian character. While many older people can still speak the Mazahua

language, most younger people speak only Spanish. Except for the
recent introduction of the seed drill, methods of agriculture have
remained fairly traditional. Plowing is done with ox-drawn plows,
planting with seed drill or digging stick, and harvesting is carried
out by hand. The agriculturalists of Puerto de las Piedras mainly
produce maize corn. The corn is used for home consumption and is
sold when families need cash. A few individuals grow forage crops,
which they use to feed their own animals or to sell to others. In
addition to corn, a minority of farmers sow beans and squash. The
production of squash and beans is relatively unusual at the present
time, although it was common in the past. Many families keep
animals. Some have a cow or two; several have sheep or goats.
Several families keep horses for plowing and cultivating. Most
families have a few chickens or turkeys, and two enterprising
families have begun to raise rabbits for home consumption.

Many food items, clothing and goods are purchased in the town
center, a twenty-minute walk from the village. On market day
almost every family sends at least one member to town to do the
weekly marketing. Foods and goods from all over Mexico are
offered for sale there. Fruits and vegetables including mangoes,
oranges, bananas, avocados, lettuce, tomatoes, carrots, cauliflower
and many others are available in season. Vendors sell barbecued
mutton and goat, tripe soup, *carnitas* (boiled pork), and smoked
fish. In addition, the local butchers do a tremendous business on
market day, selling the bulk of the beef, pork, and poultry that they
offer each week. Staples, such as beans, rice, pasta, oil, sugar, and
salt, are usually purchased in the shops on market day, as well.

The people of Puerto de las Piedras are poor.[3] The typical home is
a one or two room *adobe* dwelling with a dirt floor. Many homes
have no furnishings at all; others have a table or small chair. About
64 percent of the families have at least one bed, but in many
households the family members sleep on straw mats (*petates*) on
the floor. Cooking is usually over a wood fire. In the poorest homes
the fire is built on the floor, although many homes have a hearth
built up to waist height with *adobe*. A very few homes have oil or
gas stoves.

Superficially, there appears to be little economic stratification
within the community. On closer inspection, however, there are
differences, including differences in the number and types of
goods owned. In a peasant community such as Puerto de las Piedras
income data is difficult to obtain and usually unreliable. In order to

ascertain differences in economic standing, we inventoried a number of commodities and household goods of village families. From the household inventories we constructed an index that measures relative economic wealth. This "material style of life" scale (M.S.L.) correlates well with other economic indicators, such as estimates of income, number of animals owned, and key informants' rating of the relative wealth of their fellow villagers (cf. B.R. DeWalt, 1979). From this scale (Table I) we can see that there are actually quite important differences among families. The economic microdifferentiation stems from household differences in number of workers, amount and quality of land, health and strength of family workers, and other short-term and long-term factors.

Family Diets in Puerto de las Piedras

Corn, mainly home grown, and beans, mainly purchased from the market, are the two most important staples in villagers' diets. Most corn is consumed in the form of *tortillas*, although some is made into a thin gruel, *atole*, which is regarded as a beverage. In our interviews we asked women about the number of kilos of corn they had taken to the mill to be ground during the week preceding the interview. This is relatively easy for women to estimate since they pay for the milling process according to the number of *cuartillos* (1.5 kilos) of corn they have ground. Most women bring a fixed number of *cuartillos* to the mill very other day.

To obtain data on consumption of beans, meat, milk, and eggs, we asked women about the amounts of these items they had purchased at the market the preceding week. As with corn, the amounts purchased are usually easily remembered, for marketing tends to be a structured and significant event. The least reliable estimate is probably the amount of beans used, but only for those families who grow their own. In this minority of cases, the quantity of beans consumed that week had to be estimated by the female household head.

In order to get a rough measure of the average quantity of corn an individual consumes daily, we used the figure for the total weekly household consumption, divided by seven and divided again by the number of people in the household. Recognizing that this estimate is subject to error since adult males eat more than

TABLE I   GUTTMAN SCALE OF MATERIAL STYLE OF LIFE

Household	Scale Type	I	II	III	IV	V	VI	VII	VIII
025	1								
047	1								
003	2	X							
005	2	X							
014	2	X							
021	2	X							
024	2	X							
038	2	X							
010	2	X			X				
037	3	0	X						
001	3	X	X						
007	3	X	X						
016	3	X	X						
020	3	X	X						
026	3	X	X						
028	3	X	X						
029	3	X	X						
040	3	X	X						
041	3	X	X						
043	3	X	X						
002	4	X	0	X					
008	4	X	0	X					
045	4	0	X	X					
027	4	X	X	X					
030	4	X	X	X					
033	4	X	X	X					
039	4	X	X	X					
042	4	X	X	X					
044	4	X	X	X					
046	4	X	X	X					
051	4	X	X	X					
052	4	X	X	X					
056	4	X	X	X			X		
018	5	X	0	X	X				
019	5	X	X	0	X				
048	5	X	X	X	X				
032	5	X	X	X	X				
050	5	X	X	X	X				
049	5	X	X	X	X			X	
013	6	X	X	X	X	X			
012	6	X	X	X	X	X			X
006	6	X	0	X	0	X			
011	6	X	X	X	0	X			
015	7	X	X	X	X	X	X		
035	7	X	X	X	X	X	X		
004	7	X	X	X	0	X	X		
031	7	X	X	X	0	X	X		
036	7	X	X	X	X	0	X		
034	8	X	X	X	X	X	X	X	
009	8	X	X	X	X	0	X	X	
061	8	X	X	X	X	0	X	X	
055	9	X	X	X	X	X	X	0	X
017	9	X	0	X	X	X	0	X	X
058	9	X	X	X	X	X	0	X	X
023	9	X	X	X	X	X	X	X	X
057	9	X	X	X	X	X	X	X	X
054	9	X	X	X	X	X	X	X	X

ITEMS:

    I. Iron (electric and non-electric)   V. Sewing Machine
    II. Radio   VI. Wardrobe
    III. Bed   VII. Stove
    IV. Cooking facilities off the floor   VIII. Television

Coefficient of reproducibility $1 - \frac{22}{456} = .95$;   Mean = 4.7;   Standard deviation = 2.3.

women and children, the figure is *not* intended as an indicator of nutritional status. However, it is useful for comparative purposes since it provides an estimate of the amount of food distributed within each household. For example, if two families consume the same total quantity of corn in a week, but one household has ten members, while the other has three, individuals in the second household will almost certainly have more corn to eat than those in the first, regardless of age or sex. A similar procedure was used to obtain estimates for average consumption of beans, meat, eggs, and milk.

Two additional measures of food consumption patterns help to fill out the picture of differential food used in Puerto de las Piedras. From the data on the three-day recall of meals (obtained from the female head of household), we constructed two indices of dietary complexity. The first index (DC I) measures the total number of *different* food items consumed. In this scale, then, a food item is counted only once regardless of the number of times it was used during the three days. Scores on this index ranged from 6 to 11.

The second index (DC II) is the sum of all the different foods used by a household on each of the three days for which we have meal-plan data. It was constructed by scoring the number of different items used on each of three days. (If a particular item was used twice on the same day, it was counted only once, but if it was used on two different days, it was counted twice.) The household score is the total for the three days. In contrast with the first scale, it takes into consideration day-to-day variations. As with the average food consumption estimate, these scales do not measure nutritional adequacy, as such. However, inspection of the items suggests that the more complex diets probably contain more of the essential nutrients than do the more restricted ones.

Food Use and Economic Differentiation

Analysis of the food use data reveals large differences in the quantities and types of food consumed in the households of Puerto de las Piedras. The diets are far from homogeneous, and there are clearly quite different food use patterns within the community. The main question we want to address with our data is: how are these differences related to microeconomic variations? To examine this question, we calculated the average (individual) consumption of corn, beans, meat, milk, and eggs for our sample of sixty-two families, dividing them into quartiles based on M.S.L. scores. That is, we used the M.S.L. scale as the measure of microeconomic differentiation, in terms of which food consumption was examined. Table II shows the consumption averages for the four socio-economic categories. We also calculated correlation coefficients between consumption and M.S.L. scale score, and the results are shown in Table III.

As can be seen from the results in Tables II and III, there is a clear relationship between socioeconomic status and food intake, which is especially apparent in the contrast between the highest and

TABLE II

FOOD CONSUMPTION AVERAGES FOR THE SOCIO-ECONOMIC GROUPS

Socio-economic Groups	Corn (gms.)	Beans (gms.)	Meat & Poultry (gms.)	Eggs	Milk (ml.)
I	587	48	1.7	.2	7
II	690	32	2.7	.4	18
III	596	15	2.5	.3	18
IV	423	39	7.0	.7	28

TABLE III

PEARSON'S CORRELATIONS BETWEEN FOOD USE

AND MATERIAL STYLE OF LIFE

	Corn	Beans	Meat	Milk	Egg	DC I
M.S.L.	.20	.11	.59*	.39*	.36*	.37*

*Statistically significant at or below the .01 level.

lowest quartiles. For example, people in the lowest economic bracket have, on the average, 587 gms. per person of corn per day, which alone provides 2113 Kcals. of energy and 55 gms. of protein. Compared to the highest group, they get relatively little protein from animal sources (meat, eggs, and milk). On the other hand, the people with the highest material style of life in the village eat considerably less corn, and more than three times as much meat, on the average. Households in the second quartile (M.S.L. Level 2 in Table II) appear to be consuming more of everything (except beans) than their somewhat less fortunate neighbors. They have the highest per capita corn consumption, eat twice as many eggs, more meat and more milk than families in the first quartile. More surprising are the figures for the third (next to highest group), for they report eating less meat, less corn and less beans, than those in the next lowest group! We hypothesize that for these households, their somewhat higher standard of living may be bought at the expense of better nutrition, for this group is apparently spending less for food and more for other material items.

In general, the figures on bean consumption are quite low for the entire sample, lower than those reported for other areas of Mexico. Many families are substituting unenriched macaroni for beans, and women were reporting a much higher use of macaroni (*sopa*)[4] than we had anticipated. From key informant interviews we learned that the substitution of *sopa* for beans is a recent change. There are several reasons for this shift: (1) fewer people sow beans than was formerly the case, in part because the government development programs have stressed the cultivation of improved varieties of corn or forage crops, but not legumes; (2) the area has been invaded by insect pests that attack beans with devastating results, and (3) the cost of beans has risen very sharply in recent years, while macaroni has remained an inexpensive food item. A fourth factor, perhaps the most important, is the result of a more indirect cost. The hills around the community have become badly deforested, and people must travel long distances (as much as half a day) to collect firewood. Beans are slow-cooking and require a lot of wood. *Sopa*, however, cooks more quickly and therefore precious firewood is conserved on days when this food is used rather than beans. Women tended to stress this latter point in discussing the shift from beans to *sopa*.

Nutritionally *sopa* is inferior to beans. The protein content is lower, and it does not complement the protein derived from corn, as do beans. Since it is made from unenriched white wheat flour, it is also lower in vitamins than beans. The women in Puerto de las Piedras maintain that it is also less satisfying. They point out that one is hungry again shortly after eating a meal of *sopa*.

While the consumption of meat, milk, and eggs increases fairly steadily with an increase in M.S.L. status, it is clear that the largest increases occur in the highest group. At this level families are clearly substituting signficant amounts of other food for the corn used by families in lower levels. This is most clearly shown in the relationship between M.S.L. scale scores and scores on the Dietary Complexity indices. As can be seen in Table IV, the more well-off families are using a greater variety of foods in their diets.

TABLE IV

DIET COMPLEXITY SCORES FOR FOUR SOCIOECONOMIC GROUPS

	DC I	DC II
I	5.3	10.1
II	7.2	11.8
III	6.1	12.1
IV	11.0	14.6

Dietary Patterns of Three Village Families

Three households selected from the sample population illustrate the relationships delineated in the statistical analysis and help to provide the context for interpreting our findings. We've picked cases that represent different levels of economic status in the community. However, it should be recognized that these families are only broadly representative of families in the same general economic situation, and within each "group" there are also many differences.

Pedro and Felipa
Pedro and Felipa live in a dirt-floored *adobe* house, with three of their seven children. The older children have migrated to the city

or live nearby with their spouses. Pedro's share of *ejido* land is about average for the village, but the land is poor. When he can, he works as a day laborer for other small agriculturalists, from which he earns about $1.50 (U.S.) a day. The family is not the poorest in the community, but they are not well-off. Their economic status is reflected in their low M.S.L. score (scale type 2, in the lowest quartile).

Pedro and Felipa usually produce enough corn to meet their family's needs, but with little extra left to sell. They sow beans, although their harvest is often poor, and they buy most of the beans they consume. They own three hens and a rooster. The hens produce eggs, which are not eaten since the family is trying to start a flock. The hens are allowed to brood the eggs. At the time of the research, they had just purchased a pair of rabbits and had hopes of raising rabbits for food.

Senora Felipa buys one-fourth liter of milk nearly every day. She used sixteen kilos of corn and bought one and one-half kilos of beans the week of the interview. She also bought a chicken that the family ate early in the week. She bought six eggs that were eaten on one day (see below). Her other food purchases for the week were 200 gms. of *charales* (small, dried fish); a box of oatmeal; one kilo of sugar; one-half K. of bananas; one-fourth K. of chiles; one-half K. of tomatoes, and one K. of potatoes. When asked what she would purchase if she had more money to spend on food, Felipa replied she would like to buy more beans and *sopa*, as well as oil for cooking.

The three-day meal-plan for the Pedro/Felipa household was:

	Day One	Day Two	Day Three
First Meal:	Atole de arroz*	Atole de maizena[+]	Rice, tortillas & salsa[#]
Second Meal:	Eggs, scrambled with tomato and chile; tortillas and salsa	Potatoes with charales; tortillas & salsa	Rice with tomatoes, tortillas & salsa
Third Meal:	Tortillas & salsa, with leftover eggs	Leftover potato dish; tortillas and salsa	Tortillas & salsa

* a thick drink made from rice flour and milk

+ a thick drink made with corn starch and milk

the standard accompaniment for tortillas, a sauce made from chilis, tomatoes, onion and salt

Juan and Sara

Juan and Sara live in a new cement house close to their fields. They have moved from the village center to be closer to their land. Their house is very small, but only two of their eight children still live at home. Among their possessions two important items are a sewing machine and a farm cart. Sara earns some money by sewing, and an unmarried son in the army sends a small amount of money home every month. Their economic status is intermediate for Puerto de las Piedras (Scale type seven, on the material style of life index, the third quartile).

Juan is a careful cultivator and gets above average yields. He also has more land than the average *ejidatario*. The family produces all the corn they need, with some left over to sell. They also produce enough beans to meet their needs, and they grow a small amount of squash. Sara considers their food crops to be a kind of insurance and says that even if they had no money to buy food, they would always have beans and tortillas. Sara has a friend in another part of the valley who occasionally gives her wheat. She grinds the wheat, along with the corn/lime mixture used to make tortillas, and makes corn-wheat tortillas, a special treat. (She is the only woman we know of who does this in Puerto de las Piedras, although it is more common in wheat-growing areas of the valley.)

During the time of our study, Juan and Sara purchased several *maguey* (Agave sp.). In many parts of Mexico the sap of this plant (called *aquamiel*) is collected and made into a nutritious and moderately alcoholic beverage, *pulque*. Sara began to gather the *aquamiel* and ferment it for their own consumption. Juan drinks about three to four liters of *pulque* a day and Sara about a liter. Their extra *pulque* is sold to fellow villagers. The family also raises chickens, producing about thirty-five eggs a week. They eat the cockrels and approximately half of the eggs. Sara also adds to the family diet by gathering wild greens from the fields and hills.

Senora Sara estimates that she spends about $8.00 (U.S.) per week on food, in addition to what they grow themselves. She buys a liter of milk a day. She used nine kilos of corn and three kilos of beans during the week of the interview. In addition to one-half kilo of pork rind (which has practically no meat on it), she purchased a half a kilo of lean beef at the market. She also bought a kilo of tomatoes, three kilos of macaroni, a liter of oil, a box of oatmeal, one-half kilo of rice, a jar of chicken boullion, and two kilos of sugar. Some of these items were intended for use over a two to three week period.

If she had more money to spend Sara said that she would buy vegetables, for she feels that the family does not eat enough vegetables.

During the three days for which we have detailed data, Sara prepared the following meals for her family:

	Day One	Day Two	Day Three
First Meal:	Oatmeal with milk	Coffee with milk, beans and tortillas & salsa	Coffee with milk, beans, tortillas & salsa
Second Meal:	Broad bean soup; fried pork rind with green chilis; tortillas & salsa	Sopa; fried pork rind; beans, tortillas & salsa	Sopa; green squash sauted with spices; tortillas & salsa
Third Meal:	Coffee; tortillas & salsa	Coffee; tortillas & salsa	Coffee; tortillas & salsa

Marcos and Juana

Marcos and Juana live in a large adobe house with a stone floor. A married daughter and her child live with them, as well as four of their younger children. The family is well off by community standards. They enjoy the luxury of a gas stove and a television set. Their living standard is reflected in a high score (scale type nine, the fourth quartile) on the material style of life index.

In part, their higher living standard is due to the fact that they have more land than the average *ejidatario*. Marcos adds considerably to the family income by buying and selling animals for a profit. In addition to growing corn for home consumption (and for sale), they grow squash, tomatoes, and chard. They have twelve fruit trees, which yield more than enough for their family. They give the excess fruit away.

Senora Juana estimates that she spends $48 (U. S.) a week to feed her family of eight. She buys a kilo of meat a day; two liters of milk each day; and about eighteen eggs per week. In addition to tomatoes, chiles, rice, oil, *sopa*, and sugar, she purchased candy, wheat flour and guayava at the market during the week of the interview. When queried about what foods she would buy if she had more money to spend, Juana replied that she felt their food was adequate and that she would spend extra money on household goods, such as furniture, rather than food.

The three-day menu for Marcos/Juana's family was:

	Day One	Day Two	Day Three
First Meal:	(Unknown)	Beans, coffee, tortillas & salsa	Chicken with mole; coffee, tortillas & salsa
Second Meal:	Beef stew with vegetables; sopa; tortillas & salsa; beans	Chicken with mole* rice; beans; tortillas & salsa	Pork with nopales[+], sopa; beans, tortillas and salsa
Third Meal:	Coffee & leftovers	Coffee with milk	Coffee with milk

* A rich sauce made from chiles, chocolate and spices

+ Tender, young leaves of the opuntia cactus, with a consistency, when cooked, like okra

Discussion and Conclusions

A major focus in this paper is the importance of variations within one small, economically marginal Mexican community. From the point of view of urban people, the hundreds of small agricultural villages in rural Mexico seem very uniform in their poverty and the simplicity of life-styles, including diet. Yet underlying the seeming homogeneity are some very real differences—variations that make the difference between adequate nutrition and health-threatening deprivation. Nutritional researchers and anthropologists have often ignored such "micro" variations, for several theoretical reasons.

In examining the patterns of variation within Puerto de las Piedras, we find that a major point of interest is the way in which economic resource control, as measured by "material style of life," is an important predictor of dietary variation. That is, households in the highest economic group show much greater complexity in their diets and obtain protein from a greater variety of sources than do the families with less access to economic resources. We should note that these variations are found in an agricultural context in which land reforms, purchased by a costly and bloody revolution, were supposed to insure that within a given agricultural community, families would have equal access to production land. Access to land is not, in fact, equal (DeWalt, B. R. 1979). In many other ways, too, the households are quite different in resources.

A second point, linked to the first, is that the differences in diets of families suggest that "traditional beliefs" and "food attitudes" are not the major stumbling blocks to adequate nutrition among these people. In related research in the same valley area (DeWalt and Pelto, 1977), we found that people's ratings of food "tastiness" and "healthiness" tended strongly to favor the more nutritious foods—even though respondents were well aware that they frequently could not afford them. The people of Puerto de las Piedras are clearly not deterred from changing their diets, as the substitution of *sopa* for the more "traditional" beans demonstrates. In this case, the change appears to reflect economic factors, to the detriment of good nutrition.

Our data suggest that a strong emphasis on teaching modern nutritional ideas is not likely to produce much in the way of useful results in communities in these situations, especially if economic conditions remain unchanged. However, some economic development programs in the area may be unwittingly contributing to a further decline of nutritional status of the poorer families. Not only do agricultural "improvement programs" tend to work to the advantage of the already better-off families much of the time (DeWalt, 1979; see also Bernard and Pelto, 1972), but the widespread use of herbicides and heavy weeding in connection with agricultural projects may have effects on the availability of wild greens, an important but usually unnoticed food resource, as has been pointed out by Messer (1972). The wild greens grow in disturbed soils, in areas close to or directly among crops, but they are considered "weeds" by agricultural agents. In addition, development projects, which push for redirection of efforts away from corn production to cash crops, can work to the detriment of household food adequacy.

We do not argue that all the intracultural variation in food use in the community is due to direct economic factors. Certainly attitudes, along with many other factors, also play a part in the picture there as in other economically marginal populations. But these materials indicate that the microdifferentiation of economic resources, even in seemingly homogeneous communities, must be taken strongly into account in connection with nutrition plans and programs, as well as in projects aimed at improved health and well-being.

Notes

1. The data to be presented here are the results of eleven months of field work carried out in 1973 by Kathleen DeWalt in the community of Puerto de las Piedras. The researcher carried out extensive open-ended interviewing with a number of key informants concerning food use and health practices. During this time it was also possible to observe meal preparation and consumption including snacking as well as the interaction among parents (usually mothers), children and food. To insure a well-rounded representation of the community, however, a more structured interview was conducted with the male and female household heads of a randomly selected sample of families with access to *ejidal* land. Data from these interviews form the basis of the numerical analysis to be presented here.

2. Pseudonyms are used here for the village and individuals in order to protect to some extent the anonymity of informants.

3. While it is true that the people of El Puerto are poor by any standards, they do not represent the lowest end of the economic continuum. In fact, several isolated communities within the *municipio* of Temascalcingo have significantly fewer resources and the people of these communities are poorer than those of El Puerto. While instances of frank protein/energy malnutrition are rare or absent from El Puerto, deaths from kwashiorkor have been reported from several other villages.

4. In this study data on the amounts of wheaten products—in this community mainly *sopa*—are not included. A preliminary look at the use of *sopa* and other wheat products suggests that these foods are used by all socioeconomic groups in the community, and further that there is a small positive correlation between M. S. L. and use of *sopa* and bread.

References

Adams, R. N.
    1952   Un Analysis de la Creencias y Practicos Medicos en un Pueblo Indigena de Guatemala. Boletin Especial del Inst. Indigenista Nacional 17. Guatemala City.
    1959   Un Programa de Investigaciones Sobre Nutricion en Guatemala. Cultura Indigena de Guatemala. Seminario de Integracion Social de Guatemala.
Beaudry-Darisme, Micheline N., Lesly C. Hayes-Blend and A. G. Van Veen
    1972   The Application of Sociological Research Methods to Food and Nutrition Problems on a Caribbean Island. Ecology of Food and Nutrition I (2): 103.
Bernard, H. Russell and Pertti J. Pelto
    1972   Technology and Social Change. New York: MacMillan.
Bonfil Batalla, Guillermo
    1966   Conservative Thought in Applied Anthropology: A Critique. Human Organization 25: 89-92.
Cassel, John
    1955   A Comprehensive Health Program Among the South African Zulus. *In* Health, Culture, and Community, B. Paul, Ed. New York: Russell Sage Foundation.
Chassey, T. P., A. G. Van Veen, and F. W. Young
    1967   The Application of Social Science Research Methods to the Study of Food Habits and Food Consumption in an Industrializing Area. American Journal of Clinical Nutrition 20: 56.

Cravioto, Joaquin
    1958   Consideraciones Epidemiologicas y Bases Para la Formulacion de un
    Programa de Prevencion de la Desnutricion. Bol. Hosp. Inf. Mex. 15: 925-935.
Currier, Richard
    1966   The Hot-Cold Syndrome and Symbolic Balance in Mexican and
    Spanish-American Folk Medicine. Ethnology 5, 251-263.
DeWalt, Billie R.
    1979   Modernization in a Mexican Ejido. New York: Cambridge University
    Press.
DeWalt, Kathleen
    1971   Preliminary Investigation of the Effects of a Home Improvement and`
    Nutritional Change Program. Paper read at Northeastern Anthropological
    Association Meetings. April, 1971.
DeWalt, Kathleen and Gretel Pelto
    1977   Food Use and Household Ecology in a Mexican Community. In T.
    Fitzgerald, ed., Nutrition and Anthropology in Action. The Hague: Van
    Gorcum.
Hernandez, Mercedes, Carlos Perez Hidalgo, Juan Romirez Hernandez, Herlindo
Madrigal and Adolfo Chavez
    1974   Effect of Economic Growth on Nutrition in a Tropical Community.
    Ecology of Food and Nutrition 3 (4): 283.
Jelliffe, Derrick
    1957   Social Culture and Nutrition Cultural Blocks and Protein Malnutrition
    in Early Childhood in Rural West Bengal. Pediatrics 20: 128-138.
Jerome, N. W.
    1979   Diet and Acculturation: The Case of Black American In-Migrants. (This
    volume).
Lewis, Oscar
    1951   Life in a Mexican Village: Tepoztlán Restudied. Urbana: University of
    Illinois Press.
Messer, Ellen
    1972   Patterns of Wild Plant Consumption in Oaxaca Mexico. Ecology of
    Food and Nutrition 1: 325-332.
Perez Hidalgo, C., A. Chavez, and C. Martinez
    1969   Metodologia Simplificada de Encuestas Nutricionales. Salud Publica
    de Mexico 11: 223-238.
Wilson, C. S.
    1971   Food Beliefs Affect Nutritional Status of Malay Fisherfolk. Journal of
    Nutritional Education 2: 96-98.
    1973   Food Taboos of Childbirth: The Malay Example. Ecology of Food and
    Nutrition 2 (4): 267.
Walter, John P.
    1973   Internal-External Poverty and Nutritional Determinates of Urban Slum
    Youth. Ecology of Food and Nutrition 2: 3-10.

9

Factors Associated with Malnutrition in the Children of Western Jamaica

In: NA? Conle...

T. J. Marchione

Introduction

The problem of malnutrition, especially under-nutrition of young children in the Third World, has become a matter of urgent concern in the world today. Famines, though of tragic conse-quence, are limited in scope compared to the much more widespread under-nutrition which forms a daily pattern of death, disease, and general human misery even in relatively affluent countries. Unfortunately, explanations of how and why serious under-nutrition can exist in countries not experiencing famine tend to be either oversimplified, or unnecessarily complex. Explana-tion is confined either to broad, qualitative, macroscopic critique of the social structural background of economic exploitation (Stone, 1974), or to complexes of microscopic cultural, social,

economic and other etiological "factors" impinging on the malnourished child (Jelliffe, 1969). In practice, the first type of analysis
is often merely polemical and lacks empirical scientific basis. The
second is often short-sighted, descriptive of only a few correlations,
and generally evasive of underlying sociopolitical conditions in the
society.

To bridge the explanatory impasse requires that either social
structural elements be identified and operationalized, so they can
be seen to relate to the actual household circumstances that cause
malnutrition; or more general factors must be constructed from
correlations linking malnutrition to household variables, such that
household conditions can be viewed in the context of the structure
of the society. This chapter represents an attempt to do the latter
through the use of factor analysis.

Jamaica is certainly not one of those countries faced with
overwhelming malnutrition problems.[1] But nutritional deficiency
is perhaps the major public health problem affecting young
children. In the early 1970s, major consequences of malnutrition
were reported to be child death, morbidity and possibly mental and
behavioral retardation (Puffer, 1973; Ashworth and Picon, 1974;
Richardson, 1972). Recent efforts by the Jamaican government to
combat these problems through policy and programs suffer from a
lack of empirically based and useful theory on the social etiology of
malnutrition. As a result, untested assumptions often form the basis
of costly nutrition improvement programs.

One such effort is the island-wide "Community Health Aide
Programme" initiated in 1973 by the newly-elected Government of
Jamaica. An important objective of this effort is the reduction of
young child protein energy malnutrition (PEM) through early
detection and nutritional counseling. In the spring of 1973, the
Caribbean Food and Nutrition Institute (CFNI), in collaboration
with the Jamaican Government, undertook an evaluation of the
Community Health Aide Programme in the parish of St. James. The
initial phase of this evaluation entailed the measurement of some
dietary and anthropometric indices of nutritional status, and the
collection of household social and economic data. The evaluation
which I directed as a CFNI staff member provides the data base for
the following study of the factors underlying young child PEM. The
study, however, is not a formal evaluation, but rather a more
general effort to identify the causes of nutritional deficiency in
young children.

Child Nutrition Studies in Jamaica

Malnutrition in Children

Protein calorie malnutrition among pre-school children has been an increasing concern of Jamaican officials in recent years. Declines in kwashiorkor since 1950 have tended to be counter-balanced by increases in nutritional marasmus and intermediate forms of PEM. Community survey data suggest that lowering infant mortality rates (from 50/per 1000 live births to 30/per 1000 live births in the 1960s) have not been matched by reduced young child malnutrition (Gurney, Fox and Neill, 1972). In 1968-69, eight percent of hospital beds were filled by malnourished children (Cook, 1971). In addition to the financial cost this represents, new knowledge about possible mental and behavioral effects of young-child malnutrition gave an added urgency to the problem (Scrimshaw, 1968; Richardson, 1972).

There are a long series of hospital studies on the nutritional status of Jamaican infants and children.[2] Observations at midcentury focused on the kwashiorkor of the child during the post-weaning transition. Relatively unusual combinations of obesity and kwashiorkor were reported due to the intake of highly refined carbohydrate, low protein foods, such as sugar teas and diluted sweetened condensed milk. This gave rise to the term "sugar babies" (Jelliffe, 1968: 63-65, 117). Since the mid-1950s, hospital admissions suggest that kwashiorkor has been replaced by marasmus, or PEM viewed as a combination of protein and energy shortage, as the more prevalent form of malnutrition in Jamaica (Ashworth and Picou, 1974). Alleyne reports that over 70 percent of admissions to the University Hospital malnutrition unit* are children under 60 percent of weight for age, pointing to marasmus, while only 40 percent have signs of oedema, the *sine qua non* of kwashiorkor (1970: 33). Malnutrition accounts for one-fourth of the hospital cases of children under two years of age, and in conjunction with gastroenteritis accounts for 50 percent of deaths in this age group at the major hospitals (Ashworth and Picou, 1974).

Out in the community, the Pan American Health Organization Inter-American Investigation on Mortality in Childhood reported that malnutrition was directly responsible for or contributed to

*The Tropical Metabolism Research Unit.

slightly over half of all deaths of children under two in Metropolitan Kingston and rural St. Andrew during the period 1968-1970 (Puffer, 1973; Boodhoo, n. d.). Community prevalence surveys are now common. And since the problem is primarily one of overall growth failure, i. e., calorie deficits, surveys rely on weight standards to estimate infant and young child malnutrition. A national sample in 1970 (Table I) of 490 children under four reveals the following:

	Gomez	*Preva-lence*	*Weight for Age*
mild malnutrition	*I*	*40%*	*75-89%*
moderate malnutrition	*II*	*9%*	*60-74%*
severe malnutrition	*III*	*1%*	*under 60%*

The data also confirm a consistent finding that the peak period of weight failure begins in the latter part of the first year and proceeds through the second year (p. 654, see also Desai and Standard, 1968; Alderman, 1973).

Growth Standards in Jamaica
Unlike severe forms of malnutrition usually clinically diagnosed in hospital, we see community nutrition surveys relying heavily on anthropometric measures such as weight and height. Nutritional status is then estimated by comparisons with the Harvard Standards: distributions of body measurements for age cohorts of privileged North American white children (Nelson, 1969). Although not unquestioned, it has been shown that most populations of privileged school children around the world have similarly distributed height and weight measurements to that of Caucasian North American children at the same ages (Habicht, 1974). Generally, it appears that genetic influence is much more powerful in determining body shape and less potent in influencing height or weight (Tanner, 1970). In particular, research in Jamaica by the University of the West Indies comparing different Jamaican ethnic groups found virtually no consistent differences between the average heights and weights of "better off" school children of African, Afro-European, and European origins (Ashcroft, 1966: 36). Other body measures also support the contention that variations from the U. S. anthropometric standard are primarily nutritional

Table 1

"Proportions (Percentages, <u>sic</u>) in each age group of the children surveyed falling into different levels of malnutrition as assessed by the Gomez classification using the Harvard standard weights for age." (Gurney, Fox, Neill, 1971: 661)

Age Group (months)	Urban Children			Rural Children		
	Gomez 1	Gomez 2	Gomez 3	Gomez 1	Gomez 2	Gomez 3
0- 5	8.0	8.0	0	7.1	7.1	0
6-11	29.4	11.8	0	33.3	8.3	5.6
0-11	16.7	9.5	0	19.2	7.7	2.6
12-23	56.8	0	2.3	37.9	15.8	3.2
24-35	48.8	11.6	0	48.6	6.8	1.4
36-47	43.6	10.3	0	45.3	9.3	0
0-47	41.7	7.7	0.6	37.6	10.2	1.9

The authors see little improvement in recent years:

No change in overall nutrition of infants and young children in Jamaica between 1963 and 1970 could be detected. (Gurney, 1971: 662).

rather than genetic in origin. Among Afro-Jamaican preschoolers, triceps fat fold thicknesses fall below standards in step with decreases in weight for age (Gurney, 1971: 657-658). In this study, therefore, I will refer to the anthropometric growth status of individuals as their "nutritional status."

Etiology of Malnutrition
Once it had been accepted that Jamaican children were apparently failing to meet genetic growth potentials, a number of efforts were made to account for the deviation in growth. Of course, the most proximate environmental variable is diet in relation to nutrient needs. In the Gurney, Fox and Neill study, for example, the urban-rural weight status variation was interpreted as a reflection of the fact that protein, rather than calories, is lacking in quality and quantity in the rural diet (pp. 660-661). But a more satisfactory interpretation should include explanation about why such urban-rural dietary differences exist. In response to this, investigators have searched for etiological factors in both broad and detailed social and economic differences between and within child rearing households.

The most thorough of these studies was a five-year longitudinal study done by the Epidemiological Research Unit and the Department of Social and Preventative Medicine of the University of the West Indies. The study area was Tavern, a rural area fifteen miles north of Kingston. A cohort of 200-300 children were followed for the first five years of life. Analyses were carried out by comparing the mean height and weight of groups of children from contrasting household circumstances (Desai, 1970). The studies found that better growth was associated with the following household circumstances (pp. 140-141):

1. larger ratio of earners to dependents,
2. the father living in the home,
3. the father's occupation, other than cultivator,
4. larger areas of land under cultivation,
5. higher socioeconomic status,
6. both parents present,
7. family size under six,
8. birth interval at least twenty-four months before the birth of a subsequent child,
9. mothers with at least three years of primary school,
10. if absent, father contributes to the support of the child,
11. larger and less crowded houses, i. e., at most three persons per room and houses over three rooms in size.

Variables having no effect on weight and height were:

1. mother's presence or absence,
2. grandmother's presence or absence,
3. frequency of changing guardian,
4. occupation of mother or guardian,
5. age of the mother,
6. birth rank of the child,
7. child welfare clinic attendance.[3]

The influence of these conditions has different impacts at differing growth periods; for example, economic influences take effect after the first three to six months of life. In another study, in which the Harvard standards were used, similar results were found (Desai, 1968). The authors conclude:

> The analysis reported here emphasizes the importance of poverty, but poverty per se is rarely a cause of gross malnutrition in Jamaica. Poverty leading to inadequate care—sometimes as a direct result of economic pressures—and poverty associated with lack of knowledge and inappropriate and often-delayed treatment of disease, undoubtedly plays a major role.
>
> Irresponsibility, manifested by a small minority of Jamaican mothers, but by a much larger proportion of fathers, is clearly another important social factor contributing to undernutrition in general—and to infant malnutrition in particular. (1968, n. p.)

They conclude, further, that seasonal variations and acute diseases do not play a major role in child growth in Jamaica as they do in other parts of the world.

Unfortunately, the authors have not demonstrated how the statistically-based results lead to these conclusions about "delayed treatment" of disease, "inadequate" care or "irresponsibility." Nowhere do they show how these terms were operationalized or measured. They do not demonstrate that "poverty per se" is not directly related to malnutrition. One is left with qualitative, economic and social-psychological underlying causes and fragmented, quantitative bivariate correlations. Apparently no effort was made to generate quantitatively the general underlying factors used in the resulting explanation. Furthermore, no effort is made to relate the conditions to the broader social framework of life in Jamaica.

The St. James Study

This study was carried out during 1973 in St. James, one of Jamaica's Western parishes. It entailed a random sample survey of households containing young children. The purposes of the research were to:
(1) estimate the current level and distribution of malnutrition.
(2) identify and describe household variables which were linked to young child malnutrition.

In theoretical terms, the study proposes to contribute to our understanding of the social etiology of malnutrition in general. Although most policy research and project development research pays lip service to the notion that causes are a blend of "cultural" and economic factors, convictions tend to run in favor of either one or the other pole of argument. In this study, we gave relatively little weight to the "cultural" (i. e., knowledge, beliefs) theory of food habits, except in so far as they are reflected in the dietary recalls. Aside from practical limitations, this lack of emphasis reflects our general theoretical bias: that social and economic, or *ecological factors* are the major influence on child nutritional status. Ideational, cultural factors are more often than not outgrowths of the more powerful socioeconomic and environmental variability.

Other than this assumption, the analysis that follows takes an inductive approach. Rather than applying a cultural, ecological or structural-functional framework *a priori,* the approach taken relates the macroscopic social and economic context of the society with child nutritional status through statistical analysis. Bridges are constructed through the integration of highly specific household measures into general factors which are relatable to both young child malnutrition and national socioeconomic conditions in Jamaica. The usual process of operationalizing a concept from a body of theory is consciously being reversed by starting with explicit measurements arrived at from several sources and building from them new concepts of theoretical and applied value.

In practical terms, the research results were to provide not only specific recommendations for improving the nutritional intervention program, the Community Health Aide Programme, but at the same time could reveal the bases for choosing among more far reaching national food and nutrition policy alternatives. This requires that factors be discussed not only in the context of the household group, but also in relation to Jamaica as a national economic and social unit.

The Social and Economic Context

St. James is semi-tropical, sharing twenty miles of northern border with the Caribbean Sea. South of the coast, the parish narrows down to five miles across at its border with the adjoining parish of St. Elizabeth about twenty miles into the center of the island (see map). Flat lands along the coast formerly planted in sugar cane have rapidly given way to the growing tourist city of Montego Bay. The hilly and mountainous interior contains large areas of banana plantations in the mid-south, some cattle estates in the west, and modest cane farms in the northeast. Roughly a third of the land, often marginal in quality, is devoted to the large majority of farmers on small farms growing a mix of subsistence and cash export crops. The remote and mountainous southeastern region of the parish, home of the famous Maroons, is still relatively inaccessible. Roads radiating out of Montego Bay are better paved and maintained in comparison to the dirt and gutted roads between interior towns. Motor transport from the remotest part of the parish to Montego Bay requires about two hours, whereas travel between interior towns and villages is more difficult not only because of poor roads but also due to lack of public transportation.

The population of St. James as of the 1970 census was 100,400, about 5 percent of the country's population of 1.95 million. Politically, the parish is divided into three national parliamentary constituencies and fourteen parish council districts. Montego Bay is classified as urban with a population of around 40,000; the rest of the parish is considered rural by the census authorities, and for the purposes of this analysis as well.[4]

Montego Bay, popular for its tourist beaches, has many of the features of cities throughout the developing countries of the world. Luxury hotels and shops attest to the wealth of merchants and the investments of foreign interests. Suburban residential homes from modest to luxurious are located in lush green surroundings. Juxtaposed to this affluence are the shanty-towns sandwiched behind and between buildings or stacked on the hillsides of the town's periphery, the ports of entry for rural emigrants. From 1960 to 1970, Montego Bay grew by 60 percent. This increase is associated with massive unemployment estimated nationally to be 25 percent but rising to nearer 40 percent for younger men. Even a growing tourist industry cannot meet the urban demand for employment (Jefferson, 1972: 171-172).

PARISH OF ST. JAMES

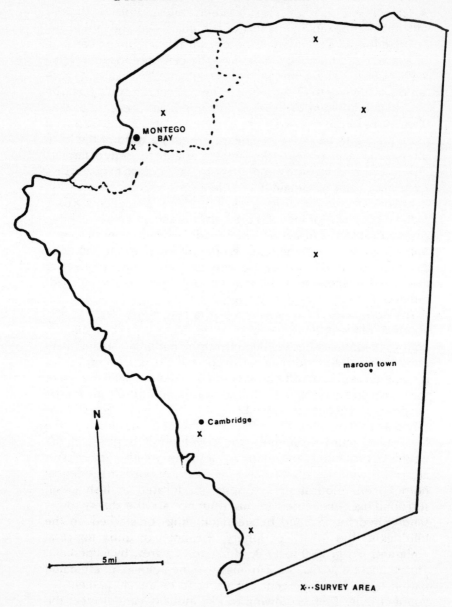

MONTEGO
BAY

maroon town

N

• Cambridge
X

5mi

X···SURVEY AREA

In the rural areas, the pattern of inequality is also quite apparent. Most households practice some form of agriculture. In keeping with its history as a plantation economy supplying agricultural products to England, Jamaica continues to favor cultivators of major export crops. Sugar estates take up 56 percent of farm land and 1 percent of all farms (Beckford, 1972: 25). In our survey area, St. James, 80.5 percent of all farms (N = 8064) were under five acres in size in 1968. These farms average 1.3 acres while utilizing only .12 percent of all cultivated land in the parish. Farms over 500 acres were .19 percent of all farms and monopolized 48.1 percent of all cultivated land. In Jamaica as a whole, 78 percent of all farms are under five acres in size, and average between 1.5 and 1.8 acres (Jefferson, 1972: 80).

In our survey, most rural households (78 percent) were found to be cultivating subsistence root crops (yam and sweet potatoes) for local consumption. Sixty percent also cultivated bananas for home use and export, while only small proportions were cultivating nutritious legumes such as the pigeon pea *cajanus cajan* (Marchione, 1973). In 1963, the Jamaican Central Planning unit reported that "40 percent of farms under 5 acres grew mainly crops for local consumption and 52 percent concentrated on export crops. In contrast, on farms over 500 acres in size, 64 percent grew mainly export crops and less than 3 percent derived income mainly from local food crops" (cited in Heywood, 1974).

It has been claimed that the average household cannot rely solely on agriculture for its income (Orde Brown, 1939: 18); Floyd, 1971: 33; cited in Heywood, 1974). Detailed household by household observations reveal a highly complex employment structure. Often more than one person provides for the needs of the household in differing seasons (Bantje, 1973a). Cultivation, public works jobs, agricultural labor (nearby or abroad), domestic service, remittances from relatives abroad, and other wage work are found singly, but more often combined, in the lower income households comprising the bulk of the parish. Seasonal labor migration, particularly to the United States and Canada, is very much desired because of the higher wage rates for manual labor compared to those anywhere in Jamaica. In 1971, the Government reported that 11,450 contract farm laborers went to the United States and Canada from Jamaica (Jamaican Government, 1971: 16).

The growth of Montego Bay is not surprising in light of the difficulties of rural life in St. James. The situation is conducive to permanent and temporary labor migration. Wage differentials from parish to parish, unemployment rates, and the land holdings of uneconomic size are cited as the major push-pull forces in Jamaica's internal migration (Adams, 1969).

Jamaica's Gross National Product is in the neighborhood of J$600 per capita annually.* Income distribution is estimated by most observers based on the household expenditure survey of 1958. At that time, the bottom 80 percent of households received 38 percent of the national income and the top 20 percent received 61.5 percent (Ahiram, 1964). There is good reason to believe that no substantial changes have occurred since then (Jefferson, 1972: 54). In the present study, it is estimated that in over 80 percent of child rearing households surveyed in St. James, the mean annual income was J$130 per household member or $2.50 per person per week (calculated from figures in Marchione, 1973: 29).

The facts above generally support the model of socioeconomic stratification of Jamaican society proposed by Stone (1973). He suggests that two classes based on a relationship to the means of production is not as useful in Jamaica as is a status formulation based on a continuum of material well being indicated by occupational hierarchies. "Capitalists constitute the most affluent stratum and manual wage labour the poorest stratum" (p. 16). Non-unionized wage labor is by far the most dispossessed element in the society, receiving the lowest wages and having the highest employment insecurity. In recent years, development combined with unionization has proved to economically differentiate the wage laborers. But small farmers still form the largest segment of the lower strata of the society today.

Survey Sample
The survey sample was drawn on the basis of 1970 census enumeration districts (ED's).[5] Fifteen of one hundred districts were randomly selected from urban and rural ED's in proportion to the population distribution.[6] In the selected ED's, all households with children from three months to thirty-six months of age were included (Table 2). In the spring and summer of 1973, these households were surveyed by locally-known female Jamaican Community Health

*(J$1 = $1.10 in 1973)

Aides. At a later predetermined time, the children from these households were weighed and measured by nutrition professionals at health facilities around the parish, and household interview schedules were collected and verified. When necessary, measurement teams visited the households not attending the measuring centers. Over 90 percent of the children selected in the original sample were weighed. Special attention was given to one year old children, the group at highest risk of malnutrition, to assess the success of their transition to the family diet. For this purpose, 24-hour dietary recalls were taken for one child:meal-maker (mm) pair in every household where they were found.

Table 2

ST. JAMES SURVEY SAMPLES COMPARED TO 1970 CENSUS DATA

	Parish Census (N=100,400)	Sample Children	
		3 mos. to 36 mos. (N=516)	one year olds (N=164)
Urban	39	37	32
Rural	61	63	67
Total	100%	100%	100%

Table 3
LOCATION OF ONE YEAR OLDS
IN THE SAMPLE

Area	Percent (N=164)
Urban (Montego Bay)	32
Rural (Cambridge)	21
(South)	11
(Central)	9
(Northeast)	15
(East Coast)	12
Total	100%

The survey sample falls into roughly six areas (see map), which reflect the ecological diversity of the parish. In Montego Bay, both middle class and shanty-town neighborhoods are represented. The rural sample includes the large towns such as Cambridge, the remote farming communities in the south, the banana plantation areas in the central area, and the coastal areas east of the city. The diversity of settlement typologies found relevant to PEM incidence by Foneroff, i.e., (1) urban, town, isolated rural, and plantation, were all represented (1969). Contrasts can be sharp. The urban residential middle class areas are inhabited by wage and salaried workers; these areas have paved roads, piped water in many houses and relatively easy access to professional medical care. On the other hand, there are isolated rural semi-subsistence farming areas accessible in large measure only over gutted tracks or rock parochial roads; piped water is distant and unreliable, and roadside cisterns filled by tank truck are inadequate for demand. Professional medical care is distant; if services are offered nearby in temporary clinic facilities, they are held infrequently (Marchione, 1973:10).

Nutritional Status of One Year Olds

The nutritional status of the one year olds, as measured by anthropometric standards, shows no severe malnutrition, but a great deal of milk and moderate PEM (Table 4). Comparison to the islandwide survey is favorable (see Table 1).[7]

Using the Gomez classification, 47 percent of the one year olds were found to be malnourished to some degree. This is mostly mild underweightedness, Gomez I, where much normal genetic variation would tend to be included. For instance, at twelve months of age, 90 percent of standard weight approximates the tenth percentile, and 80 percent of standard approximates the third percentile for

Table 4

NUTRITIONAL STATUS OF ONE YEAR OLD CHILDREN BASED ON
CLASSIFICATIONS DERIVED FROM THE HARVARD STANDARDS, SEXES COMBINED

Nutritional Status	Child's Residence		
	Urban (N=43)	Rural (N=89)	Total (N=132)
Normal	65	47	52
Gomez I	28	44	39
Gomez II	7	9	8
Gomez III	0	0	0
Total	100%	100%	100%

the Boston population.[8] In other words, one can expect 10 percent
"malnourished" by Gomez standards in a privileged, presumably
well-fed cohort of North American children. Consequently, the
third percentile has been often used to identify child malnutrition.
Using this modified cutting point, the urban-rural differences in
our sample become more pronounced; i.e., more serious malnutrition is nearly twice as prevalent in rural than in urban areas (Table
5).

Table 5

*NUTRITIONAL STATUS OF ONE YEAR OLDS EMPLOYING THE THIRD PERCENTILE
CUTTING POINT (i.e. 80% of Standard Weight for Age)*

Weight Status*	Child's Residence		
	Urban (N=43)	Rural (N=89)	Total (N=132)
normal≥90%	65	47	52
mild malnutrition 80-89%	25	36	33
moderate to severe malnutrition<80%	10	18	16
Total	100%	100%	100%

No obese (>120% of standard) one year olds were found in the sample.

Length as an index of nutritional status is not well standardized; it is hard to measure accurately, and the standard group distribution is narrowly dispersed, accentuating small measurement errors. However, it may be an excellent cumulative measure of the individual's history of nutritional status because, unlike weight, length does not fluctuate. A number of episodes of previous malnutrition would be more consistently apparent in current length deficits than in weight deficits (Seoane and Latham, 1971). Using this criteria, rural malnutrition is four times that of urban (Table 6).

Table 6

CLASSIFICATION OF STANDARD LENGTH FOR AGE OF ONE YEAR OLDS USING HARVARD STANDARDS

	Child's Residence		
Length Status	Urban (N=32)	Rural (N=82)	Total (N=114)
≥95% of Standard	94	76	81
<95%	6	24	19
Total	100%	100%	100%

Viewed this way, one sees more striking and significant differences between urban and rural children. The result mirrors the
observations made at the malnutrition ward of the Noel Holmes
Hospital in Hanover, an adjoining parish. PEM admissions there
were primarily from more rural households (Bantje, 1974b).

Although it is important to use standards, it is clear that reported
prevalences change markedly and somewhat arbitrarily with slight
changes in cutting points. A method for avoiding these difficulties
is simply to do analyses using actual weight for age or length for age
wherever possible. This approach is taken later in this analysis.

Household Measures Associated with Nutritional Status

In addition to rural versus urban location of the child's household,
data on thirty other possible etiological variables were collected
through interviews with mothers or guradians of the children in the
sample (see Appendix). That is, we wanted to assess the effects of a
series of variables on the nutritional status of the one year olds. The
variables were selected based on previous research on child
malnutrition in the Caribbean, and on certain objectives of the
Community Health Aide Programme. The measures can be roughly
categorized into the usual epidemiological classification of host (or
innate), agent, and environment. Host variables measured were
sex, age, and illness history of the child. Agent measures were food
recall records of the child for the previous day. Environmental
measures included number of siblings, household income and
food expenditure, age of the mother, agricultural resources, and
the like.

The fact that the study was done in an applied setting using
semi-skilled survey workers made it necessary to operationalize
variables in the simplest form and to precode interview schedules
for rapid, economical processing. Possible interval scales have
often been converted to nominal and ordinal types, reflecting, we
think, the level of confidence possible in this type of survey data.

As in many studies (e.g., Desai in Jamaica or Wray in Columbia),
many bivariate associations were found between nutritional and
household measures (Table 7). In fact, nineteen out of the thirty-
one measures have some kind of statistically significant correlation
with the anthropometric status. Clearly, the growth rates of
children are complexly interwoven with many aspects of their
home circumstances: the locality, the size of the household, food

Table 7

HOUSEHOLD MEASURES CORRELATED* WITH THE WEIGHT STATUS OR HEIGHT STATUS OF ONE YEAR OLDS

Household Variable	Weight Status (N=132)	Height Status (N=114)
Location	-.19	-.18
Household Size	-	-.20
Dependency Ratio	-	-.15
Agricultural Resources	-.14	-.24
Home Food Use	-.11	-.15
Food Expenses	-.24	-.20
Income	.13	-
Distance to (Piped) Water	-.14	-.18
Age of Meal-Maker	.12	-
Child's Age	.15	-.11
Diet Variety	.12	.20
Diet Complexity	.15	.13
Mother's Presence	.15	.13
Father's Presence	.21	-
Mother's Age	.14	-
Children Under Five	.10	-.15
Child Welfare Clinic Attendance	-.13	-.14
Diet Adequacy of Meal-Maker	-	.13
Diet Adequacy of Child	.10	.16

*Kendal's tau are correlations shown significant at $p < .05$

expenditures, and many other variables have, with varying strengths, elevating or depressing effect on child length and weight. The impact of poverty appears evident in the association of food expenditure and income with nutritional status (see also Table 8).

Table 8

WEEKLY FOOD EXPENDITURES VERSUS THE WEIGHT STATUS OF ONE YEAR OLDS

(Food Expenditures - Jamaican Dollars)

Gomez	Under $1 (N=29)	$1 to $4 (N=78)	Over $4 (N=25)
Normal	41	53	67
I	35	42	33
II	24	5	0
TOTALS	100%	100%	100%

$p < .01$

*At the time, one Jamaican dollar = $1.10 U. S.

Although every possible bivariate or two-way association was examined, a problem of interpretation remains—the problem of interrelationships among the household measures themselves. Examination of the matrix of interrelationships, the social ecological matrix (Table 9), displays a bewildering array of intercorrelations.

Table 9: CORRELATION MATRIX
OF
MEASURES
HOUSEHOLD

N=132

Kendal's tau rounded to nearest .05

Correlations shown have p<.05.

* "relationship"-meat-maker (mm) to child (c)
** CWC = child welfare clinic
   FPC = family planning clinic

Correlation matrix (Kendall's tau, upper-triangular; rows and columns follow the variable order below). Values rounded to nearest .05; only correlations with p<.05 shown.

#	Variable
1	location
2	household size
3	dependency ratio
4	school lunches
5	employment history
6	agri. resources
7	home food use
8	food expenses
9	income
10	dist. to water
11	dist. health fac.
12	relationship (mm-c)*
13	age of meal-maker
14	age of child
15	diet variety
16	diet sharing
17	diet. complexity
18	mother's presence
19	father's presence
20	mother's empl.
21	father's supt.
22	mother's age
23	children under five
24	mother's education
25	milk type
26	illness of child
27	CWC** attendance
28	FPC** attendance
29	sex of child
30	diet adq. (mm)
31	diet adq. (c)

Selected diagonal and legible correlation values:

Variable	Correlations (reading left→right to diagonal 1.00)
location	.00
household size	.35 | 1.00
dependency ratio	.20 | .35 | 1.00
school lunches	.40 | .65 | .30 | 1.00
employment history	-.15 | ... | 1.00
agri. resources	.30 | .15 | ... | .10 | 1.00
home food use	.35 | .25 | .20 | .50 | .10 | .15 | 1.00
food expenses	-.55 | -.70 | -.20 | -.35 | -.25 | -.20 | .15 | 1.00
income	-.25 | -.20 | -.25 | -.25 | -.15 | -.15 | .15 | .60 | 1.00
dist. to water	.50 | .30 | .15 | .20 | ... | .15 | -.20 | -.40 | -.20 | 1.00
dist. health fac.	.30 | .15 | .25 | .20 | ... | ... | -.25 | -.35 | -.25 | .35 | 1.00
relationship (mm-c)*	.20 | -.25 | .20 | .15 | ... | .20 | ... | ... | ... | .20 | .20 | 1.00
age of meal-maker	... | ... | ... | ... | ... | .20 | ... | -.20 | ... | .15 | ... | .20 | 1.00
age of child	... → 1.00
diet variety	... | .11 | 1.00
diet sharing	... | -.11 | -.10 | 1.00
diet. complexity	... | -.14 | .10 | -.14 | 1.00
mother's presence	... → 1.00
father's presence	... | .30 | 1.00
mother's empl.	... → 1.00
father's supt.	... → 1.00
mother's age	... → 1.00
children under five	... → 1.00
mother's education	... → 1.00
milk type	... → 1.00
illness of child	... → 1.00
CWC** attendance	... → 1.00
FPC** attendance	... → 1.00
sex of child	... → 1.00
diet adq. (mm)	... → 1.00
diet adq. (c)	... | .30 | 1.00

Some correlations may be merely reflections or "proxy expressions" of others, which are more powerful. For example, by controlling food expenditures, it is possible to halve the effects of urban-rural location. The correlation drops from -.19 to -.08,[9] and ceases to have substantive significance. In addition, close examination shows that variables with no apparent, direct relationships with height or weight status are always correlated with at least one other variable that does have a direct correlation (e.g., employment history is related to income and food expenditure, which are in turn related to the weight status of the child). It is probably that under proper statistical control, new associations not demonstrated would appear. Even slight changes in category cutting points or samples might cause new, low-value correlations to appear. It is dismaying that policy research often reports only bivariate correlations between malnutrition and household ecology.

Application of Factor Analysis to the Survey Data

It would be most useful if we could reduce the complexity and size of the matrix of household measures without losing potentially important variables. Factor analysis is a powerful technique for doing just this. It involves a set of mathematical procedures designed to discover the clusters of interrelationships that exist in a correlation matrix (Rummel, 1970). Factors are new variables composed of mathematical (linear) combinations of the original variables. Classical or common factor analysis, used here, presents a particular solution composed of a set of factors fewer in number than the number of variables in the matrix. Closely related variables tend to be represented in the same factors. In general, the more interrelated the original variables in the matrix, the smaller the number of factors produced. In the data from St. James, twelve factors were derived from the thirty-one variables (see Table 10). The only variable not represented in the factors is the sex of the child, which was slightly correlated with only a few matrix variables; and fortunately, it is not itself related to nutritional status.

The factor procedure also includes techniques for manipulating the interrelationships among the factors. In this case, orthogonal factors were employed; that is, the newly-derived variables are programmed to be uncorrelated with each other.[10]

[handwritten margin note: factor analysis teases out clusters of interrel.]

Table 10.

ROTATED FACTOR MATRIX (VARIMAX)
FACTOR LOADINGS* OF HOUSEHOLD MEASURES
N=132

Household Measures						Factors						
	1	2	3	4	5	6	7	8	9	10	11	12
Father's Presence	.87											
Father's Support	.72											
Mother's Presence	.50											
Mother's Employment	-.30										-.34	
Mother's Age	.25	.70										
CWC Attendance			.83									
Age of Meal Maker		.95										
Distance to Water			.32					-.59				
Location			.28					-.44				
Diet Variety				.60		.53						
Diet Adequacy (mm)				.48								
Diet Sharing				-.31								
Diet Adeq. (Child)				.25	-.25	-.29						
Milk Type				.25	-.26				.47			
Age Child					.89					.30		
Agri. Resources						.76						
Home Food Use						.73			.31			
Household Size						.41	.37					
Food Expenses						-.40		.62	.60			
School Lunches						.28						
Dependency Ratio							.69					
Children Under Five							.50					
Dietary Complex.							-.35					
FPC Attendance							.27					
Income								.68				
Empl. History											.53	
Mother's Education										.66	-.31	
Relation (mm-c)												
Illness of Child											-.46	
Distance to Hlth. Fac.												-.59
Sex of Child									.26			

*Loadings with standard error exceeding ±.1 are not reported.

Table 10 shows the twelve new variables or factors enumerated. The values in the columns are the correlation between the factors and the original variables. These are often referred to as "factor loadings." The character of a factor is determined by the variables "correlated with it" or "loading on it." Some factors are quite simple, such as factor 2 which is represented by only two variables; others, such as factor 6, are complex with seven variables loading on it. The order in which the factors are extracted is determined by the degree of internal interrelationship or strength for explaining the common matrix variance (communality). The factors are defined briefly as follows:

Factor 1: "Family Cohesion"

Household Measures	Factor Loadings
Father's Presence	.87
Father's Support	.72
Mother's Presence	.50
Mother's Employment	−.30
Mother's Age	.25

The five significant measures in factor 1 are elements that relate to the relative stability, integrity or coherence of the child's family. I have chosen to call this factor "family cohesion." It demonstrates the interrelatedness of these variables: in the one-third of households where the father of the child was not present, it was also likely that he was not a regular economic provider for his child. Also, the mother's and father's absence often occur together, as when the child resides with the grandmother in a rural area while parents reside in Montego Bay. Mother's employment is negatively loaded on the factor demonstrating that mothers are less likely to be working when fathers are present and supporting the child.

All of these associations are consistent with the wide variance in Jamaican family social structure reported in some detail by Clarke (1957) and Smith (1962). The familial structures have been classified into five or six types (Clarke, 1957:191-194). The factor reflects the types quantitatively—from the various cohabitation types where both biological parents are present to the "denuded female" type where the father is absent, to the grandparents/grandchildren type where both biological parents are absent. Furthermore, the factor supports the idea that these may be stages in family development. Since mother's age loads on the factor, older mothers are more likely to be married or settled into cohabitation with the father of her children. The father's decision to reside in the household is probably based, in part, on the older man's ability to become a financially viable farmer; get local employment, or otherwise provide a secure homestead (see also Clarke, 1957:78). The factor, family cohesion, then represents in a single measure the variance of family structure, and the socioeconomic dynamics with which family structure articulates.

Factor 2: "Mother/Guardian Maturity"

Household Measures	Factor Loadings
Mother's Age	.70
Age of Meal-Maker	.95

The high correlation between the age distribution of mother and meal-maker occurs because, more often than not, the mother of the child also makes the child's meals. Most of the mothers of the one year olds were twenty to thirty-four years of age. One in six were above thirty-four, and one in six were below twenty years old. Guardians or meal-makers tended to be older—one-third were over thirty-four. I have labeled this factor "Mother/Guardian Maturity," to suggest that the age of mother and/or guardian may relate to a biocultural element important to the growth of the children.

Factor 3: "Clinic Care Demand"

Household Measures	Factor Loadings
Child Welfare Clinic Attendance	.83
Distance to Piped Water	.32
Location	.28

This factor integrates three variables related to the demand for and availability of child health services by the mother or guardian of the child. We found that 30 percent of the children in the sample had been brought to the most recently held government child

welfare clinic in their areas. The factor seems to support the view
that rural mothers in St. James have less access to nongovernment
services, and are generally better attenders of welfare clinics.
Private doctor services were used more often than government
clinic services by all, but especially by urban mothers in our sample.

The distance of piped water from the household is probably part
of this factor for two reasons: Distance from piped water relates to
the remoteness from urban and town areas where public works
have concentrated. Also, distance from water sources is usually
related to the prevalence of gastroenteritis or other serious child
illnesses calling for curative medical attention. Most mothers do
not respect the distinction between preventative and curative
services.

The illness variable, however, does not load on the factor
because the bulk of milder child illnesses recorded by this variable
are treated with home remedies. Although Nanas may be consulted,
use of western medicine for child care is universal. Full-time folk
practitioners or "balmists" are rarely used in cases of preschool
child illness in modern Jamaica.[11]

Factor 4: "Household Diet"

Household Measures	Factor Loadings
Diet Variety	.80
Diet Adequacy of Meal-Maker	.48
Diet Sharing	-.31
Diet Adequacy of Child	.25
Milk Type	.25

This factor is labeled "Household Diet" and reveals the interrelationship of five specific measurements of dietary quality of the
mother/meal-maker and the child.

Slightly less than half of the food recall records of the meal-
makers consisted of ten or more items or were judged completely
adequate in both protein and calories using quantitative estimates.
Similarly, slightly less than half of the children had adequate diets
based on the dietary recall.

As the value and variety of the diet improves, the one year old
child is less likely to be sharing most of the items in it. More
commercial full-cream milks for children are found in more varied
household dietaries. The factor accounts for some, but not all

variation in the child's diet adequacy, that part which does not appear to be directly linked to the immediate economic circumstances of the household. That is to say, income and food expenditure are not involved in this factor.

Factor 5: "Age Transition"

Household Measures	Factor Loadings
Age of Child	.89
Milk Type	−.26
Diet Adequacy of Child	−.25

This factor is principally a measure of the child's passage from age one to two not only biologically, but also culturally. The negative loading of "milk type" reveals a transition from breast milk and powdered milk formulas, to condensed milk or no milk at all. At the same time, the overall "dietary adequacy" of the child's diet declines. Generally, the period of transition beginning in the latter part of the first year and extending into the third is a stressful one. The child moves away from the secure, immobile, breast-fed "extra gestate" fetus to the mobile, self-sufficient, young child. Jelliffe has referred to this as the "biocultural transitional" period (1968).

Factor 6: "Agricultural Subsistence"

Household Measures	Factor Loadings
Agricultural Resources	.76
Home Food Use	.73
Location	.53
Household Size	.41
Food Expenses	−.40
Dietary Adequacy of Child	−.29
School Lunches	.28

Seven variables correlated with rural peasant subsistence farming are clustered here. I have called the factor "agricultural subsistence." The variable is a measure of the degree to which the household exhibits life patterns associated with dependence upon their own agricultural pursuits.

Of course, the factor reveals that about 60 percent of households with some type of food crop or livestock resources are rural. And quite obviously those households using more home grown food items in their own diets had resources to draw from, even though the resources might be meager ones. At the same time, it should be noted that only half of those with agricultural resources actually reported using any of them in their own diets; the balance are exclusively cash-croppers.

As expected, use of home grown food is positively correlated with agricultural resources, but negatively correlated with food expenditures. Having one's own food resources reduces food costs; or alternatively, being short of cash for food purchases, one is forced to live off the land. Generally speaking, rural households spent less for food. In fact, one-fifth of the households spent less than a dollar per person on food; these were practically all rural households. Similarly, one-fifth spent more than four dollars per person; these were mostly urban households. Not surprisingly, subsistence farming households are larger in size reflecting labor needs.

The subsistence farming household evidently puts a drain on children's diets. School age children are more likely to need a subsidized school lunch, and no doubt dependence on the vicissitudes of nature takes its toll on the one year olds.

However, the standard notion that the subsistence farming family is more traditional and has a simpler, less-varied diet, is *not* borne out by the data.

Factor 7: "Dependency Stress"

Household Measures	Factor Loadings
Dependency Ratio	.69
Children Under Five	.50
Household Size	.37
Dietary Complexity	−.35
Family Planning Clinic Attendance	.27

This factor I interpret to be a measure of the stress on the household, especially due to numbers of young children and dependents under fifteen years of age. The three demographic variables—dependency ratio, number of children under five, and household size—are positively correlated. The following conditions tend to occur together: over one-third of the households contain eight or more persons. One-fifth have a dependency ratio exceeding two. And 50 percent of the mothers had more than one child under five years; 10 percent had three or more. These statistics give evidence of the frustration of Jamaican family planning workers; maternal readiness to use the contraceptives and counseling services often follows, rather than precedes, the creation of large families. Family Planning Clinic attendance increases with increase in family size and dependency ratio.

In connection with large family size, we find a decline in the complexity of the child's diet indicating more use of starch, sugar and fat at the expense of vegetables, fruits, animal protein, and commercial products. It has been observed by others that increasing size is matched by lowering per capita food expenditures and general decline in dietary adequacy; however, this analysis does not support such conclusions for St. James.

Factor 8: "Monetary Wealth"

Household Measures	Factor Loadings
Income (Weekly)	.68
Food Expenses (Weekly)	.62
Distance to (Piped) Water	-.59
Employment History	.46
Location	-.44

This factor is a cluster of five measures related to the flow of cash into the household. There was a wide range of weekly incomes in our sample. While most household incomes, per capita, were between one and six dollars weekly, one-sixth of households had less than one dollar for each household member, and one-sixth over six dollars per week. However, the factor "Monetary Wealth" should be conceptually distinguished from the weekly cash income measure. Unlike weekly income, the factor reflects a more general, overall availability of liquid assets for a period of time. For instance, we see that the regularity of the main provider's employment over the past year is included in the factor. Also, the distance to piped water decreases as the monetary wealth increases. The past cash income of the household is reflected by the ability to either purchase piped water connections or obtain gainful employment

in urban and town areas where public water supply is more
accessible. In fact, one-fourth of the children's households had
piped water connections, and they were exclusively urban households.

Another important distinction needs to be made; the factor does
not include *all* household wealth but "monetary" wealth. The
factor particularly does not include traditional forms of capital,
such as land and livestock which are reflected in another factor,
agricultural subsistence.

Factors 9-12
The last few factors appearing in the analysis become difficult to
interpret, and they are least reliable in attempts to replicate. I have
chosen not to interpret the remaining factors for this reason. In any
case, they proved not to be signficantly related to nutritional status.

Correlations of Factors with Nutritional Status

Now that a set of factors has been derived, they can be used in
further analysis. Using the factor score matrix, each child is assigned
a value for each factor replacing the original thirty-one measures
(Rummel, 1970: 433-445).

Four factors have significant correlations with the weight status,
and/or length status, of the one year olds (Table 11). Collectively,
the factors correlated (.49 and .53) quite highly with the nutritional
indicators. Because individually the factors are orthogonal (uncorrelated with each other), one can confidently interpret each
relationship with the anthropometric standards to be entirely a
result of the factor in question and not an expression of hidden
relationships. Also, because of the orthogonal factors, the square of
the correlation is the proportion of the variance explained by the
factor, a useful estimate of the strength of the relationship. For
instance, dependency stress accounts for .12 (12%) of the length
status variation. In all, the factors account for about one-fourth of
the anthropometric variation.[12] The remainder would be accounted
for by other unmeasured environmental factors, error in this
analysis, and genetic variance.

Table 11

THE CORRELATION (r) BETWEEN FACTORS AND
NUTRITIONAL STATUS OF THE ONE YEAR OLDS

Factors	Nutritional Status	
	Weight Status (N=132) (r)	Length Status (N=114) (r)
Agricultural Subsistence	-.25*	-.28*
Dependency Stress	-.22*	-.35*
Family Cohesion	.23*	.15
Mother/Guardian Maturity	.22*	.11
Clinic Care Demand	-.08	-.14
Age Transition	-.03	-.14
Monetary Wealth	.12	.07
Household Diet	.09	.03
Multiple (R)	.49	.53
Variance Accounted for	24%	28%

*Significant at $p < .05$ (Two-tailed tests)

Agricultural Subsistence and Nutritional Status

Poor nutritional status in one year olds in Jamaica is clearly related to the degree to which households live in a subsistence agricultural pattern. This consists of dietary dependence on home grown foods coupled with low food expenditures, child diets less adequate in calories and protein, and larger household size. This result does not mean that *all* farming households deleteriously affect child growth; it relates specifically to farms of the subsistence type. Children of larger cash crop farmers were not so affected.

It appears that the small, nearly landless peasantry suffers most from malnutrition. We have discussed above the colonial heritage of inequitable land distribution in St. James. Apparently the inequality has not been alleviated in the years since Jamaica's independence in 1962. In fact, from 1961 to 1968, the average size of the peasant farm in St. James fell by 27 percent (Jamaica, 1975). During the present research, it was common to see rural land areas "captured" by small farmers during the 1960s and early 1970s. These government-owned lands were simply taken over by land-hungry peasants and divided for subsistence cultivation. Following the change in government in 1972, these lands were being leased at nominal fees to the occupiers. Peasant actions to increase land resources for their households are clearly related to their general *poverty*, which affects young children. In an area adjoining the parish of St. James, Bantje has shown that an increase in cultivated land from under one-half acre to over significantly reduces young child PEM (1974a). Our result supports the conclusion that malnutrition in St. James results when a household is forced to live off an inadequate piece of land.

The problem is further complicated by the institutions of land tenure. Land is divided or held in common by heirs rather than being inherited according to principles of primogeniture or ultimogeniture (Clarke, 1957:60-69). It does not take long for land plots to become inadequate in size for the support of a reproducing unit.

In a sense, young child malnutrition is an adaptational response to scarce resources (Stini, 1971; Alland, 1970). Gross and Underwood found poor growth rates of children associated with households dependent upon low wage agricultural labor in Northern Brazil (1971:727). I am not implying that the severity of the problem in Jamaica approaches that of Brazil; however, the energy deprivations for nonproductive household members (children) seem similar.

The Jamaican peasant household must optimize the use of scarce energy resources. Under these cruel circumstances of shortage, productive members doing farm work must use greater proportions of available household energy resources to the detriment of unproductive members, such as children. For the sake of the household's overall survival, when land and weather conditions are unfavorable, energy rations must shift in favor of productive members, and child malnutrition or growth retardation occurs. No doubt this is not a conscious process and involves hardly measurable food increments. Providing severe malnutrition does not occur, this process *may* even confer an advantage to the family. Older children and adults who are growth retarded demand less energy. However, I would not advocate a risky course of "benign neglect." To rely on these adaptive mechanisms is nothing but irresponsible where severe malnutrition is a common occurrence.

This process can be seen in many households in rural St. James. One such household consists of fifteen persons, a mother and father with their ten children, two grandchildren, and one distant relative's child. Two of the children under five years of age are malnourished; one is in our target age group; he is twenty months old. The household has a narrow base of economic support. The father, a man of fifty, farms a thirty-three square yard garden plot, and when there is work, he heads bananas for a few cents a bunch at an estate. Ten chickens and three pigs are tended in the yard. A twenty year old daughter gets some child maintenance money from the father of her two children; he lives elsewhere in St. James.

This household spends less than a dollar per person per week on food, and consumes many home-grown items, such as callalu, yams, corn, and eggs. Overall the diet is simple, less than ten different items. One of the children was under 60 percent of standard weight for age, another 66 percent of standard weight. The latter exhibited signs of protein deficiency, such as flaking of the skin and ankle edema.

The household head was clearly distressed by his situation. He was attempting to find road work with the government, or a piece of adequately sized land to plant. He had applied for a five-acre piece in a small nearby government land cooperative. One of the many applicants, he was desperately hoping to be included in the final selection. In the meantime, the government food distribution program began to supply food packets for feeding the young children.

Dependency Stress and Nutritional Status

The child's growth tends to fail as the number of preschool siblings increases, dependency ratios increase, and family size grows larger. That is, malnutrition tends to occur where "dependency stress" is greatest. This result confirms similar observations of the effects of fertility and family size in the Caribbean and elsewhere.[13] Our results are also congruent with the serious situation discovered in rural St. Andrew near Kingston where Boodhoo and Standard found in 1970 that young child mortality due to malnutrition increased sharply as the number of siblings under five exceeded two.

The growth of the Jamaican population is in large measure due to declines in infant mortality rate without concomitant declines in birth rate, a common pattern throughout the Third World. Jamaica's crude birth rate (35 per thousand) is among the highest in the Americas. However, because of emigration, the annual population growth rate has been relatively low (1.5% annually). The island, of course, has never since aboriginal times been self-sustaining in food production. We are not now seeing generalized food shortage for all people due to over-population, but an overload of dependents in poor class households with marginal resources.

The dynamics of this situation seem obvious.[14] The overall nutritional and economic resources of mother and household are increasingly diluted by increasing numbers of children. However, while child diets become simpler (e.g., less animal protein), the factor does not demonstrate a decrease in food expenditure as income with stress increases. What we do see is an increase in dependency ratio with stress. This means that the fewer adults relative to children, the fewer potential earners, and the more likely that peaks and valleys in the household budget will occur. In relation to the young child, the steadiness of dietary intake is important because of his or her limited nutrient stores. It is not surprising, therefore, to see length for age (an index of the child's history of malnutrition) is more affected by dependency stress than weight for age (more an indication of current status).

The relationship between length, dependency stress, and malnutrition may also reflect the results of a natural selection process. Garrow and Pike (1967) followed up fifty-six survivors of severe young child malnutrition who were hospitalized in the Tropical Metabolism Research Unit in Kingston. They found some evidence that these children were taller than a control group made up of siblings. They suggest:

the child whose genetic make-up is such that he would grow very rapidly if well-fed, will suffer more on a restricted diet than one with more modest demands. (1967:4)

In Peru, Frishancho (1973) found that under poor economic conditions, shorter mothers had about 9 percent more surviving offspring than taller mothers. This could mean that what I have called dependency stress may, to some degree, be the discovery that short mothers have more surviving offspring who, in turn, tend to be shorter. Such interpretations, however, do represent a departure from most previous studies linking lower birth weight and higher perinatal mortality with shorter mothers (WHO, 1965).

Consider the rural family introduced above. Five adults (15 years plus) and nine children, six under age five, shared meals from the family pot. The wife of the household head, age forty-two, had ten children ranging from nine months to twenty years. Three were born in the past five years, the two youngest, twenty-five months apart. Both of these children were mildly to moderately malnourished. However, her resident grandchildren, born only fifteen months apart, were more seriously malnourished, and one of them showed clinical signs of kwashiorkor. Unfortunately, neither of these mothers had been regular attenders at the family planning clinics held in the area.

Family Cohesion and Nutritional Status

Children's growth, in particular their weight for age, is supported in cohesive family units. The child suffers least when both parents are present in the household, the father is the main provider, and the mother is not employed. In brief, a child's weight for age is better in more cohesive families.

Cohesiveness of families in Jamaica tends to increase with the age of the parents. It relates to the development of the lower class child-rearing family (Clarke, 1957). The family starts with courting relations between a young man and woman. This relationship tends to proceed to cohabitation in a neolocal residence, and eventually may become a common law or church marriage. Child rearing, however, starts early in this development. In 1964, the latest data available, 74 percent of all births were classified by the authorities as illegitimate (Jamaica, 1975). However, it is expected and customary for the biological father to maintain his children fully or partially. However, the law clearly discriminates against the illegitimate child. The amount of support required under the

Affiliation (Bastardy) Law is limited to a small, fixed amount of money (J$4.00) whereas for the legitimate child, maintenance is fixed according to the means of the father. Furthermore, " . . . affiliation orders are not, as maintenance orders are, enforceable outside of the jurisdiction. If the father goes away, no court in his place of residence can be asked to enforce payment under an affiliation order" (Cumper, 1972:35). This legal "escape hatch" encourages greater disintegration of the household when fathers are unable to provide regular maintenance.

Nevertheless, the geographical mobility of the father is economically advantageous due to the scarce, unstable employment opportunities for young men in the society. A man's decision to settle with his wife and children usually comes after he has obtained the financial ability to find a locally-based, relatively stable means of economic support (land or employment) for a homestead. This development is by no means always the case. Community pressures may encourage earlier marriage. Or in a large proportion of instances, estrangement occurs after a couple has one or two children. In these cases, the mother will become associated with other men. But she will find it increasingly difficult to find a man willing to enter into a permanent relationship because of his reluctance to support other men's children. It is not uncommon to find women with children from two or three men with little chance of finding a permanent partner.

Bantje (1974), who has done detailed community study of the social structure in relation to malnutrition, found PEM increasing over 50 percent when parents were both absent and that married family households had lower rates of child growth failure than other types of households (pp. 10-12).

It is not clear from this factor that low income is associated with uncohesive households, as one might expect from the reasoning above. No direct economic measures load on the factor. The reason for this is that the social structure is adjusting to compensate for *potentially* low income. Bantje puts the matter clearly and concisely:

> what is lost due to the absence of the parents is sometimes compensated for by the (financial) support they are able to give . . . . The fluidity of the household pattern is an adaptation to the depressed economic situation. People are forced to choose the least of two evils, and sacrifice family life to economic advancement. (1974:12)

Again to return to our case family, we find that the most serious case of malnutrition in the household was a three year old most distantly related to the household head, a "cousin's child." He had lived in the household for over a year away from both parents. This child was under 60 percent of standard weight, with a parallel length deficiency. The child was in poor condition, but not marasmic. His condition might be described as "nutritional dwarfism" (Jelliffe, 1965:192). Next were the children of the twenty year old unmarried daughter with the edemous child at 66 percent of standard weight. (This child, by the way, was nearly normal standard height for age.) Both of her children were fathered by a young man living elsewhere in St. James and providing a small maintenance every two months, or whenever he could get work. He called himself a "carpenter" doing "day work," that is, *when* he could find it; "work all around," that is, *where* he could find it. Far from standard length and weight, but best off in the household, was the young child of the household head and his wife. She was not employed except for occasional travel to Montego Bay to market garden roots and vegetables for cash. Her husband farmed and worked nearby, resided in the household, and filled the role of main provider as best he could.

Mother/Guardian Maturity and Nutritional Status
Child weight status is higher in households with mature mothers and guardians. Mothers under twenty tend to have lighter one year old children than mothers in their thirties.

This result may be a consequence of better child care experience although no nutritional measures load on the factor. The subtleties of good care and appropriate feeding were not measured in this analysis. For instance, longer and more complete breast feeding during infancy may be practiced by older mothers following more traditional patterns, whereas younger mothers may be more inclined to use costly modern foods such as formula milks, more for their convenience and prestige value than for their nutritional value.

It is also possible that the higher prematurity rates of teenage mothers may be reflected here. If younger mothers have low birth weight children, the weight and length for age of their one year olds would be somewhat reflected in the results. However, in Jamaica, Desai (1968) reports no statistically significant relationship between birth weights and later growth attainment, especially after twelve months of age.

Returning to our case, the effect of maturation of the meal-maker seems to come through clearly in the comparison of the older mother's children with those of her daughter. The 42-year-old woman had two children aged thirty-four months and nine months. Their nutritional statuses were 83.2 percent of standard and 79.2 percent of standard weight for age. The youngest was mostly breast fed, but supplemented with a commercial infant milk powder. The twenty-year-old's children were twenty and thirty-five months of age and were 66 percent and 77 percent of standard weight for age. Each mother prepared her children's meals, and whereas one might expect the grandmother to nurture her grandchildren, this unwieldy household of ten children probably made it next to impossible.

The malnourished children in our sample household show how the four factors discussed above can operate simultaneously with tragic consequences. As we see, no one factor explains all the nutritional variation in this household, but only in combination do the cases of malnutrition become understandable.

Household Diet and Monetary Wealth

It is important to note the factors that did *not* prove to be significantly correlated with nutritional status. Perhaps the most unexpected are "household diet" and "monetary wealth." There are methodological as well as theoretical reasons to explain this result. "Household diet" is composed of variables gathered in a twenty-four hour recall record, an extremely short period of measurement when one reflects on the dietary history of any one-year-old child. Just consider the weekly cycle. Over one week's time, the household diet may vary considerably; on Sunday, the family has the best meal of the week, rice and peas, perhaps fried chicken back or another meat dish. On weekdays, one is more likely to find less elaboration in the diet, soup dishes being commonly composed of combinations of starchy roots and tubers such as yam, banana, and flour dumplings. Our dietary recall records for this survey have not accounted for this weekly cycle, let alone seasonal cycles and unpredictable lean and fat periods. Furthermore, the records are largely qualitative and would not readily highlight the small, long-term, incremental deficiencies, or past, short-term, massive deficiencies. These are not serious problems in my view. Food consumption measures enter into other important factors, such as "agricultural subsistence," in more understandable ways than they do as an "independent" factor.

The lack of correlation with "monetary wealth" is harder to explain. This may be simply due to relatively unreliable data. The absence of a significant correlation could also be a result of measuring only the past week's income and not yearly income estimates. As with the dietary measures, income related measures such as food expenditure do enter into factors that are significantly correlated with nutritional status. However, for the monetary factor, there may be a powerful theoretical reason why this result was obtained. In a rapidly expanding tourist area, such as St. James, one should not be surprised to find that income of households is often diverted to expensive status foods or to other non-food prestige items. The area has been flooded with commercial advertising and promotion for many years. This represents the introduction of relatively new maladaptive cultural ideas from multinational companies operating in the region. If this is true, we should not find young child malnutrition following a simple direct (linear) relationship with income because of the diversion of income above certain levels to consumer goods, particularly inappropriate infant foods. Advertising inflates the nutritional value of infant foods such as tonic milk drinks and infant formula milks. They provide extremely costly calories and are harmful if not properly used (Grantham—Macgregor, 1971).

In this study, we found one-third of the one-year-olds' diets containing imported tonic drinks such as "Milo" and "Ovaltine," a greater proportion than those containing the nutritious and inexpensive locally grown legumes or dark green vegetables. In our case household, both tonic drinks and infant powdered milk formula were used. The tinned formula in use was one of the most prestigious and expensive United States brands, "Olac," produced by Mead Johnson. Its price per pound tin at the local shop was more than 90 percent of the household's reported weekly income! No doubt the formula was overdiluted. The family had no refrigerator, or even rat proof storage facility. The women cooked over open hearths. No doubt formulas were also contaminated with disease-bearing organisms in ways human breast milk could never be.

Another powerful reason why the monetary factor may not have been correlated with nutrition is that income effects are remote in the causal chain. For example, current income could be affecting future cultivation patterns, consumption patterns, water supply, fertility patterns, job seeking, and family structure in ways that have their effect on nutritional status at some future time.

A Theoretical Caveat

This leads me to introduce a general theoretical caveat regarding the interpretations some might draw from this analysis. It may appear that independent *causal* forces behind malnutrition have been identified. Viewed in this manner, we might conclude that malnutrition is "caused by" socioeconomic factors such as the degree of agricultural subsistence, and "caused by" sociocultural factors such as the maturity of the mother or guardian, the compatibility of parents, and differential ideal family size. Economic or material history and structure should be used to understand the socioeconomic factors, and sociocultural factors should be analyzed in the light of cultural influences or ideational history and structure. However, bear in mind that nearly all the variables in the analysis are measurements of current household circumstances; only a few questions requested recall of more than seven days. Because we avoided the difficulty of gathering reliable data on retrospective mortality, past migration, and other "historical" data, the analysis is almost exclusively a synchronic snapshot of the society.

Furthermore, there are inherent limitations in the analytical method of factor analysis using orthogonal factors. The causal chain is flattened in such a way that it is impossible to construct and test causal models. As discussed previously in connection with income, variables far removed from the dependent variable through a number of intervening causal links might be all important, but show little or no direct correlation with the outcome (cf. Woods and Graves, 1973).

It may well be that a diachronic or historical picture of the society would reveal a close, perhaps inseparable, linkage between factors. In my view, material history would go far to explain the intra-cultural variation represented in the "cultural" factors. In fact, nutritional status as a part of or reflection of material conditions, can also be a cause rather than a passive effect of cultural and socioeconomic conditions. Where wide class inequalities in income and land available have existed for centuries, sociocultural and biological adaptations to poverty become well-developed. As discussed before, "family cohesion" probably depends upon the ability of the household to support itself economically, as a single unit in one locality. Where th eopportunities for employment or land holding are locally inadequate, one or two family members must set out on migratory searches for income. Ironically, if this strategy is successful, income (per capita) is maintained somewhat and comparisons would not reveal very great income disparities between cohesive and fragmented families, although material conditions are basically responsible for the difference. What we see instead is only the biological component of the material cause, young child malnutrition. Carrying the point further, even if the stark deprivations that created this type of family no longer exist to such a degree, the cultural pattern has persisted.

Similar arguments could be advanced for possible associations between other factors, but these would be speculative in the context of this present study. Based on this analysis, we cannot honestly dismiss the fact that the results show the association of independent socioeconomic and sociocultural *factors* with nutritional status. We do not have sufficient justification to say that there is no variation in cultural knowledge and skills useful in improving a family's ability to survive and raise well-nourished children. For instance, the "mother/guardian maturity" factor seems to be an indication that some mothers are slightly better at child rearing than others. Similarly, wide variation in family size preferences appear to exist, and affect nutritional status. While in theory we have compelling reasons to expect that increase or redistributions of resources and income would greatly relieve the young child malnutrition associated with all the factors, in practice important sociocultural variations exist regardless of their origins. Most societies today are changing rapidly enough that cultural practices could persist for some time after the economic conditions to which they were responsive have changed. Conversely, new maladaptive cultural behavior can enter the society from outside. In tourist areas such as St. James, the influences of affluent life styles, including food and feeding habits, are pervasive and enticing regardless of how inappropriate they are in the context of the poor Jamaican's life. Particular maladaptive behavior may in the long term die out; in the short term it nevertheless is there and demands our attention within the current context. Being both powerless, and compassionate toward suffering children, we have little choice.

Policy Implications

Moving from the results and theory to policy is not an easy task; it is a practical as well as responsible move to stay close to empirically defensible recommendations.

(1) The clearest and least risky uses of the data would be as an aid to epidemiological research and population screening. The factors derived in this analysis could be used to identify households with a good probability of containing malnourished children. In other words, a simple set of questions could be developed that could replace expensive nutritional surveying as a means of a diagnosis of young child malnutrition in this age group.

(2) It seems clear that if one were going to recruit child nutrition counselors such as Community Health Aides, somewhat older, more mature women would take precedence over younger ones.

(3) More far-ranging implications are also evident for planners of Jamaica's food and nutrition policy. Young child malnutrition is clearly linked with agricultural land use policy. The results suggest a criticism of current policies which stress a capital intensive, export-oriented agricultural sector rather than a labor intensive agricultural sector. Large estate farms that use most prime land at the expense of the bulk of peasant farmers, not only tend to increase de-✓ pendence on foreign food imports at highly inflatable prices, but also have an insidious impact on young child nutrition. No doubt policy makers are enticed by the needs for foreign exchange, but unless export production in this area can be done without continuing the patterns of unemployment and uneconomic family farm size, the gains in foreign exchange will not be beneficial to the nutritional status of young children. Government policy instituted by the recently-elected Peoples National Party is addressing the problems of land tenure. One program known as operation GROW (Growing and Reaping Our Wealth) is a small step in the right direction. The plan consists of three parts: (a) leasing idle land from owners and releasing it to farmers; (b) Government-owned lands will be farmed on a cooperative basis; and (c) farmers of farms from five to twenty-five acres will be encouraged to grow food crops. The primary object of this plan, however, seems only to reduce food import bills, and not to make the smallest agricultural subsistence farms more economic in size. In any case, it seems clear that rural households should not be expected to live off their own home grown food unless more adequate land is provided to them.

Within the limits of their present resources, such a move will lead to increased child malnutrition in many rural households due to agricultural subsistence stress.

(4) The present study also highlights the fact that Jamaica's long-standing concern with population control is not misplaced. The integration of child welfare, nutrition, and family planning services currently taking place is wise, considering the linkage between dependency stress and child nutritional status. Achievement of a more prosperous existence for these stressed households would diminish the nutritional consequences and might even encourage a decrease in the birth rate because parents would be more confident in the survival of offspring. However, on an island the size of Jamaica, in light of the current possibilities of radical improvements in the lower class economic resources, family planning seems a practical course of action at this time.

(5) Intrafamilial food maldistribution doesn't appear to be an important element in the nutritional status of the one-year-old child. Therefore, efforts to instruct mothers on sharing greater quantities or varieties of family dietary items will not in itself make much difference in the nutritional status of these children.

(6) More regular use of clinic services as presently organized or improvements of maternal literacy *per se* do not carry any special advantages for the nutritional status of one-year-olds.

(7) The advertisement of inappropriate infant foods should be eliminated.

Summary

Young child malnutrition and general growth failure in Jamaica are associated with four independent ecological factors in the child's microenvironment. The degree of *agricultural subsistence* of the household and the *dependency stress* on the household have a negative influence on both length and weight achievement of one-year-olds. *Household cohesion* and *mother/guardian maturity* have positive effects on weight alone.

The meaning of these relationships was examined in relation to macroscopic social and economic features of Jamaican society. The connections of malnutrition with long standing inequalities of this plantation economy were discussed. However, intracultural variation such as maternal maturity, ideal family size, and food preferences appeared relevant and seemed to operate independently of current material conditions. Given the research design, it could not be shown how these may be linked to historical macroeconomic conditions. Finally, I have suggested some policy recommendations for alleviating malnutrition, which focus on problems of land reform, food import policy, family planning and nutritional programming, nutritional epidemiological screening, and food advertising.

Notes

1. Jamaica's nutritional and health status is high compared to other developing countries. (Bengoa, 1973; Puffer, 1973).

2. Many internationally known professionals in the nutrition field have interest in Jamaica. Among them is Cecily Williams, "discoverer" of kwashiorkor. She was born on an estate in western Jamaica in a small town known as Rat Trap. D. B. Jelliffe, former director of the Caribbean Food and Nutrition Institute, was her student.

Much of the notable work on young child malnutrition has been biochemical and clinical work done by the Tropical Metabolism Unit of the University Hospital in Kingston. In one popular medical text (Davidson, Passmore and Brock, 1972), the chapter on protein energy malnutrition cites nine separate studies done in Jamaica, one-fourth of all the citations in the chapter.

3. Desai and Clarke (1970b) report this in detail. Later Alderman (1973) reported positive results in a rural clinic staffed by Cornell medical students and staff.

4. Based on unpublished statistics provided by the Jamaican Government, Department of Statistics, Division of Census and Surveys.

5. This survey was phase III of a four-phase evaluation of the Community Health Aide Programme. Sample size was determined by differences in nutritional status which were expected upon resurvey.

6. This cluster sampling technique was modeled after Snedecor and Cochran (1967, p. 515). In it the approximation to a simple random sample is found if the mean differences from cluster to cluster of key variables can be estimated. Based on nutritional status data as the key variable, this sample was virtually identical to a simple random sample.

7. The results reported here should not be taken as precise prevalence measurements because the sample was reduced introducing some distortion. For instance, one case of severe malnutrition was found, but not reported here.

The reduction in sample size is the result of case-wise deletion of missing data. This was necessary because of later stages in the analysis where calculation of exact and reliable factor values requires that a value for every household variable be available in each case for the linear equations which generate the factor scores. The reduction does not upset key distributions. For instance, income, food expenditure, urban-rural, and Gomez classifications are not significantly altered, i. e., Chi square tests confirm the null hypothesis.

8. See Nelson's Textbook of pediatrics, 1969: 40. For example, at twelve months, 90 percent of standard weight for age of boys is 19.0 lbs., and that is the tenth percentile. Eighty percent of standard is 17.6 lbs., which is just under the third percentile.

9. Partial correlation was calculated after Seigel (1956: 226).

x-percent standard weight for age
y-urban vs. rural location of household
z-household food expenditure per person per week

$tau_{xy} = -.19$
$tau_{xz} = .24$
$tau_{yz} = -.50$

$$tau_{xy \cdot z} = \frac{tau_{xy} - tau_{yz} tau_{xz}}{\sqrt{(1 - tau^2_{yz})(1 - tau^2_{xz})}}$$

$$tau_{xy \cdot z} = \frac{(-.19) - (-.50)(.24)}{\sqrt{(1 - (-.50)^2)(1 - (.24)^2)}}$$

$$tau_{xy \cdot z} = -.083$$

10. Other methods were attempted, including oblique rotation and factor limitation. Oblique rotation results in factors which are intercorrelated, the assumption being that factors so derived are less complex and more realistic. In this case, however, factors were neither clearer nor easier to interpret than were the orthogonal factors. Similarly, attempts to limit the output to six factors only compounded the complexity of the factors. All programs were derived from the Statistical Package for the Social Sciences, Nie (1970) and the July 1973 update.

11. My own observations and discussions with physicians in St. James. Also, personal communication from anthropologist, Joseph Long, who did intensive field studies of balm yards just south of our study area in the early seventies. Balm yards are the "clinics" of Jamaica's indigenous medical practitioners.

12. Multiple regression analysis was tried and added little analytically. Since the factors are already uncorrelated, partial correlations with the dependent variable are identical to the zero-order correlations. Therefore, the primary use of the technique, i. e., to assess the contribution of each independent variable to the dependent variable, is preempted.

13. A documented discussion of demographic (family size) impact on nutrition of children is found in IPPF (1970). See also Antrobus, K., "Child Growth and Related Factors in a Rural Community in St. Vincent," *Journal of Tropical Pediatrics* (December, 1971). Of course the Desai (1968) report cited in this study is supported.

14. The lack of importance of the income or "monetary wealth" factor may be due to the difficulties encountered in collecting accurate data. The CHAs, being government employees, were viewed with suspicion by some householders, resulting in possibly false income reports. Also, women questioned may have had only partial knowledge of all income sources flowing into the household.

Appendix

Each child's household was interviewed using precoded interview schedules. The variables and the scale types used in the analysis are given below.

1. *Location*—urban-rural (1, 2) based upon Jamaican census tracts.

2. *Household Size*—defined as the number of persons both co-residing and sharing meals during the survey week.

3. *Dependency Ratio*—defined as the number of householders under fifteen years divided by those fifteen and over.

4. *School Lunches*— the number of school children in the household receiving a lunch at school.

5. *Employment History*—the proportion of the past twelve months in which the main economic household provider was employed.

6. *Agricultural Resources*—whether the household has access (owns, leases, or rents) any cultivable land, has livestock, or both.

7. *Home Food Use*—the degree to which home grown food was used in the family diet over the past week, i. e., none, one or two items, many items.

8. *Food Expenses*—the household food expenditure per capita over the past week.

9. *Income*—the household income in cash from all sources per capita over the past week.

10. *Distance to (Piped) Water*—the distance from the household, if not house connected, to a currently operating piped water supply.

11. *Distance to (Nearest) Health Facility*—distance to nearest Health Center, Rural Clinic, or Public Hospital.

12. *Relationship of Meal-Maker to Child*—the social relationship of the "meal-maker" and the one year old target child. Mother was

given highest numerical value, grandmother second, other adult relatives third, child relatives fourth, and non-relatives, lowest value.

13. *Age of Meal-Maker*—age in years classed into four categories: 20, 21-24, 25-34, over 35.

14. *Age of the Child*—age in months. Verified by birth records in most cases.

15. *Diet Variety*—whether or not ten or more items of different foods were found in the meal-maker's twenty-four-hour dietary recall record.

16. *Diet Sharing*—whether or not over 90 percent of the meal-maker's items appeared in the target child's dietary recall record.

17. *Diet complexity*—whether or not a nearly "complete" set of food types was represented in the child's dietary recall. These included *staples* (roots, tubers, or cereals such as yam, sweet potato, cassava, "irish" potato, bread or rice), *sugar and sweets* (such as "sweeties," soft drinks), *vegetables* (such as callalo and pumpkin), *fruits* (pawpaw, citrus and the like), *peas and beans* (including all legumes such as pigeon peas and red peas), *animal products* (including milk, eggs, cheese, meat, fish or fowl), *commercial "tonic" drinks* (canned drinks, mixed with hot water or milk, such as Milo, Horlicks, Ovaltine).

18. *Mother's Presence*—whether the mother of the target child was currently resident in the household, was elsewhere in the parish or was abroad.

19. *Father's Presence*—as above.

20. *Mother's Employment*—whether or not the mother was currently employed for wages.

21. *Father's Support*—whether the father of the child was providing economic support for the whole household, or whether he provided support for the child in whole, in part, or not at all.

22. *Mother's Age*—the age of the target child's biological mother.

23. *Children Under Five*—the number of surviving children born to the mother in the past five years.

24. *Mother's Education*—whether or not the mother of the child had at least four years of formal schooling. Bolland (1971) found this cutting point to be predictive of illiteracy in survey of rural Jamaica.

25. *Milk Type*—the most frequently used milk said to be used in the past twenty-four hours for the child. Breast milk was given

highest value, whole cream milk, which is cheapest, second, other whole cream milk third, cow's milk fourth, sweetened condensed milk fifth, dry skim milk sixth, and none, lowest numerical value.

26. *Illness of Child*—if the child was or was not ill from any cause over the past thirty days.

27. *Child Welfare Clinic (CWC) Attendance*—if the child was or was not brought to the last scheduled government clinic for that area.

28. *Family Planning Clinic (FPC) Attendance*—whether the mother of the child did or did not attend the last scheduled government family planning clinic for the area.

29. *Sex of the Child*—female was given higher numerical value than male.

30-31. *Dietary Adequacy—Meal Maker, and Child*—this measure was based upon twenty-four-hour recalls of the meal-maker regarding herself and the target child. Daily portions in the various food groups, given above in #17, were counted and were assessed for adequate or inadequate nutrient levels by a set of criteria, based on more exact surveys. Adequate diets were given highest numerical value, diets inadequate in calories, second value, protein inadequate diets, third highest, and protein and calorie inadequate diets, lowest value.

The formula was developed by Miss Helen Fox, Technical Officer/Nutrition, who has conducted extensive and intensive dietary surveys of the island. (Calories: at least four portions staples and/or sugar plus two of fats and oils. Protein: at least three portions of animal product and/or peas and beans.)

References

Adams, Nassau A.
    1969 Internal Migration in Jamaica: An Economic Analysis. Social and Economic Studies 18 (2).
Ahiram, E.
    1964 Income Distribution in Jamaica, 1958. Social and Economic Studies 13.
Alderman, Michael, et al.
    1973 A Young-Child Nutrition Programme in Rural Jamaica. The Lancet, May 26, 1973.
Alland, A.
    1970 Adaptation in Cultural Evolution: An Approach to Medical Anthropology. New York: Columbia University Press.
Alleyne, G. A.
    1970 Some Features of Infantile Malnutrition in Jamaica. The West Indian Medical Journal XIX (1).

Ashcroft, M. T., P. Heneage, and H. G. Lovell
   1966   Heights and Weights of Jamaican Schoolchildren of Various Ethnic
   Groups. American Journal of Physical Anthropology 24 (1).
Ashworth, A., and D. Picou
   1974   Nutritional Status in Jamaica 1968-1973. Paper presented at the
   Conference on Food and Nutrition Policy. Kingston.
Bantje, Han F.
   1974a   Household Circumstances and Infant Malnutrition in Western Hanover, Jamaica. Kingston, Jamaica: Caribbean Food and Nutrition Institute and
   Nutrition Unit of the Ministry of Health. (Mimeographed).
   1974b   A Follow-up Study of Cases of Infant Malnutrition and Gastroenteritis
   in the Noel Holmes Hospital, Lucea, Jamaica 1972-73, Kingston, Jamaica, CFNI
   and Nutrition Unit of the Ministry of Health. (Mimeographed).
Beckford, George L.
   1972   Persistent Poverty: Underdevelopment in Plantation Economics of the
   Third World. New York and London: Oxford University Press.
Bengoa, J. M.
   1973   The State of World Nutrition. M. Recheigle, Ed. Man, Food and
   Nutrition. Cleveland: CRC Press.
Bolland, O. Nigel
   1971   Literacy in a Rural Area of Jamaica. Social and Economic Studies 20.
Boodhoo, V. R., and K. Standard
   n. d.   An Investigation of Child Mortality in Rural St. Andrew, Jamaica, June,
   1968-May, 1970. Kingston: Department of Social and Preventative Medicine,
   University of the West Indies. (Mimeographed).
Clarke, Edith
   1957   My Mother Who Fathered Me. London: George Allen & Unwin, Ltd.
Cook, Robert
   1971   The Cost of Malnutrition in Jamaica. Ecology of Food and Nutrition 1.
Cumper, Gloria
   1972   Survey of Social Legislation in Jamaica. Jamaica: Institute of Social and
   Economic Studies, University of the West Indies.
Davidson, S., R. Passmore, and J. F. Brock
   1972   Human Nutrition and Dietetics. Baltimore: The Williams and Wilkins
   Co.
Desai, P. et al.
   1970   Socio-Economic and Cultural Influences on Child Growth in Rural
   Jamaica. Journal of Biosoc. Science 2.
Desai, P., L. Clarke, and Heron
   1970   Do Child Welfare Clinics Influence Growth? Journal of Biosoc. Science
   2.
Desai, P., W. E. Miall, and K. L. Standard
   1968   Jamaica: The Social Background of Malnutrition. Maternal and Child
   Care 4.
Fonaroff, L. S.
   1969   Settlement Typology and Infant Malnutrition in Jamaica. Trop. Geogr.
   Med 21: 117
Frishancho, A. Robert, et al.
   1973   Adaptive Significance of Small Body Size under Poor Socio-Economic
   Conditions in Southern Peru. American Journal of Physical Anthropology 2.
Garrow, J. S. and M. C. Pike
   1967   The Long-Term Prognosis of Severe Infantile Malnutrition. The Lancet
   1.

Gurney, J. M., Helen Fox, and J. Jeill
    1972   A Rapid Survey to Assess the Nutrition of Jamaican Infants and Young
    Children in 1970. Trans. of the Royal Society of Tropical Medicine and
    Hygiene 66 (4).
Grantham-McGregor, Sally M. and E. H. Back
    1970   A Note on Infant Feeding in Kingston. West Indian Medical Journal XIX
    (2).
Gross, Daniel and Barbara Underwood
    1971   Technical Change and Caloric Costs: Sisal Agriculture in Northern
    Brazil. American Anthropologist 73.
Habicht, J. et al.
    1974   Height and Weight Standards for Preschool Children. How Relevant
    Are Differences in Growth Potential? The Lancet 1.
Harman, Harry H.
    1960   Modern Factor Analysis. Chicago: University of Chicago Press.
Heywood, P.
    1974   Malnutrition and Productivity in Jamaican Sugar Cane Cutters. Ph.D.
    Thesis, Cornell University, Department of International Nutrition.
International Planned Parenthood Federation
    1970   The Relationship between Family Size and Maternal and Child Health.
    Working Paper 5, London.
Jamaican Government, Central Planning Unit
    1971   Economic Survey.
Jamaican Government, Department of Statistics
    1975   Statistical Yearbook (1974).
Jefferson, Owen
    1972   The Post-War Economic Development of Jamaica. Surrey, England:
    Unwin Brothers Limited.
Jelliffe, D. B.
    1966   The Assessment of the Nutritional Status of the Community. Geneva:
    World Health Organization.
    1968   The Pre-School Child as a Bio-cultural Transitional. Journal of Tropical
    Pediatrics 14.
    1968   Infant Nutrition in the Subtropics and Tropics. Geneva: World Health
    Organization.
    1969   Observations on Protein-Calorie Malnutrition in the Caribbean.
    Protein-Calorie Malnutrition, A. Von Muralt, Ed. New York: Spring-Verlag.
    n. d.   Commertiogenic Malnutrition.
McKenzie, H. L., H. G. Lovell, K. L. Standard, and W. E. Miall
    1967   Milbank Memorial Fund Quarterly 45.
Marchione, Thomas J.
    1973   An Evaluation of the Nutrition and Family Planning Components of the
    Community Health Aide Programme in the Parish of St. James, Jamaica.
    Kingston: Caribbean Food and Nutrition Institute. (Mimeographed Report).
Nelson, W. E.
    1969   Textbook of Pediatrics. W. E. Nelson, Ed. Philadelphia: W. B. Saunders
    Company, Ninth Edition.
Nie, N., Dale Bent, and C. Hull
    1970   Statistical Package for the Social Sciences. New York: McGraw-Hill.
Norton, A. V., and G. E. Cumper
    1966   Peasant Plantation and Urban Communities in Rural Jamaica: A Test of
    the Validity of the Classification. Social and Economic Studies.
Puffer, R. R. and Serrano
    1973   Patterns of Mortality in Childhood. Washington, D. C.: PAHO.

Richardson, Stephen A.
    1972   Ecology of Malnutrition: Malnutritional Factors Influencing Intellectual and Behavioral Development. Nutrition, The Nervous System and Behavior: Proceedings of a Seminar. Washington, D. C.: PAHO.
Rummel, R. J.
    1970   Applied Factor Analysis. Evanston: Northwestern University Press.
Scrimshaw, Nevin, and John Gordon
    1968   Malnutrition, Learning, and Behavior. Nevin Scrimshaw and John Gordon, Eds. Boston: The MIT Press.
Seoane, N. and Latham
    1971   Nutritional Anthropometry in the Identification of Malnutrition in Childhood. Journal of Tropical Pediatrics and Environ. Child Health.
Siegel, Sidney
    1956   Nonparametric Statistics for the Behavioral Sciences. New York: McGraw-Hill Book Company.
Smith, M. G.
    1966   Introduction in Edith Clarke, My Mother Who Fathered Me. Allen and Unwin, Ltd., 2nd Edition.
    1962   West Indian Family Structure. Seattle: University of Washington Press.
Snedecor, George, and William Cochran
    1967   Statistical Methods. Ames, Iowa: The Iowa State University Press.
Stini, W.
    1971   Evolutionary Implications of Changing Nutritional Patterns in a Human Population. American Anthropologist 73 (5).
Stone, Carl
    1974   Political Aspects of Post-war Agricultural Policies in Jamaica (1945-1970). Social and Economic Studies 23 (2).
    1974   Electoral Behavior and Public Opinion in Jamaica. Institute of Social and Economic Studies Publication, University of the West Indies.
Tanner, J.
    1970   Growth and Physique in Different Populations of Mankind. Evolutionary Anthropology, Blerbtreu, Ed. Boston: Allyn and Bacon, Inc.
WHO
    1965   Technical Report Series, No. 302. Geneva: World Health Organization.
Woods, C. M. and T. D. Graves
    1973   The Process of Medical Change in a Highland Guatemalan Town. Los Angeles: U. C. Latin American Center.
Wray, et al.
    1969   PCM in Candelaria, Columbia. Journal of Tropical Pediatrics 15 (3).

10

Diet and Acculturation

The Case of Black-American In-Migrants*

N. W. Jerome

Introduction and Frame of Reference

When people move from a rural to an urban environment, their diets often change. They must prepare meals quickly to meet the demands of work and school schedules. They must purchase rather than produce their food. This may mean a substantial decrease in their ability to acquire food despite equivalent or increased monetary incomes. Children develop new appetites at school; and

*This paper is based on the author's doctoral dissertation entitled "Food Habits and Acculturation: Dietary Practices and Nutrition of Families Headed by Southern-Born Negroes Residing in a Northern Metropolis," University of Wisconsin, 1967. Although the social situation in Centavia has undergone change since the community was first described thirteen years ago, the study on which this paper is based has been hailed a classic in Nutritional Anthropology. Thus, this paper is particularly meaningful here. The author was the first person to have received graduate training in both human nutrition and anthropology at a United States university and apply the methods and concepts of both disciplines to an urban setting in a modern industrialized society. This study marked the beginning of Nutritional Anthropology.

experiences away from home with different culinary styles stimu-
late new tastes. The new foodways which emerge are a clear
syncretization of long-cherished habits and new lifestyles. Diet
quality and nutritional status are easily affected by such changes
although successful nutritional adaptation to the new environment
is a biological prerequisite for socioeconomic success.

Diet is thus a sensitive index of acculturation. But the relationship
between dietary change and other types of acculturation is
complex. Social, cultural, economic, and nutritional factors are
interwoven in an intricate net. Unraveling it requires a combination of nutritional and ethnological methods of research and
analysis.

Between 1965 and 1966 I studied the dietary acculturation of
southern-born women in a Black Inner City district of Milwaukee. I
combined participant observation with nutrient analysis of the
diets of sixty-three selected families. All of the respondents were
women who had migrated from a relatively homogeneous culture
area and resided in a single twenty block census tract, typical of
Milwaukee's "inner core." Because of the *de facto* segregation
which isolated them from Milwaukee's other ethnic groups their
dietary habits were influenced more by the social and economic
conditions of urban life than by intercultural contact. Although
some dietary changes were common to the entire group, they
exhibited several distinct intracultural variations in lifestyle and
dietary habits. Through participant observation I discovered four
microcultural groups, defined on the basis of material achievement
and marital style in Milwaukee. On the basis of nutritional data, I
developed an index of dietary acculturation. In this paper, I
correlate the four microcultural groups with the different patterns
of dietary acculturation and analyze the nutritional consequences
of each.

Using this methodology, I have been able to answer the
following questions: (1) How does the southern meal pattern
evolve to a form compatible with the lifestyle of northern urban
wage-laborers? (2) How do dietary variations within the sample
reflect the ability to "make it" or not in the new environment? and
(3) What are the nutritional consequences of different patterns of
adjustment to urban life? This makes it possible to see how
nutrition and culture interact in creating small but spiralling
differences which may have great consequences for the success
black southern migrants and their inner city born children.

Living in Centavia

"Centavia," the study site, is one of the nine "highly segregated" census tracts of Milwaukee's twenty-six tract "inner core" (O'Reilly 1963:6). Between 1940 and 1960, its black population gradually increased. By 1960, 3,241 of Centavia's 3,713 residents were black. As is typical of black inner city neighborhoods, life in Centavia is characterized by economic oppression and overcrowding made bearable and congenial by proximity to networks of friends and relatives who "help each other out."

Centavia is part of an area which is regarded locally as the heart of the business district. A 1966 assessment of blight and property deterioration in Milwaukee admitted that this is also one of the city's major problem areas (*Milwaukee Journal* April 3, 1966). Centavia is flanked by a busy commercial district to its east, an expressway to its west, a housing redevelopment project to its south, and slightly better housing to the north. According to the 1960 United States census, population density was 39.9 (median) persons per acre.

Most of Centavia's educational services and a major portion of its political and economic resources come from outside the community. But the tone and direction of its religious, recreational, and life, Centavia is more self-sufficient. It contains many public facilities and community institutions. There are six churches and one "Black Muslim" mosque in Centavia; four of the churches are of the "store front" variety. Churches function as religious and social centers for the members. An elementary school and a public library are located in the heart of Centavia; and there is a parochial school on its southern boundary. Three blocks south of Centavia there is a recreational center where a well-baby clinic is held weekly.

Centavia's commercial retail area is largely white-owned and includes one large department store, two banks, a variety of small business and service centers including two drug stores. Black-owned businesses or service centers include a dental and medical office and the office of an Afro-American weekly newspaper. Other businesses and services represented are two variety stores, a bakery, two meat markets, one fish market, two laundromats, one liquor store, and several discount stores. Adjoining this area are four beauty shops, one wiggery, two filling stations, three grocery chain stores, four restaurants, and two dry-cleaning establishments. Six corner grocery stores and fifteen taverns dot the non-commercial sections of Centavia.

According to the Milwaukee Health Department, Centavia's death rate is 38.1/1,000 live births. Its infant death rate ranks sixteenth highest among the twenty-six Inner Core tracts. Its death rate for tuberculosis is 21.5/100,000 population, ranking fifth highest among the Inner Core tracts.

The mean number of years of formal education for Centavia's residents is eight. In 1960, the unemployment rate for Centavia's black men was 15.4 which compared unfavorably with the national average of 8.7. (By contrast, only 3.6 of Centavia's white males were unemployed, while the national unemployment average for white men was 4.7).

According to the 1960 United States census, 20.2 percent of Centavia's dwelling units were classified as "crowded." Yet, crowding in Centavia appears minimal, compared to other tracts in the inner core. Houses are either single-family or two-family dwelling units; with only a few multiple-family dwelling units. Housing condition was assessed as follows: 43.2 percent sound, 38.8 percent deteriorating, and 17.9 percent dilapidated. The median value of all house units in Centavia is $7,900 and median monthly gross rentals for nonwhites are $82. O'Reilly (1963:58-59) reveals that 90.8 percent of the housing was built before 1919.

Many of Centavia's houses are owned by absentee-landlords. Of the 831 nonwhite housing units, 23.8 percent were owner-occupied. This figure almost coincides with the 24.2 percent black owner-occupied units in the Inner Core as a whole. Of 227 white housing units, 22 percent are owner-occupied. Some Centavia residents reside in tumbledown "rear" cottages, many of which have been condemned as uninhabitable by the city.

Most of the respondent families live in two-apartment houses made of wood-frame, sometimes disguised with asphalt or imitation brick siding. Unlighted passages and creaky, winding stairs, often without handrails, lead to upper floor apartments. Outside stairs lead directly to the living rooms of all apartments in two-unit buildings, and to "street side" apartments in four-unit buildings. Outside stairs lead directly to the kitchenettes of back apartments.

Apartments are uniform in structure, layout, and design. Most have high ceilings. The broken glass of the windows is patched with board and insulated with plastic. Individual space heaters and/or oil furnaces supply heat.

Meal preparation takes place in a kitchen-dinette equipped with a gas or electric stove, refrigerator, sink, storage cupboards, and one or two tables and chairs. In some apartments a storage pantry adjoins the area. A few respondents own upright or box-type freezers, and many own small kitchen appliances.

Most apartments have only two bedrooms to accommodate the families which average six members in size. Due to the railroad flat layouts, inter-room traffic is high, especially in the toilet-bathroom and kitchen-dinette areas. Adequate physical requirements for health, study, family living, privacy, and pets are lacking.

Family attitudes and values are manifest in the ability to overcome the inadequacies of the physical structure through resourcefulness and ingenuity in decorating homes and apartments. They are expressed also in the interpersonal relationships of Centavia residents. The Centavia resident is enmeshed in a network of kinship and friendship ties that is psychologically gratifying and practically helpful.

Some of these ties are established even before individuals move to Centavia. Most residents begin social life in the city even before they move. Their first Milwaukee residence is often in the homes of friends and relatives. They move out only after they have obtained a job and formed additional social ties in the city. Often they make their own homes close to friends and relatives.

When asked if they missed anything in the South, the usual answer was "relatives and weather." Those who had close relatives in the neighborhood remarked "only the weather and the taste of good southern food." These attachments are reflected in attitudes toward Centavia. A subsample of twenty-three respondents were asked if they would like to move from the area. Twenty-one said no. (The other two stated that they would like to move farther north in the city where better housing is available.) The feelings of my respondents bear out the conclusions of O'Reilly, Downing, and Pflangzer (1965) that Centavia residents are generally satisfied. Of course, feelings of satisfaction are both relative and practical.

Methodology

Because the methodology demanded a close working relationship between researcher and informant, true randomness had to be sacrificed to considerations of rapport. The responding women had to cooperate fully, keeping detailed dietary records and sharing intimate sociocultural and psychological data. I, in turn, had to be familiar with my informants' daily lives, and understand why they shopped, cooked, served, and ate as they did.

I collected data for a period of seven months. Since I lived within walking distance to Centavia (five blocks north), it was very convenient to observe and participate in the daily activities of the residents. Data collected during early phases of the study were of a general nature, while detailed information on food use was collected later.

Women of sixty-three households[1] provided general, qualitative data in an early phase of the study. Subsequently, I obtained detailed, quantitative data from women of twenty-three households who had major responsibility for the purchase, selection, distribution or preparation of the family's meals, and who had migrated from the South at least three months prior to the investigation.

During an intensive three-week observational period of Phase I, I spent a great deal of time in learning the neighborhood, its people, its social, educational, recreational, and religious life, its shopping centers and service centers, its small neighborhood stores and "store-front" churches. This led to the introductory period of Phase II. I met women in sixty-three households by ringing doorbells and requesting information on food use and southern cooking. I was invariably greeted with a smile and "Come on in. I'd be glad to tell you what I know." Introductions lasted from one to three hours and included informal discussions on general food use, diet patterns, southern cooking, the "taste of city food" or the "taste of food up here." This phase culminated with either the granting of an appointment to begin intensive interviews, or the offering of apologies for the family's inability to cooperate with the study. Much of the quantitative data, therefore, are derived from the women of twenty-three households, comprising 130 individuals and secured in Phases III, IV, and V of the study. Only households of two or more persons were included.

In the intensive interviews of Phase III, I used a semi-structured, largely open-ended interview schedule which yielded data on the following:

(a) family food practices: those dealing with total dietary selection and patterning, consumer practices, and values and beliefs which guide the family's dietary behavior;

(b) continuities and changes in food practices: respondents' reconstruction of diet patterns of the premigration period, identification of diet patterns and food practices currently followed and/or abandoned;

(c)   opinions: on a variety of topics relating to the exigencies of living in a new environment;

(d)   family characteristics: pertinent social characteristics of family members and opportunity for contact in the dominant culture;

(e)   life histories: voluntary description of particular life events relevant to a particular subject under discussion.

I also participated in family activities and in various aspects of family life surrounding birth, marriage, illness, death, separation and divorce and observed and recorded a variety of food practices in the homes of respondents.

Upon completing the interview schedule, I secured additional information from the female household head on the frequency with which family members selected certain food items at the morning and evening meals. This marks Phase IV of the study. Graded on a ten-point scale, the test took into account all of the knowledge I had gained in earlier phases on the respondents' dietary practices.

The Food Frequency Tests aided in the description of the respondents' meal patterns. Information gathered through this instrument also helped to identify the basic components of the meal pattern on a daily, weekly, monthly and annual cycle.

Approximately two weeks after completing the Food Frequency Tests, the respondents further cooperated in the study by keeping records on family food use and meals for seven consecutive days. This represented Phase V of the study.

I assumed responsibility for weighing, measuring and recording all food and beverages on hand on the first and last day of the week's undertaking. I left record sheets with the female household head and visited each household every other day to assist in recording additional foods and beverages obtained in the interim. The records provided quantitative data on the total food consumed in each of the twenty-three participating households. Nutrient analyses were also computed from the data.

The method of this study permits comparison of diet and food use in the pre-migration and contemporary periods. It is also sensitive to elucidating factors associated with diet continuity and change in the new environment. It further serves as a useful

strategy for determining intracultural variations in dietary patterning and adequacy, especially where these variations indicate
differential adjustments to a new environment.

Characteristics of Respondents

The respondent population consisted of women who were first
generation in-migrants from the southeastern section of the
United States. They all had some important responsibility for
family meals, although most were not primary financial supporters.
They had grown up in the South between 1900 and 1940, had lived
in Milwaukee from three months to thirty years, and were married
to men who held semiskilled or unskilled positions.

The sample represents adults who migrated from rural and
urban areas of Mississippi, Arkansas, Alabama, Louisiana, Georgia,
and Tennessee in order of descending representation. Eighty-
seven percent of the household heads (twenty households) are of
rural farm origin, 9 percent (two households) of urban origin, and
4 percent of rural non-farm origin.

Table 1 compares some socioeconomic characteristics of the
respondents with similar data provided by the United States
Bureau of Labor Statistics and the United States Bureau of the
Census for the city of Milwaukee. Blanks indicate that data were
not provided for the specific category.

Table 1 indicates that there are many similarities between
socioeconomic characteristics of the study sample and Milwaukee's
Negro or non-white population (United States Census). The study
sample also reflects many of the characteristics shown by the
randomly selected Negro sample (United States Bureau of Labor
Statistics). The greatest difference lies in the occupational classification of the study sample.

The Study

By reconstructing the format of meals served in the respondents'
homes during the pre-migration period, and comparing it with
contemporary meal patterns, I was able to discern changes in the
structure of the latter. It was also possible to tentatively identify
stages in which change occurred.

TABLE 1
SOCIOECONOMIC CHARACTERISTICS, STUDY
SAMPLE, BUREAU OF LABOR STATISTICS, UNITED STATES CENSUS
Milwaukee

Socioeconomic Characteristics	Per Cent of Sample		
	Study Sample 1965 (Negro)	Bureau of Labor Statistics 1963 (Negro)	U.S. Census 1960 (Negro-Non-white)
Occupation			
Semiskilled and Unskilled	100	--	49
Money Income after Taxes (dollars)			
(Average Income	$6,011	$5,721	$4,842)
2,000 - 2,999	8.7	--	10.7
3,000 - 3,999	8.7	--	11.9
4,000 - 5,999	17.4	--	28.0
6,000 - 9,999	60.9	--	27.1
10,000 and above	4.3	--	6.8
Poverty			
2,000 - 4,000	17.4	--	22.8
Deprived			
4,000 - 6,000	48.0	--	28.1
Per Cent Expenditure on Food	29.52*	25.1*	--
Housing			
House type, 1-2 units	55.5	--	70.0
Home Owners	30.4	--	24.3
Per Cent Expenditure for Rent	15.9*	14.9*	20.6*

TABLE 1   (Continued)

Socioeconomic Characteristics	Per Cent of Sample		
	Study Sample 1965 (Negro)	Bureau of Labor Statistics 1963 (Negro)	U. S. Census 1960 (Negro-Non-white)
Education (years)**			
5-7	29.2	--	18.8
8	22.0	--	17.9
High School, 1-3	36.6	--	25.1
High School, 4	12.2	--	17.6
Average Family Size	5.7*	5.0*	--
Aid to Families of Dependent Children	13.0	--	49.6[2]

*   These values do not represent percentages of samples, but are included since these values are pertinent to this table.

**   Values are for heads of household (male and female) of the study sample. U. S. Census data considered all persons over 14.

The Traditional Southern Diet and Meal Plan—a Review

Various researchers have concluded that there is a distinct Southern dietary pattern.[3] This traditional diet is exemplified by Vance's report of an analysis of 150 menus of Negro and white Southern farm families which show a preponderance of pork fats, starches and sweets and the frequent inclusion of hot breads and fried foods. Notably lacking are green salads, milk, and eggs (Vance, 1932). Dry beans, peas, nuts and cereals are also commonly eaten among families in the Southeastern states.

While affirming that the staple foods are basically the same for Negroes as for whites, Cussler and De Give see the racial problem as an integral part of the nutritional picture. "The whole social and economic level of the Negroes is lower than that of the whites. Their diet is less varied; they have fewer and smaller gardens, less canning, less livestock, just as their income (usually as tenants) is less" (Cussler and De Give, 1941).

The United States Department of Agriculture report on the 1935-36 food consumption in the United States showed a basic similarity between white and Negro families in the Southeast. For both, outlays for food increased with additional income, but the food selection patterns differed for the two groups. Negro families tended to spend relatively more of their food money for meat and less for milk, vegetables, and fruit than white families of comparable income and family type in the same communities (Stiebeling et al., 1941). More recent studies indicate slight modifications in the basic pattern outlines. However, most of the migrants in this study brought with them the dietary practices of the time period in the studies cited.

The Basic Meal Pattern—in Milwaukee

Analysis of the data indicates that the meal pattern consists of three basic components—the "core" or staple items of a particular meal, the "secondary core" or those items which are either added to or substituted for the basic core, and the "peripheral diet"[4] or those items which are used infrequently by most people. Items included in the peripheral diet are considered special or "ceremonial foods" or they may be items discriminated against due to the specific food ideology.

Breakfast. Meat, eggs, cereals and cereal products, butter, beverage and sweet condiments form the core items at breakfast; secondary core items may be substituted or added to the core items. There are four variations of the breakfast pattern based on either the exclusion of meat and eggs or in the manner in which these items are included in the meal. Patterns whereby the meat component is excluded are rare in the adult dietary. Hot biscuits and white bread or toast are essential cereal products in the day's first meal. The beverage, or "something to drink" may be milk, coffee, hot chocolate, chocolate milk, fruit drink or juice or a carbonated drink. Most individuals or families who consume fruit drinks and juices at breakfast include them in late breakfasts and as alternative beverages to the exclusion of milk or coffee. Generally, hot beverages and cold beverages of the "non-acid" type, e. g., apple juice and mixed fruit drinks, are preferred with early breakfasts. A sweet condiment is usually included in the breakfast meal.

Lunch. Two layers of white bread form the core of most noon meals, especially those packed at home. From a nutritional standpoint, the type of filling appears to be secondary to the bread itself since, in many cases, spreads of little or no protein value constitute the sandwich filling. On the other hand, aesthetic and organoleptic characteristics seem to be of primary consideration in the selection of sandwich fillings. All other luncheon patterns are subsidiary to the sandwich-beverage type. This is the only meal in which fresh fruits, soup, and crackers are included.

Dinner. Many core foods and two preparation methods are utilized as important factors in the planning and preparation of dinner. Meat, vegetables, dry legumes, cornbread, butter, and a beverage form the core items for this meal, and boiling and frying are decisive in determining the meal plan. For main dish meals, boiling is linked with vegetable or legume preparation; meats, i. e., neckbones, ham hocks, salt pork, etc., serves purely as flavoring agents, while greens or dry beans serve as the main dish. Frying is reserved for dinner meals when meats, i. e., chicken, pork chops, pork steak, etc., serve as the principal ingredient and vegetables, if any, clearly take a secondary role. Thus, method of preparation functions as a prime determinant of protein supply and quality for ? the dinner meal.

There are two or three boiling days each week; usually, they coincide with the day's schedule for heavy domestic work, and with low home supplies. Vegetables and dry legumes form the core of the meal on these days. Dinner on a boiling day constitutes one of several green leafy vegetables or dry beans or peas boiled with a meat item. Vegetable items may be collards, mustard greens, kale, cabbage sprouts or turnip greens, and the meat items may be salt pork, bacon, ham hocks, pig's tail or ham. The other days are designated frying days. Meat—fried chicken, fried pork chops, fried ham and occasionally fried beef or pork steak—forms the core of these meals. Baked or candied sweet potatoes, rice, fried corn, mashed or fried white potatoes may be included with fried meats. Few households include a "non-starchy" vegetable on those days. A fourth dinner pattern includes a non-starchy vegetable in the fried dinner pattern. In such cases, left-over greens, English peas, string beans, or sliced tomatoes may be added, but this pattern is not frequently encountered on a weekday. Irrespective of the meal patterns and preparation method, three items—cornbread and occasionally biscuits, butter, and an iced drink—are added to complete the meal. Determinants of the breakfast, lunch, and dinner patterns are shown in tables 2, 3, and 4, respectively.

Weekend Variations in the Basic Meal Pattern

Similarities between the basic and weekend meal patterns stem from the constant factors influencing those patterns (i. e., core items and preparation methods), and conformity in their breakfast patterns. Variations are based on disparity within the factors involved. The core food items of the weekend pattern differ somewhat from the core items of the basic meal pattern, and an additional method is utilized in food preparation.

Saturday and Sunday breakfast meal patterns differ from that of the basic in only one respect—the inclusion of pancakes with the core items.

Saturday dinner is non-specific and informal and includes such items as hamburgers, sandwiches, hot dogs, pizzas, meat sauces, spaghetti, fruit drinks, and iced beverages. The informal, unstructured, experimental, indulgent nature of the Saturday dinner indicates that that meal is a prime entree for acculturation based on intercultural contact, and for the introduction of snack foods of variable nutritional value.

The Sunday dinner meal pattern is comprised of the following core items: meat, English peas, string beans, white and sweet potatoes, biscuits, rolls, cake, pie, and an iced beverage. Frying and roasting are methods generally employed in the preparation of meat for Sunday dinner. The specialness of the Sunday dinner sets it apart from the basic (weekday) and Saturday dinners. Method of preparation is of essence here; this factor is associated with time, food selection, quality and cost. The Sunday dinner thus represents the ideal in quality food preparation. The basic components of the Sunday dinner meal pattern are shown in table 5.

Snack Items in the Meal Pattern

Any food which can be eaten with a minimum of preparation is considered a snack. Thus, the terms lunch and snack are used interchangeably by respondents. Except for a few items shown

TABLE 2

MEAL COMPONENTS AND PREPARATION METHODS: DETERMINANTS OF THE BREAKFAST PATTERN

Components			Preparation Method	Meal Patterns
"Core Items"	"Secondary Core"	"Peripheral" diet		
Meat				I
Ham				Meat
Bacon	Cheese			Baked products or
Chicken				cooked cereal
Pork chops				Butter
Sausage				Beverage
				Sweets
Eggs			Frying	
				II
				Eggs
Dry cereal with milk				Baked cereal
				products or
Baked Cereal products				cooked cereal
White bread	Pancakes			Butter
Biscuit	Toast			Beverage
				Sweets
Cooked cereal	Cream of wheat			
Rice	Oatmeal			III
Grits				Meat and eggs
				Baked cereal
Beverage	Fruit drink			products
Coffee	Fruit juice	Citrus		Beverage
	Chocolate milk	juice		Sweets
	Carbonated beverages			
	Hot chocolate			IV
Sweets				Dry cereal
Syrup	Fried sweet potatoes			with milk
Jelly	Fried apples			
Preserves	Fruits			

TABLE 3

MEAL COMPONENTS OF THE LUNCH PATTERN

"Core Items"	Components "Secondary Core"	"Peripheral" diet	Meal Patterns
Bread and fillings[5]			I
Soup with crackers			Sandwich Beverage
Left-overs			Dessert
Dry cereal with milk			II
Beverage			Soup with
Milk	Fruit juice		crackers
Fruit drink	Carbonated beverage		Dessert
	Chocolate milk		III
			Left-overs
Dessert			Dessert
Fresh fruit	Potato chips		IV
Cake	Fritos		Dry cereal
Pastry	Pickles		with milk
Cookies			Dessert
Doughnuts			V
			Variety of combinations utilizing core and secondary core items

TABLE 4

MEAL COMPONENTS AND PREPARATION METHODS: DETERMINANTS OF THE DINNER PATTERN

Components		"Peripheral" diet	Preparation Methods	Meal Patterns
"Core Items"	"Secondary Core"			
Meat	Liver	Meat casseroles	Boiling	**I**
Pork	Fish	Pig's head	and	Meat
Beef		Other poultry	Frying	Cornbread, butter
Chicken				Beverage
Seasoned	Baked sweet potato	Vegetable salad		**II**
Vegetables	String beans	Other vegetables		Seasoned vegetables
Collards	English peas	Baked Irish		Cornbread, butter
Mustard greens	Okra	potatoes		Beverage
Cabbage sprouts	Fried corn			Dessert
Turnip greens	Mashed potatoes			
Kale	French fried potatoes			**III**
	Home fried potatoes			Seasoned dry beans
	Rice			or peas
Seasoned dry beans	Macaroni			Cornbread, butter
or peas	Spaghetti			Beverage
	Sliced tomatoes			Dessert
Cornbread	Biscuit			**IV**
				Meat
Butter	Margarine			Vegetables
				Cornbread, butter
Beverage	Carbonated beverage	Milk		Beverage
Kool Aid	Iced tea			Dessert
Fruit drink	Water			
	Dessert			
	cake			
	pie			

TABLE 5

COMPONENTS OF THE MEAL PATTERN AND FACTORS INVOLVED IN DETERMINING THE SUNDAY DINNER

"Core Items" Meal: Sunday Dinner	Components "Secondary Core"	"Peripheral" diet	Preparation Method	Meal Patterns
Meat			I	I
Beef or pork roasts	Fried chicken	Wild game	Frying and Roasting (Meats)	Roast chicken with cornbread dressing
Beef or pork steaks	Fried pork chops			Potatoes
Roast chicken with cornbread dressing				Vegetables
Roast ham				Butter
				Baked cereal products
				Beverage
				Desserts
Potatoes			Quick boiling (Vegetables)	II
Sweet				Roast ham with sweet potatoes
Irish				Vegetables
				Baked cereal products
				Butter
				Beverage
				Desserts
Vegetables	Lettuce and Tomato	Brussel sprouts		III
English peas	Cabbage	Fruit salad		Smothered beef or pork steaks
String beans	Cole slaw	Tossed salad		Potatoes
Mixed vegetables	Potato salad	Molded salad		Vegetables
				Baked cereal products
				Butter
				Beverage
				Desserts
Baked Cereal Products				
Brown-and-serve rolls				
Biscuits				
Butter	Margarine			
Beverage		Fruit punch		
Sweet iced drink				

TABLE 5 (Continued)

"Core Items"	Components "Secondary Core"	"Peripheral" Diet	Preparation Methods	Meal Patterns
				IV
Dessert				Roast beef or pork
Ice cream	Jello			Potatoes
Canned peaches				Vegetables
Cake				Baked cereal product
Pie				Butter
Cobbler				Beverage
				Desserts

below, e. g., juices, snacks may be eaten at any time during the day
and before retiring.

SNACK FOODS

Beverages (all)	Fruit (all)	Popsicle
Cake	Hamburger	Potato chips
Candy	Ice cream	Prunes
Cheese	Leftovers	Sandwiches (all)
Cookies	Milk	Raisins
Cornflakes	Peanut Butter	TV dinners
Crackers	Pie	Wieners
Doughnuts	Pizza	

Like the Saturday dinner, snack foods provide an avenue for
acculturation and for the introduction of a high level of calories of
variable nutritional value.

Seasonal Variations in the Basic Meal Pattern
Summer and Winter.
Many respondents, especially those with children of school age,
have reported that the general Saturday meal plan of self-service
and informality is observed during the hot summer months, and
not more than one hot meal each day is prepared during that time.

The summer meal pattern entails an increased use of fresh fruits
and garden vegetables, lunch meats, sandwiches, potato salad,
iced tea, and other iced beverages. Tomatoes, generally purchased
by bushel amounts at this time, appear frequently as an accessory
food item. Another feature of importance during the hot summer
months is the reduced consumption of pork, dried beans, and
peas. These food items are considered "too heavy" and "too hot"
for summer consumption. "Boiled foods" made from dry legumes
are therefore largely limited to the cool months. In cases where
the food supply is marginal, nutritional consequences could be
fairly severe.

There is a seasonal fluctuation in food consumption which is
somewhat unrelated to the availability of particular foods. The
reduced consumption of pork and dry legumes during the hot
months of summer is followed by an increase in the consumption
of these items during winter; neither is related to the phenomenon
of supply. However, the reduced consumption of fresh tomatoes
appears to be related to the absence of a farmer's market where
they are obtained in large quantities during summer.

The more regular eating habits of winter—especially in households with children of school age—appear to be related to schedules as well as to general atmospheric conditions. It is strongly believed that the body needs nutritious and protective foods on a regular basis during the cold months for protection against colds and other illnesses.

Holiday Variations in the Dinner Pattern

The meal pattern at Thanksgiving, Christmas and Easter differs from the basic dinner in that it conforms to the traditional American pattern. For Thanksgiving and Christmas, roast turkey and dressing (cornbread) and the "usual" trimmings are featured. Baked ham is the featured main dish at Easter. Holiday dinners are elaborate and varied. They are regarded as special meals, in keeping with the spirit of the occasion.

Variations in the Basic Meal Pattern When Entertaining Guests

Variations in the meal pattern when guests are being entertained seem to differ with family attitudes and ideals. Thirteen respondents stated that guests were usually served the family's Sunday meal pattern, but for others the quality did not change appreciably. All changes were based on the number of people to be served. Generally, it appears that the occasion and the day of the week dictated a guest's menu pattern. When guests were being entertained on Sundays and holidays, the occasions most frequently mentioned, the guest meal pattern differed from the basic pattern mainly because the patterns in themselves usually changed, irrespective of the presence of guests.

The Meal Pattern as Determined by Frequency Tests

Figures 1 and 2 depict the frequency of occurrence of selected food items in the breakfast and dinner meal patterns of the twenty-three responding households, as revealed by replies to the frequency tests. Data obtained by this technique support the descriptions of the breakfast and dinner patterns made in tables 2, 3, and 4. All core items appear with greater frequency on the graph than do secondary core items. Food items which were shown to assume a "peripheral" place in the meal pattern appear with lowest frequencies. Thus, the graphs encompass the numerous factors and

variations which affect the total food consumption and, consequently, the meal pattern may be defined in relation to the cyclical
fluctuations of a year.

Aspects of Change

Change in the food habits of the respondent group can be
recognized in the following areas: (a) source of the food supply, (b)
food preservation practices, (c) use of commercially prepared foods,
(d) changes in preparation methods, (e) meal pattern, and (f)
traditional beliefs concerning food.

The Food Supply

A majority of the respondents (87 percent) have experienced a
sudden change from being food producers to being total food
purchasers. Most of the respondents stated that they had produced
almost all of their food in the South. Meat, milk, vegetables, fruits,
fat, and some grain and sugar were produced by these respondents.
Food purchases had been limited to wheat flour, tea, coffee, salt and
certain canned goods—e. g., peaches, salmon, and sardines—which
are sources of emotional satisfaction and prestige in rural areas. In
addition to farming, many exploited the food resources of the rivers,
streams, and hinterland by fishing, hunting, and gathering
wild fruits and vegetables. Food was generally purchased only once
per week, on Saturdays, as this entailed travelling a number of miles
to the village grocery store.

The food supply in the old environment assumed an annual cycle.
Fresh fruits and vegetables were consumed in large amounts during
summer and early fall. The period between late winter and early
spring, when winter stores were exhausted, was considered "the
lean months," when pork, dry beans and peas, corn meal, and home
preserved fruits and vegetables were the major foods. Chitterlings
and lesser parts of the pig were usually eaten at slaughtering time in
the fall.

In Centavia, the food supply is quantitatively and qualitatively
constant throughout the year. Respondents unanimously agreed
that their dietary practices have improved because of the availability
of their favorite foods throughout the year.

Figure 1.

Frequency of occurrence of 33 selected food
items in the Breakfast pattern.

Score Legend

230..........Every morning
207..........4 - 6 times per week
184..........2 - 3 times per week
161..........Once per week
138..........3 times per month
115..........Once - twice per month
 92..........Every other month
 69..........3 - 5 times per year
 46..........Once - twice per year
 23..........Never

Figure 1.

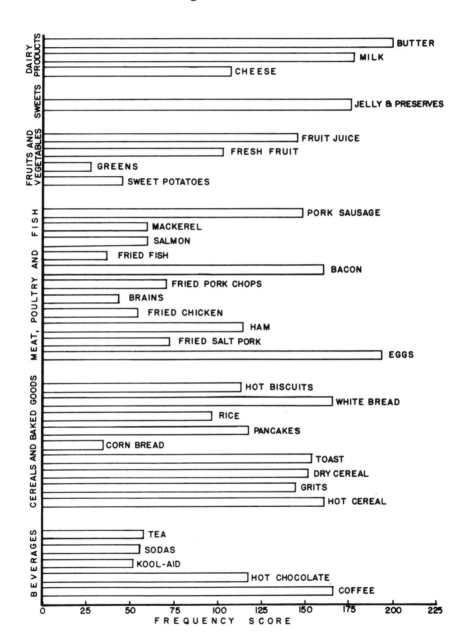

Figure 2.

Frequency of occurrence of 60 selected food
items in the Dinner pattern.

<u>Score</u> <u>Legend</u>

230..........Every evening
207..........4 - 6 times per week
184..........2 - 3 times per week
161..........Once per week
138..........3 times per month
115..........Once - twice per month
 92..........Every other month
 69..........3 - 5 times per year
 46..........Once - twice per year
 23..........Never

Figure 2.

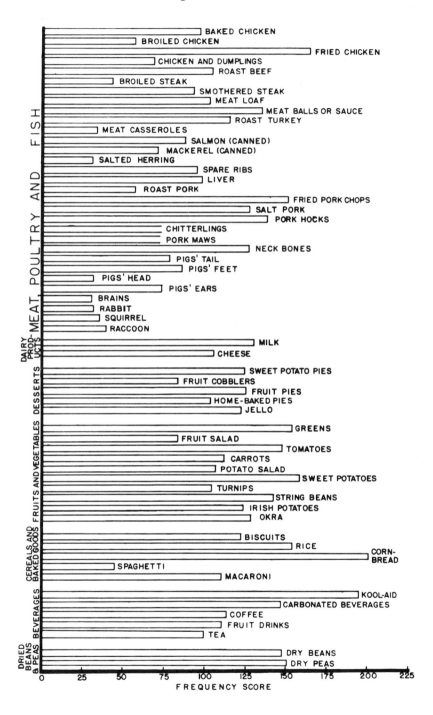

Food Preservation Practices

Home food preservation practices in the South differed greatly from present methods. Former practices involved home canning many hundred quarts of fruits, vegetables and meat annually; drying of beans, peas and some fruits, salting and smoking of meats, and some freezing. Respondents now do very little home food preservation. Freezing has been substituted for salting, smoking, drying and most of the home canning. However, some of the older respondents continue to use canning techniques. These changes coincide with the accessibility of freezers and the lack of seasonal fluctuations in the food supply. There is a change in emphasis on the kinds and amount of foods preserved. Meat, vegetables and legumes were emphasized in the old environment. Today the accent is on freezing meat and, to a lesser extent, freezing vegetables.

Use of Commercially Prepared and Preserved Foods

Many new semi-prepared and ready-to-serve items have been incorporated into the meal pattern. "Light" bread, refrigerator biscuits, brown-and-serve rolls, frozen meat pies, frozen pizzas, commercially prepared cakes and cake mixes, jellies and preserves, baby foods, some frozen vegetables, and a variety of canned foods have been identified as the new items in current use. Most of these foods are used by young families. "Light" bread, which substitutes for home-made biscuits, appears to be the first modification recognized by the respondents. Frozen vegetables are usually introduced after a long period of residence in the new area.

Preparation Methods

Introduction of canned and frozen vegetables is attended by certain modifications in the preparation and seasoning of these items. Commercially canned vegetables (generally disliked) are heated for a short time and seasoned with butter, while the frozen variety are cooked according to package directions and seasoned with butter, bacon, or bacon fat. In a few cases, bacon has been substituted for salt pork in the seasoning of fresh vegetables.

Modes of seasoning and cooking commercially canned and frozen vegetables serve to illustrate how traditional methods of food preparation (i. e., boiling fresh vegetables) yield to the new. Processing method and style of presentation (i. e., container and directions for preparation) make familiar items seem new and different modes of preparation, appropriate.

Meal Pattern

There is evidence that the old meal pattern has undergone substantial change in the new environment. Initial changes are apparent in the terminology of meals; breakfast, dinner and supper are now labelled breakfast, lunch, and dinner. The change in terminology is followed by changes in meal schedules and patterns.

In the traditional pattern, the first meal, breakfast, consisted of fried meats of various kinds, rice, grits, biscuits, gravy, fried sweet and Irish potatoes, coffee and milk. Children of school age usually carried a portion of breakfast to be eaten as lunch. Dinner, eaten at mid-afternoon by the adults, consisted of boiled vegetables or dry legumes seasoned with meats, cornbread, sweet potatoes, a sweet beverage or milk. This was termed a heavy "boiled" dinner. This pattern was sometimes repeated in a late supper but more often, leftovers from dinner were served as supper. Raw fruits were usually eaten as snacks.

Current terminology designates the three meals as breakfast, lunch, and dinner. Breakfast usually consists of eggs, or bacon or sausage with eggs, hot biscuits, "light" bread, and coffee. When compared with the traditional breakfast pattern, the respondents consider this a "light" breakfast. The change from fried chicken and pork chops to fried eggs and bacon has doubtlessly been engineered by occupational requirements. However, ideas that the ideal breakfast is comprised of bacon and eggs, or sausage and eggs, must have much to do with the change in pattern. The "heavy breakfast" of the South, it was found, continues up to at least one year's residence in Milwaukee. In such cases, lunch consists of leftovers from breakfast, dry cereal with milk, and fruit drinks. Thus, the luncheon pattern (breakfast leftovers) replaces the old supper pattern (dinner leftovers).

The emergence of a new breakfast pattern in the urban area is accompanied by a change in the luncheon pattern. The presence of children of school age tends to accelerate changes in the meal pattern, since family meal times generally follow that set by school schedules, and the food preferences of children are usually honored by mothers. Thus, breakfast leftovers yield to sandwiches, beverages, soup, fruit, and crackers.

The new dinner pattern emerges as a combination of the old breakfast (fried meats) and dinner (boiled vegetables or legumes) patterns. Instead of five "boiling" days as described in the traditional dinner pattern, there are now two or three; this leaves room for two or three "frying" days to replace the old breakfast pattern. The general absence of vegetables in the current "frying" pattern is probably accounted for by this shift, since there were no vegetables in the old breakfast pattern.

Thus, change in the nomenclature of meals and in meal times are expressed in meal components and in nutrient content. Differences in nutritional content of the two diets cannot be measured, however, because of seasonal variations in the traditional fare. It would seem, however, that the year-round availability of foods and the improved economic conditions of the in-migrant have mitigated any ill effects which might have arisen from changes in the meal patterns.

Concepts of Food and Nutrition

The advice of a physician now appears to be the paramount determinant of dietary restrictions during pregnancy, lactation, the *post partum* period, and during illnesses. Changes in infant feeding practices—from breast to formula—are associated with available medical and hospital facilities and services and the high esteem in which the physician's advice is held. The prevailing attitude towards physicians is reflected in the following statement by a respondent: "The doctors up here treat you like a real person. They make you feel that you are a human being and they want to see you get better."

The textural qualities of certain foods seem to determine when they will be used. For example, unemployed people tend to consume relatively less of "heavy foods" such as cornbread, greens and dried beans, and relatively more "light foods" such as fruits, "light" bread and frozen pot pies.

The use of some foods seems to be related to respondents' self-esteem and perception of their place in the total social structure. Recipients of public welfare, for example, tend to feel that certain foods (asparagus, lamb chops), some methods of preparation (unseasoned vegetables) and some methods of serving ("a little bit of this and a little bit of that") are beyond their reach. They tend to serve only two items and a beverage at each meal. Conversely, when socioeconomic status improves, respondents often introduce "a salad or a vegetable when frying" or include "boiled and fried foods" at the same meal.

Areas of Stability—Ideology

There appears to be great persistence in certain values, beliefs and attitudes which effect food selection, distribution and meal preparation. Relations between food and health were emphasized by all respondents and associations between vegetable consumption and good health were especially exemplified by the primary position given to vegetables whenever foods were being enumerated.

The theme of food and health entered every discussion of food especially in its relationship to children. In reference to food, children are considered the most important members of the family "because they need food for growth and strength" or "because they are small and need much of the right kinds of food for vitamins," and also, "for them to be healthy." One respondent gauges the efficacy of her dietary practices by illness in the family. "I don't cook like they taught me in school," she said, "but I know that I feeds them right because they ain't never sick. Now if they were sick all the time, then I would know they need better food."

In connection with adults, health is analogous to strength; and "for strength" adults need the "right foods." According to nineteen respondents, vegetables constitute "food for strength." Other strengthening foods listed were meat, milk, and eggs, by seven, five, and two respondents, respectively. Each of the following items, potatoes, soups, beans, and bread was considered as a source of strength by one respondent. One informant also advocated the use of bread every day "to keep you healthy."

On subjects relating food and vitamins to health, fifteen respondents regarded vegetables as being desirable "because of their richness in vitamins." Other foods falling into that category were milk, listed by nine respondents; orange juice, listed by five; fruit and eggs each listed by four; meats and cereals listed by three and two respondents, respectively; and desserts and beans each listed by one respondent.

On the question of essentiality of foods, that is foods which respondents considered as "necessary" to health, the following data were obtained.

Respondents saw a direct relationship between health and the consumption of pork. Some regarded this association from a positive standpoint and others viewed it negatively. One respondent said that her husband reported that he had a "feeling of weakness" whenever he abstained from pork for a week or more and regained "his strength" as soon as it was included in the menu. However,

TABLE 6

FOODS REGARDED AS BEING ESSENTIAL TO HEALTH BY RESPONDENTS

Foods	Number of Respondents
Vegetables	17
Meat	11
Milk	9
Fruits	4
All foods	4
Liver	2
Cornbread	2
Bread	2
Citrus fruits	1
Juices	1
Eggs	1
Cereal	1

seven respondents claimed abstinence from pork items since they were regarded as being causative factors in high blood pressure. ("Pork runs up your blood.")

Notwithstanding a general lack of awareness of deficiency diseases and conditions which arise from the failure to include certain items of food in the diet, one condition, anemia or "low blood" seemed to be of particular concern to respondents. Many respondents knew of "relatives down south" who had had the condition and confessed that they, too, at one time, had been victims of the disease. The relationship between anemia and food as recognized by respondents is shown in Table 7. Three respondents advocated the exclusion of fats, starches, and sugars to

TABLE 7

FOOD AND OTHER ITEMS CONSIDERED ESSENTIAL TO THE PREVEN-
TION AND CURE OF ANEMIA BY RESPONDENTS

Foods	Number of Respondents
Liver	12
Beets	6
Rare steak or hamburger	4
Milk	4
Meat	3
Eggs	2
Spinach	2
Carrots	1
Green vegetables	1
Tomato juice	1
Orange juice	1
Grape juice	1
Raisins	1
Prunes	1
Other	
"Tonic"	1
Beef, iron and wine	1
Iron tablets	1

alleviate the condition. On the whole, the data indicate general awareness of a positive relationship between health and food. However, most respondents were unsure of the multiple ways by which health may be affected by dietary practices. Many respondents admitted that various family members had taken vitamin pills on the advice of physicians. However, of the 130 individuals represented in the twenty-three households, only three infants were being given vitamin drops during the period of the study.

The importance of proper flavor, the efficacy of proper seasonings, and consideration of individual preferences—southern influences on the diet—persist among the respondents.

There are other tangible areas of persistence. Most of the core items of the dinner pattern and a few core breakfast items remain essentially southern. There is also some stability regarding the seasonal consumption of certain foods. Such practices were related to seasonal availability in the old environment but bear no relationship to current supply. They include a summertime reduction in the consumption of pork and dried peas and beans.

Finally, the presence of back yard gardens planted with various types of deep-green leafy vegetables, tomatoes, and beans may be regarded as an element of stability in the food habits of the in-migrant group.

Further evidence of stability and change in the food habits of the respondents is shown in Table 8. This table portrays the 1955 household consumption pattern of selected food items by the North Central and Southern regions and according to the areas of origin and destiny of respondents. These values are compared with those obtained from the group being studied. The table illustrates essential differences in consumption practices between the North Central region and the South. It also reaffirms the major differences in food consumption between the North Central Urban area and the Southern Rural Farm area. Household food consumption practices of the respondents will be analyzed by comparing trends and directions in consumption in relation to the North Central Urban and Southern Rural Farm areas. Trends are recognized on a "high" or "low" consumption pattern using the values of the two areas as reference points, since differences in sample size do not permit absolute comparisons.

On the above basis, it appears that the consumption pattern of the respondents adheres to the traditional (Southern Rural Farm) in the following items: pork, chicken, fish, eggs, cornmeal, sugars and

TABLE 8

RELATION BETWEEN HOUSEHOLD CONSUMPTION OF SELECTED FORMS TO REGION AND URBANIZATION

	North Central	North Central Urban [a]	South Rural Farm	South [b]	Study Sample
			Amount per Household		
Fluid milk (quarts)	12.39	11.68	9.82	16.79	8.22
Beef (pounds)	5.01	4.87	3.00	2.87	4.69
Pork (pounds)	4.06	3.90	4.45	4.98	8.68
Chicken (pounds)	1.94	2.02	2.35	2.61	7.58
Fish (pounds)	1.05	1.05	1.33	1.74	1.23
Eggs (dozen)	2.05	1.87	2.23	2.85	2.20
Lard (pounds)	.32	.13	1.04	2.39	.38
Cornmeal (pounds)	.16	.13	2.45	5.37	2.41
Sugars and Sweets (pounds)	4.22	3.49	4.98	7.54	5.65
White potatoes (pounds)	6.80	5.76	4.24	6.35	4.56
Sweet potatoes (pounds)	.12	.15	.33	.36	2.75
Dark-green leafy vegetables (pounds)	.29	.34	.89	1.34	2.35
Tomatoes (pounds)	1.07	1.12	1.42	1.49	.74
Citrus fruits (pounds)	4.42	4.73	3.20	2.41	5.41
Dry beans & legumes (pounds)	.20	.14	.77	1.30	1.27

[a] Household Food Consumption Survey, 1955, Report No. 3.

[b] Household Food Consumption Survey, 1955, Report No. 4.

sweets, sweet potatoes, dark-green leafy vegetables, and dry beans, peas and legumes. Consumption of fluid milk, beef, eggs, lard, Irish potatoes, tomatoes, and citrus fruit is more closely related to the North Central Urban pattern. This apparent shift in orientation, from rural South to Urban North Central really reflects the more frequent inclusion of certain food items (tomatoes and citrus fruits) available to the respondents throughout the year but which are included seasonally in the South. The shift in consumption pattern is closely associated with the component classification of certain foods—whether they are "core items"—Southern emphasis—and consequently used by all persons almost every day, or whether they are secondary or peripheral and therefore used less frequently by the group.

Intragroup Variation—Indices of Microcultural Groups

In terms of education, occupation, and income, most residents of the area might be placed at the bottom of the tripartite class structure congruent with the working-class occupational delineation. However, in terms of values, attitudes, practices and beliefs, four microcultural groups emerge. Group assignments are based upon such factors as family background and tenancy in the South, receipt of public welfare, marital status, personal traits, age, completion of high school, continuation of formal education in adult classes, degree of contact with the wider community, migration pattern, selection of recreational activities, church affiliation, leadership in church and group life, food habits, family life, reading habits, and tenure of housing. Some or all of the groups are similar in a few details, but there are important differences in living patterns among members of each group. Some salient characteristics which classify members in the four microcultural groups are shown in Table 9.

Group I—New Residents "Surviving." Female adults of this group fall within the middle age bracket and are relatively recent migrants to Milwaukee. Their migration pattern was direct, partly because of family size, and partly because they entered with the intention of establishing a home in the city. Families in this group are large with as many as eleven children. These families may be complete with a male and female head or one or the other may be absent. The median number of years of schooling completed is seventh grade

TABLE 9

AVERAGE PERCENTAGES OF THE WEEK'S FOOD ALLOWANCE ALLOCATED TO EACH FOOD GROUP
BY THE FOUR MICROCULTURES

Microcultural Groups	Dairy products	Meat Poultry Fish	Eggs	Peas Dry Beans Nuts	Flour Cereals Baked Goods	Potatoes	Citrus Fruit Tomatoes	Dark-Green, Deep-Yellow Vegetables	Other Vegetables, Fruits	Fats and Oils	Sugars and Sweets
						FOOD GROUPS					
I	5.39	42.21	5.18	2.83	14.16	1.03	.51	2.85	5.51	5.17	15.37
II	12.06	37.55	5.08	2.73	11.37	1.85	4.41	4.96	6.19	6.09	7.73
III	10.56	36.97	4.41	2.45	12.51	1.54	2.95	3.00	6.03	6.30	13.02
IV	9.40	43.35	4.68	2.85	14.03	1.33	8.90	1.60	5.77	1.84	9.28
All Groups	9.87	38.84	4.44	2.60	12.93	1.47	3.90	3.00	5.68	5.27	12.00

for the woman and sixth grade for the man. Family income, dependent upon family stability and earning capacity, may be inadequate; consequently, the axis of life is generally centered around survival and adjusting to the various demands of the new environment. Food, obtainable from certain relief organizations, and some guidance from relatives, may be the only stable source of sustenance at this critical time. The family's ability to successfully overcome this period of crisis and adjustment is the determining factor in its emergence from this group and movement to Group II or III. Failure to surmount the many barriers to success may lead to acceptance of defeat and movement to Group IV.

Group II—"Making It." Women in Group II are in their late twenties or early thirties and have completed high school in a southern state. They are married to men of their age group who have completed elementary school but not high school. These men are employed in heavy or light industry as unskilled or semiskilled workers, and they earn an average wage totalling $5,000 a year. Couples have migrated from a rural area or town in one of the represented states, spent from six months to two years in an urban area of the South or North, and finally settled in Milwaukee some five years previous to the study. They have from two to seven children and expect them to have "the better things in life."

Families so classified reside in two-bedroom apartments rented at $65 per month exclusive of utilities. They own a four-year old sedan—necessary for transportation to the men's place of employment and for family trips to the south or to neighboring areas in the north. Women of this group feel that they are needed at home to take care of their children; however, they may accept part-time employment whenever extra money is needed. Social life and leisure activities, which are centered around relatives or friends from their home state, include holiday dinners, small parties at home, card games, informal visiting, and membership in small social clubs.

Subscription to a local daily or weekly newspaper and one national (non-black) women's or family magazine is customary. Adults attend a local Baptist church occasionally. The attendance of older children at Sunday School seems mandatory "for good training." In addition to urging their children to make good use of current educational opportunities, these women express the desire to enter vocational training to equip themselves for future employment. Their neat apartments, decorated with modern furniture, reflect economical and thoughtful purchasing habits while the many small kitchen appliances reveal the urge to compensate for the obsolete design and layout of their apartments.

Group III—"Enjoying It." The women of this group are in their late thirties or mid-forties. Their migration pattern approximates that of Group II, but they settled in Milwaukee about eleven years prior to the study with their present or former mate. They completed an average of two years of high school in their home state. Their mates have an equivalent education or less. Husbands of this group are steadily employed and earn an average of $6,000 per year. In many cases, a relative, roomers, or foster children reside with the family. Couples of this group are house owners; such investments were made approximately eight years previously, at a cost of about $8,900. Women in this group seldom work outside the home, especially when there are foster children in the family. However, it is not unusual to find these women "helping out" neighbors by baby-sitting. Many are leaders in either the Baptist or Holiness churches, and they derive great satisfaction in contributing their time and energy to church activities. Reading material is limited to the Bible, a medical encyclopedia, and an occasional newspaper. Many families make an annual trip in the family car to visit relatives down South.

Since most of the children have left home, members of these families feel they can now relax and make luxury purchases. Many own fairly new cars, food freezers, boats, fur pieces, pianos, and large television sets.

Home interiors reflect the gradual increase in material possessions. Furniture in the crowded living rooms, bought piecemeal over the years, is uncoordinated. A sofa, usually protected with a throw cover, dominates the living room. Photographs of relatives, vacation souvenirs, houseplants, artificial flowers, large television consoles, pianos, chairs, and lamps complete the furnishings. Although some family-owned homes have separate dining rooms, these are used only on Sundays, holidays, and special occasions. Thus, as with the younger group, the kitchen serves as the family room, for most activities other than television viewing.

Group IV—"Living Passively." Generally, women of Group IV may be characterized as those who have failed to adjust to the requirements of the new environment and have yielded to frustration. The average age of these women is thirty years. On the average they obtained nine years of schooling and might have been married to men who had completed five years of education in a southern state. The average family comprises four children, and the current adult male head is an itinerant mate, either because the children are recipients of public welfare, because he is unemployed and has "lost face," or because there is domestic strife. The average income fluctuates since it is dependent upon welfare payments, or the presence, employment, luck at games of chance, or generosity of the titular male head. Ordinarily, income increases during the spring and summer months, when men are employed as laborers on construction projects, and declines during winter, when the male's income, if any, is derived mainly from unemployment compensation. Despite these inconstancies, it was possible to derive an average income of $4,000 for this group.

The majority of women within this group migrated directly to Milwaukee, and they have been residents of Milwaukee for periods varying from seven months to sixteen years. A major proportion of families within this group obtain some form of public support. They are children of share-cropper tenants on southern plantations, and they visit their homes or are visited at regular intervals. They claim no local church affiliation, and their social life and leisure activities, though generally unplanned and unorganized, are of frequent occurrence. They include getting together at home for card games, beer, television, and socializing in taverns. Most contact with the wider world is through the mass media, television, radio, and less often newspapers and entertainment magazines. The physical structure of their apartments, and the contract rent are similar to that of Groups I, II, and III; but interior furnishings reflect Centavia's blight. Plastic draperies hang from doors and windows. Walls are covered with screen idols and family photographs. Used and broken furniture scantily furnish the two bedrooms, living room, and kitchen-dinette; the living room sofa serves as bed at night. Two items of importance in these homes are a small record player and a television set. Since many women in this group do not work outside the home, these items are said to be necessary for "company" during the day.

Life appears to be one of mere existence; most actions are geared toward immediate gratification of needs and wants and reflect an inability to mobilize personal or group resources for intermediate or long-term gains.

Differences in the Meal Patterns of the Four Microcultural Groups

Despite a basic uniformity in the overall meal pattern, many differences based on the microcultural index of respondents exist. The meal patterns furnish a means of expressing traditional beliefs and convictions, new attainments and ideas, and a lifestyle commensurate with individual or family values.

The meal pattern of Group I is close to the traditional southern pattern. This may be due to their relatively recent migration and the consequent low level of adjustment to the new environment. Age, family size, and income are important variables accentuating the continuation of procedures and patterns which, in the past, led to desired goals. The following meal patterns predominate among members of this microcultural group: Breakfast and Luncheon Patterns I and III (Tables 2 and 3) and Dinner Patterns II and III (Table 4).

Generally, the women in Group II and those of Group III who have attended vocational school or have been exposed to principles of scientific nutrition in work situations adhere to practices which reflect an understanding of basic nutritional concepts. Group II women use all five patterns illustrated in Tables 2, 3, and 4; however, all members of this group tend to provide more dinners of Pattern IV.

A majority of the women in Group III exhibit conservatism and traditionalism in their food habits. For these women, variety in the meal pattern is achieved mainly through their propensity to add new food items and more foods to their menus. This practice is in keeping with their relatively higher spending power and their inclination to spend more money on consumer items. Their discussions of family meal patterns do not reveal a recognition of the necessity to plan and consume balanced meals. Every meal pattern may be found within this microcultural group.

In Group IV irregularity, inconsistency, and speed in preparation seem to be the dominant themes affecting the meal patterns. Much money is spent on food, but such expenditure is cyclical. This results in a period of high food consumption and a varied diet when there is money available, followed by a period of low food consumption and a monotonous diet. There may be a psychological tendency to spend a great deal of money on food whenever there is available money as a measure of security against future lean days.

Values sanction the expenditure of a minimum amount of time in meal preparation and the incorporation of many prepared, semiprepared, and ready-to-serve items in the menu. Thus, fruits, ice cream, and frozen meat pot pies and soups are popular with members of this group; fried meats are also very popular menu items. There is a tendency to reduce the number of "boiled dinners" and to limit the use of cornbread and home-made biscuits. Every meal pattern may be discovered within this microcultural group with some reduction in the number of dinners in Patterns II, III, and IV and the substitution of luncheon patterns in their place.

Microcultural factors, it was shown, functioned as an important variable in food selection and distribution. Table 9 illustrates how these factors affected the distribution of food expenditures among the eleven food groups during the report week. A high percentage of expenditure on meat items typifies the group as a whole. The four microcultural groups show similar expenditure patterns for most of the food groups. Exceptions are dairy products, citrus fruits and tomatoes, dark-green and deep-yellow vegetables, and sugars and sweets. In the case of dairy products, contrasts are greatest between microcultural Groups I and II; Group II had the highest percentage expenditures for dairy products and dark-green and deep-yellow vegetables, while Group I had highest percentage expenditures for sugars and sweets. There are major differences among all groups in expenditure patterns for citrus fruits and tomatoes, dark-green and deep-yellow vegetables, and sugars and sweets. Group I and IV show extremes, low and high, in expenditure patterns for citrus fruits and tomatoes, respectively; Groups II and IV show similar extremes for dark-green and deep-yellow vegetables, and Groups I and II for sugars and sweets. Groups II and III show similar expenditure patterns for all food groups except sugars and sweets. Obviously, variations in food selection and expenditure patterns appear to be closely related to microcultural orientation.

How relevant are these variations in food selection and expenditure patterns to average food costs?

Table 10 relates microcultural classifications to family income, size, and food costs.

The percentage of average income spent on the week's food supply appears to be similar for groups I, II and IV. However, as

TABLE 10

FAMILY INCOME, FAMILY SIZE, FOOD COSTS IN RELATION TO MICROCULTURES

RANGE AND AVERAGE VALUES

Microcultural Group	Family Income $	Family Size	Food Expenditure Units $	Income Spent on Food %
I	4,000-6,000 4,997	5 - 13 9.6	3.69 - 5.06 4.23	21.00 - 49.58 35.46
II	3,552-6,550 5,351	3 - 9 5.3	6.47 - 9.00 8.09	22.52 - 40.98 32.58
III	3,427-13,000 6,917	2 - 8 5.1	4.00 - 8.52 6.34	11.29 - 65.18 25.28
IV	2,013-6,500 4,330	2 - 8 4.7	4.43 - 7.35 5.75	13.82 - 62.59 36.89

shown for food selection practices in Table 9, microculture appears to be associated with food costs. Group I, the New Residents with large families, show the lowest food costs, and Group II, those who are "Making It," have the highest food costs. Family size in Group II is similar to Group III, those "Enjoying It," and to Group IV, the "Passive Livers." However, the two latter groups spend less money on the week's food supply than does Group II.

In view of the relationships between food costs and nutritive quality of the diet, it is expected that there would be an analogous association between microculture and diet quality. Table 11 relates nutritional data to the four microcultures.

The data show that all the members of Group II met or exceeded the recommended levels for all nutrients. In view of their general attitudes toward selecting food items which ensure a balanced diet and the data on their food selection provided in Table 9, the results are not surprising.

Table II also reveals that 31 and 15 percent of households in Group III fell below two-thirds the recommended levels of calcium and ascorbic acid, respectively. The levels for ascorbic acid were the lowest encountered in the sample, and the low values are related to the selection pattern shown in Table 9. A large proportion of older adults in this group indicated that they use milk in food preparation only and not as a beverage; this must account for the low level of calcium intake for that group. It has been shown that a balanced diet is not the main objective of a majority of the homemakers in this group. Diversity in the diet is accomplished solely through a propensity to secure more food as a result of a stable income and a settled way of life.

Members of microcultural Group I departed farthest from recommended levels of ascorbic acid and calcium. Data in Table 9 are relevant to this finding. Also relevant to the nutritional data are the large family size, unvaried meal pattern, low income, and low level of adjustment which characterize members of this group.

Twenty-five percent of the members of microcultural Group IV failed to attain recommended levels of calcium and ascorbic acid. Despite a high expenditure distribution toward citrus fruits and tomatoes, and an average distribution toward dairy products, the relatively low consumption of dark-green vegetables (Table 9) accounts for the low levels of ascorbic acid and calcium in the dietary. Preparation methods of the dark-green and deep-yellow vegetables generally consumed by respondents warrant a considerable expenditure of time or require some planning to coordinate

TABLE 11

NUTRITIVE QUALITY OF THE DIET FOR EACH MICROCULTURE

Percentage of Households Receiving Designated Levels of Food Energy and
Eight Nutrients on the Basis of the Recommended Dietary Allowances

Micro-cultural Group	Calories II	Calcium II	Calcium III	Iron II	Vitamin A Value II	Riboflavin II	Niacin II	Ascorbic Acid II	Ascorbic Acid III
I	33	--	100	33	33	33	--	33	67
II	--	--	--	--	--	--	--	--	--
III	8	31	31	--	15	8	8	23	15
IV	--	--	25	--	--	--	--	--	25

Legend

II . . . . 66.66-99.99 per cent of the RDA
III . . . . Below 66.66 per cent of the RDA

household chores during their preparation. Therefore, emphasis on quick meals, as accented by members of this microculture, reduces considerably the consumption of such foods. Generally, it appears that the supply of foods were adequate but for all groups, the selection of foods influence nutritional adequacy of the food supply.

The group's relatively high achievement level of nutritional adequacy leads to a consideration of the possibility of over-supply of nutrients in the respondents' diets. It is pertinent to recall that recommended levels of nutrients "are designed to afford a margin of sufficiency above average physiological requirements to cover variations among essentially all individuals in the general population" (NRC, 1964:4). In the words of Scrimshaw,

> If recommended dietary allowances are correctly determined few individuals in the population need intakes as those specified. Thus, even population groups with average intakes well below the recommended allowances may contain few individuals who are actually deficient in a certain nutrient. (1962: 333)

Since microculture appears to influence food selection and nutritional adequacy, Table 12 was constructed to determine how this factor affects the excess supply of nutrients. Microcultural classification ascertains the relevance of this variable by revealing important factors influencing nutrition of the group. Nutritional adequacy is closely associated with excess supply of nutrients, and the excess supply of nutrients is related to the food energy of the diet. Group II obtained nutritional adequacy at the expense of an excessive dietary supply of kilocalories. The supply of kilocalories in the diet of Group I was close to recommended levels, but both calcium and ascorbic acid were limiting in the diets of this group. A similar trend is shown for Groups III and IV. In general, when the data are viewed in terms of microcultural (and by inference, food selection patterns), it appears that dietary ascorbic acid and calcium levels are associated with an excess of recommended allowances of kilocalories. Vitamin A value, riboflavin, and niacin equivalents also follow this pattern.

It is obvious that the balance usually attained by combining quality with quantity has not been acquired by the cultural subgroup studied. Foods selected for nutritional reasons are *added* to those selected to provide emotional satisfaction, but very few items are removed from the food pattern.

TABLE 12

AVERAGE PERCENTAGES OF FOOD ENERGY AND EIGHT NUTRIENTS SUPPLIED BY THE DIET IN EXCESS OF
RECOMMENDED LEVELS ACCORDING TO MICROCULTURAL CLASSIFICATIONS

Micro-cultural Group	Food energy	Protein	Calcium	Iron	Vitamin A value	Thiamine	Ribo-flavin	Niacin eq.	Ascorbic Acid
				PERCENTAGE ABOVE RECOMMENDED LEVELS					
I	2.33	21.80	--	49.76	41.21	51.10	22.33	45.22	--
II	42.67	56.07	31.29	53.10	71.22	72.23	59.54	64.42	55.92
III	28.33	34.95	--	13.11	46.21	57.74	39.42	55.85	34.78
IV	36.40	59.09	.81	36.22	54.15	81.74	42.17	56.65	71.92
All Groups	26.82	39.45	--	33.85	51.43	63.34	39.96	41.05	38.25

Conditions of Change in Dietary Practices

Rural-urban migration serves as a means of introducing the in-migrant to a new mode of life in a new physical and social environment. Under conditions facilitating intercultural contact, the in-migrant can assume new values and gain experiences which are expressed in dietary behavior. Thus, it may be inferred that the degree of dietary change will be consistent with the amount and type of stimuli received by the in-migrant in the new physical and social setting. However, actual acceptance of change depends on more than contact and exposure in the new setting. In the case of food practices, there is the consideration of availability of both traditional items (usually physical availability) and desired new items (more apt to be a matter of economic availability).

In the situation under study, it was anticipated that stimulus for change would be limited to the respondents' immediate physical and social environment, because housing and living conditions minimize opportunities for effective primary intercultural contact within the city. Thus, factors producing culture change would be limited by established physical, economic, social, and educational restrictions which obtain in the new cultural milieu. In addition, it was expected that traditional food habits would tend to be maintained along with other beliefs and values which go unchallenged in the new environment including *de facto* segregation which reinforces the old and separate way of life. In situations where familiar foods are available, everything else being equal, it is likely that the content will be retained. However, lack of items, especially "core" ones would lead to certain modifications with the resultant preservation of the form rather than the content.

Eighty-seven percent of the respondents had migrated to Milwaukee from southern rural farming areas where they were engaged in a variety of agricultural pursuits and service enterprises. In addition to the major difference between the urban and rural way of life, there are numerous elements in the culture of the new environment which differ from those left in the respondents' area of origin. Among these are general climatic conditions, house type, occupational pursuits, health, education and welfare facilities, social and economic conditions, and sources of food supply. Such differences warrant adjustments and accommodations of the accustomed mode of living to the exigencies of the new setting.

While it was anticipated that changes in general food habits would accompany adjustments in general living patterns, it was fully expected that personal characteristics of the respondents would encourage differential adaptive strategies. Change and adjustment to the new environment is dependent upon family and individual characteristics, and on the ability to make requisite psychological adaptations to the new social climate. The individual or group can regulate certain forces (however limited) which he controls to permit the achievement of some goals.

Guided by different principles, individuals within a microculture demonstrate a different style of adaptation which is reflected by variations in food selection and consumption patterns and in the nutritive content of the diet.

Change Processes

Differences in use and emphasis of selected food items emphasizing the southern rural traditions are shown for the four microcultural groups in Table 13. This helps to illustrate the dynamics of change.

When Table 13 is compared with Table 8, microcultural Group II, those "Making It," shows a tendency towards the food consumption style of the North Central Urban area. This indicates processes involving *rejection* (lard), *addition* (beef, tomatoes), and *integration* (continued use of dark-green leafy vegetables, and sweet potatoes). The food consumption pattern of microcultural Group I, the New Residents, essentially demonstrates a traditional southern rural farm orientation. The diet emphasizes "core" items. Microcultural Group IV, the "Passive Livers," is of dual orientation; consumption patterns for some items are inclined toward the North Central region, while for other items a Southern rural farm orientation is obvious. It is possible to identify dynamics of *semirejection* (sweet potatoes) *without substitution* but with *addition* (citrus fruit). Food consumption patterns of microcultural Group III, those "Enjoying It," demonstrate an *incorporation* and *integration* of the two regional patterns in the process of adapting to the new environment.

Direction of Change

From the foregoing pages it appears that change in food habits appears with time. The direction of change depends upon the characteristics of the individual or group, type of adjustment to the new environment, assumption of values transmitted by economic, social, educational, and mass communication systems of the new

TABLE 13

RELATION BETWEEN HOUSEHOLD CONSUMPTION OF SELECTED FOODS TO
MICROCULTURAL CLASSIFICATION

	Microcultural Groups			
	I	II	III	IV
	Amounts per Household			
Fluid milk (quarts)	6.25	11.56	8.93	9.49
Beef (pounds)	2.08	7.25	4.51	2.75
Pork (pounds)	14.83	8.83	6.46	11.25
Chicken (pounds)	11.91	8.68	7.46	5.37
Fish (pounds)	.53	.50	1.07	2.80
Eggs (dozen)	2.75	3.10	2.30	.92
Lard (pounds)	1.16	--	.38	.06
Cornmeal (pounds)	5.41	1.03	2.25	1.56
Sugars & Sweets (pounds)	8.58	6.25	5.51	3.87
White potatoes (pounds)	6.41	6.33	4.75	1.25
Sweet potatoes (pounds)	6.16	4.08	2.50	--
Dark-green leafy vegetables (pounds)	1.66	3.33	2.28	2.37
Tomatoes (pounds)	1.00	1.38	.55	.62
Citrus fruits (pounds)	--	4.41	4.44	13.50
Dry beans & peas (pounds)	4.00	.50	1.50	2.08

environment, amount, quality and effectiveness of primary intercultural contact in the new environment. The direction of change is toward an elaborate, high caloric but varied diet in which many traditional items are retained.

Summary and Conclusions

There is evidence of both stability and change in the diet of the cultural subgroup. The current dietary pattern represents a composite of the traditional Southern rural diet pattern and the North Central urban diet pattern. This synthetic pattern is based on the general availability of familiar items, lack of primary intercultural contact, improved economic conditions, exposure (via marketing channels) to desired food products, and to the requisite adjustments to work and school schedules in the new setting.

The basic or week day diet consists of three components: "core items—essentially Southern rural in origin except in the luncheon pattern; "secondary core" items—those items added to the basic core to provide variety; and the "peripheral diet"—fancy foods or semiceremonial foods, included on special or ceremonial occasions. At least four meal patterns for breakfast and dinner and five for lunch have been discerned. Foods are prepared mainly by boiling and frying, and main meals are determined by the day's preparation method.

Food selection styles, diet patterns, dietary change, and the nutritive quality of the diet vary among four microcultural groups identified in the study. Microcultural placement is closely associated with the change process and the direction of change. In general, change towards a balanced diet integrating food habits of the areas of origin and destiny are shown for Groups II and III. Except for calcium and ascorbic acid, the diet of these groups meet or exceed levels of nutrients recommended by the National Research Council. Very little change has been encountered in the dietary pattern of microcultural Group I. Recommended levels of nutrients were attained for only protein and thiamine. Change in the diet of members of Group IV illustrate an erratic tendency towards both regions. This diet is slightly below recommended levels of calcium and ascorbic acid.

Generally, with the exception of calcium, National Research Council recommended allowances were met by a majority of the households. Calcium and ascorbic acid were the most limiting nutrients in the diet. However, average values showed that the dietary supply of all nutrients but calcium exceeded recommendations established by the National Research Council. High nutritive quality was always achieved at very high caloric intakes.

Change processes identified for Group II are *rejection* (lard), *addition* (e.g., beef, tomatoes), *integration* (dark-green leafy vegetables, sweet potatoes); for Group III, *integration* (all aspects of the meal pattern); for Group IV, *semirejection* (sweet potatoes) *without substitution but with addition* (citrus fruit).

The direction of change is toward an elaborate, high caloric varied diet retaining many elements of the past.

Notes

1. This term will be used synonymously with family in subsequent sections of this paper. For purposes of this study, a household is characterized as a residential group of at least two persons who share a common domicile where a majority of the meals are prepared.

2. Data for 1960 but provided by the Milwaukee County Department of Public Welfare.

3. Davis, A. et al. *Deep South.* Chicago: University of Chicago Press. 1941. Haag, W.G. "Aborigine Influence on the Southern Diet." *Pub. Health Rep.* 70:920. 1955. Langsworthy, C.F. "Food Customs and Diet in American Homes." U.S. Dept. Agric. Office of Exp. Sta. Circ. 110. 1911. Rubin, M. *Plantation Country.* Chapel Hill, N.C.: University of North Carolina Press. 1951.

4. The terms "core," "secondary core," and "peripheral" used to describe the dietary pattern were borrowed from Bennett (1943:651-652). However, the description of the diet pattern according to the above terms differs substantially from Bennett.

5. Sandwich spreads of various types, cheese, and lunch meat.

References

Bennett, J.W.
     1942 "Food and Culture in Southern Illinois." *American Sociological Review* 7:645-660.
Cussler, M. and M.L. DeGive
     1941 "Interrelations Between the Cultural Pattern and Nutrition." U.S. Dept. of Agriculture Ext. Ser. Circ. 336.
     1952 *'Twixt the Cup and the Lip.* New York: Twayne Publishers.
Milwaukee Journal
     April 3, 1966, p. 6.
O'Reilly C.T.
     1963 *The Inner Core—North: A Study of Milwaukee's Negro Community.*

O'Reilly, C.T., W.E. Downing, and S.I. Pflangzer
  1965 *The People of the Inner Core—North.* New York: Le Play Research, Inc.
Scrimshaw, N.S.
  1962 "Significance of the Appraisal of the Nutrient Intake and the Nutritional Status of Man." *American Journal of Clinical Nutrition* 11:331-334.
Stiebeling, N.K. et al.
  1941 Family Food Consumption and Dietary Levels. Consumer Purchases Study (Urban and Village Series). Five Regions (1935-1936 data). U.S. Dept. of Agriculture Misc.
Vance, R.B.
  1932 *Human Geography of the South.* Chapel Hill, N.C.: University of North Carolina Press.

11

The Health Food Movement

Social Revitalization or Alternative Health Maintenance System?

R. F. Kandel
G. H. Pelto

Introduction

A new convert to yoga stops eating meat. A wealthy lawyer buys organic cows prepared for freezing. A student goes off to college with a six-month supply of brewer's yeast. A housewives' lobby, organizing an economic boycott, adds meatless main dishes to their repertoire. An early morning jogger pops a multivitamin capsule before starting a two-mile run.

What do these people have in common? All of them are active participants in the contemporary health food movement. They, and many others like them, are on the forefront of a major change in American dietary habits.

Over the past decade several social concerns have coalesced to produce a large-scale interest in health foods and vegetarian diets. The widespread interest in ecology and environmental quality has been an important factor. Since 1962, when Rachel Carson's *The Silent Spring* aroused popular awareness of impending environmental destruction, the ecology of food and nutrition has been a growing concern. Anxieties have been expressed about the safety and nutritional quality of contemporary foods, especially highly processed foods and those grown with chemical pesticides. A second factor is the consumer rights movement. A number of consumer advocates and organizations such as Center for Science in the Public Interest; Council on Children, Media and Advertising; and Center for Study of Responsive Law have prodded a growing consumer consciousness. Consumerism is being reflected in rebellion against cosmetic food additives and a rising emphasis on preventive medicine and health maintenance. A third force is the legacy of th so-called Hippie Movement and the Anti-Vietnam War protests, which created interest in, and empathy with Far Eastern cultures. Expatriate Indian and Oriental gurus have preached philosophies of meditation, mysticism, and vegetarianism throughout the United States and found an eager following. The prolonged national economic recession, which has brought a series of food and energy crises and spiralling food costs, has been yet another influential force. Economic difficulties have been a strong motive to deviate from a "meat and potatoes" diet. Thus, the social, cultural, economic, and health motivations behind contemporary health food use run broad and deep.

Interest in health foods has probably helped to raise the "nutritional consciousness" of North Americans generally. Guiding this change in nutritionally-sound directions is an immediate and urgent challenge to nutritionists, other health-care workers, and some applied anthropologists. Since many health food users are people who are working actively to change their own food consumption patterns, it is important to learn as much as possible about the phenomenon.

Young vegetarians, through their gastronomic experimentation, are evolving some of the nonmeat dietary patterns that conform to American palates, food preparation techniques, and mealtime hours. Moreover, they have evolved a grass roots method for promoting dietary change that is more effective than most traditional nutrition education programs. This group of innovators should be viewed as a significant resource for understanding biobehavioral change associated with diet and nutrition.

Health food users could provide information for the agricultural specialists and economic planners who seek to rationalize the long-range production of foodstuffs. Lester Brown writes:

> We must begin by placing some upper limits on the total demand for food as dictated by the finite capacities of the ecosystem. One way to reduce agricultural pressure . . . is to lower the position of high income man on the food chain . . . We may be eventually forced into substituting beans for steak and meat with soybean derived imitations. (1972:231)

Some nutritionists have raised the possibility that studying the children of health food users may be one way to assess the effects of food additives on children. Medical institutions in and around universities, who treat large numbers of young adult health food users and their families, are in an ideal position to engage in longitudinal studies of these children from birth through the early school years, if they are provided with sufficient descriptive data to properly coordinate research efforts. At the same time, as a nutritionally concerned group, health food users are an ideal population for nutrition education programs if applied nutritionists and dietitians have sufficient information to work with them rather than against them.

Approaches to Health Food Users

Unfortunately, health food users have not received the type of serious study they deserve. Many nutritionists and dietitians have misjudged the importance of the movement by dismissing health food users as "faddists" and "freaks" and argue that the fad would soon disappear or at least assume new and different styles at frequent intervals. In part, the professionals' mistrust stems from the fact that the dietary patterns of health food users are nutritionally serendipitous and so defy comprehension or classification. In addition, many leaders of the health food movement are mis-informed, motivated by profit or committed to rigid ideological systems. For these reasons, the nutritionists' scorn is well deserved.

But much of the misunderstanding derives from a lack of information and inadequate theoretical orientation. In the past, vegetarian diets in the United States have most often been practiced by religious groups, such as Trappist Monks, Hindu Brahmins, and Seventh Day Adventists. When diet deviation was not sanctioned by religion, it frequently bore the stigma of medical quackery. Assuming that contemporary health food use is merely more of the same, most researchers have relegated its study to the realm of exotica. There is, however, another perspective. As diverse as health food diets are from a nutritional vantage point, they are explicable and unified from the perspective of a social scientist. In the following pages we describe health food use from a perspective that suggests it is a significant social phenomenon.

Several researchers have examined sociocultural aspects of contemporary health food use. New and Priest (1966) interviewed health food users in Boston. They discovered differences between "general users," who tried a variety of health food store products, and "unitary users," who subscribed to a folk nutritional system, interacted socially and followed a charismatic leader. They noted that the "unitary" group tended to splinter, forming competing factions around different charismatic leaders.

Erhard (1971, 1973) described the folk nutritional systems of several health food and vegetarian groups in San Francisco. She demonstrated that scientific nutritional information could be expressed in the vocabularies of these groups. Dwyer et al. (1974a, 1974b) who studied 100 "new vegetarians" in the Boston area, demonstrated that differences in dietary patterns and lifestyles exist between independent vegetarians and those who follow charismatic leaders.

These studies have been an excellent beginning, but we need to expand the focus beyond the categorizing of individual users or describing isolated vegetarian-oriented groups. Our approach in this paper, therefore, is to take a "systems approach" to the health food movement in Southern New England.

Research Methods

The data on which our analysis is based was gathered between 1971 and 1973. Kandel conducted research in the Greater Boston area, and Pelto conducted research in a rural university center. After conclusion of the data gathering phase, we pooled our data for analysis.

In the Greater Boston area two research strategies were employed. First, Kandel conducted extensive participant observation research with a network of vegetarian and health food-oriented groups. Cultural, social and economic aspects of these groups were thoroughly investigated. Participant observation was supplemented with informal interviews. Dietary data were collected through twenty-four-hour recall diet histories, observation by the researcher, and dietary records kept by selected informants. The second strategy was a survey, sponsored by Miles Laboratories, and conducted by a team from the Department of Nutrition, Harvard School of Public Health, which included Jean Mayer, Johanna Dwyer, Laura Mayer and Randy Kandel. Independent vegetarians as well as group affiliated ones were included in the sample of 100. Twenty-four-hour recall dietary intake data were collected from the majority of subjects.

In the rural university area, the major research strategy was a survey conducted by Gretel H. Pelto and Pertti J. Pelto in conjunction with a course on research methods in anthropology at the University of Connecticut. In addition to observation and casual interviewing at the health food stores and the vegetarian food line at the university dining hall, structured interviews, lasting an hour or more, were conducted with thirty-two health food users contacted mainly through the health food stores. Another sample of twenty-eight persons, also contacted through the health food stores, was interviewed with a modified semantic differential technique in order to reveal some major dimensions of the respondents' beliefs and attitudes (Nishizawa, n. d.).

Participant observation research in both the urban and rural areas began with the search for health food users at the health food stores, health food and vegetarian restaurants, vegetarian food lines at schools, and vegetarian and health food-oriented ashrams and communes. There, we contacted workers, residents, and regular and infrequent patrons. Through them, we "plugged" ourselves into the health food network, following individual introductions, recommendations, and leads from person to person and group to group. All informants, except for some thirty who responded to an ad for subjects printed in a university newspaper, were contacted in this way. We also "tracked" key informants, following them as they modified their diets or switched affiliation from one group to another.[1] We thus roughly recreated an accelerated version of a deeply involved participant's experience in the health food movement.

Since there is no "membership list" for the health food movement, we could not ascertain total population size, and since participants are not united by common residence, traditional sampling techniques could not be used. Therefore, although we believe we obtained a fair picture of a network of committed health food users in our areas, the data cannot be taken as a comprehensive account of health food use in New England, nor generalized without further research to the country as a whole.

Theoretical Framework

In considering the total body of information from the research sites, we found two concepts to be particularly useful for organizing and analyzing the data. First, it appears that the present health food movement can be viewed as a movement of social revitalization or transformation. Secondly, it can be viewed as an alternative health maintenance system. These two perspectives are clearly related. The health food movement derives much of its popularity from the combination of medical and social concerns. Food may be used simultaneously to cure or prevent illness, as a religious symbol and to forge social bonds. Frequently health food users are trying to improve their health, their lives, and, sometimes, the world as well.

Several years ago the anthropologist A. F. C. Wallace outlined the features of what he called "revitalization movements." Revitalization movements are attempts by people to radically restructure their cultural beliefs and practices in order to construct a more satisfying way of life (Wallace, 1956). From their studies of several social movements, including Pentecostalism and Black Power, Luther Gerlach and Virginia Hine have extracted a set of characteristics that appear to apply to a wide range of such movements (Gerlach and Hine, 1970a, 1970b). The list below, which we will use to analyse the health food movement, is based on their work, with some modifications and additions.

Social movements are characterized by:

1. An *ideology* that provides a conceptual framework for interpreting events and codifying values. The ideology exists in the form of a theme with variations. Members of the movement are bound together by their belief in ideas that are new and different from those of the social establishment. Individuals, however, may

subscribe to different variations and permutations of these ideas.

2. *Deep personal commitment*—Members of the movement recognize one another by a bond of "subjectively perceived commitment." Initiation into the movement is generated by a bridge-burning act or transforming experience which separates the convert in some significant way from the established order, or his previous place in it, identifies him with a new set of values, and commits him to changed patterns of behavior.

3. *Real or perceived opposition*—from the society at large or that segment of the established order within which the movement has arisen. Members of the movement feel a common sense of purpose in their desire to combat the opposition. Thus, the opposition itself motivates and energizes the movement. Consequently, the force and antagonism of the "opposition" may be exaggerated by the movement leaders for their own purposes.

4. *A combination of face-to-face recruitment and impersonal recruitment through books and mass media.* Committed individuals use their own pre-existing social, professional, and kinship networks to win new converts to the movement. At the same time, publicity by and about the movement attracts isolated individuals who then seek out its social groups or follow its doctrine.

5. *A segmented, polycephalous, cellular socioeconomic organization.* The social and economic organization of the movement consists of a collectivity of differently-sized independent groups or "cells." These groups have largely separate leadership and membership. They share the common "umbrella" ideology but may disagree radically on points of doctrine, method, or specific goals. The groups of the movement are linked in several ways. These include friendship and kinship ties maintained across the groups; overlapping, non-exclusive, and sequential membership; proselytizing trips and tours by leaders and members of various groups; and common participation in mass events. In addition, they are linked through the indirect communication channels of books, articles, and television appearances by the leaders.

The groups of the movement stand in an ambivalent relationship toward one another. At times they compete for power and membership, and at times they cooperate to achieve common goals. They frequently support one another's financial enterprises. This results in a kind of "influence flow" so that personnel, ideology, and tactics diffuse from group to group.

The groups are in a continuous state of flux. Changes in

ideological focus, personalities, or particular programs of a given group may result in attrition or accretion of its membership and in fission, fusion, or realignment of groups and coalitions of groups.

6. *Multiple types of participation or involvement in the movement* ranging from minimal to total social and cultural involvement. Because the movement spreads through both face-to-face and indirect communication, cultural and social participation may be separated. Some individuals may be intensely socially involved with the movement membership, but subscribe in only a limited way to its practices; while others may fanatically adopt the practices but not have much social interaction with other members of the movement.

7. *Rapid change*—Ideological variations propagate and hybridize quickly and differently in different areas; and many phases of the movement seem to be happening simultaneously. Individuals follow idiosyncratic courses through the movement, picking and choosing among ideas and groups. In pursuit of personal goals, they move in and out of component groups, varying intensity of involvement. Thus, not only groups but individuals differ from one another in the movement variations they practice and believe.

The overall pattern of a social movement is thus that of a theme with variations, represented by both independent members and organized groups. The paths of individuals criss-cross the network of organized groups.

Ideological Unity and Diversity

On the whole, people who define themselves or label themselves as "health food users" eat less animal flesh, fewer processed and convenience foods and often, more highly concentrated doses of vitamins than do other Americans. They pursue their dietary habits because they believe that such diets are better for them physically, psychologically and/or spiritually. Many also believe that their eating patterns are more compatible with a healthy environment and balanced ecology. For most health food users, as indeed for most people, foods are not simply aggregates of proteins, fats, carbohydrates, vitamins and minerals. Foods have symbolic and psychological value and, in some cases, mystical properties are also attributed to them. In the following paragraphs we describe aspects of the belief system of the health food movement. The features of three "key ideas" discussed below were abstracted from the interview materials, both formal and informal.

1. *The natural food idea*—Diets are chosen for their health-related properties. This includes both the selection of specific foods believed to have positive value because of their nutritional content or purported physiological and psychological effects, and the avoidance of foods considered of negative value because of their deleterious nature or contents. Subsumed under the *natural food idea* are three motifs: the *vitamin motif,* the *organic motif,* and the *mystical motif.*

In the application of the *vitamin motif,* nutritional requirements are conceptualized in terms similar to those used by nutritional scientists (proteins, vitamins, etc.). But participants may believe they need certain nutrients in quantities far in excess of those normally recommended by nutritional scientists and take large doses of these vitamin and mineral supplements daily. They may also avoid foods considered of meager nutritional value (relative to their caloric contents) such as starchy vegetables, or foods that have lost nutritional value in processing, such as bleached flour and white rice.

In the *organic motif* a distinction is made between foods classified as "organic" and those classified as "chemical." Chemical foods are those that have received some additive, especially inorganic fertilizer in the growing soil, or food additives, preservatives, or artificial flavoring and coloring agents used in processing. Growth hormones given to cattle or poultry are considered "chemical" agents; canning, as a processing technique, is generally considered to be less acceptable, organically, than freezing. In general, the less human intervention there has been with a foodstuff prior to cooking, the more "organic" it is. Application of the *organic motif* involves the avoidance of processed foods, foods containing additives, foods grown with chemical fertilizers and meat from animals that have been fed hormones. It involves the inclusion of vegetables grown and animals raised on "organic" farms, and raw, fresh foods that have received a minimum of processing prior to reaching the home kitchen. The *organic motif* is applied with varying degrees of strictness, ranging from only the avoidance of foods containing "artificial" or "synthetic" ingredients to the purchase of all foodstuffs from health food stores and organic farms.

The *mystical motif* involves the attribution of beneficial qualities to foods for their symbolic properties rather than their scientific nutrient contents. Raw food eaters and fruitarians frequently justify their diets by reference to the "life energy" contained in uncooked foods. Sprout eaters talk about the "growth force" of their dietary staples. They like to pick the sprouts immediately before eating so the force that provides the energy to make the sprouts grow is still active to give them energy. Macrobiotic vegetarians attribute an ideal balance of positive and negative forces—Yin and Yang, activity and passivity, expansion and contraction—to brown rice. Those who subscribe to the *mystical motif* appear to believe the symbolic properties of foods may be transferred from the food to the eater by a combination of sympathetic and contagious magic. Thus, eating "energetic" foods makes the eater energetic; eating balanced foods results in a balanced soul and psyche.

2. *The vegetarian idea*—Diets are characterized by avoidance of animal proteins, to varying degrees. Individuals who call themselves "vegetarians" range from those who avoid only "red" meat (beef, pork, lamb) but eat chicken and/or fish and seafood; to lacto and/or ovo vegetarians; to strict vegans; and those who further modify veganism, eating only raw foods or only grains. Reasons for the avoidance of animal protein include beliefs about its unhealthiness for the human body; its psycho-physical effects on cognition; humanitarian concerns about killing; and ecological concerns about the high energy cost of producing animal protein.

3. *The spiritual idea*—Diets are a means for achieving a balanced and righteous life. They may be a necessary, but are rarely a sufficient, method of achieving this goal. Application of the *spiritual idea* is often associated with the practice of yoga, meditation, or various types of prayer. The *spiritual idea* differs from the *mystical motif* (above) in that the food itself need have no special symbolic or magic properties. For example, when the spiritual idea is associated with the natural food idea, the doctrine may be that a nutritionally balanced diet makes one physically healthy and mentally alert to pursue one's spiritual discipline. When the spiritual idea is associated with the vegetarian idea, the doctrine may be that concern with the preservation of all life increases one's sense of continuity with the rest of God's creatures.

These three key ideas are not always found in association. The dietary beliefs of any individual or organized group are idiosyncratic to the extent that they represent a personal combination of these ideas. This may be illustrated with several examples.

The members of one station of the "Holy Brotherhood," a neo-Catholic order with a heavy emphasis on occult study, suggested that a health food diet was necessary in order to keep one's body well and active in the service of God. They also said that a vegetarian diet was the most spiritually purifying. They themselves, however, eat meat three times a week, in order to keep their "spiritual vibrations" down to the level of the "common man" so they can communicate with him in their missionary work. If they were to become vegetarian, they believe, such a rarefied aura would exude from them that potential converts would be frightened away.

The profit-sharing restaurant, "Tree of Life," provides another example. Most members of the group attempt to follow fruitarian diets personally, although they also serve cooked grain dishes in the restaurant. The proprietors stated that there is a separation between their spiritual and dietary concerns. Yet they also stated that the restaurant itself is a form of meditation. For a time they rang a gong hourly in the restaurant to draw the workers together spiritually.

Formal Organizations of the Health Food Movement

The formal organizations of the health food movement may be divided into two types: (a) revitalization cults and (b) other communication-distribution centers.

The anthropologist, Anthony F. C. Wallace, defined revitalization as "a deliberate, organized, conscious effort by members of a society to construct a more satisfying culture" (1956: 265). Within the health food movement there are groups that fulfill this comprehensive definition and subscribe to such a mandate of messianic change. The ideologies of these revitalization cults include not only dietary, but metaphysical and moral tenets, as well as strictures about proper lifestyle and attitude. Socially, they are well-organized, and membership often means passing through an initiation rite, taking an oath, or joining a brotherhood. Many of them are actively proselytizing, have formal political organizations, own and operate businesses, and maintain communal residences or ashrams. Some of these revitalization cults have only local influence, while others are organized on a national or international scale.

The other type of organization, the communication-distribution centers, include health food stores and restaurants, organic farms, and vegetarian food lines at schools. These places serve multiple functions. They are sources of food, and the eating habits of health food users may thus be heavily influenced by the inventories of health food stores in their localities. They are meeting places where health food users come together, both those who belong to revitalization cults and those who do not. They are also sources of information: most sell books, pamphlets and periodicals; shoppers often chat together exchanging ideas about diet, and health food store proprietors are consulted for dietary guidance.

Geographical area appears to play a part in determining the relative importance of revitalization cults and other communication-distribution centers. In Boston, and probably in other urban centers, there is sufficient population to sustain the revitalization cults, and their proselytizing efforts influence the diets of many individuals who do not actually belong to them. In less-populated areas there are no revitalization cult headquarters, and the influence of the other communication-distribution centers is more strongly felt. In the rural area studied, the most significant formal organizations include two health food stores, a bakery that specializes in whole grain breads, an independent health food restaurant, and numerous small farms selling "organically grown vegetables in season" and "organically grown chickens."

In the rural area, the close proximity of farms seems to exert a significant influence on diet in several ways. The proportion of meat-eating health food users in the rural sample was higher than in the urban sample; possibly a reflection of the accessibility of fresh organic meats. The option to purchase foodstuffs directly from the farms also lessens health food users' dependence on stores and restaurants. In the rural area most health food users apparently prefer to "do it themselves," a characteristic that tends to discourage the development of commercial health food bakeries and restaurants.

Types of Participation in the Movement

Our participant observation research in the two areas revealed that health food users become socially and economically involved in the movement to varying degrees. The following four types of social involvement can be noted.

1. A *reservoir* of potential members, coming primarily from the young adult, formally educated middle class. These individuals are partisans to the movement by virtue of their interest in the ecological, political, and spiritual concerns that spawned it. They may be recruited to the movement by friends, or by reading the popular literature of the movement.

2. *Independent or "reading and eating" members* who subscribe to the ideology and follow health food diets without intense social interaction with other dieters.

3. *Peripheral social members*—In addition to eating and reading about health foods, peripheral social members "hang out" at the communication-distribution centers and occasionally attend the organized meetings of the revitalization cults. Many of their friends may be actively involved in the movement. However, peripheral social members do not live in the residences or work in the stores, restaurants or farms of the movement, and they are substantially socially and economically independent of it.

4. *Joiners*—For the joiners, participation in the movement is a major part of life and a mainstay of social and financial support. They may devote almost all their time to the movement, living in communal residences, working in health food stores, businesses and residences, choosing their friends primarily from among the members of the movement, and attending organized meetings. In addition, they may devote themselves to the doctrine of a re-vitalization group with religious fervor, and make living in ac-cordance with its ideology a major goal and focus of their lives. Thus, some joiners have told us "I belong to (this group) because it answers all the questions I have about life," and "I belong to (this group) because it is telling me all I need to know to live right now."

Although, as a rule, social involvement and dietary strictness tend to go together, there is no necessary relationship between them. We found independents who conscientiously followed strict diets, and committed joiners who casually indulged in delicatessen meats and candy store sweets.

These categories are fluid, for an individual may be an inde-pendent one week and a joiner the next, or move casually from one group to another. It is therefore necessary to learn the career history of any individual within the movement. For examples of types of involvement and health food career histories, the reader is referred to the case histories below.

Leadership in the Health Food Movement

Leadership within the movement may be divided into two types: (a) social leaders and (b) asocial leaders. *Social leaders* influence the beliefs and behavior of their followers through personal face-to-face contact. Social leaders include both the gurus who generate the systems and control the larger economic enterprises, their top-ranking apostles, and the proprietors of the smaller enterprises. These social leaders are charismatic figures, not only for their close followers but for many of the "independents" and "reservoir individuals" in their localities.

In the revitalization cults, dominant ideological leadership belongs to a few charismatic leaders. Many of them are middle aged, and most are from India or the Far East. Nearly all of them are foreign born. They write books, give lectures, and maintain study houses or institutes. They own and operate food stores, restaurants, and other financial enterprises, which both promote their products and bring money to their organizations. A portion of this money is used to support some of their followers, who, in turn, return part of it to the organization through the purchase of foodstuffs and other products. Social leaders provide tutelage and financial support, and act as counselors and advisors to their followers.

The structure of most of the revitalization cults is hierarchical. Secondary leadership usually belongs to a few apostles in each cult. These apostles have considerable freedom, and take initiative in organization and maintenance. They may expand and modify doctrine and diet, but they do so under the mandate of interpretation and exegesis, and describe their activities primarily in administrative or missionizing terms.

Asocial leaders are those who influence large numbers of health food users through their books, articles, and public appearances but do not act as political leaders for an organized following. The names of some familiar asocial leaders are Adelle Davis, Lelord Kordel, Bob Hoffman, and Euell Gibbons.

Demographic factors seem to play a large part in determining the relative importance of social and asocial leadership in any area. The social leaders tend to establish headquarters in more heavily populated areas where there is sufficient interest to make their organizations economically successful. Health food users who wish to study with these leaders, in turn, migrate to the urban areas. This leaves a relative absence of social leadership in the rural area, where health food users predominantly turn to the writings of the asocial leaders for their dietary guidance.

Communication within the Movement

There are four major channels of communication through which new diets and ideas spread in the health food movement. These are:

1. Books, articles and television appearances by health food movement leaders.

2. Proselytizing trips and tours by social leaders and their apostles.

3. Health food stores, restaurants, and other communication-distribution centers which act as information channels by recommending books and diets, spreading community gossip, and bringing independents, peripheral social members, and joiners of various groups together.

4. Person-to-person communication by members of the movement through (a) friendship and kinship networks, (b) common participation in mass events, and (c) movement from one revitalization cult to the next, bringing along the ideas of the previous group and introducing them to the new one.

Through these four communication channels a vast health food information network is maintained, linking all types of participants, and all types of groups, throughout the United States.

A Network Analysis of the Movement

An analysis of the interaction among individuals and groups in the urban area illustrates how the "segmented, polycephalous, cellular organization" of the health food movement operates and influences food-related behavior. The part of the movement examined is a network of six health food groups that dominate the communication-distribution centers in the area. We have termed this network the "Vega-net." Within the Vega-net the flow of membership, ideology and finances from group to group is especially marked. The six groups of the Vega-net are:

1. The Macrobiotics, who combine an interpretation of the Oriental philosophical dialectic of Yin and Yang with a vegetarian diet in which brown rice and miso soup are the most important staples. In the urban area they form a socioeconomic community

surrounding Michio, their charismatic leader. (They have been described elsewhere. See Kandel and Kandel, 1971; Kandel, 1972, 1975).

2. The "Way of the Mouth," a natural food restaurant and bakery operated by volunteer workers, some of whom live communally.

3. The "Tree of Life," a profit-sharing vegetarian restaurant operated by a group of young people under the leadership of a woman called "Karma."

4. The "Holy Brotherhood," one station of a national neo-Catholic, occult-oriented proselytizing order who live in a communal house. They are under the leadership of the Father of the order, based in San Francisco, and "Father Richard," head of the station.

5. The "Grecian Health Resort," a raw food eating institute and guest house, incorporated as a non-profit religious institution, and occupying a large mansion. It is directed by "Dr. Jane," a graduate of several institutes of drugless therapy, and her disciple "Igor."

6. The Divine Light Mission, a locally based ashram devoted to the internationally influential Indian spiritual leader, Satguru Maharaj Ji. Three obligations are placed upon initiates into the movement: meditation, service, and *satsang* (group meditational sessions). The philosophy emphasizes love, peace, and joy, and a lacto-vegetarian diet is recommended. Many of the local following live in the communally run ashram. Others visit regularly to attend *satsang*.

Several small, privately owned health food stores, and some other revitalization cult groups, including the Process People and Hare Krishna People are peripheral members of the Vega-net. Though these cult groups are colleagues in spirit, overlapping membership is extremely limited. This is, in part, due to the history of personal friendship and the geographical location of the various cult headquarters. It is also due to the fact that these peripheral groups require their members to make a more permanent, binding and exclusive commitment, symbolized by a religious oath or participation in an initiation rite.

At its periphery, the Vega-net is bounded by two types of receptive and supportive institutions. They are:

1. Sellers of goods and services who encourage business with the health food movement, including wholesale food sellers, Chinese and Japanese grocery stores, landlords, restaurant supply dealers, and a church that offers its hall for meetings. While the economic

flow is basically outward from the network, members of the Vega-net have established advantageous patron-client bonds.

2. Other health food oriented, spiritualist, and folk medical groups whose contact with the Vega-net does not result in exchange of ideas or personnel. This includes the Seventh Day Adventist Hospital where many Vega-net members deliver their babies, and a chain of vitamin-pill oriented health food stores. These institutions support the Vega-net, largely unintentionally, by making available essential goods and services.

Major structural features within the network include four restaurants, two food stores, one book store, one wholesale food processor, one ashram, two newspapers, a periodical, two communal apartments, and a shifting number of boarding houses officially maintained by one or another of the Vega-net groups. There are also a number of residences shared by or exchanged among members of the Vega-net.

The social leaders of the Vega-net are Michio, head of Macrobiotics, and Dr. Jane, founder of the Grecian Health Resort, both of whom resided in the area throughout the study period; and Satguru Maharaj Ji, who was out of the area during most of the study period, and had never been personally seen by many of his local followers. Karma exercised charismatic leadership over the Tree of Life group but was not widely known in the Vega-net.

Secondary social leadership in the Vega-net is also clearly localized with about ten apostles. These include a group of Macrobiotics who edit the newspapers and periodical, and manage the study houses, restaurants, and store; Igor, who works closely with Dr. Jane and acts as her culture broker with the young adults; Father Richard, head of the Holy Brotherhood station, and "Helena," unofficial housemother of the Divine Light ashram, whose personal warmth and managerial ability keep her group together.

There are at least four significant spatial "cluster areas" where several Vega-net institutions are located within a city block of each other. These are:

1. *Downtown area*—includes both Macrobiotic restaurants, the Macrobiotic retail store and bookstore, an independent health food store, and the Grecian Health Resort.

2. *"Main Square"* area—includes the "Tree of Life" communal apartment and the Holy Brotherhood station.

3. *"Stillman Square"* area—includes the Way of the Mouth, a seafood store and restaurant popular with Vega-net members, and two peripherally related groups.

4. *Michio area*—includes Michio's own residence where classes and lectures are held, two of his study houses, and many apartments occupied by Macrobiotics.

Only the Divine Light Mission is located by itself, approximately fifteen miles outside of Boston. With the exception of the Divine Light Mission and the Michio area, clustering is determined primarily by the low rents and landlords' permissive attitudes. Secondarily, however, the proximity of different groups results in influence flow. Notably, the downtown cluster permits individuals to literally run back and forth between the Grecian and Macrobiotic enterprises; allows the immediate diffusion of their innovations to the smaller stores; and allows peripheral social members and reservoir individuals who come to shop or gawk to circulate among the several institutions in a short time. The Stillman Square cluster area enables several small operations to be financially viable by sharing a common clientele who would not be attracted to the area by the presence of one of these institutions alone. Conversely, the continuing financial difficulties experienced by the Tree of Life restaurant result partially from its geographical isolation in another section of town.

All members of the Vega-net are not equal. Originally dominance was maintained by the Macrobiotics, who described themselves as a "community," had the largest membership, the most highly structured organization, and control of the newspapers and periodical. The Macrobiotics were also the largest wholesale health food suppliers in the Boston area, so that all the health food stores were forced by necessity to obtain some of their products from the Macrobiotics.

The Grecian Health Resort, although smaller, is older, financially solvent, well known and respected by all members of the Vega-net. It has an additional recruitment reservoir in the large number of elderly people who turn to the Grecian diet as a cure for degenerative and psychosomatic ills.

The Divine Light Mission, although originally small, gained rapidly increasing membership as part of a burgeoning international cult. The local chapter had originally been started by a group of friends who split off from the Macrobiotic community. A steady recruitment to the Mission through personal friendship links with the Vega-net continued throughout the study period. Membership flow was periodically intensified by mass proselytizing *satsang* held by Divine Light leaders visiting the area. Although the Divine Light Mission was less organized than Macrobiotics on a local level, it was much more highly organized on a national level. By the end of the study period, its membership was probably as large as, or larger than, that of the Macrobiotics.

The Holy Brotherhood, although also a national organization, has only about twenty initiated members in the study area and is not well known. The Tree of Life and the Way of the Mouth groups each comprise, at any one time, no more than fifteen members each, and each member is trying to do "his own thing" within the movement. At all times, these two groups struggle for financial survival and internal ideological cohesion.

Beliefs and practices in the Vega-net are dominated by the doctrines of its strongest members. Three of these are most important. First is the Divine Light Mission version of the spiritual idea. This involves initiation into a state of joy and peace, which then has to be maintained by meditation and diet. Second, is the Macrobiotic version of the mystical motif. In Macrobiotic theory, harmony with the Order of the Universe may be attained through the proper balance of Yin and Yang in the diet. Third is the raw food version of the mystical motif. In this theory, life energy and spiritual purity may be obtained by eating fruits, salads, and freshly picked sprouts. This theory is exemplified in the Vega-net primarily in the doctrine of the Grecian Health Resort.

In order to share a common clientele each group makes concessions to the others. One macrobiotic restaurant provides a special "vegetarian" section on its menu with raw food items; the Tree of Life, although leaning towards fruitarianism, also serves Macrobiotic-style cooked grain dishes; and the Way of the Mouth serves modified Macrobiotic cuisine. Proprietors of the small health food stores must cater to both Macrobiotics and raw food patrons. Food items are sold by the stores to independent users.

The growing popularity of Divine Light and the large degree of overlapping membership between it and other Vega-net groups has resulted in an increased emphasis on spirituality within the Vega-net. The Macrobiotic newspaper eventually became a vehicle for the entire urban spiritual community, and many Macrobiotics came to conceive of their diet as a route to spiritual well being. Influence flow has also operated in the other direction. New followers of the Satguru Maharaj Ji introduce raw food and macrobiotic patterns into the local Divine Light diet.

Through distribution of the newspapers in health food stores and by street hawkers, these ideas have ultimately flowed to independent health food users in the area.

Basic changes in the beliefs and practices of each of the local groups have also resulted from their cross-contact. For example, the dietary system of the Grecian Health Resort combines a folk medical system of Eastern European derivation with a fundamentalist version of Christianity slightly influenced by Dr. Jane's indirect contact with Christian Science. Therapy focuses primarily on physical curing and the insurance of longevity. The root of all bodily ills is seen to lie in gastrointestinal disturbances resulting from eating bad foods. The core of the diet is a "complete meal salad" of freshly picked sprouts (grown in window boxes), and avocados. The sprouts have health-giving properties by virtue of their "growth energy" and the chemical similarity of chlorophyll to hemoglobin. Therapy also includes the use of blended wheat grass juice as an emetic. The Grecian Health Resort appealed mainly to elderly people suffering from psychosomatic or degenerative diseases and obesity, prior to the current interest in health foods. Traditional prayer meetings and mild calesthenics had been optional aspects of therapy. Dr. Arnold Ehret is a popular asocial leader among the Grecian guests.

Through the Vega-net and similar health food networks many young, healthy health food users have been led to Dr. Jane's door. She recognizes the value of these people as proselytizers and takes a motherly interest in those few who are trying to recuperate from heavy drug use. She employs a number of them at Grecian; paying them room, board, and a few dollars weekly, in exchange for a few hours of daily work devoted to planting sprouts, making beds for the paying guests, or providing clerical services.

Examples of Vega-net Collaboration
In addition to the informal flow of diets, ideas, and people described above, members of the Vega-net sometimes collaborate in an organized fashion. Some collaborative efforts fail, but others have permanent results. The eight examples below, which came to the researchers' attention within a period of several months, probably represent a good sample of the cooperative ventures that have occurred.

1. Purchasers for the Macrobiotic restaurant, dissatisfied with the quality of tofu (bean curd) they were obtaining from a retail grocery store in Chinatown, complained to the owner. He told them that the majority of his customers wanted low cost rather than high quality and recommended a manufacturer who sold a superior, more expensive product. As the price of the superior tofu

was too high for the Macrobiotics, the restaurant purchaser formed a cooperative that included most of the Vega-net stores and restaurants, and the Chinese grocer, in order to buy the better quality tofu at reduced prices. The buying cooperative proved unsuccessful, when all involved decided that their customers were unable to discriminate between better and lesser quality tofu.

2. "Hibiscus House," a reducing resort in the northern part of the state was taken over by a new owner. His assistants activated their. personal contacts with members of the Grecian Health Resort staff to recruit personnel and patrons to their institution. This resulted in several cooperative efforts, including a joint weekend seminar at Hibiscus House with the social leaders of Hibiscus, Macrobiotics, and Grecian.

3. Half-a-dozen Macrobiotics who began lunching regularly at the Grecian Health Resort were converted, and a few became members of Dr. Jane's staff. One of them continued simultaneously to work at the Macrobiotic retail store, introducing several Grecian products to the store inventory. He also introduced several Macrobiotic products to the Grecian guests.

4. Karma and her Tree of Life followers, after reading Dr. Arnold Ehret's books, sought out Igor for dietary advice. They established a patient-therapist relationship with Igor, contributed to the ongoing Easternization at Grecian by sharing their ideas with him, considerably modified their own diets, and added several new Grecian-style items to the Tree of Life menu.

5. Out of curiousity, several Tree of Lifers began attending open masses at the Holy Brotherhood station. They soon established friendships with the brothers and discussed their mutual problems. The brothers were interested in winning converts. The Tree of Life group was in financial straits. The Holy Brotherhood, licensed as a religious institution, had tax exempt status. They agreed to missionize the Tree of Life apartment, thereby granting them tax exempt status as well. One of the Holy Brotherhood priests transferred his residence to the apartment and converted one of the rooms into a chapel. In exchange, the brothers agreed to eat a diet more compatible with the Tree of Life group's. The Tree of Life people admitted that the liaison was primarily an economic one. Their own religious leanings, they confided, lay towards Hindu-Buddhism. In turn, the holy Brotherhood people felt that their religious example would ultimately have an effect on the Tree of Lifers, although they themselves only followed a vegetarian diet

when at the Tree of Life apartment. On several occasions the researchers found raw-food-eating Tree of Life people gleefully dining on chicken soup and french fries with ketchup at the Holy Brotherhood station. Assured of attaining financial success with their new tax status, the Tree of Life people were soon pursuing the purchase of a large farm.

6. The manager of the Macrobiotic restaurant interpreted the Macrobiotic doctrine to include an emphasis on ecology. He established procedures for recycling restaurant wastes. The Process People, a mendicant order, were looking for places to obtain free food. The Process People established a relationship with the restaurant whereby they could obtain leftover food at the end of the day. A relatively rich organization since members pay a tithe, they would arrive at the restaurant in the early morning by taxi, dressed in their silk uniforms and silver crosses, to return the plastic bowls they had borrowed the previous evening. As a result, the Process People, who were health food users, were introduced to a number of Macrobiotic items. However, there was little verbal exchange between the members of the two groups.

7. The Satguru Maharaj Ji visited the area and held a mass satsang that was publicized through fliers, on bulletin boards at the communication-distribution centers, at schools, and in the Macrobiotic press. Large numbers of independents and Vega-net members attended the satsang, and were initiated into the Divine Light Mission. Few residence changes took place, but a large number of double memberships ensued. Among those initiated was an editor of one Macrobiotic newspaper. He published a long article on the ceremony and intensified his coverage of the Divine Light Mission and other spiritually-oriented groups in the succeeding months. These events ultimately led to increased interaction among proponents of the vegetarian and spiritual ideas.

8. Members of the Vega-net groups and a number of peripherally associated spiritual groups formed an informal Sunday Morning meeting of the Spiritual Community, which met regularly at the Tree of Life restaurant with varying degrees of Vega-net participation.

When we examine the extent of network involvement we find that three events involved only a portion of the groups in the Vega-net, while five involved some or all of the Vega-net, as well as peripheral members or outsiders. None of the events involved the entire Vega-net to the exclusion of outsiders. This indicates that the

Vega-net is composed of shifting, situationally-conditioned subnets. A group might participate simultaneously in several subnets, thus facilitating the flow of information through the entire network.

Leaders were actively involved in only two events, while apostles and rank and file members were involved in six events out of the eight. The Vega-net events included purely socioeconomic and purely ideological interchanges, but the personal contact that occurs among members of the various groups appears to result in some shifts of cult membership. There are individuals who move out of one group and into another, at least partially as a result of contacts made through the Vega-net.

From the foregoing analysis we find that the structure of the health food movement in the urban area conforms well to the general characteristics of social movements outlined above. There is considerable communication among the various cult groups, yet they retain their independence both ideologically and organizationally. Occasionally small groups splinter off from the established cults. Outside the social network of the joiners and peripheral social members are the independents, adherents to the movement who are tied into the network through its books and the mass media.

Association of Ideological Focus, Participation Type, and Diet: Case Histories

In their analysis of the data on urban vegetarians, Dwyer et al. found that there were a number of statistically significant differences between independents and joiners (1973, 1974). Independents reported losing less weight on their new diets, reported fewer allergies or sensitivities to certain foods, shopped less often in vegetarian and health food stores, and used conventional eating utensils more than joiners. Our data indicate that joiners smoke marijuana less frequently than independents in both the urban and rural areas. In addition, our data suggest that health food users who place primary emphasis on the *vitamin motif* get much of their dietary guidance from reading and do not make an effort to participate in social relationships with other dieters; while those who place primary emphasis on the *mystical motif* and the *spiritual idea* tend to associate themselves more frequently with revitalization cults. On the other hand, there appear to be no clear correlations among ideological focus, type of participation and dietary behavior.

The case histories that follow demonstrate the heterogeneity and diversity of diet, ideology, and behavior among the health food users in the urban and rural areas studied in our research.

Helena

Ideological Focus: Vegetarian Idea, Spiritual Idea
Participation Type: Joiner
Location: Urban

Helena first became a member of the health food movement when she was drawn into the social network by friends who followed the local Macrobiotic leader. Over a period of several months her diet became more and more strictly vegetarian and "classically" Macrobiotic, with a limited intake of fruits and dairy products, and a heavy intake of brown rice, other whole grains, and miso soup. During that time her primary ideological focus was on the mystical motif of the natural food idea. She describes that period as the "healthiest" period of her life, and remembers happily how slim she was in those days. But, "It was too much," she recalls. "We would go out and binge once in a while on chocolate ice cream, come home and be terribly sick." During her Macrobiotic period, Helena and her husband attended a lecture given by the Satguru Maharaj Ji, international leader of the Divine Light Movement. They were immediately attracted to him. Helena became initiated into Divine Light, and for a time, retained joint affiliation in both Divine Light and Macrobiotics. Gradually, she severed her connection with Macrobiotics, though retaining a number of Macrobiotic friends. Also gradually, during this transitional time, her diet changed from a Macrobiotic one, to one that substantially followed the lacto-vegetarian diet recommended by the new group, and believed to induce receptivity to the meditative state.

At the time of our study, Helena was the cook in an ashram devoted to the Satguru Maharaj Ji. She did almost all of the cooking for the ashram residents, and sometimes baked as many as twelve whole grain breads in a single day. Although she substantially follows a lacto-vegetarian diet, thus combining the vegetarian and spiritual ideas, she freely eats processed foods and refined sweets, and is especially fond of Howard Johnson's chocolate ice cream and onion rings. She says, "There are so many things more important than food; especially love and meditation."

Helena's Food Intake: 24 Hour Period

Breakfast 9:30	Lunch 2:00	Dinner 7:00

1 pretzel stick
¼ cup Wheatena with
1/8 cup milk
	2 cups coffee
	4 t white sugar
	3 T of melloream
	1 cup french-fried
	  onion rings
		½ cup brown rice
		1 cup nituke sauteed
		  spinach (corn oil,
		  tamari, garlic)

Snack 10:45	3 t catsup 1 lrg slice chocolate	**Snack 9:00**

2 walnuts	fudge cake w/fudge
	  icing
	2 lrg scoops vanilla
	  ice cream
	¼ cup chocolate fudge
	  sauce
	5 saltine crackers
	8 oz. water
		1 cup mu tea
		3 walnuts

Teresa

Ideological Focus: Vegetarian Idea, Natural Food Idea, Mystical Motif
Participation Type: Joiner
Location: Urban

Teresa first discovered the health food movement during a confused period of her life. On the verge of a divorce, she and her friends were involved in both drugs and Eastern spiritualism. She found herself vacillating between emotional extremes.

Then I read a copy of Zen Macrobiotics which a friend had left at my house, by mistake. I discovered Ohsawa! Suddenly, all the pieces fit. I knew he was right. Everything seemed to make sense. I just had to learn more. This was my answer. Macrobiotics seemed like a way to return to all the happiness of my childhood. I gave up all plans for a career in commercial art. I left the frenzied world of art because Ohsawa said in one of his books that the emotional extremes of the artist were best maintained by eating the extreme Yin and Yang foods but that by following the middle path one could reach a new calmer and higher happiness. First I began eating macrobiotically. Then I heard about Michio (the charismatic leader of Macrobiotics) and I moved to Boston to study Macrobiotics and become his student. Now I have even started painting again but it's coming from a different part of me. A calmer, deeper part.

Teresa strictly follows the whole grain and vegetable diet characteristic of Macrobiotics. Brown rice and miso soup are her principal dietary staples. She conscientiously attempts to balance each meal in terms of the proportion of Yin and Yang elements. She is very reflective and analyzes the emotional effect that each item of diet has upon her. She faithfully attends the lectures and seminars given by her leader, participates in cooking classes offered by the leader's wife, and experiments with new macrobiotic recipes.

During the study period Teresa, who lived only with her four-year-old daughter, began to feel lonely. She turned to her spiritual leader for advice. He informed her there was an opening for a cook in one of his study houses. She was hesitant, but Michio looked directly into her eyes, pointed a thin finger at her, and said, "You are afraid of responsibility. I know you can do it, or I wouldn't send you." She accepted the job, and, despite many second thoughts, worked diligently at it to please Michio.

At the conclusion of our study, Teresa was still employed as a study house cook. She was responsible for food purchasing and meal planning as well as cooking. She was spending the greater portion of her day in the kitchen, for which she received a reduced cost for room and board and a small salary.

The direction of Teresa's career within the movement thus appears to be more increasingly committed socially, economically, and dietarily to this one revitalization group.

Teresa's Food Intake: 24 Hour Period

Breakfast	Lunch	Dinner
1 cup bancha tea	1½ cups buckwheat	1 cup kasha
1 cup miso soup (carrots, onions, bean curds)	½ cup vegetable sauce onions, celery, chinese cabbage, carrots	1 cup summer squash
		1 cup brown rice
		1 cup lentil soup

Snack

1 cup bancha tea
2 cigarettes

Robert

Ideological Focus: Vegetarian Idea, Natural Food Idea, Organic and
Mystical Motifs
Participation Type: Joiner
Location: Urban

Robert was gradually absorbed into the health food movement during his "Hippie days." While hitchhiking around the United States, he discovered a network of organic farms that took in people like himself, allowing them to work temporarily for their room and board. During this period, he ate whatever he was served, usually some type of organic vegetarian diet and learned the ideology of the health food movement from the people with whom he lived and the books they lent him. When he decided to go to Boston, he was told about the "Grecian Health Resort." At the time of the study he had been living at the Grecian Health Resort for about two months, doing clerical work and household chores in exchange for room, board, and a small salary. At that time he was totally committed to the strict raw foods diet and the detailed food beliefs of the cult. He voraciously read all available literature on the virtues of raw food diets or fasting. He also ate voraciously and snacked frequently on fruits, nuts, and seeds. Most of his social life seemed to center around the Grecian Health Resort. It is impossible to predict how his diet might evolve from this point, though one suspects that when his wanderlust urges him to move on to another city, his diet might make an equally great change.

Robert's Food Intake: 24 Hour Period

Breakfast 7:30-8:15

Juice of ½ lrg lemon
   mixed with ½ qt water
   and 3 T honey
½ oz. wheat grass juice
½ cup of equal portions
   lentil sprouts, mung
   bean sprouts, chick
   peas with ¼ t almond
   oil, pinch of kelp
2 scallions
4 apples
½ cup winter wheat sprouts
¼ cup Persian raisins
7 dried dates
3 dried figs
1 dried peach
1/8 cup dried pears
½ cup sunflower seeds
1 T shredded coconut

Lunch 3:30

3 apples
3 dried dates
¼ cup Persian raisins
¼ cup sunflower seeds
¼ cup chick peas
   sprouts

Dinner 6:00

Salad of:
2/3 avocado
1 tomato
1/5 cup lentil sprouts
1/3 cup Mung bean sprouts
1/6 cup tahini sauce (sesame
   seeds, chick peas, lemon
   juice, and rejuvalac pureed
   in blender)
½ cup shredded carrots
¼ carrot in sticks
½ stalk celery
1/5 green pepper
1 floweret broccoli
2 thin slices turnip

Snack 9:00

1 apple
1 grapefruit

Snack - Intermittent

Sunflower seeds
Dried dates
Dried figs

Jenifer

Ideological Focus: Natural food idea
Participation Type: Independent
Location: Rural

Jenifer is a graduate student, working on a Ph.D. in a biological science. Divorced, she lives with her eleven year old daughter and six year old son in a comfortable, but somewhat sparsely-equipped old house. Her interest in health food use is a fairly recent development, stemming from several different sources. She credits a course in biochemisty as the major influence in her decision to avoid foods with preservatives, while new cooking styles were learned from a Chinese friend. In addition to reading about nutrition in textbooks, she relies heavily on advice from the proprietor of a small, local health food store.

Jenifer is the daughter of a German-American family; her father is professionally educated and holds a Ph.D.; her mother is a college graduate. She is moderately active in liberal political causes and a dedicated environmentalist; her ideology is reflected in household maintenance activities, such as recycling all bottles, paper, and cans, as well as the lead around wine bottles. She doesn't smoke and drinks no alcohol except for an occasional glass of wine. Baking breads and "healthy" desserts are her favorite hobbies, but the demands of her educational program and work schedule (research assistant in an animal lab) leave her with little time for recreational activities.

Jenifer is evolving a fairly stable new style of food use, which, she says, differs considerably from that of her natal family. In food preparation she makes extensive use of items such as honey and unbleached flour, but is not dedicated to the more "exotic" aspects of health foods, such as brewer's yeast and soy products. As can be seen in the diet data that follows, she continues to eat many foods that purists would find unacceptable.

Jenifer's Food Intake: 24 Hour Period

Breakfast	Lunch	Snack
8 oz. grape juice	Peanut butter and honey	handful of
1 slice homemade bread,	sandwich on homemade	potato chips
toasted, with peach	white bread	black coffee
jam	1 cup tea with 2 t. honey	
1 cup coffee	1 apple	
	3 chocolate cookies	
Dinner		**Evening Snack**
4 oz. ground round		5 crackers
3/4 cup broccoli		2 slices cheese
1 baked potato		small glass liquer
5-6 dates		
8 oz. ginger ale		

George

Ideological Focus: Natural Foods, Vitamin Motif
Participant Type: Independent
Location: Rural

George represents an unusual type of participant in the health food movement—a health care professional, who, in mid-career, has become interested in the role of nutrition in health maintenance. A practicing dentist, he became interested in nutrition, in part, as a result of a growing concern with preventive dentistry. He has worked to establish dental hygiene programs in the area schools, as well as to develop an education program for his patients. In connection with the education component of patient care, his dental hygienist convinced him that it was important to teach patients about good nutrition, and he began to acquire more knowledge about himself. The assistant gave him a book by Adele Davis, which he read with considerable interest. Following that he made an effort to read articles on nutrition in the dentistry journals, attended sessions on nutrition at professional meetings, and joined a statewide nutrition group.

George's eating habits are in a state of rapid transition. His interest in nutrition is, he admits, very new, and he is in the process of acquiring more knowledge. At the time of the interview, his diet had recently taken a radically different direction since he was experimenting with eating a great deal of liver. As a reflection of his incomplete knowledge, he admitted ruefully that he had been eating yeast, stirring it into orange juice, until he discovered that he was using baker's yeast, not brewer's yeast. He is committed to improving his knowledge, as well as using it toward the goal of preventive dentistry. It seems probable that his own diet will continue to undergo considerable change as he begins to establish new eating patterns that are different from the heavy-carbohydrate diet he consumed prior to his new-found interest in nutrition.

George's Food Intake: 24 Hour Period

Breakfast	Lunch	Dinner
16 oz. V-8 juice	sandwich of rye bread	8 oz. beef liver,
8 oz. skim milk with	with 4 slices pressed	fried in corn oil,
2 T powdered skim	ham	with ketchup
milk stirred in	1 hard-boiled egg	1 cup mixed frozen
3 oz. beef liver,	2 oz. cashew nuts	vegetables
fried in corn oil	1 cup Sanka	6 oz. wine
		small liquer glass
		of B&B

Sarah

Ideological Focus: Natural Foods, Organic Motif, and Vitamin Motif
Participant Type: Independent
Location: Rural

Sarah is a committed, *second-generation* health food user, whose food habits have been sharply influenced by the constraints of dormitory life. To make up for what she perceives as the poor nutritional quality of food in the dormitory, she supplements her diet liberally with vitamins and other tablets. Like the majority of students, she returns home on weekends, where her family's meals are more in accord with her nutritional principles. Her family is committed to eating organic foods as much as possible, and they avoid eating liver and kidneys because of the possible harmful effects of DES residues. At home, they do not eat processed foods, but make extensive use of wheat germ, brewer's yeast, and soy products.

Sarah credits her father with being the major influence on her eating habits. He was a premed student whose studies were interrupted by the Second World War, and he became a piano tuner to support his family, never returning to school. Sarah's mother is a high school home economics teacher, who, she claims, learned the principles of good nutrition from her husband (rather than from her college training). Sarah works hard at learning more about nutrition: she regularly reads *Prevention* magazine and, in high school, carried out a number of independent projects in nutrition-related subjects. She is also very active physically, was a member of her high school field hockey team, and now swims daily. As a freshman she is still uncertain of her long-range career goals, but she has declared herself as a fine arts major and expects to pursue art and theatre as major interests.

Sarah and her family appear to represent one stereotype of the health food user. They are very concerned about environmental issues, recycle papers and bottles, and try to create a healthy environment in their home. They don't smoke; they drink alcohol very moderately, and use prescription drugs as little as possible. Sarah doesn't use marijuana (although she is not against it morally). In adjusting to dormitory life, Sarah attempts to maintain her principles, to the fullest extent possible. As a result, she is thought of as "odd" or "different" by other students, an evaluation that she finds amusing. Sarah appears to be making an effective compromise,

and one would expect that her long-standing dietary habits will not
be greatly changed by her college experience.

Sarah's Food Intake: 24 Hour Period

Breakfast	Lunch	Dinner
12 oz. orange juice	3/4 c. egg salad	2 bites of spare rib
1 scrambled egg	with lettuce	3/4 c. squash
1 banana, sliced	6 oz. vegetable soup	3 helpings of salad
with 4 oz. milk	8 oz. yogurt	with Green Goddess
	16 oz. milk	dressing
	1 apple	24 oz. milk
Snack	handfull of sunflower	
	seeds	
one small piece of		
sesame seed candy		

Health Food Use as an Alternative Medical System

Within the United States there have always been forms of medical
practice that are alternatives to the "mainline," allopathic medicine
practiced by licensed physicians. In spite of legal restrictions,
herbalists, faith healers, *santeros, curanderos,* and other folk-
curers carry out healing activities for a considerable clientele.
Although Latin and American Indian curers are perhaps the best
known, folk medicine is not confined to the rural backlands, the
poor, or ethnic minority groups. Rather, it is present throughout
the United States today, for North American society has always
contained many people who have serious doubts about the
efficiency, the honesty, the approachability, and the costs of
modern medicine.

Increasingly, the health food movement offers an enticing
alternative medical system. Of course, the use of food-as-medicine
is not new. Many societies, from simple, hunting-gathering groups
to complex, industrialized nations, have sets of beliefs about the
role of food in health maintenance and illness management. While
some of these beliefs have scientifically-established validity, others
may be incorrect, but innocuous, while still others may be seriously
detrimental to health—as in the case of the Malaysian peasants who
withhold all green and yellow fruits and vegetables from a child
with symptoms of xerophthalmia (vitamin A deficiency), on the
belief that the worms blamed for the eye symptoms feed on these
foods (McKay, 1971).

Health food use, as an alternative medical system, is perhaps particularly appealing because it provides several features not always evident in the "mainline" system of modern medicine. It is a *system of preventive medicine* that offers a complete theory of health and disease and provides holistic treatment in which the patient takes an active role in cure and health maintenance. It is a system that has physical, psychological, spiritual, and social properties.

Apart from "well-baby clinics," childhood innoculations, and other special services, the great majority of people probably encounter the modern medical doctor only when they are sick. Modern medicine is thus associated far more with disease than with health. Generally, the physician acts upon the passive patient, except in the case of chronic illness when a more active patient role may be encouraged. Rarely does the healthy patient receive a "prescription" to keep him well, or a technique to reduce his anxiety about possible future sickness.

Food is the most direct, deliberate, continually recurrent, and easily available means through which the well individual maintains or alters his health status. Many Americans remember clearly that during their childhood, they were told again and again that eating the right foods would keep them healthy. That lesson is being resurrected in new form by the adherents of the movement and exploited by movement spokesmen who emphasize that special diets may decrease the risk of heart attack, cancer, "tiredness," and other more and less serious disabilities.

Many health food systems place explanations for treatment within a theoretical framework the patient can understand, and provide a therapeutic ritual that can be performed unassisted. Macrobiotics, for example, follow a know-thyself pragmatism. Our informants report that they constantly re-examine their own state of health and emotional feelings to learn their yin-yang makeup. By making dietary choices particularly right for the individual, a Macrobiotic can alter his constitution, put himself in harmony with the world, and control his destiny.

Many health food users consider scientific medicine to be "fragmented," and "dehumanized." They feel that treatment is aimed at the disease rather than the individual, and they seek a system with "all the answers." Where modern medicine fails, many health food theorists step in. The "holistic" theory of nutrition and health outlined in some of the health food literature has the further inducement that it speaks not only to the organic, physical condition, but also to matters of psychological health and well-being. A text on the Macrobiotic system expresses a holistic philosophy of healing:

> The Supreme Medicine . . . is educational, biological, physiological and a dialectical technique, aims to permit the ailing person to discover all by himself the constitution-conception of life and the world. It cures, decidedly, not only all the diseases of the present and to come but every misfortune too. (Oshawa, 1966)

The Future of the Health Food Movement[2]

The process of commitment and the presence of strong opposition are particularly important to the survival and growth of social movements. The act of commitment involves three components:

(1) a highly emotional experience which changes an individual's self-identity;
(2) bridge-burning acts, which cut the individual off from his previous behavior patterns; and
(3) a social context which reinforces and supports these changes.

Opposition plays a major role in supporting the commitment process as well as serving as a force against which to unite the movement. Gerlach and Hine note that it is the ideology of the movement which "defines the opposition" (1970:xvii). The perception of opposition may give momentum to the movement as satisfactorily as real opposition. The nature of the opposition is subject to continual redefinition as the movement progresses, and the relationship between "insiders" and "outsiders" changes.

To what extent are commitment and opposition present in the health food movement? In the first place, basic changes in food habits can be difficult, emotion-laden experiences for many people. Giving up tempting sweets, succulent steaks, and many ethnically and culturally valued foods requires continued reinforcement. For health food users who turn to vegetarianism there must be a fairly radical change in food habits that has the potential for bridge-burning acts of commitment.

For others, health food use is perceived as a means of taking self-responsibility for health maintenance and transcending the pill-popping neurosis of our society, again implying a major redefinition of self-image, role, and one's relationship to others.

Such commitments, however, can be retracted or erased unless there is social support for the continuance of the new food regimen.

The presence of organizations, especially residence groups and supporting infrastructures such as exist in the Vega-net are a first line of defense for the movement in checking the tendencies to slip back into old dietary patterns. The initiation rites and prescribed behavioral codes of some of these groups are clear symbols of commitment. The employment and recreational opportunities they offer support continued health food use. Many joiners mentioned that their diets were most important to them for social reasons. For example, the cook in one health food restaurant said: "I know every day when I get out of bed what I am going to do and it is important. It gives me a meaningful role to perform working here and a status to have as cook. I get to meet almost everyone in the community this way."

As such individuals advance within the hierarchies of the revitalization cults, health food use actually becomes a career for them, in the popular sense of the word. Health food use affords career opportunities also for enterprising individuals who seize the chance to open small stores and restaurants that are not in direct competition with larger businesses.

Individuals within the Vega-net system may maintain their commitments to health food use through "lateral movement" within the network. They have many options, all supported by social networks, living groups, strong charismatic leaders, and the rest of the movement paraphernalia.

At least some of the organized groups show every evidence of permanent viability. Divine Light and Hare Krishna, among the religiously-oriented groups, are nationally organized, financially solvent, and steadily winning converts. Like the Church of the Latter Day Saints and Unitarianism, before them, they are evolving into distinctively American established churches, within which the contemporary version of health food diets will continue to be followed by at least a minority of Americans.

Erewhon, the Macrobiotic food company, and several others, have grown into multi-million dollar concerns. With the reorganization consequent upon financial success, however, may come a compromise of health food ideals with operational efficiency. These firms may, like the Kellogg Corporation did several decades ago, join the ranks of the large food producing corporations.

Food companies appear uncertain, at this point, on what stand to take towards the health food movement. A number of companies are now marketing "natural cereals." Many committed health food users, however, distrust these products and prefer to patronize their own food stores. Although several of these cereals have gained a large measure of popularity, the market for them is limited. In general, food manufacturers expand their markets by creating new forms of processed foods. The income from "natural" products may be insufficient to offset the loss in sales on other items, which would result from a widespread health food movement. In such a case, we could certainly expect to see a well-financed, well-organized food industry lobbying for tighter and tighter FDA controls of health foods.

Moreover, each new concession that the industry makes to the health food movement, be it the cellophane packaging of brown rice and raw sugar or a televised testimonial advertisement from a well-known personality such as the late Euell Gibbons, which reaches the large market of the health food reservoir, draws ambivalent individuals conceptually into the health food camp, changing their consumer demands even as they are filling the coffers of the food companies. Thus, the two sides are continuously redefining their relationship to each other.

The strength of the food industry opposition will, no doubt, be proportional to the perceived threat. At this time, the threat does not appear to be particularly great. However, each new attack encourages the health food movement to coalesce its latent powers. The greater the economically motivated opposition, the greater the likelihood that health food users will be joined by physicians, nutritionists, and other prestigious health professionals. The health food controversy may be played out in the political arena, under the banners of "Consumerism" and "Human Rights." It may end in the establishment of higher nutritional standards for food products and more stringent controls on harmful additives, preservatives, and insecticides.

On the eve of the 1980s, the major problem confronting American society appears to be economic recovery in the face of an ever-shrinking world supply of natural resources. Counter-cultural activity has waned in the face of more mundane financial preoccupations. If this continues, the health food movement may have its permanent results through evolutionary rather than revolutionary forms of change. Participation in the health food movement may prove to be one of the most successful preadaptations to life in the coming century. Members of the health food movement are developing diets based on a lower consumption of animal products, and fresh rather than processed foods, which are produced with a high energy cost. They are comfortable cooking whole grain products from scratch, used to nutrition-conscious menu planning and to making radical changes in their diets. As parents, they will raise their children in a dietary and culinary tradition more compatible with the economic, ecological, and political demands of the future world.

Notes

1. Names of all individuals and groups which appear in quotation marks are pseudonymous. The authors have used their judgment in determining when anonymity should be retained.

2. As described above, the data for this study were collected between 1971 and 1973, and the analysis followed shortly thereafter. The descriptive materials were written in the "ethnographic present" of the early 1970s. From our perspective at the end of the decade the behavioral phenomena we have described under the rubric of the "health food movement" continues to be a visible feature of the contemporary scene. We feel that developments of the past five years support our analysis and that the current situation represents the continuing evolution of a significant social movement.

References

Brown, L.
    1972   "Population Growth, Food Needs and Environmental Stress." *Ecology of Food and Nutrition* 3:225-233.
Dwyer, J. T., L. F. Meyer, V. H. Dowd, R. F. Kandel, and J. Meyer
    1974   "The 'New' Vegetarians." *Journal of the American Dietetic Association* 65: 529-534.
Erhard, D.
    1973   "The New Vegetarians." Part One. *Nutrition Today.* November/December:4-12.
Gerlach, L.P. and V.H. Hine
    1970   *People, Power, Change: Movements of Social Transformation.* Indianapolis: The Bobbs-Merrill Company, Inc.
    1970   "The Social Organization of a Movement of Revolutionary Change: Case Study. *Black Power in Afro-American Anthropology.* N.E. Whitten, Jr. and J.F. Szwed, eds. New York: The Free Press.
Kandel, R.F. and J. Kandel
    1971   "Repersonalization and Revitalization in American Medicine: Lamaze Childbirth and Macrobiotics." Read at 70th Annual Meeting of the American Anthropological Association. New York.

Kandel, R.F.
    1972   "Doctrine and Diet in an Urban American Medical Cult. Read at 71st Annual Meeting of the American Anthropological Association. Toronto.
    1974   "Doctrine and Diet in an Urban Medical Cult." Unpublished Ph.D. dissertation. City University of New York.
McKay, D.
    1971   "Food, Illness and Folk Medicine: Insights from Ulu Trengganu, West Malaysia. *Ecology of Food and Nutrition* 1:67-72.
New, P. Kong-Ming and R.P. Priest
    1967   "A Sociological Study of Food Cultists." *Journal of the American Dietetic Association* 1:13-19.
Nishizawa, M.
    n.d.   "Cognitive Aspects of Health Food Users." Unpublished Paper, University of Connecticut, Department of Anthropology.
    8:20-21.
Oshawa, G.
    1966   *The Book of Judgment.* Ignoramus Press.
Wallace, A.F.C.
    1956   "Revitalization Movements." *American Anthropologist* 58:264-281.

Additional References on the Topics Discussed in the Introduction and in Chapters 1-3

Abelson, P. H.
   1975 Food: Politics, Economics, Nutrition and Research.
   Washington: American Association for the Advancement
   of Science.

Adams, R. N.
   1959 Nutrition, Antrhopology and the Study of Man.
   Nutrition Reviews 17:97-99.

   1960 Early Civilization, Subsistence and Environment.
   City Invincible: A Symposium on Urbanization and
   Culture Development in the Ancient Near East.
   Kraeling and Admas, Eds. Chicago: University of
   Chicago Press.

Adelson, S. F.
   1960 Some Problems in Collecting Dietary Data from
   Individuals. Journal of the American Dietetic
   Association 36:453-461.

   1968 Changes in Diets of Households, 1955 to 1965.
   Journal of Home Economics 60:448-455.

Ahmed, M. J. M. and van Veen, A. G.
   1968 A Sociological Approach to a Dietary Survey and
   Food Habit Study in an Andean Community. Tropical
   Geographical Medicine 20:88-100.

Almy, T. P.
   1975 Evolution, Lactase Levels and Global Hunger. New
   England Journal of Medicine 292:1183-1184.

American Ethnologist
   1975 Sex Roles in Cross-Cultural Perspectives 2:587-769.

Anderson, J. N.
   1974 Ecological Anthropology and Anthropological Ecology.
   Handbook of Social and Cultural Anthropology.
   Honigmann, Ed. Chicago: Rand McNally.

Annegers, J. F.
   1973 Seasonal Food Shortages in West Africa. Ecology of
   Food and Nutrition 2:251-257.

Arroyo, P., et al.
    1972 Correlation Between Family and Infant Food Habits by
          Scalogram Analysis. Ecology of Food and Nutrition
          1:127-130.

Aylward, F.
    1953 The Indigenous Foods of Mexico and Central America.
          Proceedings of the Nutrition Society 12:48-58.

Bailey, K. V.
    1962 Rural Nutrition Studies in Indonesia, 5: Field
          Surveys--Procedure and Background. Tropical and
          Geographical Medicine 14:1-10.

Baker, G. L.
    1969 Nutrition Survey of Northern Eskimo Infants and
          Children. American Journal of Clinical Nutrition
          22:612-616.

Baker, P. T. and Mazess, R. B.
    1963 Calcium: Unusual Sources in the Highland Peruvian
          Diet. Science 142:1466-1467.

Barnicot, N. A.
    1969 Human Nutrition: Evolutionary Perspectives.
          The Domestication of Plants and Animals. Ucko and
          Dimbleby, Eds. Chicago: Aldine Publishing.

Barth, F.
    1956 Ecologic Relationships of Ethnic Groups in Swat,
          North Pakistan. American Anthropologist 58:1079-1089.

Bass, M. A. and Wakefield, L. M.
    1974 Nutrient Intake and Food Patterns of Indians in
          Standing Rock Reservation. Journal of the American
          Dietetic Association 64:36-41.

Bassir, O. and Umoh, I. B.
    1973 The Nutritive Adequacy of Some Nigerian Peasant
          Diets. Ecology of Food and Nutrition 7:297-306.

Beals, A. R.
    1964 Food Is to Eat: The Nature of Subsistence Activity.
          American Anthropologist 66:134-136.

Beaudry-Darisme, M. N., Hayes-Blend, L. C. and van Veen, A. G.
    1972 The Application of Sociological Research Methods to
          Food and Nutrition Problems of a Caribbean Island.
          Ecology of Food and Nutrition 1:103-119.

Behar, M.
    1967 Geographic Peculiarities of Nutrition: Central
          America and Panama. Seventh International Congress of
          Nutrition, Hamburg, 1966, Vol. 3. New York: Pergamon
          Press.

1968 Food and Nutrition of the Maya Before the Conquest
and the Present Time. Biomedical Challenges Presented
by the American Indian. Scientific Publication No. 165.
Washington, D. C.: Pan American Health Organization,
World Health Organization.

Bell, W. H. and Castetter, E. F.
1937 The Utilization of Mesquite and Screwbean by the
Aborigines in the American Southwest. Bulletin No. 314.
Albuquerque: University of New Mexico.

Bennett, J. W.
1946 An Interpretation of the Scope and Implications of
Social Scientific Research in Human Subsistence.
American Anthropologist 48:553-573.

1946 Subsistence Economy and Foodways in a Rural Community:
A Study of Socio-Economic and Cultural Change. (Ph.D.
Dissertation 1946, University of Chicago.)

1976 The Ecological Transition: Cultural Anthropology
and Adaptation. New York: Pergamon Press.

Berg, A., et al.
1973 Nutrition, National Development and Planning. Cambridge,
Massachusetts: MIT.

1973 The Nutrition Factor: Its Role in National Development.
Washington, D. C.: Brookings Institution.

Bergstrom, G.
1973 The Food and the Population Dilemma. North Scituate,
Massachusetts: Duxbury Press.

Berkes, F. and Farkas, C. S.
1978 Eastern James Bay Cree Indians: Changing Patterns of
Wild Food Use and Nutrition. Ecology of Food and Nutrition
7:155-172.

Bicchieri, M. G., Ed.
1972 Hunters and Gatherers Today. New York: Holt, Rinehart
and Winston.

Billard, J.
1970 The Revolutions in American Agriculture. National
Geographic 2:137.

Blake, E. C. and Durnin, J. V. G. A.
1963 Dietary Values from a 24-Hour Recall Compared to a
7-Day Survey on Elderly People. Proceedings of the
Nutrition Society 22:i.

Blanton, J. H., et al.
   1966   A Dietary Study of Men Residing in Urban and
          Rural Areas of Puerto Rico. American Journal of
          Clinical Nutrition 18:169-175.

Bronte-Steward, B., et al.
   1960   The Health and Nutritional Status of the !Kung Bushmen
          of Southwest Africa. South African Journal of Laboratory
          and Clinical Medicine 6:187-216.

Brown, H. B.
   1971   Food Patterns that Lower Blood Lipids in Man.
          Journal of the American Dietetic Association 58:303-311.

Brown, L. R. and Finsterbusch, G.
   1972   Man and His Environment: Food. New York: Harper and
          Row.

Brown, M. L., et al.
   1968   Health Survey of Nepal: Diet and Nutritional Status
          of Nepalese People. American Journal of Clinical
          Nutrition 21:876-881.

   _____
   1970   Diet and Nutrition of Pre-School Children in Honolulu.
          Journal of the American Dietetic Association 57:22-28.

Brush, S. D.
   1977   Mountain, Field and Family. The Economy and Human
          Ecology of an Andean Valley. Philadelphia: University
          of Pennsylvania Press.

Burk, M. C. and Pao, E. M.
   1976   Methodology for Large-Scale Surveys of Household and
          Individual Diets. Home Economics Research Report No. 40.
          Washington, D. C.: United States Department of Agriculture,
          ARS.

Burke, B. S.
   1967   The Dietary History as a Tool in Research. Journal of
          the American Dietetic Association 23:1041-1046.

Call, D. A.
   1972   The Changing Food Market: Nutrition in a Revolution.
          Journal of the American Dietetic Association 60:384-388.

Call, D. and Levinson, F. J.
   1973   A Systematic Approach to Nutrition Intervention
          Programs. Nutrition, National Development and Planning.
          Cambridge, Massachusetts: MIT.

Carneiro, R. L.
   1960   Slash-and-Burn Agriculture: A Closer Look at Its

Implications for Settlement Patterns. Men and Cultures:
Selected Papers of the Fifth International Congress
of Anthropological and Ethnological Sciences, September, 1956.
Wallace, Ed. Philadelphia: University of Pennsylvania Press.

_____
1968 Slash-and-Burn Cultivation Among the Kuikuru and
Its Implications for Cultural Development in the
Amazon Basin. Man in Adaptation: The Cultural Present.
Cohen, Ed. Chicago: Aldine Publishing.

Caster, W. O.
1962 Use of a Digital Computer in the Study of Eating
Habit Patterns. American Journal of Clinical Nutrition
10:98-106.

Chalmers, F. W., Clayton, M. M. Gates, L. O., Tucker, A. W.,
Wertz, A. W., Young, C. M. and Foster, W. D.
1952 The Dietary Record--How Many and Which Days. Journal
of the American Dietetic Association 28:711-717.

Chartkiff, J. L.
1974 Causes of Adaptive Change and the Origins of Food
Production in the Near East. (Ph.D. Dissertation 1974,
University of California - Los Angeles.)

Chassy, J. P., van Veen, A. G. and Young, F. W.
1967 The Application of Social Science Research Methods to
the Study of Food Habits and Food Consumption in an
Industrialized Area. American Journal of Clinical
Nutrition 20:56-64.

Clark, F.
1974 Recent Food Consumption Surveys and Their Uses.
Federation Proceedings 33:2270-2274.

Clements, F. W.
1970 Some Effects of Different Diets. The Impact of
Civilization on the Biology of Man. Boyden, Ed.
Toronto: University of Toronto Press.

Cohen, M. N.
1977 The Food Crisis in Prehistory. New Haven: Yale
University Press.

Collazos, C., et al.
1953 Dietary Surveys in Peru, 1: San Nicolas, a Cotton
Hacienda. Journal of the American Dietetic Association
29:883-889.

_____
1954 Dietary Surveys in Peru, 3: Chancan and Vicos,
Rural Communities in the Peruvian Andes. Journal of the
American Dietetic Association 30:1222-1230.

Collis, W. R. F., et al.
  1962 On the Ecology of Child Nutrition and Health in
        Nigerian Villages, 2: Dietary and Medical Surveys.
        Toprical and Geographical Medicine 14:201-229.

Colson, E.
  1959 Plateau Tonga Diet. Rhodes Livingstone Lournal 24:51-67.

Committee on Food Habits
  1945 Manual for the Study of Food Habits. National Research
        Council Bulletin No. 3. Washington, D. C.: NAS-NRC.

  1946 Food Acceptance Research. Manual 17-9. Washington, D. C.:
        Quartermaster Food and Container Institute.

Committee on Nutrition Surveys
  1949 Nutrition Surveys: Their Techniques and Value.
        Report of the Committee on Nutrition Surveys, National
        Research Council, National Academy of Sciences,
        Bulletin No. 117. Washington, D. C.: NAS-NRC.

Contribution of Anthropology to the Assessment of Nutritional Status
  1977 Symposium of the American Institute of Nutrition
        61st Annual Meeting of the Federation of American Societies
        for Experimental Biology, Chicago, Illinois, April 6, 1977.

Cook, O. F.
  1919 Olneya Beans: A Native Food Product of the Arizona
        Desert Worthy of Domestication. Journal of Heredity
        10:321-331.

Cook, S. F.
  1941 The Mechanism and Extent of Dietary Adaptation Among
        Certain Groups of California and Nevada Indians.
        Ibero-Americana 18:3 Pl 59 pgs. including Tables.
        Berkeley: University of California Press.

  1946 Human Sacrifice and Warfare as Factors in the Demography
        of Pre-Colonial Mexico. Human Biology 18:81-102.

Corkill, N. L.
  1954 Seasonal Dietary Change in a Sudan Desert Community.
        Journal of Tropical Medicine 57:257-269.

Cowan, J. W.
  1965 Dietary Surveys in Rural Lebanon. Journal of the
        American Dietetic Association 47:466-469.

Cravioto, J., DeLicardie, E. R. and Birch, H. G.
  1966 Nutrition, Growth and Neurointegrative Development:
        An Experimental and Ecological Study. Pediatrics 38:319.

Cuthbertson, W. F. J.
  1966 Problems in Introducing New Foods to Developing Areas.
        Food Technology 20:634-636.

Dahlquist, P. A.
  1972 Kohdo Mwenge: The Food Complex in a Changing Ponapean
        Community. (Ph.D. Dissertation 1972, Ohio State University.)

Dare, R.
  1974 The Ecology and Evolution of Food Sharing. California
        Anthropologist 2:13-25.

Davenport, C. B.
  1945 The Dietaries of Primitive People. American
        Anthropologist 47:60-82.

Davenport, E.
  1964 Calculating the Nutritive Value of Diets. United
        States Department of Agriculture, Agricultural Research
        Service, Bulletin No. 62-10-1. Washington, D. C.:
        United States Government Printing Office.

Davis, C. M.
  1928 Self-Selection of Diets by Newly Weaned Infants:
        An Experimental Study. American Journal of Diseases
        of Children 36:651-679.

de Castro, J.
  1952 The Geography of Hunger. Boston: Little, Brown and
        Company.

de Garine, I.
  1978 Population, Production and Culture in the Plains
        Societies of Northern Cameroon and Chad: The
        Anthropologist in Development Projects. Current
        Anthropology 19:42-65.

Dehavenon, A. L.
  1977 Rank Ordered Behavior in Four Urban Families: A
        Comparative Video-Analysis of Patterns of Superordination
        in Request Compliance and Food Control Behavior in
        Two Black and White Families. (Ph.D. Dissertation 1977,
        Columbia University.)

Dema, I. S.
  1968 Some Reflections Upon the Nutritional Problems of
        Dense Farm Populations in Parts of Nigeria. The
        Populations of Tropical Africa. Caldwell and Okonjo, Eds.
        New York: Columbia University Press.

Denevan, W. M.
  1971 Campa Subsistence in the Gran Pajonal, Eastern Peru.
        Geographical Review 61:498-518.

Descartes, S. L., et al.
    1941 Food Consumption Studies in Puerto Rico. Bulletin No. 59.
        Rio Piedras, Puerto Rico: Agricultural Experiment Station.

Dickins, D.
    1927 A Study of Food Habits in Two Contrasting Areas of
        Mississippi. Bulletin No. 245. Jackson: Mississippi
        Agricultural Experiment Station.

    1946 A Regional Approach to Food Habits and Attitude
        Research. Food Acceptance Research, Manual 17-9.
        Washington, D. C.: Quartermaster Food and Container
        Institute.

Dickins, D. and Gillaspie, B. V.
    1953 Menu Patterns in the Delta Cotton Area. Journal
        of Home Economics 45:169-173.

Dornstreich, M. D.
    1973 Food Habits of Early Man: Balance Between Hunting
        and Gathering. Science 179:306-307.

Dove, W. F.
    1946 Developing Food Acceptance Research. Science 103:187-190.

    1947 Food Acceptability--Its Determination and Evaluation.
        Food Technology 1:39-50.

Draper, H. H.
    1978 Nutrition Studies: The Aboriginal Eskimo Diet--A
        Modern Perspective. The Eskimo of Northwestern Alaska:
        A Biological Perspective. Jamison, Zegura and Myelin,
        Eds. Stroudsburg, Pennsylvania: Dowden, Hutchinson and
        Ross.

Drews, R. A.
    1952 The Cultivation of Food Fish in China and Japan: A
        Study Disclosing Contrasting National Patterns for
        Rearing Fish Consistent with the Differing Cultural
        Histories of China and Japan. (Ph.D. Dissertation 1952,
        University of Michigan.)

Durnin, J. V. G. A. and Passmore, R.
    1967 Energy, Work and Leisure. London: Heinemann.

Eggan, F. and Pijoan, M.
    1943 Some Problems in the Study of Food and Nutrition.
        America Indigena 3:9-22.

Eindhoven, J. and Peryam, D. R.
    1959 Measurement of Preference for Food Combinations. Food
        Technology 13:379-382.

Eppright, E. S., Patton, M. B., Marlott, A. L. and Hathaway, L. H.
1952 Dietary Study Methods, 5: Some Problems in Collecting
Dietary Information About Groups of Children. Journal of
the American Dietetic Association. 28:43-48.

Ernster, M., McAleenan, M. and Larkin, F.
1976 Social Research Methods Applied to Nutritional
Assessment. Ecology of Food and Nutrition 5:143-151.

Evers, S. and McIntosh, W. A.
1977 Social Indicators of Human Nutrition: Measures of
Nutritional Status. Social Indicators Research 4:185-205.

Factors for Converting Weights of Specified Foods to Equivalent
Weights
1955 Survey of Food Consumption of Households in the United
States, Spring, 1955. United States Department of
Agriculture, Household Economics Research Branch
Publication FE 102 (10/6/55).

Filer, L. J.
1971 Commentary: Infant Feeding in the Nineteen-Seventies.
Pediatrics 47:489-490.

Firth, R.
1934 The Sociological Study of Native Diet. Africa 7:401-414.

Fischer, R., Griffin, F., England, S. and Garn, S. M.
1961 Taste Thresholds and Food Dislikes. Nature 191:479.

Fonaroff, L. S.
1965 Was Huntington Right About Human Nutrition? Annals
of the Association of American Geographers 55:365-376.

Forbes, R. J.
1965 Foods in Classical Antiquity. Studies in Ancient
Technology, Vol. 3. Leiden: E. J. Brill.

Fortes, M. and Fortes, S. L.
1936 Food in the Domestic Economy of the Tallensi.
Africa 9:237-276.

Foster, G. M.
1973 Traditional Societies and Technological Change.
New York: Harper and Row.

Fox, F. W.
1926 Diets in South Africa. South African Medical Journal
10:25-36.

Fox, R. H.
1953 A Study of the Energy Expenditure of Africans Engaged
in Various Activities, with Special Reference to Some
Environmental and Physiological Factors which May
Influence the Efficiency of Their Work. (Ph.D. Dissertation
1953, University of London.)

Freeman, H. E., Klein, R. F., Kagan, J. and Yarbrough, C.
    1977 Relations Between Nutrition and Cognition in Rural
          Guatemala. American Journal of Public Health 67:233-239.

Friend, B. and Clark, F.
    1959 Changes in Sources of Nutrients. Food: The Yearbook
          of Agriculture. Washington, D. C.: United States
          Department of Agriculture.

Frisch, R. and Revelle, R.
    1969 Variation in Body Weights and the Age of Adolescent
          Growth Spurt Among Latin American and Asian Populations
          in Relation to Calorie Supplies. Human Biology 41:185-212.

Fry, P. C.
    1957 Dietary Survey on Rorotonga, Cook Islands, 2: Food
          Consumption in Two Villages. American Journal of
          Clinical Nutrition 5:260-273.

Gallagher, C. R., Molleson, A. L. and Caldwell, J. H.
    1974 Lactose Intolerance and Fermented Dairy Products.
          Journal of the American Dietetic Association 65:418-419.

Garn, S. M.
    1973 Stature Norms and Nutritional Surveys. Ecology of
          Food and Nutrition 2:79-82.

Geertz, C.
    1963 Agricultural Involution: The Processes of Ecological
          Change in Indonesia. Berkeley: University of California
          Press.

Gilbert, A.
    1974 Latin American Development: A Geographical Perspective.
          Baltimore: Penguin Books.

Gilbert, B. M.
    1969 Some Aspects of Diet and Butchering Among Prehistoric
          Indians in South Dakota. Plains Anthropologist 14:277-294.

Glegg, C. G.
    1945 Native Food in Tanganyika. Tropical Agriculture
          22:32-38.

Gortner, W. A.
    1975 Nutrition in the United States 1900 to 1974. Cancer
          Research 35:3246-3253.

Graedon, T. L. F.
    1976 Health and Nutritional Status in an Urban Community of
          Southern Mexico. (Ph.D. Dissertation 1976, University of
          Michigan.)

Greene, L. W.
    1976 Nutrition and Behavior in Highland Ecuador. (Ph.D.
          Dissertation 1976, University of Pennsylvania.)

Grivetti, L. E.
1978 Nutritional Success in a Semi-Arid Land: Examination of Tswana Agropastoralists of the Eastern Kalahari, Botswana. American Journal of Clinical Nutrition 31:1204-1220.

Groen, J. J., et al.
1964 Nutrition of the Bedouins in the Negev Desert. American Journal of Clinical Nutrition 14:37-46.

Haas, J. and Harrison, G. G.
1977 Nutritional Anthropology and Biological Adaptation. Annual Review of Anthropology, Vol. 6. Siegel, Ed. Stanford: Stanford University Press.

Hackenberg, R. A.
1962 Economic Alternatives in Arid Lands: A Case Study of the Pima and Papago Indians. Ethnology 1:186-196.

Hardesty, D. L.
1975 The Niche Concept: Suggestions for Its Use in Human Ecology. Human Ecology 3:71-85.

Harlan, J. R.
1967 A Wild Wheat Harvest in Turkey. Archaeology 20:197-201.

Harris, D. R.
1967 New Light on Plant Domestication and the Origins of Agriculture. Geography Review 57:90-107.

Harrison, G. G.
1975 Primary Adult Lactase Deficiency: A Problem in Anthropological Genetics. American Anthropologist 77:812-835.

Hart, J. A.
1978 From Subsistence to Market: A Case Study of the Mbuti Net Hunters. Human Ecology 6:325-353.

Haviland, W. A.
1967 Stature at Tikal, Guatemala: Implications for Ancient Maya Demography and Social Organization. American Antiquity 32:316-325.

Hawley, F. M., Pijoan, M. and Elkin, C. A.
1943 An Inquiry into the Food Economy in Zia Pueblo. American Anthropologist 45:547-556.

Hayes, S. P., Jr.
1959 Measuring the Results of Development Projects: A Manual for the Use of Field Workers. Monographs in the Applied Social Sciences, UNESCO, Paris.

Hegsted, D. M.
1972 Problems in the Use and Interpretation of the Recommended Dietary Allowances. Ecology of Food and Nutrition 1:255-265.

1975 Editorial: Dietary Standards. New England Journal
      of Medicine 292:915.

Heiser, C. B.
1973 Seed to Civilization: The Story of Mans' Food.
      San Francisco: W. H. Freeman.

Heizer, R. F.
1955 Primitive Man as an Ecological Factor. Kroeber
      Anthropology Society Papers 13:1-31.

Helm, J.
1962 The Ecological Approach in Anthropology. American
      Journal of Sociology 67:630-639.

Hesse, F. G.
1959 A Dietary Study of the Pima Indian. American Journal
      of Clinical Nutrition 7:532-537.

Hipsley, E. H. and Kirk, N.
1965 Studies of Dietary Intake and the Expenditure of
      Energy by New Guineans. Noumea, New Calodonia: South
      Pacific Commission Technical Paper No. 147.

1966 An Integrated Approach to Nutrition and Society: The
      Case of the Chimbu. Australian National University: New
      Guinea Research Unit Bulletin No. 9.

Holmberg, A.
1950 Nomads of the Long Bow. Washington, D. C.: Institute
      of Sociological Anthropology, Smithsonian Institute
      Publication No. 10.

Holmes, S. A.
1954 Qualitative Study on Family Meals in Western Samoa
      with Special Reference to Child Nutrition. British
      Journal of Nutrition 8:223-239.

Hrdlicka, A.
1908 Physiological and Medical Observations Among the
      Indians of Southwestern United States and Northern
      Mexico. Washington, D. C.: Bureau of American
      Ethnology, Smithsonian Institute Bulletin No. 34.

Huenemann, R. L. and Turner, D.
1942 Methods of Dietary Investigation. Journal of the
      American Dietetic Association 18:562-568.

Huenemann, R. L., et al.
1954-55 Nutrition and Care of Young Children in Peru. Journal
         of the American Dietetic Association 30:554ff, 1101ff and
         31:1121ff.

1957 A Dietary Survey in the Santa Cruz Area of Bolivia.
American Journal of Tropical Medicine and Hygiene
6:21-31.

Hunter, J. M.
1967 Seasonal Hunger in a Part of the West African Savanna:
A Survey of Bodyweights in Nangodi, Northeast Ghana.
Transactions of the Institute of British Geographers
41:167-185.

Insull, W., Jr., et al.
1968 Diet and Nutritional Status of Japanese. American
Journal of Clinical Nutrition 21:753-777.

Irvine, F. R.
1952 Food Plants of West Africa. Economic Botany 6:23-40.

1957 Wild and Emergency Foods of Australian and Tasmanian
Aborigines. Oceania 28:113-142.

1959 Bibliography of Wild Food Plants of United States
Indians. Washington, D. C.: Bureau of American Ethnology,
Smithsonian Institute.

1970 Evidence of Change in the Vegetable Diet of Australian
Aborigines. Diprotodon to Detribalisation. Pilling and
Waterman, Eds. East Lansing, Michigan: Michigan State
University Press.

Issac, E.
1970 Geography of Domestication. Englewood Cliffs, New Jersey:
Prentice-Hall.

Jelliffe, D. B.
1962 Culture, Social Change and Infant Feeding: Current
Trends in Tropical Regions. American Journal of
Clinical Nutrition 10:19-45.

1966 The Assessment of the Nutritional Status of the
Community, Monograph No. 53. Geneva: World Health
Organization.

Jelliffe, D. B., Bennett, F. J., Jelliffe, E. F. P. and White, R.
1964 The Ecology of Childhealth Among the Karamajory of
Uganda. Archaeology and Environmental Health 9:25-30.

Jelliffe, D. and Jelliffe, E. F. P.
1975 Human Milk, Nutrition and the World Resource Crisis.
Science 188:557-561.

Jelliffe, D. B., Woodburn, J., Bennett, F. J. and Jelliffe, E. F. P.
    1962 The Children of the Hadza Hunters. Journal of
    Pediatrics 50:907-912.

Jerome, N. W.
    1975 On Determining Food Patterns of Urban Dwellers in
    Contemporary United States Society. Gastronomy: The
    Anthropology of Food and Food Habits. Arnott, Ed.
    The Hague: Mouton Publishers.

    1978 Frozen (TV) Dinners - Modern Staple Emergency Meals?
    Food Technology 32:48-51.

    1979 Changing Nutritional Styles within the Context of
    the Modern Family. Family Health Care, Vol. 1.
    New York: McGraw-Hill.

Jitsuchi, M.
    1945 Changing Food Habits of the Japanese in Hawaii.
    American Sociological Review 10:759-765.

Jocano, F. L.
    1967 The Relevance of Anthropology to Nutrition Research.
    Phillippine Journal of Nutrition 20:202-210.

Jones, L. V., Peryam, D. R. and Thurston, L. L.
    1955 Development of a Scale for Measuring Soldiers' Food
    Preferences. Food Research 20:512-520.

Joy, L.
    1966 The Economics of Food Production. African Affairs
    65:317-328.

Kallen, D. J.
    1971 Nutrition and Society. Journal of the American Medical
    Association 215:94-100.

Kariel, H. G.
    1966 A Proposed Classification of Diet. Annals of the
    Association of American Geographers 56:68-79.

Karvonen, M, J., et al.
    1961 Diet and Serum Cholesterol of Lumberjacks. British
    Journal of Nutrition 15:157-164.

Katz, S. H., Hediger, M. L. and Valleroy, L. A.
    1974 Traditional Maize Processing Techniques in the New
    World. Science 184:765-773.

Kemp, W. B.
    1971 The Flow of Energy in a Hunting Society. Scientific
    American 224:116-131.

Kight, M. A., et al.
1969 Nutritional Influences of Mexican-American Foods in
Arizona. Journal of the American Dietetic Association
55:557-561.

Kraut, H. and Cremer, H. D., Eds.
1969 Investigations into Health and Nutrition in East
Africa. Ifo-Institut fur Wirtschartsforschung, Afrika
Studien, No. 42. Munchen: Weltforum Verlag.

Krogh, A. and Krogh, M.
1951 A Study of the Diet and Metabolism of Eskimos Undertaken
in 1908 on an Expedition to Greenland. Medd. om Grønland
2:1-52.

Kuhnlein, H. V. and Calloway, D. H.
1977 Contemporary Hopi Food Intake Patterns. Ecology of
Food and Nutrition 6:159-173.

Lappe, F. M.
1971 Diet for a Small Planet. New York: Ballantine Books.

Latham, M. C.
1972 Planification et Evaluation des Programmes de Nutrition
Appliquée. Etudes de Nutrition de la FAO 26:129.

Latham, M. C. and Staare, F. J.
1967 Nutritional Studies in Tanzania. World Review of
Nutrition and Dietetics 7:31-71.

Leary, P. M.
1969 A Nutritional Assessment of Pedi School Children.
South African Medical Journal 43:1170-1174.

———
1969 The Use of Percentile Charts in the Nutritional
Assessment of Children from Primitive Communities.
South African Medical Journal 43:1165-1169.

Lee, R. B.
1968 What Hunters Do for a Living, Or How to Make Out on
Scarce Resources. Man the Hunter. Lee and DeVore, Eds.
Chicago: Aldine.

———
1974 Mongongo: The Ethnography of a Major Wild Food
Resource. Ecology of Food and Nutrition 2:307-321.

Lee, R. B. and DeVore, I., Eds.
1976 Kalahari Hunter-Gatherers: Studies of the !Kung San and
Their Neighbors. Cambridge: Harvard University Press.

Leopold, A. C. and Ardrey, R.
1972 Toxic Substances in Plants and the Food Habits of
Early Man. Science 176:512-513.

1972 Early Man's Food Habits. Science 177:833-835.

Levinson, F. J.
   1974 Morinda: An Economic Analysis of Malnutrition Among
         Young Children in Rural India. International Policy
         Series, Cambridge, Massachusetts. Cornell: MIT.

Macpherson, K. K.
   1966 Physiological Adaptation, Fitness and Nutrition in the
         Peoples of the Australian and New Guinea Regions. The
         Biology of Human Adaptability. Baker and Weiner, Eds.
         New York: Oxford University Press.

Malhotra, M. S.
   1966 People of India Including Primitive Tribes: A Survey
         on Physiological Adaptation, Physical Fitness and Nutrition.
         The Biology of Human Adaptability. Baker and Weiner, Eds.
         New York: Oxford University Press.

Mann, G. V., et al.
   1962 The Health and Nutritional Status of Alaskan Eskimos.
         American Journal of Clinical Nutrition 11:31-76.

Margen, S. and Oger, R. A., Eds.
   1978 Progress in Human Nutrition, Vol. 2. Westport,
         Connecticut: Avi Publishing Company.

Masek, J.
   1974 Man and the Trends of Modern Civilization. Ecology
         of Food and Nutrition 3:55-59.

Massieu, G. H., et al.
   1951 Nutritive Value of Some Primitive Mexican Foods.
         Journal of the American Dietetic Association 27:212-214.

Mata, L.
   1977 Environmental Determinants and Origins of Malnutrition.
         Malnutrition and the Immune Response. Suskind, Ed.
         New York: Raven Press.

Mata, L., Kronmal, R. A., Urrutia, J. and Garcia, B.
   1976 Antenatal Events and Postnatal Growth and Survival
         of Children in a Rural Guatamalan Village. Annals of
         Human Biology 3:303-315.

May, J.
   1958-1972 Studies in Medical Geography (a number of volumes on
         the Ecology of Malnutrition in Various Regions of the World,
         Vol. 1 - Vol. 11.

May, J. M.
   1974 The Geography of Nutrition. The Geography of Health
         and Diseases. Hunter, Ed. Chapel Hill: University
         of North Carolina Press.

Mayberry, R. H. and Lindeman, R. D.
1963 A Survey of Chronic Disease and Diet in Seminole
Indians in Oklahoma. American Journal of Clinical
Nutrition 13:127-134.

Mayer, J.
1973 United States Nutrition Policies for the 70's.
San Francisco: W. H. Freeman.

Mazess, R. B. and Baker, P. T.
1964 Diet of Quechua Indians Living at High Altitude,
Nunoa, Peru. American Journal of Clinical Nutrition
15:341-351.

McArthur, M.
1960 Food Consumption and Dietary Levels of Groups of
Aborigines Living on Naturally Occurring Foods. Records
of the American-Australian Scientific Expedition to
Arnhem Land, 1948 2:90-136.

McCann, M. B. and Trulson, M. F.
1957 Our Changing Diet. Journal of the American Dietetic
Association 33:358-365.

McCarthy, M. C.
1966 Dietary and Activity Patterns of Obese Women in Trinidad.
Journal of the American Dietetic Association 48:33-37.

McCay, B. J.
1978 Systems Ecology, People Ecology and the Anthropology of
Fishing Communities. Human Ecology 6:397-422.

McCracken, R. D.
1971 Lactase Deficiency: An Example of Dietary Evolution.
Current Anthropology 12:479-517.

McCulloch, W. E.
1929 Inquiry into Dietaries of Hausas and Town Fulani of
Northern Nigeria, with Some Observations of Effects on
National Health with Recommendations Arising Therefrom.
West African Medical Journal 3:36.

Mead, M.
1943 Anthropological Approach to Dietary Problems.
Transactions of the New York Academy of Science 5:177-182.

_____

1946 Changing Food Habits in the Post-War Period. Nutrition
for Young and Old. Legislative Document No. 76. New York
State Joint Legislative Committee on Nutrition.

_____

1964 Food Habits Research: Problems of the 1960's.
Publication No. 1225. Washington, D. C.: NAS-NRC.

1970 The Changing Significance of Food. American Scientist
      58:176-181.

Meadows, D. H., et al.
1972 The Limits to Growth. New York: Universe Books.

Meggitt, M.
1957 Notes on the Vegetable Foods of the Walbiri of Central
      Australia. Oceania 28:143-145.

Meredith, A., Matthews, A., Zickefoose, M., Weagley, E.,
Wayave, M. and Brown, E. G.
1951 How Well Do School Children Recall What They Have
      Eaten. Journal of the American Dietetic Association
      27:749-751.

Merwe, A. le R. van der
1969 Isolated Homogenous Groups in Nutritional Studies.
      South African Medical Journal 43:331-336.

1971 A Comparative Study of Rural and Urban Venda Males.
      South African Medical Journal 45:1281-1323.

Messer, E.
1972 Patterns of "Wild" Plant Consumption in Oaxaca, Mexico.
      Ecology of Food and Nutrition 1:325-332.

Metz, J., et al.
1971 Iron, Folate and B_{12} Nutrition in a Hunter-Gatherer
      People: A Study of the !Kung Bushman. American Journal
      of Clinical Nutrition 24:229-242.

Millan, S.
1942 Dietary Condition in Some Mexican Rural Communities.
      Journal of the American Dietetic Association 18:521-523.

Mitchell, D. D.
1976 Land and Agriculture in Nagovisi, Papua, New Guinea.
      Monograph No. 76.3. Boroko, Papua, New Guinea: Institute
      of Applied Social and Economic Research.

Montagu, M. R. A.
1957 Nature, Nurture and Nutrition. American Journal of
      Clinical Nutrition 5:237-244.

Montgomery, E.
1973 Ecological Aspects of Health and Disease in Local
      Populations. Annual Review of Anthropology, Vol. 2.
      Siegel, Ed. Stanford: Stanford University Press.

Montgomery, E. and Bennett, J. W.
1978 Anthropological Studies of Food and Nutrition: The
      1940's and the 1970's. The Uses of Anthropology.
      Goldschmidt, Ed. Washington, D. C.: American
      Anthropological Association.

Moore, F. W.
   1964 Methodologic Problems of Cross-Cultural Dietary
        Research. Journal of the American Dietetic Association
        45:415-419.

Moore, W. N., et al.
   1972 Nutrition, Growth and Development of North American
        Indian Children. Publication No. (NIH) 72-76.
        Washington, D. C.: Department of Health, Education and Welfare.

Mountford, C. P.
   1960 Anthropology and Nutrition. Records of the American-
        Australian Scientific Expediation to Arnhem Land, Vol. 2.
        Melbourne, Australia: Melbourne University Press.

Murdock, G. P.
   1968 The Current Status of the World's Hunting and Gathering
        Peoples. Man the Hunter. Lee and DeVore, Eds. Chicago:
        Aldine.

Murrill, R. I.
   1954 Racial Blood Pressure Studies: A Critique of Methodology,
        with Special Reference to the Effect of Age, Nutrition,
        Climate and Race on Blood Pressure in Puerto Rico.
        (Ph.D. Dissertation 1954, Columbia University.)

National Academy of Sciences
   1977 World Food and Nutrition Study: The Potential
        Contributions of Research. Washington, D. C.: NAS-NCR.

   _____
        1975 Arid Lands of Sub-Saharan Africa. Staff Final Report
        on an Advisory Panel of the Board on Science and Technology
        for International Development, Commission on International
        Relations. Washington, D. C.: NAS-NCR.

Newman, M. T.
   1962 Ecology and Nutritional Stress in Man. American
        Anthropologist 64:22-34.

Nicol, B. M.
   1949 Nutrition of Nigerian Peasant Farmers. British Journal
        of Nutrition 3:25-43.

Niehoff, A.
   1969 Changing Food Habits. Journal of Nutrition Education
        1:10-11.

Nietschmann, B.
   1972 Hunting and Fishing Focus Among Miskito Indians,
        Eastern Nicaragua. Human Ecology 1:41-67.

   _____
        1973 Between Land and Water: The Subsistence Ecology of the
        Miskito Indians, Eastern Nicaragua. New York: Seminar Press.

1974 When the Turtle Collapses, the World Ends. Natural
History 83:34-43.

Oddy, D. J.
1970 Food in the Nineteeth Century in England: Nutrition
in the First Urban Society. Proceedings of the Nutrition
Society 29:150-157.

Ohlson, M. A.
1969 Dietary Patterns and Effect on Nutrient Intake. World
Review of Nutrition and Dietetics 10:13-43.

Omololu, A.
1972 Changing Food Habits in Africa. Ecology of Food and
Nutrition 1:165-168.

Oomen, H. A. P. C.
1971 Ecology of Human Nutrition in New Guinea. Ecology of
Food and Nutrition 1:3-18.

Orr, J. B.
1936 Problems of African Native Diet: Forward. Africa
9:145-146.

Ostwald, R. and Gebre-Medhin, M.
1978 Westernization of Diet and Serum Lipids in Ethiopians.
American Journal of Clinical Nutrition 31:1028-1040.

Parrack, D. W.
1969 An Approach to the Bioenergetics of Rural West Bengal.
Environment and Cultural Behavior. Vayda, Ed.
Garden City, New York: Natural History Press.

Peel, R. M.
1958 Dietary Methodology. Comparison of Seven-Day Dietary
Record and 24-Hour Recall Methods. Food and Nutrition
Notes and Reviews 15:9.

Pelto, G. H. and Jerome, N. W.
1977 Intracultural Diversity in Nutritional Anthropology.
Health and the Human Condition: Perspectives in Medical
Anthropology. Hunt and Logan, Eds. Boston: Duxbury Press.

Peryam, D. R. and Pilgrim, F. J.
1957 Hedonic Scale Method of Measuring Food Preference.
(Symposium, Studies in Food Science and Technology,
1: The Methodology of Sensory Testing.) Food
Technology 2:9-14.

Pi, J. S. and Groves, C.
1972 The Importance of Higher Primates in the Diet of
the Fang of the Rio Muni. Man 7:239-243.

Pilgrim, F. J. and Kamen, J. M.
1959 Patterns of Food Preferences Through Factor Analysis.
Journal of Marketing 24:68-72.

Pirie, N. W.
1969 Food Resources, Conventional and Novel. Baltimore:
Penguin Books.

Polunin, I. V.
1967 Health and Disease in Contemporary Primitive Societies.
Diseases in Antiquity. Brothwell and Sandison, Eds.
Springfield, Illinois: C. C. Thomas.

Psychology Today
1974 The New Food Conciousness 10:62-106.

Quin, P. J.
1964 Nutrition of the Pedi. South African Medical Journal
38:369.

Raphael, D.
1973 The Role of Breast-Feeding in the Bottle-Feeding World.
Ecology of Food and Nutrition 12:121-124.

Rappaport, R. A.
1971 The Flow of Energy in an Agricultural Society.
Scientific American 224:104-115.

Read, M.
1938 Native Standards of Living and African Culture Change.
Africa 9:1-64.

Revelle, R.
1974 Food and Population. Scientific American 231:160-170.

Rivera, T.
1949 Diet of a Food-Gathering People, with Chemical Analysis
of Salmon and Saskatoons. Indians of the Northwest.
Smith, Ed. Columbia University Contributions in
Anthropology 36:19-36.

Roberts, L. J. and Waite, M.
1925 A Dietary Study Made in a Day Nursery by the
Individual Method. Journal of Home Economics 17:80-88.

Robinson, W. D., et al.
1944 A Study of the Nutritional Status of a Population
Group in Mexico City. Journal of the American Dietetic
Association 20:289-297.

Roch, J.
1975 Les Migrations Économiques de Saison Sèche en Bassin
Arachidier Sénégalais, Cah. ORSTOM, Serv. Sc. Hum.
21:55-80.

Rodahl, K.
  1967 Changes in Eskimo Nutrition by Imported Foods.
        International Congress of Nutrition, 7th, Hamburg,
        1966, Vol. 3. New York: Pergamon Press.

Roth, W. E.
  1901 Food: Its Search, Capture and Preparation.
        N. Queensland Ethnog. Bulletin No. 3, Brisbane,
        Australia.

Roy, J. K. and Rao, R. K.
  1962 Diets of Some Indian Tribes. Indian Journal of
        Medical Research 50:905-915.

Sadre, M., Emami, E. and Donoso, G.
  1971 The Changing Pattern of Malnutrition. Ecology of
        Food and Nutrition 1:55-60.

Schlegel, S. and Guthrie, H. A.
  1973 Diet and the Tiruray Shift from Swidden to Plow
        Farming. Ecology of Food and Nutrition 2:181-192.

Scientific American
  1976 Food and Agriculture 235:30-205.

Scrimshaw, N. S.
  1964 Ecological Factors in Nutritional Disease. American
        Journal of Clinical Nutrition 14:112-122.

  _____
  1968 Food: World Problems. International Encyclopedia of
        the Social Sciences 5:502-508.

  _____
  1974 Myths and Realities in International Health Planning.
        American Journal of Public Health 64:792-798.

Scrimshaw, N. S., Taylor, C. E. and Gordon, J. E.
  1968 Interactions of Nutrition and Infection. Monograph No. 57.
        Geneva: World Health Organization.

Scudder, T.
  1971 Gathering Among African Woodland Savannah Cultivators.
        A Case Study: The Gwembe Tonga. University of Zambia,
        Institute for African Studies, Zambian Papers No. 5,
        Manchester, England.

Sen Gupta, P. N.
  1952 Investigations into the Dietary Habits of the Aboriginal
        Tribes of the Abor Hills. Indian Journal of Medical
        Research 40:203-218.

Simoons, F. J.
  1966 The Geographic Approach to Food Prejudices. Food
        Technology 30:42-44.

1970 Primary Adult Lactose Intolerance and the Milking
Habit: A Problem in Biologic and Cultural Interrelations,
II: A Culture Historical Hypothesis. American Journal
of Digestive Diseases 15:695–710.

1973 The Determinants of Dairying and Milk Use in the
Old World: Ecological, Physiological and Cultural.
Ecology of Food and Nutrition 2:83–90.

1974 Rejection of Fish as a Human Food in Africa: A
Problem in History and Ecology. Ecology of Food and
Nutrition 3:80–105.

1978 The Geographic Hypothesis and Lactose Malabsorption:
A Weighing of the Evidence. American Journal of
Digestive Diseases 23:963–980.

Sims, L., Paolucci, B. and Morris, P.
1972 A Theoretical Model for the Study of Nutritional
Status: An Ecosystem Approach. Ecology of Food and
Nutrition 1:197–205.

Sims, L. S. and Smiciklas-Wright, H.
1978 An Ecological Systems Perspective: Its Application to
Nutritional Policy, Program Design and Evaluation. Ecology
of Food and Nutrition 7:173–179.

Sinclair, H. M.
1953 The Diet of Canadian Indians and Eskimos. Proceedings
of the Nutrition Society 12:69–82.

Smith, P. E. L.
1972 The Consequences of Food Production. Addison Wesley
Modular Publication in Anthropology, Vol. 31, Reading,
Massachusetts.

1976 Food Production and Its Consequences. Menlo Park,
California: Cummings Publishing Company.

Solby, H. A.
1970 Continuities and Prospects in Anthropological
Studies. Current Directions in Anthropology.
Fischer, Ed. Bulletin of the American Anthropological
Association 3:35–53.

Sorre, M.
1962 The Geography of Diet. Readings in Cultural Geography.
Mikesell and Wagner, Eds. Chicago: University of
Chicago Press.

Spooner, B.
1972 Population Growth: Anthropological Implications.
Cambridge, Massachusetts: MIT.

1973 The Cultural Ecology of Pastoral Nomads. Addison
      Wesley Module in Anthropology, Vol. 31, Reading,
      Massachusetts.

Sprauge, G. F.
   1975 Agriculture in China. Science 188:549-555.

Stefansson, V.
   1937 Food of the Ancient and Modern Stone Age Man.
         Journal of the American Dietetic Association 13:102-119.

Steele, B. F., Franklin, R. E., Smudski, V. L. and Young, C. M.
   1951 Use of Checked Seven-Day Records in a Dietary Study.
         Journal of the American Dietetic Association 27:957-959.

Steinhart, J. S. and Steinhart, C. E.
   1974 Energy Use in the United States Food System. Science
         184:307-316.

Stenfanik, P. A. and Trulson, M. F.
   1962 Determing the Frequency Intakes of Foods in Large
         Group Studies. American Journal of Clinical Nutrition
         11:335-343.

Steward, J. H.
   1938 Basin-Plateau Aboriginal Socio-Political Groups.
         Bureau of American Ethnology, Smithsonian Institute
         Bulletin No. 120. Washington, D. C.: Smithsonian
         Institute.

   1955 The Concept and Method of Cultural Ecology. Theory
         of Culture Change. Urbana: University of Illinois Press.

   1968 Cultural Ecology. International Encyclopedia of
         Social Science 4:337-344.

Stini, W. A.
   1971 Evolutionary Implications of Changing Nutritional
         Patterns in Human Populations. American Anthropologist
         73:1019-1030.

Sullivan, R. J.
   1942 The Ten'a Food Quest, Vol. 2. Catholic University
         of America, Anthropology Service, Washington, D. C.

Suttles, W.
   1960 Affinal Ties, Subsistence and Prestige Among the
         Coast Salish. American Anthropologist 62:296-305.

   1968 Coping with Abundance: Subsistence on the Northwest
         Coast. Man the Hunter. Lee and DeVore, Eds. Chicago:
         Aldine.

Swaminathan, M.
1968 The Nutrition and Feeding of Infants and Preschool
Children in the Developing Countries. World Review of
Nutrition and Dietetics 9:85-123.

Sweeney, G.
1947 Food Supplies of a Desert Tribe. Oceania 17:289-299.

Swezey, S.
1975 The Energetics of Subsistence-Assurance Ritual in
Native California. Contribution 23:1-46. Berkeley:
Archaeology Research Facility, Department of Anthropology, University of California.

Symposium: Contribution of Anthropology to the Assessment of
Nutritional Status
1978 Fed. Proc. 37:47-76.

Teitelbaum, J. M.
1976 Human Versus Animal Nutrition: A Development Project
Among Fulani Cattlekeepers of the Sahel of Senegal.
Nutrition and Anthropology in Action. Fitzgerald, Ed.
Assen, Netherlands: Royal Van Gorcum.

Telaki, G.
1975 Primate Subsistence Patterns: Collector-Predators
and Gatherer-Hunters. Journal of Human Evolution
4:125-184.

Thomas, R. B.
1973 Human Adaptation to a High Andean Energy Flow System.
Occasional Papers in Anthropology No. 7, Department of
Anthropology. University Park: Pennsylvania State
University.

Thompson, M. J., et al.
1957 Dietary Studies in Ecuador. American Journal of
Clinical Nutrition 5:295-304.

Townsend, P. K.
1971 New Guinea Sago Gatherers: A Study of Demography in
Relation to Subsistence. Ecology of Food and Nutrition
1:19-24.

Townsend, P., Liao, S-C. and Konlande, J.
1973 Nutritive Contributions of Sago Ash Used as a
Native Salt in Papua, New Guinea. Ecology of Food
and Nutrition 2:91-97.

Trulson, M. F.
1955 Assessment of Dietary Study Methods, 2: Variability of
Eating Practices and Determination of Sample Size and
Duration of Dietary Surveys. Journal of the American
Dietetic Association 31:797-802.

1959   The American Diet--Past and Present.   American Journal
       of Clinical Nutrition 7:91-97.

Truswell, and Hansen, J. D. L.
1968   Medical and Nutritional Studies of !Kung Bushmen in
       North-West Botswana: A Preliminary Report.   South African
       Medical Journal 42:1338.

Truswell, A. S., et al.
1969   Nutritional Status of Adult Bushman in the Northern
       Kalahari, Botswana.   South African Medical Journal
       43:1157-1158.

Turbott, I. G.
1949   Diets, Gilbert and Ellice Island Colony.   Journal of
       the Polynesian Society 58:36-46.

Valassi, K. V. and Reynolds, J. W.
1966   Dietary Studies of the Civilian Population of Uruguay.
       American Journal of Clinical Nutrition 18:203-228.

Van Arsdale, P. W.
1978   Population Dynamics Among Asmat Hunter-Gatherers of
       New Guinea: Data, Methods, Comparisons.   Human Ecology
       6:435-467.

Van Itallie, T. B. and Campbell, R. G.
1972   Multidisciplinary Approach to the Problem of Obesity.
       Journal of American Dietetics 61:385-390.

Van Veen, M. S.
1971   Some Ecological Consideration of Nutritional Problems
       on Java.   Ecology of Food and Nutrition 1:25-38.

Vayda, A. P., Ed.
1969   Environment and Cultural Behavior.   Garden City:
       Natural History Press.

Waite, B. and Roberts, L. J.
1932   Studies in Food Requirements of Adolescent Girls, II:
       Daily Variations in the Energy Intake of the Individual.
       Journal of the American Dietetic Association 8:323-331.

Wakefield, E. G. and Dellinger, S. C.
1936   Diet of the Bluff Dwellers of the Ozark Mountains and
       Its Skeletal Effects.   Annals of Internal Medicine
       9:1412-1418.

Wakefield, L. M. and Merrow, S. B.
1967   Interrelationships Between Selected Nutritional,
       Clinical and Sociological Measurements of Pre-Adolescent
       Children from Independent Low-Income Families.
       American Journal of Clinical Nutrition 20:291.

Warnick, K. P., Bring, S. V. and Woods, E.
1955 Nutritional Status of Adolescent Idaho Children, I: Evaluation of Seven-Day Dietary Records. Journal of the American Dietetic Association 31:486-90.

Warnick, K. P., et al.
1965 Nutritional Status of School Children 15 and 16 Years of Age in Three Idaho Communities. University of Idaho Agricultural Experiment Station, Research Bulletin No. 33.

Waterman, T. T.
1920 Yurok Geography. University of California Publication in American Archaeology and Ethnology 16:177-314.

Wax, R. H.
1971 A Historical Sketch of Fieldwork. Doing Fieldwork: Warnings and Advice. Chicago: University of Chicago Press.

Wehmeyer, A. S., et al.
1969 The Nutrient Composition and Dietary Importance of Some Vegetable Foods Eaten by the !Kung Bushmen. South African Medical Journal 43:1529-1530.

Wenkam, N. S., et al.
1970 A Half Century of Changing Food Habits Among Japanese Hawaii. Journal of the American Dietetic Association 57:29-32.

Westermann, D.
1936 Problems of African Native Diet: A Note on the General Situation. Africa 9:146-149.

Wetterstrom, W. E.
1976 The Effects of Nutrition on Population Size at Pueblo Arroyo Hondon, New Mexico, Vol. 1 and 2. (Ph.D. Dissertation 1976, University of Michigan.)

Whiteman, J.
1966 The Function of Food in Society. Nutrition 20:4-8.

Whiting, M. G. A.
No Date Suggestions for Anthropologists for the Collection of Information Concerning Diet and Health. Washington, D. C.: United States Public Health Service, United States Department of Health, Education and Welfare.

Whittlesey, D.
1936 Major Agricultural Regions of the Earth. Annals of the Association of American Geographers 26:199-240.

Wiehl, D. and Reed, R.
1960 Development of New or Improved Dietary Methods for Epidemiological Investigations. American Journal of Public Health 50:824-828.

Wilson, A. T. M.
    1961 Nutritional Change. Some Comments from Social Research.
          Proceedings of the Nutrition Society 20:133-137.

Wilson, C. S.
    1974 Child Following: A Technic for Learning Food and
          Nutrient Intakes. Journal of Tropical Pediatrics and
          Environmental Child Health 20:9-14.

Wiser, C. V.
    1955 The Foods of a Hindu Village of North India. Annals of
          the Missouri Botanical Garden 42:303-412.

Wittmann, W., Moodie, A. D. Fellingham, S. A. and Hansen, J. D. L.
    1967 An Evaluation of the Relationship Between Nutritional
          Status and Infection by Means of a Field Study. South
          African Medical Journal 41:664-682.

Wolf, E.
    1955 The Types of Latin American Peasantry. American
          Anthropologist 57:452-470.

Wright-St. Clair, R. E.
    1972 Diet of the Maoris of New Zealand. Ecology of Food and
          Nutrition 1:213-224.

Yanovsky, G.
    1936 Food Plants of the North American Indians,
          Bulletin No. 237. Washington, D. C.: United States
          Department of Agriculture.

Young, C. M., Chalmer, F. W., Church, H. N., Clayton, M. M.,
Murphy, G. C. and Tucker, R. E.
    1953 Subjects Estimation of Food Intake and Calculated
          Nutritive Value of the Diet. Journal of the American
          Dietetic Association 29:1216-1220.

Young, C. M., Chalmer, F. W., Church, H. N., Clayton, M. M.,
Tucker, R. E., Wertz, A. W. and Foster, W. D.
    1952 A Comparison of Dietary Study Methods, 1: Dietary
          History Versus Seven-Day Record. Journal of the
          American Dietetic Association 28:124-128.

Young, C. M., Franklin, R. E., Foster, W. D. and Steele, B. F.
    1953 Weekly Variation in Nutrient Intake in Young Adults.
          Journal of the American Dietetic Association 29:459-464.

Young, C. M., Hagen, G. C., Tucker, R. E. and Foster, W. D.
    1952 A Comparison of Dietary Study Methods, 2: Dietary
          History Versus Seven-Day Record Versus 24-Hour Recall.
          Journal of the American Dietetic Association 28:218-221.

Young, C. M., Smudski, V. L. and Steele, B. F.
    1951 Fall and Spring Diets of School Children in New York
          State. Journal of the American Dietetic Association 27:289-292.

Young, C. M. and Trulson, M. F.
    1960 Methodology for Dietary Studies in Epidemiological
          Surveys, 2: Strengths and Weaknesses of Existing Methods.
          American Journal of Public Health 50:803-814.

Yousif, M.
    1967 Nutritional Study of Hog Yousif Rural Community (Sudan).
          Tropical and Geographical Medicine 19:192-198.

Yudkin, J.
    1951 Dietary Surveys: Variation in the Weekly Intake of
          Nutrients. British Journal of Nutrition 5:177-194.

Yudkin, J. and McKenzie, J. C.
    1964 Changing Food Habits. London: MacGibbon and Kee.

Zarur, G.
    1975 Seafood Gatherers in Mullet Springs: Economic Rationality
          and the Social System. (Ph.D. Dissertation 1975, University
          of Florida.)

Additional References on the Topics Discussed in Chapters 4 and 5

Allison, M. J., Mendoza, D. and Pezzia, A.
    1974 A Radiographic Approach to Childhood Illness in
          Pre-Columbian Inhabitants of Southern Peru. American
          Journal of Physical Anthropology 40:409-416.

Armelagos, G. J., Mielke, J. H. and Winter, J.
    1971 Bibliography of Human Paleopathology. Research
          Report No. 8, Department of Anthropology, University
          of Massachusetts, Amherst, Massachusetts.

Bartholomew, G. A., Jr., and Birdsell, J. B.
    1953 Ecology and the Protohominids. American Anthropologist
          55:481-498.

Borhegyi, S. and Scrimshaw, N. S.
    1957 Evidence for Pre-Colombian Goiter in Guatemala.
          American Antiquity 23:174-176.

Breuil, H.
    1932 The Sinanthropus Deposit at Chou-Kou-Tien (China) and
          Its Remains of Fire and Tools. Anthropos 27:1-8.

Brothwell, D. R.
    1959 Teeth in Earlier Human Populations. Proc. Nutr. Soc.
          18:59-65.

1967 The Bio-Cultural Background to Disease. Diseases in
      Antiquity. Brothwell and Sandison, Eds. Springfield,
      Illinois: C. C. Thomas.

1969 Dietary Variations and the Biology of Earlier Human
      Population. The Domestication and Exploitation of
      Plants and Animals. Ucko and Dimbleby, Eds. Chicago:
      Aldine.

Brothwell, D. and Brothwell, P.
1969 Food in Antiquity: A Survey of the Diet of Early
      Peoples. London: Thames and Hudson.

Bryant, V. M.
1974 The Role of Coprolite Analysis in Archaeology. Texas
      Archaeology Society Bulletin 45:1-28.

Callen, E. O. and Cameron, T. W. M.
1960 A Prehistoric Diet Revealed in Coprolites. New
      Scientist 8:35-40.

1965 Food Habits of Some Pre-Colombian Mexican Indians.
      Economic Botany 19:335-343.

Carneiro, R. L. and Hilse, D. F.
1966 On Determining the Probable Rate of Population
      Growth During the Neolithic. American Anthropologist
      68:177-180.

Cassidy, C. M.
1972 A Comparison of Nutrition and Health in Pre-
      Agricultural and Agricultural Amerindian Skeletal
      Populations. (Ph.D. 1972, The University of Wisconsin -
      Madison.)

Chaney, R. W.
1935 The Food of Peking Man. Carnegie Institute Washington
      Bulletin 3:199-202.

Clark, J. D.
1972 Paleolithic Butchery Practices. Man, Settlement and
      Urbanism. Ucko, Tringham and Dimbleby, Eds. London:
      G. Duckworth.

Crain, J. B.
1971 Human Paleopathology: A Bibliographic List.
      Sacramento Anthropology Society Paper No. 12,
      Sacramento, California.

Heizer, R. F.
1960 Physical Analysis of Habitation Residues. The
      Application of Quantitative Methods in Archaeology.
      Heizer and Cook, Eds. Chicago: Quadrangle Books.

1963 Domestic Fuel in Primitive Society. Royal
Anthropology Society 93:186-194.

1969 The Anthropology of Great Basin Human Coprolites.
Science in Archaeology, 2nd Edition. Brothwell and Higgs,
Eds. London: Thames and Hudson.

Heizer, R. F. and Napton, L. K.
1969 Biological and Cultural Evidence from Prehistoric
Human Coprolites. Science 165:563-568.

Helbaik, H.
1950 Tollun Man's Last Meal. Aarb∅ger for Nordisk
Oldkyndighed og Historie 311-344.

1951 Seeds of Weeds as Food in the Pre-Roman Iron Age.
Kuml 1951, Aarhus, 65-71.

1961 Studying the Diet of Early Man. Archaeology 14:95-101.

Hoyme, L. and Bass, W. M.
1962 Human Skeletal Material Remains from Tollifero
(Ha-6) and Clarksville (Mc-14) Sites, John H. Kerr
Reservoir Basin. Virginian Bureau of American
Ethnology. Smithsonian Institute Bulletin 182:329-400.

Issac, G. L.
1971 The Diet of Early Man: Aspects of Archaeological
Evidence from Lower and Middle Pleistocene Sites in
Africa. World Archaeology 2:278-299.

1973 Meat Eating and Human Evolution: Aspects of the
Archaeological Evidence from East Africa. Paper presented
at the 72nd Annual Meeting of the American Anthropology
Association, New Orleans, Louisiana.

Jolly, C. J.
1970 The Seed Eaters: A New Model of Hominid Differentiation
Based on a Baboon Analogy. Man 5:5-26.

Kliks, M.
1975 Paleoepidemiological Studies on Great Basin
Coprolites: Estimation of Dietary Intake and Evaluation
of the Ingestion of Anthelmintic Plant Substances.
Archaeology Research Facility, Department of Anthropology,
University of California, Berkeley, California.

1976 Paleodietetics: A Review of the Role of Dietary Fiber
in Pre-Agricultural Human Diets. Fiber in Human

Nutrition. Spiller and Amens, Eds. Springfield, Illinois:
C. C. Thomas.

Krieger, H.
1942 Aboriginal Land Utilization and Food Economy in the
Antilles. Proceedings of the 8th American Scientific
Congress, Vol. 2.

Koreber, A. L.
1962 The Nature of Land-Holding Groups in Aboriginal
California. University of California Archaeology
Survey Report 56:19-58.

Kunitz, S. J. and Euler, R. C.
1972 Aspects of Southwestern Paleoepidemiology.
Prescott Coll. Anthropology Report No. 2, Flagstaff,
Arizona.

Lange, F. W.
1971 Marine Resources: A Viable Subsistence Alternative
for the Prehistoric Lowland Maya. American Anthropologist
73:619-639.

MacNeish, R. S.
1967 A Summary of the Subsistence. The Prehistory of the
Tehucan Valley, Vol. 1. Byers, Ed. Austin: University
of Texas Press.

McHenry, H. M.
1975 Fossils and the Mosaic Nature of Human Evolution.
Science 190:425-431.

McHenry, H. M. and Schulz, P. D.
1975 Harris Lines, Enamel Hypoplasia and Subsistence
Change in Prehistoric Central California. Ramona,
California: Ballena Press.

Moseley, M. E.
1975 The Maritime Foundations of Andean Civilization.
Menlo Park, California: Cummings Publishing Company.

Movius, H. L.
1966 The Hearths of the Upper Perigordian and Aurignacian
Horizon at the Abri Pataud, Les Eyzies (Dordogne) and
Their Possible Significance. American Anthropologist
68:296-325.

Oakley, K. P.
1956 Fire as a Paleolithic Tool and Weapon. Proc. Prehist.
Soc. 21:36-48.

_____
1956 The Earliest Tool Makers and the Earliest Fire-Makers.
Antiquity 30:4-8, 102-107.

Perlman, S. M.
    1977 Optimum Diet Models and Prehistoric Hunter-Gatherers:
    A Test on Martha's Vineyard. (Ph.D. 1977, University of
    Massachusetts.)

Reidhead, V. A.
    1976 Optimization and Food Procurement at the Prehistoric
    Leonard Haag Site, Southeastern Indiana: A Linear
    Programming Approach. (Ph.D. 1976, University of
    Indiana.)

Roney, J. G.
    1959 Paleopathology of a California Archaeological Site.
    Bull. Hist. Med. 33:97-109.

Ruffer, M. A.
    1921 Studies in the Paleopathology of Egypt. Moodie, Ed.
    Chicago: University of Chicago Press.

Saul, F. P.
    1973 Disease in the Maya Area: The Pre-Columbian Evidence.
    The Classic Maya Collapse. Culbert, Ed. Albuquerque:
    University of New Mexico Press.

Smith, C. E., Jr.
    1967 Plant Remains. The Prehistory of the Tehuacan
    Valley, Vol. 1: Environment and Subsistence. Byers, Ed.
    Austin: University of Texas Press.

Wells, C.
    1964 Bones, Bodies and Disease. London: Thames and Hudson.

    1967 A New Approach to Paleopathology: Harris's Lines.
    Disease in Antiquity. Brothwell and Sandison, Eds.
    Springfield, Illinois: C. C. Thomas.

White, T. E.
    1953 A Method of Calculating the Dietary Percentage of
    Various Food Animals Utilized by Aboriginal
    Peoples. American Antiquity 18:396-398.

Wilke, P. J. and Hall, H. J.
    1975 Analysis of Ancient Feces: A Discussion and Annotated
    Bibliography. Archaeology Research Facility, Department
    of Anthropology, University of California, Berkeley,
    California.

Yudkin, J.
    1969 Archaeology and the Nutritionist. The Domestication
    and Exploitation of Plants and Animals. Ucko and
    Dimbleby, Eds. Chicago: Aldine.

Additional References on the Topics Discussed in Chapters 6-10 and on the Anthropology of Food

Abelson, P.
    1975 Food: Politics, Economics, Nutrition and Research.
          American Association for the Advancement of Science.
          Washington: Academic Press.

Aichinger, E.
    1966 Food Habits and Taboos. Inst. Laticinios Candido
          Tusles 21:16-17.

Anderson, E. N. and Anderson, M.
    1969 Cantonese Ethnolohoptology. Ethnos 34:107-117.

Arnott, M. L.
    1975 Gastronomy: The Anthropology of Food and Food Habits.
          Chicago: Aldine.

Arroyave, G.
    1975 Nutrition in Pregnancy in Central America and Panama.
          American Journal of Diseases of Childhood 129:427-430.

_____
    1976 Nutrition in Pregnancy: Studies in Central America
          and Panama. Arch. Latinoameri. Nutr. 26:129-157.

Au Coin, D., et al.
    1972 A Comparative Study of Food Habits: Influence of Age,
          Sex and Selected Family Characteristics. Canadian
          Journal of Public Health 63:143-157.

Bailey, F. L.
    1940 Navaho Foods and Cooking Methods. American Anthropologist
          42:270-290.

Barber, E. M.
    1948 The Development of the American Dietary Pattern. Journal
          of the American Dietetic Association 24:586-591.

Barry, H., et al.
    1959 Relation of Child Training to Subsistence Economy.
          American Anthropologist 61:51-63.

Basta, S.
    1977 Nutrition and Health in Low Income Urban Areas of
          the Third World. Ecology of Food and Nutrition
          6:113-124.

Bell, F. L. S.
1931 The Place of Food in the Social Life of Central Polynesia.
      Oceania 2:117-135.

Bennett, J. W.
1943 Food and Social Status in a Rural Society. American
      Sociology Review 8:561-569.

_____
1943 Some Problems of Status and Solidarity in a Rural
      Society. Rural Sociology 8:396-408.

Bennett, J. W., Smith, H. L. and Passin, H.
1942 Food and Culture in Southern Illinois--A Preliminary
      Report. American Sociology Review 7:645-660.

Bennett, M. K.
1941 International Contrasts in Food Consumption. Geographical
      Review 31:365-376.

Bensaid, A., et al.
1966 Besoins Nutritionnels et Politique Économique.
      Réflexion a Partir d'une Enquate Détaillée dans Trois
      Vallages Sénégalais. Inst. des Sciences Economiques
      Appliquées, Dakar.

Blair, R.
1956 The Food Habits of the East Slavs. (Ph.D. Dissertation
      1956, University of Pennsylvania.)

Blanc, J., Coly, F., et al.
1967 Situation Médico-Sociale de l'Arrondissement de
      Khombole, Sénégal. Conditions de Vie de l'Enfant in
      Milieu Rural en Africa, Dakar, Centre International de
      l'Enfance, Réunions et Conférences 14:41-55.

Boek, J. K.
1956 Dietary Intake and Social Characteristics. American
      Journal of Clinical Nutrition 4:239-245.

Boggs, E. V.
1929 Nutrition of Fifty Colored Familes in Chicago.
      (Unpublished Master's Thesis 1929, University of
      Chicago.)

Bolton, J. M.
1972 Food Taboos Among the Orang Asli in West Molaysia: A
      Potential Nutritional Hazard. American Journal of
      Clinical Nutrition 25:789-799.

Bornet, L.
1968 Foods and Their Place in Folklore. Let's Dance 35:8-10.

Bourke, J. C.
1895 The Folk Foods of the Rio Grande Valley and of Northern
      Mexico. Journal of American Folklore 8:41-71.

Bristowe, W. S.
    1953 Insects as Food. Proceedings of the Nutrition Society
          12:44-48.

Bronson, B.
    1966 Roots and the Subsistence of the Ancient Maya.
          Southwestern Journal of Anthropology 22:251-279.

Brown, M. L., et al.
    1969 Infant Feeding Practices Among Low and Middle Income
          Families in Honolulu. Tropical and Geographical
          Medicine 21:53-61.

Brownfain, J. J.
    1956 Menus and Motives. Journal of the American Dietetic
          Association 32:1157-1161.

Bruch, H.
    1963 Social and Emotional Factors in Diet Changes. Nutrition
          News 26:1, 14.

Bruhn, C. M., et al.
    1970 Reported Incidence of Pica Among Migrant Families.
          Journal of the American Dietetic Association 58:417-420.

Brunson, R. T.
    1962 Socialization Experiences and Socio-Economic
          Characteristics of Urban Negroes as Related to Use of
          Selected Southern Foods and Medical Remedies. (Ph.D.
          Dissertation 1962, Michigan State University.)

Burgess, A.
    1961 Nutrition and Food Habits. International Journal of
          Health Education 4:55-58.

Burgess, A. and Dean, R. F. A., Eds.
    1962 Malnutrition and Food Habits. New York: The Macmillan
          Company.

Camp, J. C.
    1978 America Eats: Toward a Social Definition of American
          Foodways. (Ph.D. Dissertation 1978, University of
          Pennsylvania.)

Campbell, D.
    1965 Man and His Food: Some Non-Nutrient Aspects of Food
          Consumption. Journal of the New Zealand Dietetic
          Association 19 : 30.

Campbell, R. M. and Cuthbertson, D. P.
    1963 Factors Influencing Man's Selection of Food. Progress
          in Nutrition and Allied Sciences. Cuthbertson, Ed.
          Edinburgh: Oliver and Boyd.

Cannon, P.
    1964   Revolution in the Kitchen with Some Notes on the
           Anthropology of Food. Saturday Review 47:54-57.

Cantrelle, P., Diagne, M., Raybaud, N., Villod, M-Th., et al.
    1967   Mortalité de l'Enfant en Zone Rurale au Sénégal.
           Conditions se Vie de l'Enfant en Milieu Rural en
           Afrique, Dakar, Centre International de l'Enfance,
           Réunions et Conférences 14.

Cassel, J.
    1957   Social and Cultural Implications of Food and Food
           Habits. American Journal of Public Health 47:732-740.

Chang, K-C., Ed.
    1977   Food in Chinese Culture. New Haven: Yale University Press.

Chase, H. P. and Martin, H. P.
    1970   Undernutrition and Child Development. New England
           Journal of Medicine 282:933-939.

Chavez, A., Martinez, C. and Bourges, H.
    1975   Role of Lactation in the Nutrition of Low Socio-Economic
           Groups. Ecology of Food and Nutrition 4:159-169.

Childs, A. B.
    1933 Some Dietary Studies of Poles, Mexicans, Italians and
           Negroes. Child Health Bulletin 9:84-91.

Ciparisse, G.
    1978   An Anthropologic Approach to Socio-Economic Factors of
           Development: The Case of Zaire. Current Anthropology
           19:37-65.

Clark, F. L. G.
    1944   Food Habits and How to Change Them. Lancet 247:53-55.

    _____ 1947   The Vicious Circle of Austerity: Adjusting Our Food
           Habits. Lancet 252:721-722.

    _____ 1968   Human Food Habits as Determining the Basic Patterns of
           Economic and Social Life. Nutrition 22:134-141.

    _____ 1968   Food Habits as a Practical Nutrition Problem. World
           Review of Nutrition and Dietetics 9:56-84.

Coffee, E. and Clark, F.
    1959   Food Plans at Different Cost. Food: The Yearbook of
           Agriculture. Washington, D. C.: Unites States
           Department of Agriculture.

Committee on Food Habits
  1943 The Problem of Changing Food Habits. National
        Research Council Bulletin No. 108. Washington, D. C.:
        NAS-NRC.

Cornely, P. B., Bigman, S. K. and Watts, D. D.
  1963 Nutritional Beliefs Among a Low Income Urban Population.
        Journal of the American Dietetic Association 42:131-135.

Cosminsky, S.
  1975 Changing Food and Medical Beliefs and Practices in a
        Guatemalan Community. Ecology of Food and Nutrition
        4:183-191.

Crapuchet, S. and Paul-Pont, I.
  1967 Enquête sur les Conditions de Vie de l'Enfant en
        Milieu Rural au Sénégal et en Gambie. l'Enfant en
        Milieu Tropical 39:3-24.

Cummings, R. O.
  1941 The American and His Food. Chicago: University of
        Chicago Press.

Currier, R. L.
  1966 The Hot-Cold Syndrome and Symbolic Balance in Mexican
        and Spanish-American Folk Medicine. Ethnology 5:251-263.

Cushing, F. H.
  1920 Zuni Breadstuffs. New York: Heye Foundation, Museum of
        the American Indian.

Cussler, M. T. and de Give, M. L.
  1941 Interrelations Between the Cultural Pattern and Nutrition.
        Extension Service No. 366. Washington, D. C.: United
        States Department of Agriculture.

  _____
  1952 'Twixt the Cup and the Lip. New York: Twayne
        Publishers.

Damas, D.
  1972 Central Eskimo Systems of Food Sharing. Ethnology 11:22-240.

Darby, W. J., Ghalloungui, P. and Grivetti, L.
  1977 Food: The Gift of Osiris. New York: Academic Press.

Davenport, C. B.
  1947 The Dietaries of Primitive Peoples. American
        Anthropologist 47:61-82.

de Garine, I.
  1971 Food Is Not Just Something to Eat. Ceres 4:46-51.

1969 Socio-Cultural Aspects of Food Behaviour. Essay on
      Classification of Food Prohibitions. FAO/OAU Scientific,
      Technical and Research Commission Report No. 7.
      Rome: FAO.

1972 The Socio-Cultural Aspects of Nutrition. Ecology of Food
      and Nutrition 1:143-163.

de Give, M. L.
1943 Social Interrelation and Food Habits in the Rural
      Southeast. (Ph.D. Dissertation 1943, Radcliffe
      College.)

Delgado, G., Brumback, C. L. and Deaver, M. B.
1961 Eating Patterns Among Migrant Families. Public Health
      Reports 76:349-355.

Demory, B. G. H.
1976 An Illusion of Surplus: The Effect of Status Rivalry
      Upon Family Food Consumption. (Ph.D. Dissertation
      1976, University of California - Berkeley.)

Dentan, R. K.
1965 Some Senoi Semai Dietary Restrictions: A Study of Food
      Behavior in a Malayan Hill Tribe. (Ph.D. Dissertation
      1965, Yale University.)

Devadas, R. P.
1970 Social and Cultural Factors Influencing Malnutrition.
      Journal of Home Economics 62:164-171.

Devadas, R. P., et al.
1964 A Dietary and Nutritional Survey of a Small Village
      Community in South India. Indian Journal of Nutrition
      and Dietetics 1:110-113.

de Vries, A.
1952 Primitive Man and His Food. Chicago: Chandler Book
      Company.

Dickins, D.
1927 A Study of Food Habits of People in Two Contrasting
      Areas of Mississippi. Mississippi Agricultural
      Experiment Station Bulletin No. 254.

1927 A Nutrition Investigation of Negro Tenants in the
      Yazoo Mississippi Delta. Mississippi Agricultural
      Experiment Station Bulletin No. 254.

1941 Home Production of Food for Family Consumption.
      Mississippi Farm Research 4:1-8.

1943   Food Preparation of Owner and Cropper Farm Families in
        the Shortleaf Pine Area of Mississippi. Social Forces
        22:56-63.

1944   Vegetable Preferences of White and Negro Children.
        Mississippi Farm Research 7:7.

1945   Changing Pattern of Food Preparation of Small Town
        Families in Mississippi. Mississippi State College
        Agricultural Experiment Station Bulletin No. 415.

1945   Some Effects of a White Cornmeal Shortage. Journal
        of the American Dietetic Association 21:287-288.

1961   Food Purchases and Use Practices of Families of
        Gainfully Employed Homemakers. Mississippi Agricultural
        Experiment Station Bulletin No. 620.

Douglas, M.
1972   Deciphering a Meal. Daedalus (Winter):61-81.

1974   Food as an Art Form. Studio International 188:83-88.

1975   Preface. Implicit Meanings. Boston: Routledge and
        Kegan Paul.

Dove, W. F.
1935   A Study of Individuality in the Nutritive Instincts and
        the Causes and Effects of Variations in the Selection
        of Foods. American Naturalist 69:469-544.

1943   The Relative Nature of Human Preferences, with an
        Example of the Palatability of Different Varieties of
        Sweet Corn. Journal of Comparative Psychology 35:219-226.

Driskell, J. A. and Price, C. S.
1974   Nutritional Status of Pre-Schoolers from Low Income
        Alabama Families. Journal of the American Dietetic
        Association 65:280-284.

Du Bois, C.
1971   Attitudes Toward Food and Hunger in Alor. Language,
        Culture and Personality: Essays in Memory of Edward
        Sapir. Spier, Hallowell and Newman, Eds. Menasha,
        Wisconsin: Sapir Memoiral Publishing Fund.

Additional References 405

Edholm, O. G.
1970 The Changing Pattern of Human Activity. Ergonomics
13:625-633.

Eppright, E. S.
1947 Factors Influencing Food Acceptance. Journal of the
American Dietetic Association 23:579-587.

FAO
1953 Maize and Maize Diets. Rome: FAO Nutritional Studies
No. 9.

1966 Rice, Grain of Life. Rome: FAO World Food Problems
Series No. 6.

Family Food Consumption in Three Types of Farming Areas of the
South I
1950 An Analysis of 1947 Food Data. Southern Cooperative
Series Bulletin No. 7.

Family Food Consumption in Three Types of Farming Areas of the
South II
1951 An Analysis of Weekly Food Records, Late and Early
Spring, 1948. Southern Cooperative Series Bulletin No. 20.

Fathauer, G. H.
1960 Food Habits--An Anthropologist's View. Journal of the
American Dietetic Association 37:335-338.

Ferro-Luzzi, G. E.
1973 Food Avoidances at Puberty and During Menstruation in
Tamilnad. Ecology of Food and Nutrition 2:165-172.

Ferro-Luzzi, G. E.
1973 Food Avoidances of Pregnant Women in Tamilnad. Ecology
of Food and Nutrition 2:259-266.

1975 Food Avoidances of Indian Tribes. Anthropos 70:385-428.

Firth, R.
1975 An Appraisal of Modern Social Anthropology. Annals
of Review of Anthropology 4:1-25.

Fitzgerald, T. K., Ed.
1977 Nutrition and Anthropology in Action. Assen/Amsterdam:
van Gorcum.

Flores, M. and Garcia, B.
1960 The Nutritional Status of Children of Pre-School Age in
the Guatemalan Community of Amatitlan, 1: Comparison
of Family and Child Diets. British Journal of
Nutrition 14:207-215.

Fomon, S. J. and Anderson, T. A.
  1972 Practices of Low Income Families in Feeding Infants
        and Small Children with Particular Attention to
        Cultural Subgroups. Washington, D. C.: Public
        Health Service, Department of Health, Education and
        Welfare.

Freedman, R. L.
  1968 Wanted: A Journal in Culinary Anthropology. Current
        Anthropology 9:62-63.

Futrell, M. F., Kilgore, L. and Windham, F.
  1975 Nutritional Status of Black Pre-School Children in
        Mississippi. Journal of the American Dietetic
        Association 66:22-27.

Garetz, F. K.
  1973 Socio-Psychological Factors in Overeating and Dieting
        with Comments on Popular Reducing Mehtods. Practitioner
        210:671-676.

Garn, S. M. and Clark, D. C.
  1974 Economics and Fatness. Ecology of Food and Nutrition
        3:19-20.

Garn, S. M., Shaw, H. A. and McCabe, K. D.
  1978 Effect of Socio-Economic Status on Early Growth as
        Measured by Three Different Indicators. Ecology of
        Food and Nutrition 7:51-55.

Ghassemi, H., et al.
  1970 Food Budgeting for Adequate Nutrition in Tehran, Iran.
        Journal of the American Dietetic Association 58:219-224.

Godelier, M.
  1971 Salt Currency Among the Baruya of New Guinea. Studies
        in Economic Anthropology. Dalton, Ed. Washington, D. C.:
        American Anthropological Association.

Goldblith, S. A.
  1970 Food Habits and Taboos and the Potentials of Twentieth-
        Century Food Science and Tehcnology. Evaluation of
        Novel Protein Products. Proceedings of the International
        Biological Programme (IBP) and Wenner-Gren Center
        Symposium held in Stockholm, September, 1968. Bender,
        Kihlberg, Lofqvist and Munck, Eds. New York: Pergamon
        Press.

Gonzalez, N. L.
  1963 Breast Feeding, Weaning and Acculturation. Journal of
        Pediatrics 62:577-581.

  1964 Beliefs and Practices Concerning Medicine and Nutrition
        Among Lower-Class Urban Guatemalans. American Journal
        of Public Health 54:1726-1734.

   1972 Changing Dietary Patterns of North American Indians.
         Nutrition, Growth and Development of North American
         Indian Children. Moore, Silverberg and Read, Eds.
         Washington, D. C.: United States Government Printing
         Office.

Gonzalez, N. S. and Behar, M.
   1966 Child-Rearing Practices, Nutrition and Health Status.
         Milbank Memorial Fund Quarterly 44:77-95.

Gonzalez, N. S. and Scrimshaw, N. S.
   1957 Public Health Significance of Child Feeding Practices
         Observed in a Guatemalan Village. Journal of
         Tropical Pediatrics 3:99-104.

Goode, J. G.
   1977 Ethnic Dietary Change Variation in Nutritional
         Consequences. Paper delivered at the 77th Annual
         Meeting of the American Anthropological Association,
         Houston, Texas, November 30, 1977.

Gordon, J. E.
   1969 Social Implications of Nutrition and Disease. Food,
         Science and Society. New York: The Nutrition
         Foundation.

Graham, G. G.
   1972 Environmental Factors Affecting the Growth of Children.
         American Journal of Clinical Nutrition 25:1184-1188.

Grantham-McGregor, S. M. and Black, E. H.
   1970 Breast Feeding in Kingston, Jamaica. Archives of
         Disease in Childhood 45:404-409.

Graubar, M.
   1942 Food Habits of Primitive Man. Scientific Monthly
         55:342-349, 453-460.

   1943 Man's Food: Its Rhyme and Reason. New York: The
         Macmillan Company.

Gross, D. R. and Underwood, B. A.
   1971 Technological Change and Caloric Costs: Sisal
         Agriculture in Northeastern Brazil. American
         Anthropologist 73:725-740.

Gross, I. H.
   1925 A Survey of Food Habits in a Hungarian Mining Town.
         Journal of Home Economics 17:315-321.

Gussler, J. D.
   1975 Nutritional Implications of Food Distribution Networks in
         St. Kitts. (Ph.D. Dissertation 1975, Ohio State
         University.)

Haag, W. G.
    1955 Aborigine Influence on the Southern Diet. Public Health
          Reports 70:920-921.

Hacker, D. B.
    1951 Food Patterns in New Mexico. Public Health Nursing
          43:589-591.

Hallman, E.
    1936 Urban Native Food in Johannesburg. Africa 9:277-290.

Hamburger, W. W.
    1958 The Psychology of Dietary Change. American Journal of
          Public Health 48:1342-1348.

Harding, T. S.
    1931 Food Prejudices. Medical Journal and Record 133:67-70.

Harper, R.
    1963 Some Attitudes to Vegetables and Their Implications.
          Nature 200:14-18.

Harris, M.
    1974 Cows, Pigs, Wars and Witches: The Riddles of Culture.
          New York: Random House.

Harris, R. S.
    1962 Influences of Culture on Man's Diet. Archives of
          Environmental Health 5:144-152.

Harrison, G. G.
    1976 Socio-Cultural Correlates of Food Utilization and Waste
          in a Sample of Urban Households. (Ph.D. Dissertation
          1976, University of Arizona.)

Hart, D. V.
    1969 Bisayan Fillipine and Malayan Humoral Pathologies.
          Southeast Asia Program,

Harwood, A.
    1971 The Hot-Cold Theory of Disease: Implications for
          Treatment of Puerto Rican Patients. Journal of the
          American Medical Association 216:1153-1158.

Hendel, G. M., Burk, M. C. and Lund, L. A.
    1965 Socio-Economic Factors Influence Children's Diets.
          Journal of Home Economics 57:205-208.

Henry, J.
    1951 The Economics of Pilaga Food Distribution. American
          Anthropologist 53:187-219.

Hilliard, S. B.
    1972 Hog Meat and Hoe Cake: Food Supply in the Old South,
          1840-1860. Carbondale: Southern Illinois University
          Press.

Hunter, J.
1973 Geography in Africa and the United States: A Culture-
Nutrition Hypothesis. The Geographical Review
63:171-195.

Jalso, S. E., Burns, M. M. and Rivers, J. M.
1965 Nutritional Beliefs and Practices. Journal of the
American Dietetic Association 47:203-208.

Jelliffe, D. B.
1957 Social Culture and Nutrition. Pediatrics 20:128-138.

_____ 1967 Parallel Food Classifications in Developing and
Industrialized Countries. American Journal of
Clinical Nutrition 20:279-281.

Jelliffe, D. B. and Bennett, F. J.
1961 Cultural and Anthropological Factors in Infant and
Maternal Nutrition. Federation Proceedings 20:185-187.

Jerome, N. W.
1967 Food Habits and Acculturation: Dietary Practices of
Families Headed by Southern-Born Negroes Residing in a
Northern Metropolis. (Ph.D. Dissertation 1967,
University of Wisconsin.)

_____ 1968 Changing Meal Patterns Among Southern-Born Negroes in a
Midwestern City. Nutrition News 31:9, 12.

_____ 1969 Northern Urbanization and Food Consumption Patterns of
Southern-Born Negroes. American Journal of Clinical
Nutrition 22:1667-1669.

_____ 1970 American Culture and Food Habits. Dimensions of
Nutrition. Dupont, Ed. Boulder: Colorado
Associated University Press.

_____ 1972 Adaptive Responses to Poverty in Relation to Food Use
and Consumption Patterns. Proceedings of the Symposium
on Breaking the Cycle of Poverty and Malnutrition.
United States Department of Health, Education and
Welfare Publication No. (HSM) 72-8110.

_____ 1975 Flavor Preferences and Food Patterns of Selected United
States and Caribbean Blacks. Food Technology 6:46-51.

1977 Taste Experience and the Development of a Dietary
      Preference for Sweet in Humans: Ethnic and Cultural
      Variations in Early Taste Experience. Taste and
      Development: The Genesis of Sweet Preference.
      United States Department of Health, Education and
      Welfare Publication No. (NIH) 77-1068.

1978 Nutrition Education: An Anthropological Viewpoint.
      Thresholds in Education 4:6-8.

Jerome, N. W., Kiser, B. B. and West, E. A.
  1972 Infant and Child Feeding Practices in an Urban
        Community in the North-Central Region. Practices of
        Low Income Families in Feeding Infants and Small
        Children, with Particular Attention to Cultural
        Subgroups. Fomon and Anderson, Eds. Rockland,
        Maryland: Maternal and Child Health Service, United
        States Public Health Service.

Johnson, C. C. and Futrell, M. F.
  1974 Anemia in Black Plack Pre-School Children in Mississippi.
        Journal of the American Dietetic Association 65:536-541.

Kallen, D. J., Ed.
  1973 Nutrition and the Community. Nutrition, Development
        and Social Behavior. United States Department of
        Health, Education and Welfare Publication No. (NIH)
        73-242.

Kelley, L., Ohlson, M. A. and Quackenbush, G. G.
  1956 Nutritional Evaluation of Food Purchased by 146 Urban
        Families During 1953. Journal of Home Economics
        48:355-358.

Khare, R. S.
  1976 Hindu Health and Home. Durham: Carolina Press.

Knutsson, K. and Selinus, R.
  1970 Fasting in Ethiopia. American Journal of Clinical
        Nutrition 23:956-969.

Kolata, G. B.
  1974 !Kung Hunter-Gatherers: Feminism, Diet and Birth Control.
        Science 185:932-934.

Laird, D. A. and Breen, W. J.
  1939 Sex and Age Alterations in Taste Preferences.
        Journal of the American Dietetic Association 15:549-550.

Langdon, T. A.
  1976 Food Restrictions in the Medical System of the Barasana
        and Taiwano Indians of the Colombian Northwest Amazon.
        (Ph.D. Dissertation 1976, Tulane University.)

Langsworthy, C. F.
  1911 Food Customs and Diet in American Homes. United
        States Department of Agriculture Office of
        Experiment Station Circular No. 110.

Lantis, M.
  1962 Cultural Factors Influencing Children's Food Habits.
        Proceedings of the Nutrition Education Conference,
        January 29-31, 1962. Miscellaneous Publication
        No. 913. Washington, D. C.: United States Department
        of Agriculture.

Lappé, F. M. and Collins, J.
  1977 Food First: Beyond the Myth of Scarcity. Boston:
        Houghton Mifflin Company.

Lea, D.
  1969 Some Non-Nutritive Functions of Food in New Guinea.
        Settlement and Encounter. Gale and Lawton, Eds.
        London: Oxford University Press.

Leach, E.
  1976 Culture and Communication: The Logic by Which Symbols
        Are Connected. London: Cambridge University Press.

Lebenthal, E., Antonowicz, I. and Schwachman, H.
  1975 Correlation of Lactase Activity, Lactose Tolerance
        and Milk Consumption in Different Age Groups.
        American Journal of Clinical Nutrition 28:595-600.

Lee, D.
  1957 Cultural Factors in Dietary Choice. American Journal
        of Clinical Nutrition 5:166-170.

Lévi-Strauss, C.
  1969 The Raw and the Cooked. New York: Harper and Row.

Lippe-Stokes, J.
  1973 Eskimo Story-Knife Tales: Reflections of Changing
        Food Habits. Ecology of Food and Nutrition 2:27-34.

Loeb, M. B.
  1951 The Social Functions of Food Habits. Journal of
        Applied Nutrition 4:227-229.

Logan, M.
  1972 Humoral Folk Medicine: A Potential Aid in Controlling
        Pellagra in Mexico. Ethnomedizin 1:397-411.

Mackinnon, C. F.
  1955 Changing Food Habits: The Dietitian's Dilemma.
        Journal of the American Dietetic Association 31:566-569.

Marett, R. R.
    1934 Food Rites. Essays Presented to C. G. Seligman.
          Evans-Pritchard, Ed. London: Kegan Paul, Trench
          and Trubner.

Markham, J. E.
    1966 Sociological Aspects of Alcohol and Food Deviations.
          Annals of the New York Academy of Science 133:814-819.

Marriott, M.
    1968 Caste Ranking and Food Transactions. Structure and
          Change in Indian Society. Singer and Cohn, Eds.
          Chicago: Aldine-Atherton.

Martin, M. K. and Voorhies, R.
    1975 Female of the Species. New York: Columbia University
          Press.

Maslow, H. H.
    1937 The Influence of Familiarization on Preference. Journal
          of Experimental Psychology 21:162-180.

Mata, L. J. and Behar, M.
    1975 Malnutrition and Infection in a Typical Rural
          Guatemalan Village: Lessons for the Planning of
          Preventive Measures. Ecology of Food and Nutrition
          4:41-47.

Mata, L. J., Kronmal, R. A. Garcia, B., Butler, W., Urrutia, J.
and Murillo, S.
    1976 Breast Feeding, Weaning and the Diarrhoeal Syndrome in a
          Guateemalan Indian Village. Acute Diarrhoea in
          Childhood. Elsevier: Ciba Foundation Symposium 42.

Mauss, M.
    1967 The Gift. New York: Norton.

Mayberry-Lewis, D.
    1958 Diet and Health in an Acculturated Tribe. Proceedings
          of the 32nd International Congress of Americanists.
          Copenhagen: Munksgaard.

Mazess, R. B.
    1968 Hot-Cold Food Beliefs Among Andean Peasants.
          Journal of the American Dietetic Association
          53:109-113.

McKenzie, J. C.
    1967 Social and Economic Implications of Minority Food
          Habits. Proceedings of the Nutrition Society
          26:197-205.

Mead, M.
    1943 The Factor of Food Habits. Annals of the American
          Academy of Political and Social Science 225:136-141.

1943   Dietary Patterns and Food Habits. Journal of the
       American Dietetic Association 19:1-5

1949   Cultural Patterning of Nutritionally Relevant Behavior.
       Journal of the American Dietetic Association 25:677-680.

1950   Cultural Contexts of Nutritional Patterns. Collected
       Papers Presented at the Centennial Celebration,
       American Association for the Advancement of Science,
       Washington, D. C., 1948.

              , Ed.
1955   Cultural Patterns and Technical Change. UNESCO.
       New York: The New American Library.

1957   We Don't Like What We Don't Eat. Cypress Medical
       Journal 9:90-93.

1964   Food Habits Research: Problems of the 1960's.
       Publication No. 1225. Washington, D. C.: National
       Academy of Sciences.

1976   Comments on Division of Labor in Occupations Concerned
       with Food. Journal of the American Dietetic
       Association 68:321-325.

Milam, D. F. and Darby, W. J.
  1945   The Average Diet of a Southern County and Its
         Effects on Nutritional Status. Southern Medical
         Journal 38:117-124.

Molony, C. J.
  1975   Systematic Valence Coding of Mexican Hot-Cold
         Food. Ecology of Food and Nutrition 4:67-74.

Montgomery, G. E.
  1972   Stratification and Nutrition in a Population in
         Southern India. (Ph.D. Dissertation 1972, Columbia
         University.)

Moodie, A. D., et al.
  1972   Environmental Stress and the Underprivileged Child.
         Ecology of Food and Nutrition 1:95-101.

Moore, H. B.
  1957   The Meaning of Food. Americal Journal of Clinical
         Nutrition 5:77-82.

Moore, M. C., Purdy, M. B., Gibbens, E. J., Hollinger, M. E. and
Goldsmith, G.
   1947 Dietary Habits of Pregnant Women of Low Income in a
         Rural State. Journal of the American Dietetic
         Association 23:847-853.

Moore, W. M., Silverbert, M. M. and Read, M. S., Eds.
   1972 Nutrition, Growth and Development of North American
         Indian Children. United States Department of Health,
         Education and Welfare Publications No. 72-76.

Moser, A. M.
   1935 Food Consumption and Use of Time for Food Work Among
         Farm Families in South Carolina. South Carolina
         Agricultural Experiment Station Bulletin No. 300.

_____ 1942 Food Habits of South Carolina Farm Families. South
         Carolina Agricultural Experiment Station Bulletin No. 343.

Munoz, M., Arroyo, P., Gil, S. E. P., Hernandez, M., Quiroz, S. E.,
Rodriguez, M., Hermelo, M. P. and Chavez, A.
   1974 The Epidemiology of Good Nutrition in a Population
         with a High Prevalence of Malnutrition. Ecology of
         Food and Nutrition 3:223-230.

Murdock, G. P.
   1937 Comparative Data on Division of Labor by Sex. Social
         Forces 15:551-553.

Murphy, G. H. and Wertz, A. W.
   1954 Diets of Pregnant Women: Influence of Socio-Economic
         Factors. Journal of the American Dietetic Association
         30:34-38.

Murphy, R. F.
   1971 The Dialectics of Social Life: Alarms and Excursions in
         Anthropological Theory. New York: Basic Books.

Nashito, H. and Harris, M. B.
   1958 Family Food Habits in the Ryukyus. Proceedings
         of the Ninth Pacific Science Congress, 1957, 15:72-74,
         Bangkok.

Newton, M.
   1971 Psychologic Differences Between Breast and Bottle
         Feeding. American Journal of Clinical Nutrition
         24:993-1004.

Niehoff, A. H.
   1967 Food Habits and the Introduction of New Foods.
         Journal of the Washington Academy of Science 57:30-37.

Neihoff, A. and Meister, N.
    1972 The Cultural Characteristics of Breast Feeding: A
         Survey. Journal of Tropical Pediatrics and Enviornmental
         Child Health 18:16-20.

Pangborn, R. M. and Bruhn, C. M.
    1971 Concepts of Food Habits of "Other" Ethnic Groups.
         Journal of Nutrition Education 2:106-109.

Parrish, J. B.
    1971 Implications of Changing Food Habits for Nutrition
         Educators. Journal of Nutrition Education 3:140-146.

Passin, H. and Bennett, J. W.
    1943 Social Process and Dietary Change. The Problem of
         Changing Food Habits. National Research Council
         Bulletin 108. Washington, D. C.: NAS-NRC.

Peryam, D. R.
    1963 The Acceptance of Novel Foods. Food Technology 17:33-37.

Phillips, V. and Howell, E. L.
    1920 Racial and Other Differences in Dietary Customs.
         Journal of Home Economics 41:396-411.

Pijoan, M.
    1942 Food Availability and Social Function. New Mexico
         Quarterly Review 12:418-423.

_____
    1944 The Importance of a Cultural Approach in Ameliorating
         Nutritional Defects in the Southwest. Application of
         Anthropology to Problems of Nutrition and Population.
         Washington, D. C.: Committee on Food Habits, National
         Research Council.

Plank, S. J. and Milanesi, M. L.
    1973 Infant Feeding and Infant Mortality in Rural Chile.
         Bulletin of the World Health Organization 48:203-210.

Pollitt, E.
    1975 Failure to Thrive: Socio-Economic, Dietary Intake and
         Mother-Child Interaction Data. Fed. Proc. 34:1593-1597.

Pollock, N. J.
    1970 Breadfruit and Breadwinning in Namu Atoll, Marshall
         Islands. (Ph.D. Dissertation 1970, University of
         Hawaii.)

Pumpian-Mindlin, E.
    1954 The Meanings of Food. Journal of the American Dietetic
         Association 30:576-580.

Queen, G. S.
    1952 Culture, Economics and Food Habits. Journal of the
          American Dietetic Association 33:1044-1052.

Quin, P. J.
    1959 Foods and Feeding Habits of the Pedi. Johannesburg:
          Witwatersrand University Press.

Rappaport, R. A.
    1967 Ritual Regulation of Environmental Relations Among a
          New Guinea People. Ethnology 6:17-30.

_____
    1968 Pigs for the Ancestors. New Haven: Yale University
          Press.

Rawson, I. G. and Valverde, V.
    1976 The Etiology of Malnutrition Among Preschool Children
          in Rural Costa Rica. Journal of Tropical Pediatrics
          22:12-17.

Rawson, I. R.
    1975 Cultural Components of Diet and Nutrition in Rural
          Costa Rica. (Unpublished Ph. D. Dissertation 1975,
          University of Pittsburgh.)

Redfield, R.
    1942 Cultural Factors in Indian Diet. Boletin Indigenista
          2:14-15.

Rees, J. L.
    1959 The Use of Meaning of Food in Families with Different
          Socio-Economic Backgrounds. (Ph.D. Dissertation 1959,
          Pennsylvania State University.)

Remington, R. E.
    1936 The Social Origins of Dietary Habits. The Scientific
          Monthly 43:193-204.

Renaud, E. B.
          Influence of Food on Indian Culture. Social Forces 10:97-101.

Renner, H. D.
    1944 The Origin of Food Habits. London: Faber and Faber.

Reyer, J.
    1959 Note on Rural Surveys Covering Food Consumption and
          Household Expenditures in Tropical West Africa.
          Monthly Bulletin of Agricultural and Economic
          Statistics 8:1-6.

Rice, T. B.
    1944 The Emotional Factor in Nutrition. Hygeia 22:100-101.

Richards, A. I.
1932 Hunger and Work in a Savage Tribe: A Functional Study of Nutrition Among the Southern Bantu. London: Routledge and Sons.

———
1939 Land, Labour and Diet in Northern Rhodesia: An Economic Study of the Bemba Tribe. London: Oxford University Press.

Richards, A. I. and Widdowson, E. M.
1936 A Dietary Study in North-Eastern Rhodesia. Africa 9:166-196.

Ritenbaugh, C.
1978 Human Foodways: A Window on Evolution. Anthropology and Health. Bauwens, Ed. St. Louis: Mosby.

Rose, M. S.
1937 Racial Food Habits in Relation to Health. Scientific Monthly 44:257-267.

Sakr, A. H.
1971 Dietary Regulations and Food Habits of Muslims. Journal of the American Dietetic Association 58:123-126.

Sanjur, D., Cravioto, J. and Van Veen, A. G.
1970 Infant Nutrition and Socio-Cultural Influences in a Village in Central Mexico. Tropical and Geographical Medicine 22:443-451.

Sanjur, D. and Scoma, A. D.
1971 Food Habits of Low Income Children in Northern New York. Journal of Nutrition Education 2:85-95.

Schaefer, O.
1971 When the Eskimo Comes to Town. Nutrition Today 6:8-16.

Schultz, G.
1964 Food Taboos. Today's Health 42:28-32.

Scrimshaw, N. and Gordon, J. E., Eds.
1968 Malnutrition, Learning and Behavior. Proceedings of an International Conference at MIT, 1967. Cambridge: MIT.

Sebrell, W. H., et al.
1959 Appraisal of Nutrition in Haiti. American Journal of Clinical Nutrition 7:538-584.

Seifrit, E.
1961 Changes in Beliefs and Food Practices in Pregnancy. Journal of the American Dietetic Association 39:455-466.

Severance, C. J.
   1976 Land, Food and Fish: Strategy and Transaction on a
         Micronesian Atoll. (Ph.D. Dissertation 1976,
         University of Oregon.)

Shack, D. N.
   1969 Nutritional Processes and Personality Development Among
         the Gurage. Ethnology 8:292-300.

Simoons, F. J.
   1960 Eat Not This Flesh. Madison: University of Wisconsin
         Press.

   _____
   1967 Food Avoidances in the Old World. Madison: University
         of Wisconsin Press.

   _____
   1974 Rejection of Fish as Human Food in Africa. Ecology of
         Food and Nutrition 3:89-105.

Singer, J.
   1967 Taboos on Food and Drink. Open Court 41:368-380.

Snapper, I.
   1955 Food Preferences in Man: Special Cravings and Aversions.
         Annals of the New York Academy of Science 63:92-106.

Snow, L. F.
   1978 Folklore, Food, Female Reproductive Cycle. Ecology of
         Food and Nutrition 7:41-49.

Stefansson, V.
   1920 Food Tastes and Food Prejudices of Men and Dogs.
         Scientific Monthly 11:540-543.

Stevenson, G. T.
   1960 The Effect of Cultural Background on Meal Plans.
         Introduction to Foods and Nutrition. New York:
         John Wiley.

Steward, J. H.
   1936 The Economic and Social Basis of Primitive Bands.
         Essays in Anthropology Presented to A. L. Kroeber.
         Lowie, Ed. Berkeley: University of California Press.

Stiebeling, H. K.
   1939 Food Habits, Old and New. Yearbook of Agriculture.
         Washington, D. C.: United States Department of
         Agriculture.

Sukhatme, P. V.
   1972 India and the Protein Problem. Ecology of Food and
         Nutrition 1:267-278.

Sweeny, M.
1942 Changing Food Habits. Journal of Home Economics
34:457-462.

Tannahill, R.
1973 Food in History. New York: Stein and Day.

Taylor, K. I.
1972 Sanuma (Yanoama) Food Prohibitions: The Multiple
Classification of Society and Fauna. (Ph.D. Dissertation
1972, University of Wisconsin - Madison.)

Thomas, W. J., Ed.
1972 The Demand for Food: An Exercise in Household Budget
Analysis. Manchester, England: Manchester University
Press.

Trant, H.
1954 Food Taboos in East Africa. Lancet 2:703-705.

Turner, V.
1975 Symbolic Studies. Annual Review in Anthropology
4:145-161.

Valverde, V. and Rawson, I. G.
1976 Dietetic and Anthropometric Differences Between Children
the Center and Surrounding Villages of a Rural Region
of Costa Rica. Ecology of Food and Nutrition 5:197-203.

Van Veen, A. G., et al.
1971 Some Nutritional and Economic Considerations of Japanese
Dietary Patterns. Ecology of Food and Nutrition 1:39-44.

Vaughn, W. T.
1940 Why We Eat What We Eat. Scientific Monthly 50:148-154.

Wallen, R.
1943 Sex Differences in Food Aversions. Journal of Applied
Psychology 27:288-298.

_____ Food Aversions of Normal and Neurotic Males. Journal of
Abnormal and Social Psychology 40:77-81.

Walter, J.
1973 Internal External Poverty and Nutritional Determinants
of Urban Slum Youth. Ecology of Food and Nutrition
2:3-10.

Wellin, E.
1955 Cultural Factors in Nutrition. Nutrition Reviews
13:129-131.

Whiting, M. G.
   1958   A Cross-Cultural Nutrition Survey of 118 Societies
          Representing the Major Cultural Areas of the World.

Wiehl, D. G.
   1942   Medical Evaluation of Nutritional Status, 7: Diets
          of High School Students of Low Income Families in
          New York City. Milbank Memorial Fund Quarterly 20:61-82.

Wiehl, D. G. and Berry, K.
   1959   Medical Evaluation of Nutritional Status, 15: Essential
          Nutrients in Diets of High School Students According
          to Sex and for Four Different Cultural Groups in
          New York City. Milbank Memorial Fund Quarterly
          23:353-385.

Willoughby, N.
   1963   Division of Labor Among the Indians of California.
          University of California Archaeology Survey
          Report 60:7-79.

Winton, M. Y.
   1969   The Secular Essential Nature of Diet in Some South
          American Indians. (Ph.D. Dissertation 1969, University
          of California - Berkeley.)

Wilson, C. S.
   1971   Food Beliefs Affect Nutritional Status of Malay
          Fisherfolk. Journal of Nutrition Education 2:96-98.

_____
   1973   Food Taboos of Childbirth: The Malay Example. Ecology
          of Food and Nutrition 2:267-274.

_____
   1973   Food Habits: A Selected Annotated Bibliography. Journal
          of Nutrition   Education 5:38-72.

Wilson, M. L.
   1943   Nutrition, Food Attitudes and Food Supply. Post-War
          Economic Problems. Harris, Ed. New York: McGraw-
          Hill.

Wilson, M. M. and Lamb, M. W.
   1968   Food Beliefs as Related to Ecological Factors in Women.
          Journal of Home Economics 60:115-118.

Wolff, R. J.
   1965   Meanings of Food. Journal of Tropical and Geographical
          Medicine 17:45-51.

Additional References **421**

Worsley, P. M.
1961 The Utilization of Natural Food Resources by an
Austrlian Aboriginal Tribe. Acta Ethnographica
10:153-190.

Zetterstrom, M. H.
1962 Psychological Factors Influencing Food Habits of the
Elderly. Mental Hygiene 47:479-485.

Zimmer, R. A.
1976 Small-Scale Retail Food Cooperatives: Fragile Mutual
Associations Exploiting Marginal Economic Niches.
(Ph.D. Dissertation 1976, University of California -
Los Angeles.)

Additional References on the Topics Discussed in Chapter 11

Brown, J.
1973 Diet and the Now Drugs: Eating Habits of Some Drug
Users. Ecology of Food and Nutrition 2:21-26.

Brown, P. T. and Bergan, J. G.
1975 The Dietary Status of Practicing Macrobiotics: A
Preliminary Communication. Ecology of Food and
Nutrition 4:103-107.

Dwyer, J. T., et al.
1978 Pre-Schoolers on Alternate Life-Style Diets.
Journal of the American Dietetic Association 72:264-270.

Guggenheim, R., Weiss, Y. and Fostick, M.
1962 Composition and Nutritive Value of Diets Consumed
by Strict Vegetarians. British Journal of Nutrition
16:467-474.

Hardinge, M. G. and Stare, F. J.
1954 Nutritional Studies of Vegetarians. American
Journal of Clinical Nutrition 2:73-82.

Harland, B. F. and Peterson, M.
1976 Nutritional Status of Lacto-Vegetarian Trappist
Monks. Journal of the American Dietetic Association
72:259-264.

Hongladarom, G. C.
1976 Health Seeking within the Health Food Movement.
(Ph.D. 1976, University of Washington.)

Kandel, R. F.
   1976 Rice, Ice Cream and the Guru: Decision-Making and
         Innovation in a Macrobiotic Community. (Ph.D. 1976,
         University of New York.)

Koo, L.
   1976 Nourishment of Life: The Culture of Health in
         Traditional Chinese Society. (Ph.D. 1976, University
         of California - Berkeley.)

Majumder, S. K.
   1972 Vegetarianism: Fad, Faith or Fact. American
         Scientist 60:175-179.

Mirone, L.
   1954 Nutrient Intake and Blood Findings of Men on a
         Diet Devoid of Meat. American Journal of Clinical
         Nutrition 2:246-251.

New, P. K. and Priest, R. P.
   1967 Food and Thought: A Sociologic Study of Food Cultists.
         Journal of the American Dietetic Association 51:13-18.

Peryam, D. R.
   1963 The Acceptance of Novel Foods. Food Groups Technology
         17:33-39.

Register, U. D. and Sonnenberg, L. M.
   1973 The Vegetarian Diet. Journal of the American Dietetic
         Association 62:253-261.

Robson, J. R. K., Konlande, J. E., Larkin, F. A. and O'Connor, P. A.
   1974 Zen Macrobiotic Dietary Problems in Infancy. Pediatrics
         53:326-329.

Sims, L. A.
   1978 Food-Related Value-Orientations, Attitudes and Beliefs
         of Vegetarians and Non-Vegetarians. Ecology of Food and
         Nutrition 7:23-35.

Wolff, R. J.
   1973 Who Eats for Health. American Journal of Clinical
         Nutrition 26:438-445.

Author Index

426   **Nutritional Anthropology**

Subject Index

ACC/SCN (ACC Subcommittee for Nutrition), 80
Adaptation, 87, 88, 92, 95; Neolithic, 90; defined, 148; nutritional, 276, 287, 293
Adaptive strategies, 321
Additives, 17, 361
Affluence, diseases of in the United States, 37
Africa, 119, 139
Afro-Jamaican preschoolers, nutritional status, 228
Agricultural development policies: nutritional effects, 76; and women, 76, 80
Agricultural Export Plan, 35
Agricultural populations, early: life expectations, 105; and nutrient imbalance, 101; nutritional status, 102, 103; resource distribution, 102; transition from hunting-gathering, 102
Agricultural populations, past images, 117, 118
Agriculturalists: diet, 140; food supply, 120, 141; health, 119; malnutrition, 119, 120; population size, 120; protein, 129
Agriculture, industrialized, 36-39; food production systems of: definition, 36; developing nations, 37-39; and diseases of affluence, 37; and market demands, 36, 37
Agriculture, origins of, 91, 94
Altar de Sacrificios, 103
Aleutian Islands, 92-94, 98, 99; Umnak Islands in, 93
Aleuts, 93, 94, 99
American University, 188
Americans, on Miskito coast, 158
Amino acids, 87-89, 91, 95, 96, 100
Andes, 98
Anti-Vietnam War movement, 328
Arabia, 188
Archaeological data, 106
Archaeological inference, 94, 99
Archaeological reconstruction, 107
Archaeologists, 88, 90, 91, 102
Archaic age, 122
Ashram, 331, 342, 343
Atlantic-Boreal transition, 89
Australia, 184
Azande, the, of Africa, 185

Banana companies, effect on Miskito, 158
Bantu: care of cattle, 191; kwashiorkor and sexual taboos, 18
Banyoro of Central Africa: care of cows, 191
Baptist Church, 310, 311
Bemba land, 186
Bengladesh, 188
Black power, 332
Blain site, 129
Bluefields, 149, 169, 174
Brazil, 78
Brazil, northeastern: cash-cropping, 33-34
Britain, diet, 189
Broad spectrum subsistence, 88, 90
Bugandu, kwashiorkor (obwasi) and sexual taboo, 18-19
Bushmen, 138. See also !Kung Bushmen

Caloric insufficiency, 174
Canada, 233
Cape Gracias á Dios, 153, 155
Caribbean, 149, 159, 165, 169; diet, 189; CFNI (Caribbean Food and Nutrition Institute), 224
Cash crops, 32-33, 106: effect on workload of women (Africa), 63; and food adequacy, 219
Central America, 139
Chemical pesticides, 328
Chibchan languages of South America, 152
Chimbu, the, of New Guinea, 190
China, traditional, 189
Chukchee, the, of Siberia, 184
Coastal Adaptations, post-Pleistocene, 90
Colombia, 78; coast, 106; Amazonian region, 107
Colonial exploitation in Africa, 62-64
Community-based research. See Research, community-based
Community Health Aide Programme, 224, 234-35, 240
Community nutrition surveys, 226
Community research, ethnographic aspects, 51
Companies, foreign-owned, 156-58; effect on Miskito, 163-64, 169, 174-76
Copper Eskimo, 16, 23, 25, 27; food distribution (piqat), 23; food taboos, 24